"If you are looking for an introduction to the New Testament that is beautifully illustrated, handles well the essential background issues, and provides an excellent survey of the content of each book, then this is the survey you have been looking for! This book will serve well as a college textbook, or as a resource for a local church that wants to help its congregation get a better grasp of God's gift of the New Testament."

—**Daniel L. Akin,** *president, Southeastern Baptist Theological Seminary*

"*Approaching the New Testament* combines academic scholarship with a practical readability to provide an introduction and survey that will be a welcome resource for a wide array of Bible reading and study. Whether you are a pastor working on a sermon, a student taking a Bible class, or someone studying the Bible for your personal enrichment, this book will serve you well!"

—**Brian Autry,** *executive director, SBC of Virginia*

"Rigorous in scholarship yet accessible in its approach, this New Testament survey delivers on what it promises: to provide an easy-to-read introduction to the writings of the New Testament in their historical setting. This book is a must-read for all who are interested in a truly biblically grounded understanding of the New Testament writings."

—**David Alan Black,** *Dr. M.O. Owens, Jr. Chair of New Testament Studies, and senior professor of New Testament and Greek, Southeastern Baptist Theological Seminary*

"Most New Testament introductions never get to the point of asking or answering the question of relevance and application of the New Testament to the situations we face in the twenty-first-century church. This introduction does precisely that consistently throughout this volume with its 'Connection Points' sections. For pastors and laypeople who do not have time for long discussions of original context with little guidance on how to apply the material today, in other words those who want a volume that 'cuts to the chase' hermeneutically speaking and addresses the issues of today from God's Word, this is the introduction for you."

—**Ben Witherington III,** *Jean R. Amos Professor of New Testament for Doctoral Studies, Asbury Theological Seminary, and emeritus professor of New Testament, St. Andrews University, Scotland*

APPROACHING THE NEW TESTAMENT

APPROACHING THE NEW TESTAMENT

A GUIDE FOR STUDENTS

ADAM McCLENDON AND JOHN CARTWRIGHT

Approaching the New Testament

Copyright © 2022 by P. Adam McClendon and John Beck Cartwright Jr.

Published by B&H Academic
Nashville, Tennessee

All rights reserved.
ISBN: 978-1-0877-2912-1

DEWEY: 220.6
SUBHD: BIBLE. N.T.--CRITICISM / BIBLE. N.T.--STUDY AND TEACHING

Unless otherwise noted, all Scripture quotations are taken from the Christian Standard Bible®, Copyright © 2017 by Holman Bible Publishers. Used by permission. Christian Standard Bible® and CSB® are federally registered trademarks of Holman Bible Publishers.

Scripture quotations marked DARBY are taken from the Darby Translation (public domain).

Scripture quotations marked ASV are taken from the American Standard Version of the Bible. Public domain.

Scripture quotations marked KJV are taken from the King James Version of the Bible. Public domain.

Scripture quotations marked *The Message* are taken from *THE MESSAGE*, copyright © 1993, 2002, 2018 by Eugene H. Peterson. Used by permission of NavPress. All rights reserved. Represented by Tyndale House Publishers, Inc.

Scripture quotations marked NASB1995 are taken from the New American Standard Bible®, Copyright © 1960, 1971, 1977, 1995 by The Lockman Foundation. All rights reserved.

Scripture quotations marked NIV are taken from THE HOLY BIBLE, NEW INTERNATIONAL VERSION®, NIV.® Copyright © 1973, 1978, 1984, 2011 by Biblica, Inc.® Used by permission of Zondervan. All rights reserved worldwide. The "NIV" and "New International Version" are trademarks registered in the United States Patent and Trademark Office by Biblica, Inc.®

The web addresses referenced in this book were live and correct at the time of the book's publication but may be subject to change.

Cover design by Jay Smith–Juicebox Designs. Cover image: Temple of Apollo—Design Pics Inc / Alamy Stock Photo

Printed in the United States of America
2 3 4 5 6 7 8 9 10 VP 26 25 24 23 22

CONTENTS

Abbreviation Lists ... ix
Introduction ... 1
    John Cartwright

1. Influences on the New Testament World ... 5
    Matthew Kimbrough

2. Matthew ... 21
    Russell Small

3. Mark ... 39
    Russell Small

4. Luke ... 57
    Dottie Rhoads

5. John ... 73
    Cara L. T. Murphy

6. A Case for the Resurrection ... 89
    Gary Habermas

7. Acts ... 93
    Adam McClendon

8. Romans ... 109
    A. Chadwick Thornhill

9. 1 Corinthians ... 131
    Leo Percer

10. 2 Corinthians ... 151
    Leo Percer

11. Galatians ... 167
    Leo Percer

12. Ephesians 185
    Benjamin Laird
13. Philippians 199
    A. Chadwick Thornhill
14. Colossians 213
    Eunice J. Chung
15. 1 and 2 Thessalonians 227
    Jeffrey R. Dickson
16. 1 and 2 Timothy and Titus 245
    Mark Allen and Jack Carson
17. Philemon 273
    John Cartwright
18. Hebrews 281
    Matthew Kimbrough
19. James 297
    A. Chadwick Thornhill and Emily C. Page
20. 1 Peter 309
    Adam McClendon
21. 2 Peter 323
    Chris Hulshof
22. 1, 2, and 3 John 335
    Monte Shanks
23. Jude 353
    Chris Hulshof
24. Revelation 363
    Jeffrey R. Dickson

Conclusion 379
John Cartwright

Subject Index 383

ABBREVIATION LISTS

BOOKS OF THE BIBLE

Old Testament

Gen	Genesis	Song	Song of Songs (or Solomon)
Exod	Exodus	Isa	Isaiah
Lev	Leviticus	Jer	Jeremiah
Num	Numbers	Lam	Lamentations
Deut	Deuteronomy	Ezek	Ezekiel
Josh	Joshua	Dan	Daniel
Judg	Judges	Hos	Hosea
Ruth	Ruth	Joel	Joel
1–2 Sam	1–2 Samuel	Amos	Amos
1–2 Kgs	1–2 Kings	Obad	Obadiah
1–2 Chr	1–2 Chronicles	Jonah	Jonah
Ezra	Ezra	Mic	Micah
Neh	Nehemiah	Nah	Nahum
Esth	Esther	Hab	Habakkuk
Job	Job	Zeph	Zephaniah
Ps(s)	Psalms	Hag	Haggai
Prov	Proverbs	Zech	Zechariah
Eccl	Ecclesiastes	Mal	Malachi

New Testament

Matt	Matthew	Mark	Mark

Luke	Luke	1–2 Tim	1–2 Timothy
John	John	Titus	Titus
Acts	Acts	Phlm	Philemon
Rom	Romans	Heb	Hebrews
1–2 Cor	1–2 Corinthians	Jas	James
Gal	Galatians	1–2 Pet	1–2 Peter
Eph	Ephesians	1–2–3 John	1–2–3 John
Phil	Philippians	Jude	Jude
Col	Colossians	Rev	Revelation
1–2 Thess	1–2 Thessalonians		

Journal and Commentary Series

ABC	Anchor Bible Commentary
AYBC	Anchor Yale Bible Commentary
BECNT	Baker Exegetical Commentary on the New Testament
HNTC	Holman New Testament Commentary
ICC	International Critical Commentary
JSOT	*Journal for the Study of the Old Testament*
JETS	*Journal of the Evangelical Theological Society*
NAC	New American Commentary
NICNT	New International Commentary on the New Testament
NIGTC	New International Greek Testament Commentary
NIVAC	New International Version Applicational Commentary
NTS	New Testament Studies
PNTC	Pillar New Testament Commentary
TNTC	Tyndale New Testament Commentary
WBC	Word Biblical Commentary
ZECNT	Zondervan Exegetical Commentary on the New Testament

INTRODUCTION

JOHN CARTWRIGHT

When this project was nothing but a conversation, I wondered to myself, *Does the world really need another New Testament survey book?* After all, any Google or Amazon search will prove the world does not suffer for lack of New Testament surveys. However, as the idea of this project gave birth to a vision for a unique approach, the answer was wholeheartedly yes!

So, what is so unique about this book that sets it apart from what is already available? To grasp what this book is, let's take a look at what it is *not*. First, this book is not a commentary. Does it contain lots of useful information, such as cultural backgrounds or key word studies? It does. However, this book is not exhaustive when it comes to these sorts of things, nor is it intended to be. Commentaries have their place, but that is not the purpose of this book. Second, this book is not a devotional. Does it drive home important thoughts along the lines of application for you as you interact with it? It sure does. But it is not written solely for that purpose.

You see, more often than not, books such as New Testament surveys tend toward one end of the spectrum or the other: they are either highly informational or highly spiritualized concerning application. Seasoned students find commentaries useful, but what about students who are fairly new to Bible study? Often, new students of the Word are left with more spiritualized devotional books about the Bible because they have not studied the Bible enough to make use of the more scholarly commentaries.

So, what is this book? This book is designed to bridge the gap between the highly informational commentary and those resources that lean toward application. It was born out of a desire to create an introduction to the New Testament that includes the critical information and framework for understanding the whole while still connecting God's Word to the believer's everyday life. Here are some of the features that you will encounter in each chapter.

CONNECTION POINT

Each chapter begins by answering one simple question about the New Testament book it covers: What relevance does this first-century writing have for us today? Right out of the gate, the chapter's author seeks to connect you with God's Word. Each of these sections invites you to pray as you begin the journey to understanding that particular book.

SETTING

Once a connection point is established, each chapter conveys very basic but critical information necessary for understanding the backstory behind the New Testament book being studied. For instance: Who wrote the book? To whom was it written? What are the key themes and passages, and what was the author's purpose for writing the book? While most commentaries contain these features, they are important for even an introductory study of God's Word. After all, correct application begins with an accurate understanding of the book.

HIGHLIGHTS

After the setting of each New Testament book is established, the chapter will take you on a brief journey through the book. However, unlike most commentaries, this volume is more like a highlight reel than an exhaustive study. Rather than a line-by-line, verse-by-verse discussion of the entire book, each chapter focuses on the most critical passages of that book. Additionally, the authors of the individual chapters have sought out opportunities for you to reflect on possible points of application in your own personal life.

EXTRA FEATURE

One other element is worth mentioning here: the first chapter of this book, which focuses on New Testament backgrounds. The point of this chapter is to discuss briefly the first century AD, in which the New Testament was written. We will explore seven primary influences of this New Testament world. This exploration is given to help you understand the influences running behind the scenes and under the surface of the New Testament text. Hopefully this background will help you better grasp the historical context of what is being said.

Our great desire is that this book will not just be an avenue for you to "know your stuff." While knowledge is important and is the foundation for learning (2 Pet 3:18), we have found that many people know truth but have a harder time understanding the relevance of that truth in their modern context. With that in mind, it is our desire that through your learning you will fall in love with the divine Author and surrender your life more fully to him. I will paraphrase something one of my favorite professors, Paul Fink (who is now in heaven), used to say: it's never merely a matter of whether or not you have the Word; it's also a matter of whether or not the Word has *you*.

1

INFLUENCES ON THE NEW TESTAMENT WORLD

MATTHEW KIMBROUGH

What relevance does the first-century world have for us today? Think about the major life experiences that have shaped who you are today. Maybe a high school teacher noticed your talent and encouraged you to pursue college. Tragedy and loss may have profoundly impacted how you view the world. Above all, your family has influenced your values and worldviews, whether you like it or not.

In the same way, the New Testament authors did not write in a vacuum. After the final events recorded in the Old Testament, the world changed drastically. The Greeks and Romans overtook Persia as supreme world powers. New classes of political and religious leaders appeared in Israel. Idolatry no longer seemed to haunt the Hebrew people as it did throughout the Old Testament. Especially noteworthy is the change from Hebrew as the primary language of the Old Testament to Greek in the New Testament. So how did this new normal come about? What events fertilized the fields in which the gospel message would eventually flourish? To answer these questions, we will explore seven influences on the New Testament world, following a primarily chronological sequence.

With this in mind, consider making this your prayer as you read and study this chapter:

Thank you, God, that you are sovereign over history. Help us to see your guiding hand as we consider the world of the New Testament. May it cause us to trust you with the circumstances of our lives, even when we feel discouraged. Most of all, thank you for preparing the way for the coming of Christ and the spread of the gospel message. Amen.

THE OLD TESTAMENT COVENANTS

The New Testament is act 2 of the biblical story, so we must understand the Old Testament before reading the New. While we cannot review the scope of Old Testament theology, we will consider four covenants that shaped the early church's understanding of Jesus.[1] In the ancient world, a covenant was a legal agreement initiated by a superior party.[2] Likewise, God initiated the following four covenants with his people.

The Abrahamic Covenant

In Gen 12:1–3 God calls Abraham to leave his family and land but then issues three covenant promises.[3] First, God will provide a land, which Israel begins to inhabit in the book of Joshua. Second, Abraham will become a great nation. As the story progresses, we learn that Abraham and his wife are childless—a shameful and seemingly cursed state in the ancient world. Yet, by Exod 1:7, Abraham's descendants have become numerous and filled the land of Egypt. The third promise is that God will bless Abraham so that "all the peoples on earth will be blessed through you" (Gen 12:3). Unlike the other two promises, the Old Testament ends without even a hint that Israel (i.e., Abraham's family) has become a blessing to all nations.

---

[1] The apostle Paul speaks of "covenants" in the plural in Rom 9:4; Eph 2:12.

[2] This broad definition does not cover every Old Testament occurrence of the term *berit* ("covenant"), particularly those between individuals. However, the covenants between God and Israel follow the model of an ancient Near Eastern suzerain-vassal treaty in which a superior nation creates a contract with a vassal state. The conquering suzerain nation agrees to protect the vassal, who swears allegiance to the suzerain. For a relatively brief introduction to the biblical covenants, see John H. Walton, *Covenant: God's Purpose, God's Plan* (Grand Rapids: Zondervan, 1994).

[3] His name is Abram until Gen 17:5, when God changes it to Abraham. For simplicity, we will use the name Abraham throughout.

The apostle Paul, however, recognized that when the era of faith in Jesus came, God made the blessings of the Abrahamic covenant available to all who follow Abraham's example of faith. Paul wrote in Gal 3:7, "You know, then, that those who have faith, these are Abraham's sons," adding in v. 29, "And if you belong to Christ, then you are Abraham's seed, heirs according to the promise." The family line, in other words, is no longer rooted in blood relations. Faith is the family trait of Abraham's children, and all that God promised is available to the children of faith—believers in Jesus.

> **Covenant Sign of Circumcision**
>
> In Genesis 17, God clarifies that Abraham's presently unborn descendants are party to the covenant promises. However, as in most ancient covenants, God demands a sign for the males in Abraham's family line to demonstrate their obedience. That sign is circumcision. The idea of circumcision as a religious rite seems odd to us (and other ancient nations considered it strange too), but the practice had symbolic value. According to Gen 17:14, God warns that any male who does not *cut off* the foreskin will be *cut off* from the family of Abraham for breaking the covenant. Centuries later, early Christians would debate the relationship between their newfound faith in Jesus and God's ancient command to practice circumcision, especially as it relates to Acts 15, Romans 3–4, and Galatians 2–5.

The Mosaic Covenant

God initiated the second major Old Testament covenant with Israel using Moses as a mediator. The book of Exodus tells the story of God forming Abraham's family into a nation by freeing them from captivity in Egypt and establishing an intricate system of laws (i.e., *Torah* or *the Law*; Exod 3:7–11; 20:1–17). Israel's new constitution codifies three critical aspects of Israelite worship: rules for everyday living (summarized in the Ten Commandments), a new class of priests who will mediate between Israel and God, and the construction of a tabernacle where God's presence will dwell. Centuries later, Solomon would replace the worn-out tabernacle with an impressive temple in Jerusalem. The coming of Christ, however, changed the role of all three components of the Mosaic covenant. The Spirit provides the moral compass for everyday living (Gal 5:16–18). Jesus is the perfect Priest who mediates between God and the believer (Heb 10:19–22). And the family of God serves as the corporate temple where God's presence dwells (1 Cor 3:16).

The Davidic Covenant

David is famous in pop culture for defeating Goliath, but the story in 2 Samuel 7 is even more important for biblical theology. David has united Israel and defeated most of his enemies, so he decides to move on to a new task: building God a "house" (i.e., a temple). God refuses but promises to build David a "house" (i.e., a dynasty) through a son whose reign will never end. Those of us who have always lived in a democracy may not understand why the promise of an eternal king would excite Israel. But consider the Roman civil wars prompted by the death of Julius Caesar, and you will understand the risk a nation faced every time its king died. A forever king meant peace, prosperity, and a right relationship with God (which the king mediated). Scholars refer to Israel's longing for the fulfillment of 2 Samuel 7 as the "messianic hope," a hope that the son of David will appear and reign forever.

Statue of King David playing the harp

Consequently, after Jesus miraculously healed a demon-possessed man in Matthew 12, the Jews asked, "Could this be the Son of David?" (v. 23). The answer to their question became clear in the preaching of the apostles. According to Acts, Paul preached to Jews using Scripture to show that Jesus was the Son of David, the Messiah sent to offer salvation. Paul concludes in Acts 13:36–38, "For David, after serving God's purpose in his own generation, fell asleep, was buried with his fathers, and decayed, but the one God raised up did not decay. Therefore, let it be known to you, brothers and sisters, that through this man forgiveness of sins is being proclaimed to you." Jesus's resurrection proved that he was the promised "forever King."

The New Covenant

The final covenant we will consider is unique in that the Old Testament only anticipated it. No covenant mediator is announced (compare the roles of Abraham, Moses, and David). No initial fulfillment takes place. The new covenant is a mere hope as the Old Testament closes. We could point to several new covenant passages in the Old Testament prophetic books, but the clearest is Jer 31:31–34. Jeremiah wrote at a time when it appeared that all of God's promises had failed: the land was devastated, the population had been reduced to a shadow of its former self; the temple lay in ruins, and no son of David ruled in Jerusalem. Yet, as Israel hit rock bottom, God promised a new covenant with two life-altering benefits. First, God would not only issue rules, as with the Mosaic covenant, but would enable obedience to the extent that religious teachers were no longer required. Second, God would grant total amnesty, the complete forgiveness of sins for his people. The book of Hebrews declares that Jesus's sacrificial death inaugurated the new covenant so that believers can experience the forgiveness of sins now (Heb 10:11–18).

In Eph 2:12–13, Paul reminds his Gentile audience of the time before they believed in Jesus: "At that time you were without Christ, excluded from the citizenship of Israel, and foreigners to the covenants of promise, without hope and without God in the world. But now in Christ Jesus, you who were far away have been brought near by the blood of Christ." Only in Jesus can believers experience the benefits of all God has promised throughout history. Or as Paul says in 2 Cor 1:20, "For every one of God's promises is 'Yes' in him."

THE EXILE AND RETURN

The prophet Jeremiah spoke of a new covenant during the exile, a dreadful period when God removed his people from the Promised Land. Before we discuss the exile, let's rewind to the reign of Solomon. As David's son, Solomon inherited a powerful, united kingdom of Israel. Unfortunately, Solomon fell into idolatry, so God promised he would split Israel into two nations after Solomon's death. The larger, northern kingdom produced a line of evil, idolatrous kings. God's judgment fell upon the northern kingdom in 722 BC when the Assyrians conquered their land and kicked them out. The southern kingdom, Judah, enjoyed some godly kings but ultimately faced exile for their idolatry. By 586 BC, the Babylonians conquered Judah with three important effects. First, the Babylonians forced the noble and educated

> ### *Josephus*
>
> The Jewish historian Flavius Josephus (c. AD 37–100), recorded the history of Judaism, including the war with Rome. The former Pharisee became a Roman sympathizer who attempted to defend the Jewish way of life and fasten guilt for the Jewish War on the Zealots rather than the Jewish nation. Much of our information about the intertestamental period comes from Josephus. For example, Josephus explained why the Jews are no longer called Israelites, writing, "So *the Jews* prepared for the work: that is the name they are called by from the day that they came up from Babylon, which is taken from the tribe of Judah, which came first to these places, and thence both they and the country gained that appellation." See Josephus, *Jewish Antiquities* 11.5.7 §173, trans. Flavius Josephus and William Whiston, *The Works of Josephus: Complete and Unabridged* (Peabody, MA: Hendrickson, 1987), 297.

in Judea, including Daniel and Ezekiel, to move to Babylon. Second, the Babylonian army destroyed the walls of Jerusalem, leaving the city defenseless. Third, Solomon's majestic temple was destroyed, which symbolized the removal of God's presence from his people.

Graciously, God promised through his prophets that exile would not end Israel's story. While the northern kingdom was lost, scattered throughout the world, the Judean exiles remained together in Babylon. Persia soon defeated the Babylonians and began sending Judean exiles back to their land by 537 BC, approximately seventy years after the Babylonians deported the first wave of Jewish exiles to Babylon. By 516 BC, those who returned rebuilt Jerusalem's walls and completed the second temple, marking the beginning of what scholars refer to as the Second Temple period (516 BC to AD 70). As the Old Testament closes, only a fragment of the

Jewish Exiles in Babylonia

former southern kingdom of Judah, now referred to as Jews, remained.[4] At the same time, the paganism and idolatry that had led Israel into disaster from the beginning of its nationhood no longer plagued the Jews. The fiery pain of exile had refined God's people, though new vices would arise.

Centuries later, Peter identified his audience as "exiles" scattered throughout modern-day Turkey (1 Pet 1:1). Since they did not live in their "homeland," whether literally in the land of Israel or metaphorically in their heavenly home, they were to live lives set apart for God. Peter wrote, "Dear friends, I urge you as strangers and exiles to abstain from sinful desires that wage war against the soul" (1 Pet 2:11).

ALEXANDER AND HIS GENERALS

At this point we move past the Old Testament narrative to the time between the Old and New Testaments, often called the intertestamental period. As the exile and return demonstrated, kingdoms in the ancient world often rose and fell. Within a 200-year period we saw Assyria, Babylonia, and Persia each conquer the world. None, however, conquered as quickly or formed so vast a kingdom as Alexander the Great.

Alexander's father, Philip II, set the stage for his son's success by uniting the disparate city-states of Greece into an unbeatable army. Alexander's army blazed a path of conquest from Greece to Persia in only three years.[5] Along the way, they exported two central aspects of Greek culture: urbanization and the Greek language. As Alexander conquered new lands, he founded cities designed to mimic the famous cities of Greece. These new cities grew rapidly at a time in world history when rural life was the norm. Centuries later, the apostle Paul's ministry revolved around large ancient cities, such as Corinth, Ephesus, and Syrian Antioch.

Alexander made Greek the *lingua franca* (i.e., common language) of the ancient world. Even hundreds of years after Alexander's death, when the Latin-speaking Romans had firm control of the world, Greek remained the language of trade and commerce throughout the Roman world. During his missionary journeys, Paul spoke in Greek not only to preach the gospel message but also to surprise and befriend his captors at one point (Acts 21:37).

---

[4] Psalm 137 reflects on the horrors of exile. In verse 4, the psalmist declares, "How can we sing the LORD's song on foreign soil?"

[5] For a map of Alexander's empire, see Thomas V. Brisco, *The Holman Bible Atlas* (Nashville: B&H, 1998), 174–75.

Diaspora Jews, who were relocated during the exile, benefitted from the spread of Greek because many had lost their ability to understand and speak Hebrew. As Diaspora Jews gathered in synagogues to worship, someone would read the Hebrew Bible aloud, but few knew what the words meant. Consequently, Jews in Alexandria, Egypt translated the Hebrew Bible (i.e., the Old Testament) into Greek around 200 BC, producing the Septuagint (often abbreviated LXX). Paul's missionary preaching later benefited from the Septuagint translation as he preached to Diaspora Jews throughout the Roman world. Also, unlike what Paul would have experienced before Alexander's conquest, the apostle did not need to learn new languages as he traveled between regions, since most Gentiles and Jews knew some Greek. In all, the cultural empire Alexander built lasted a millennium.[6]

THE MACCABEAN ERA

Alexander's impact is all the more impressive, considering his untimely death in 323 BC, less than a decade after his conquest began. He left behind no heir, so his generals split the newly conquered kingdom. Most important for our purpose is the Seleucid dynasty, which ruled Syria and Judea.[7] The policies of one Seleucid ruler changed Judea for over a century. His name was Antiochus IV, and he nicknamed himself "Epiphanes," believing that he was the earthly manifestation of a god. Antiochus's first strike against the Jewish people came when he installed a Hellenistic Jew (i.e., a Jew in religion but a Greek in lifestyle) as the high priest in Jerusalem. This attack on Jewish worship was unacceptable, so when Roman advances on his territory distracted Antiochus, the Jews quietly reinstalled the rightful high priest. Once the gaze of Antiochus IV turned back toward Jerusalem, however, conflict was inevitable.

Antiochus IV punished Judea in the 160s BC with two acts: the abolishment of Jewish religion and the defilement of the temple. First, Antiochus abolished Jewish religion, outlawing central practices such as circumcision and changing Judea's government structure. Second, he looted the temple, stealing the treasures stored there in order to pay his family's debts, and

---

[6] Not until Islam took over the world in the seventh century AD did the influence of Greek culture fade.

[7] The empires of Seleucus and Ptolemy vied for power over Judea throughout this period. For a map of the initial division, see Brisco, *The Holman Bible Atlas*, 176–77.

Influences on the New Testament World

then erected an altar to Zeus in the temple. This abomination against the central symbol of Jewish faith lasted from 167 to 164 BC.

One Jewish family refused to accept the new status quo. Mattathias, a priest from the Hasmonean family, and his five sons conducted a guerilla warfare campaign against Antiochus's army. Mattathias's son, Judas, earned the nickname Maccabeus, which likely means, "the hammer." The distracted Seleucid army could not quell the Maccabean onslaught. By 164 BC, the Maccabean family and their small army removed the Seleucids from Jerusalem, restored Jewish religion, and rededicated the temple. According to Maccabean writings, God miraculously allowed one day's supply of sacred oil to last eight days while new oil was consecrated, an event Jews still celebrate called Hanukkah. During Hanukkah, also called

Selected Events in the Maccabean Revolt

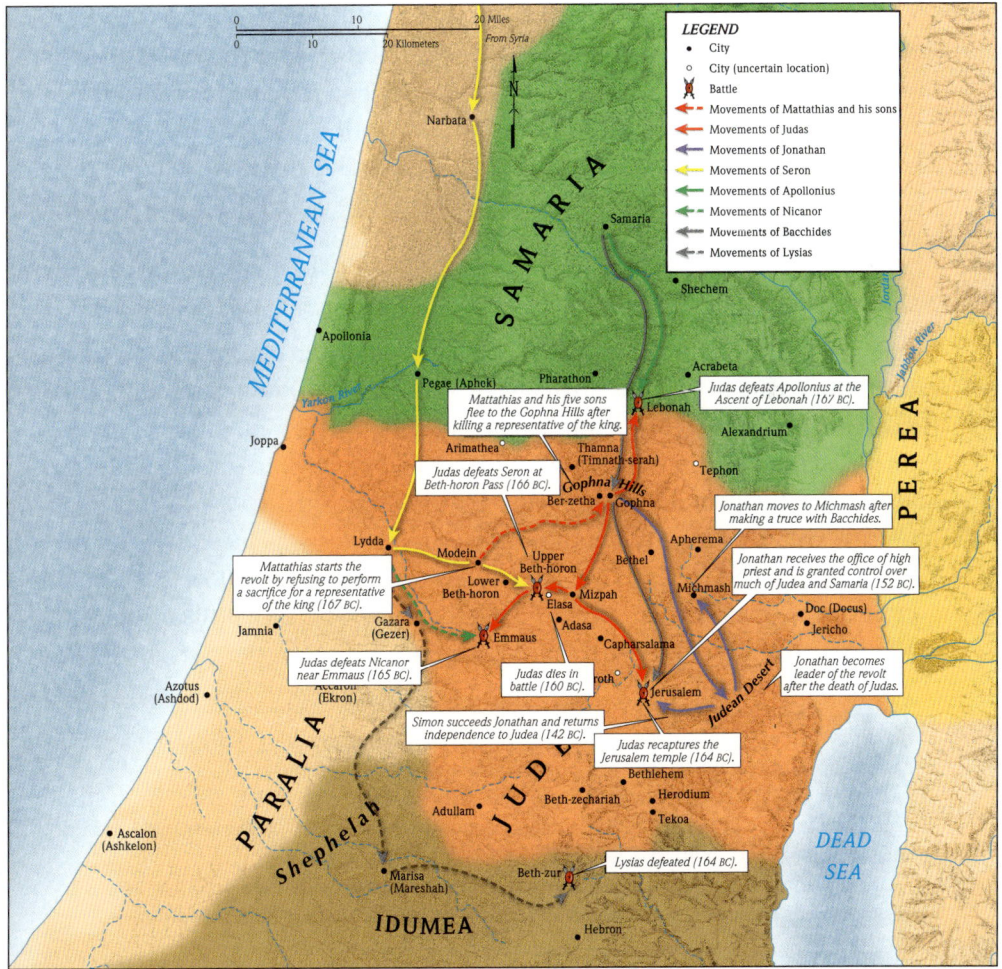

the "Festival of Dedication," Jesus claimed, "I and the Father are one," infuriating his Jewish audience (John 10:22–39).

The rule of Mattathias' family lasted a century and must have looked like the fulfillment of God's promises to Israel.[8] Later, two great-great-grandsons of Mattathias fought for power over the kingdom and appealed to the Roman general Pompey for help. Pompey took advantage of the opportunity and conquered Judea, leaving the land of Israel in Roman hands for centuries to come. Still, Jews held out hope that a new messiah would arise and, like the Maccabeans, overthrow pagan rule, restoring the Jewish nation to a state of autonomy. When the inhabitants of Jerusalem lined the streets on Palm Sunday to welcome Jesus, they likely believed he would soon end Roman rule. But Jesus had a greater world power—the power of sin—in his sights.

JEWISH SECTS

The exile and Maccabean era planted the seeds that would grow into various Jewish sects. Much like Christian denominations today, each group wrestled with how to be holy in an unholy world: "Should we embrace secular ideas to be culturally relevant? Or would we be better off sequestering ourselves from outside influence?" Jews of the Second Temple period answered these questions very differently.

Pharisees

The Pharisee movement arose during the Maccabean era, but it was the exile that most profoundly affected the Pharisees' approach to Judaism. Recall that God exiled his people as punishment for their idolatry, a fate the returning Jews never wished to face again. Therefore, to curry God's favor and prevent further punishment, the Pharisees worked to avoid all ritual impurity.[9] Yet the Law, given a thousand years earlier, was not easy to apply. For example, Exod 16:29b says, "Remain every man in his place; let no man go out of his place on the seventh day" (NASB1995). Does this mean that a Jew living in AD 30 must remain inside his house on the Sabbath? The

---

[8] "They began as insignificant country priests and became high priests and kings, the rulers of an independent state. They pursued an aggressive foreign policy, seeking alliance with Rome against the Seleucids and carving out for themselves a kingdom larger than that of David and Solomon." Shaye Cohen, *From the Maccabees to the Mishnah*, 3rd ed. (Louisville: Westminster John Knox Press, 2014), 3.

[9] Ritual impurity is not the same as sin, but refers to factors that preclude access to God, including touching a dead body, menstruation, and suffering from skin diseases.

Jesus confronted by the Pharisees

Pharisees did not believe the law was so restrictive, but they also refused to leave such a critical command up to each individual's conscience. Therefore, they looked to the "tradition of the elders," a set of Scripture interpretations they believed a series of teachers had passed along verbally since the time of Moses, later recorded in a Jewish writing called the Mishnah.[10] According to this "oral tradition," a Jew could travel 2,000 cubits (.56 miles) on the Sabbath. The average first-century Jew would have thanked the Pharisees for relaxing a rigid rule, but Jesus accused them of putting their human traditions above God's Word (Matt 15:1–6).

Sadducees

Another sect named in the Gospels is the Sadducees. They began as advisors to the Maccabean family and eventually formalized their rule as members of the Sanhedrin, the council of Jewish leaders. By the New Testament era, the "Sadducees" referred to the powerful, wealthy, high-priestly families (often called the "chief priests" in the Gospels). They maintained their power by appealing to the interests of Rome, making them unpopular with pious Jews. Yet, who could oppose them? They controlled the temple, its treasury, the temple guards, and political power in Jerusalem. They were

---

[10] Mishnah, *Eruvin* 5.

the "one-percenters" of the Jewish world. Their wealth and connection to the temple, however, became their downfall during the war with Rome.

Theologically, Sadducees held to an old-fashioned form of Judaism. They rejected the tradition of the elders, which created conflict with the Pharisees (Acts 23:6–8). The Sadducees prioritized the first five books of the Old Testament over the Prophets. They also denied "new" doctrines such as the resurrection of the righteous, a hope the prophets and psalmists hinted at that developed significantly during the intertestamental period. The resurrection hope that Jesus preached caught the attention of the Sadducees (Matt 22:23–33), but the political ramifications of Jesus's actions threatened them the most. John 11:48 records their concerns about Jesus: "If we let him go on like this, everyone will believe in him, and the Romans will come and take away both our place and our nation."

Essenes

As the line between political power and the priesthood blurred, some Jews felt the Jewish temple and priesthood were too corrupt to continue. Many such people became Essenes, a group not mentioned explicitly in the Gospels.[11] The Essenes desired to worship God purely and simply without the ostentations and corruption of politics in Jerusalem. Therefore, they fled to the desert and established communities much like those of later Christian monks. Their communes were quiet, moderate, and worshipful, and they valued hard work. Many Essene communities only admitted adults, and some promoted celibacy among all members. Above all, the Essenes were religious fundamentalists, emphasizing the *right* interpretation and application of Scripture. Their obsession with purity laws, for example, made food production meticulous. Consequently, individuals excommunicated for rule breaking often starved to death because they refused to eat impure foods but did not have the means to maintain strict purity laws. Some scholars believe that John the Baptist's unique clothing and diet point to his association with an Essene community.[12]

---

[11] Scholars debate the relationship between the Essenes and the Qumran community, which produced the Dead Sea Scrolls. See Brisco, *Holman Bible Atlas*, 213–14.

[12] More likely, John's look and food choices played a prophetic role, recalling the garments of Old Testament prophets and the end-times promises recorded in books such as Joel (i.e., John ate the "locusts" to show that God would soon defeat Israel's enemy).

The Zealots

The final sect we will mention did not become influential until after Jesus's death and resurrection, but their impact on Jewish history makes them worthy of mention. While many different types of "zealots" existed in the first century AD, the Zealot party attempted to imitate the Maccabeans by restoring purity to Israel through violence. The Zealots believed that their holy obligation was to overthrow their pagan oppressors, the Romans, and restore full control of the Promised Land to Israel. These rebels hated Rome, and any Roman sympathizers such as the Sadducees, even killing a high priest in AD 68. They provoked the war with Rome and were wiped out at its conclusion. As the Roman army closed in on their final stronghold at Masada, the remaining Zealots killed themselves rather than face captivity in Rome.

A New Sect

Jesus interacted with each of these groups in different ways. He provoked the Pharisees and weathered their criticism throughout his ministry. The Sanhedrin, composed of Pharisees and Sadducees, demanded his crucifixion. Jesus confronted the ideology of the Zealots when he prohibited violence for his sake (Matt 5:43–48; 26:51–52), and his jubilance would have drawn the ire of the solemn Essenes (Matt 11:19). Yet the most crucial contribution of these sects was that the Jews of Jesus's day accepted a variety of approaches to holiness and worship. Therefore, when Jesus began preaching and healing, the people were open to a new sect (Acts 24:14).

THE HERODIAN DYNASTY

The Pharisees and Sadducees were not the only power brokers in first-century Judaism. In fact, the family with the most direct authority over the Jewish people was not even Jewish but Idumean, descendants of the patriarch Jacob's (i.e., Israel's) brother, Esau. The first Herodian king over Judea was Herod the Great, who gained the position because of his father's friendship

> **High Priests**
>
> After Augustus deposed Herod Archelaus, Rome began appointing the Jewish high priests. Rome first selected Annas son of Seth, whose family produced six additional high priests throughout the next sixty years (mentioned in John 18:13; Acts 4:6). Annas's son-in-law, Caiaphas, remained the high priest for eighteen years (AD 18–36) because he knew how to appease Rome. Matthew 26:3 names Caiaphas, the chief priests (i.e., the high-priestly family), and the elders of the people (the Sanhedrin) as officiants at Jesus's trial. In AD 68 Zealots killed the final high priest in Annas' family line, Annas the Younger.

with Julius Caesar. Herod the Great set himself apart as a great builder, even initiating a majestic, gold-laden renovation of the temple in Jerusalem in 19 BC.[13] For those who have read Matthew's Gospel, however, Herod is most infamous for his murder of the baby boys in Bethlehem in a paranoid attempt to kill the newborn king, Jesus (Matt 2:16). His act of fearful desperation corresponds with the accounts of other ancient historians who recorded that Herod killed at least one of his wives and three of his sons, all under suspicion of plotting against him.

Herod the Great died in March of 4 BC (sometime after the birth of Jesus), bringing his more than three-decade reign to an end. Three sons survived him, and Rome split the Promised Land between them.[14] The most lucrative and influential region, Judea, went to Archelaus, who was so terrible that Mary and Joseph refused to return to Bethlehem during his reign (Matt 2:22). After nine years the Jews demanded that Caesar Augustus depose Archelaus. In response, the emperor placed Judea under the direct

The Roman Empire in the Age of Augustus

---

[13] Herod's contribution may seem like an act of piety, but the wealthy and powerful obligated themselves to serve as public benefactors in the ancient world. Sponsoring building projects was one way to gain honor, the most valuable commodity of the day. Herod also paid for pagan temples and public buildings to be erected in Sparta and Rhodes.

[14] See the map in Briscoe, *Holman Bible Atlas*, 208.

rule of a Roman bureaucrat (i.e., a procurator), the most famous of whom was Pontius Pilate. The land northeast of Galilee went to Philip, whose region provided a safe haven for Jesus during his ministry. A major turning point in the Gospel narratives occurs in Philip's region at Caesarea Philippi, where Peter first confesses Jesus as Messiah (Mark 8:27–30). The third division of land went to Herod Antipas, who received Galilee and Perea (east of the Jordan River). Antipas famously married his brother's wife, Herodias, incurring the judgment of John the Baptist, whom Antipas later beheaded (Mark 6:17–29). Also, Luke 23:6–12 records the involvement of Herod Antipas at a politically motivated hearing during the trials of Jesus.

ROMAN RULE

We have seen the final influence on the New Testament world looming in the background since we discussed the Maccabean revolt. The Roman general Pompey conquered Judea in 63 BC as part of a campaign the Romans dubbed the *pax Romana*, or "Roman peace." Before the *pax Romana*, pirates roamed the seas and bandits struck on land, making travel dangerous and trade difficult. By flexing Rome's military muscles, however, Pompey and Roman rulers after him created a world where someone like the apostle Paul could travel in relative safety.[15] Of course, that safety came with a price: the subjugation of defeated ethnic groups and oppressive taxation. In order to maintain control of a vast empire, Rome constructed an impressive system of highways designed for quick military travel. Travelers and missionaries, including the apostle Paul, also utilized these roads. Thus, while the Romans did not intend to help Christianity flourish, the *pax Romana* and Roman roads greatly aided early Christian missions.

First-century Jews enjoyed a generally positive relationship with the Roman Empire. Tensions between the Jews and Romans came to a head in AD 66 when the Roman procurator of Judea looted the temple. The Jews revolted, so the Roman general Vespasian began targeting rebel outposts on his march toward Jerusalem.[16] The death of Nero and subsequent battle for power stalled Rome's efforts, but Vespasian finally became emperor and tasked his son Titus with the subjugation of Jerusalem. By the summer of

---

[15] See Josephus, *Jewish Antiquities* 20.1.1.
[16] Fleeing zealots escaped to the walled protection of Jerusalem, where conflict with the Sadducees was inevitable. In AD 68, a group of Zealots killed the high priest, Annas the Younger, and dragged his body through the streets of Jerusalem.

AD 70, Titus ended a long siege of Jerusalem by penetrating its walls, slaughtering the remaining Zealots, and destroying the temple.

After Titus conquered Jerusalem, Judaism transformed. What later emerged was a Judaism led by the Pharisees that emphasized studying Scripture rather than offering sacrifices. Modern Judaism grew out of the seed of Pharisaism as the Sadducees, Zealots, and Essenes all disappeared. Most significant was that AD 70 marked a decisive split between Christianity and Judaism. Christian evangelism to the Jews quickly faded, and the church became predominantly Gentile. Consequently, church conflicts between believing Gentiles and Jewish Christians so prominent in Romans, Galatians, and Ephesians receded into the background by the final decades of the first century.

CONCLUSION

In Gal 4:4, Paul wrote, "When the time came to completion, God sent his Son, born of a woman, born under the law." The time was complete because God had fully prepared the world for the coming of Jesus and the spread of the gospel message. The Jewish people awaited the fulfillment of God's covenant promises, seeking a messiah who would usher in the new covenant. The presence of Jewish sects and the broadly acknowledged corruption of the priesthood meant that Jesus's audiences were open to change. After his death and resurrection, the apostles spread the gospel message throughout the known world, aided by Roman roads, large cities built by Alexander the Great, and the commonality of the Greek language Paul used to write to churches across Asia Minor and Rome. God had sovereignly prepared the world through the highs and lows of history in order to provide a Savior for all.

BIBLIOGRAPHY

Brisco, Thomas V. *The Holman Bible Atlas*. Nashville: B&H, 1998.

Bruce, F. F. *New Testament History*. New York: Doubleday, 1969.

Cohen, Shaye. *From the Maccabees to the Mishnah*, 3rd ed. Louisville: Westminster John Knox Press, 2014.

Josephus, Flavius. *Jewish Antiquities* 11.5.7 §173. Translated by Flavius Josephus and William Whiston. In *The Works of Josephus: Complete and Unabridged*. Peabody: Hendrickson, 1987.

Walton, John H. *Covenant: God's Purpose, God's Plan*. Grand Rapids: Zondervan, 1994.

2

MATTHEW

RUSSELL SMALL

CONNECTION POINT

What relevance does this first-century writing have for us today? Have you ever encountered a teacher who changed your life? Have you ever heard a message that gave your life deeper meaning, purpose, and direction? Jesus's teaching has changed countless lives and given meaning to so many. How can we find access to his teaching?

The Gospel of Matthew gives us a unique opportunity to hear directly from Jesus. This Gospel is arranged so that the teachings of Jesus confront us and allow us the opportunity to hear these ancient words from him in a fresh way. Jesus's teaching encourages and challenges our current perspectives. While most of us seek to find some level of fulfillment in life, Jesus revealed the means to live in a state of perpetual blessedness. His teaching beckons the reader to not merely live a life for self-centered pursuits but to learn to participate in God's greater kingdom work. Once the reader has listened to Jesus and learned from him, the path of genuine discipleship is opened. The disciple who has learned well from Jesus has not merely filled his or her head with knowledge but has a heart transformed by God himself. The disciple begins to possess a true inside-out righteousness. Desires and motivations are radically changed through an encounter with Jesus. Hear these live transforming words of Jesus, and be challenged at the deepest level of your heart by his message.

With this in mind, consider making this your prayer as you read and study this chapter:

> *Jesus, may we pray as you taught us: "Our Father in heaven, your name be honored as holy. Your kingdom come. Your will be done on earth as it is in heaven. Give us today our daily bread. And forgive us our debts, as we also have forgiven our debtors. And do not bring us into temptation, but deliver us from the evil one.* [The NASB1995 adds:] *For yours is the kingdom and the power and the glory forever. Amen."* (Matt 6:9b–13)

SETTING

Recipients

Matthew, the tax collector in Capernaum, appears to have been writing shortly before AD 70 to an emerging group that was in a strained relationship with the religious establishment.[1] This new community was

---

[1] R. T. France, *Matthew: Evangelist and Teacher* (Downers Grove, IL: InterVarsity Press, 1989), 66. France says, "Matthew is not one of the better known of Jesus's first followers. In fact all that is known about him from the New Testament is that he was a tax–collector in Capernaum, that he was also called Levi, that he was one of the twelve, and (at least this seems a reasonable assumption!) that he was a Jew." Because Matthew was a tax collector of Capernaum (Matt 9:9; 10:3; Luke 5:27), what would give the evidence that he was the author of the Gospel of Matthew? First, there seem to be certain features in the Gospel of Matthew that betray special interest in matters of money and trade (Matt 17:24–27; 18:23–35; 20:1–16; 26:15; 28:11–15). See Robert Gundry, *Matthew: A Commentary on His Handbook for a Mixed Church*, 2nd ed. (Grand Rapids: Eerdmans, 1994), 620. Second, a tax collector would possess certain skills. One of those skills would be the ability to keep records and make accounts. The person would likely be skilled in writing and would be reasonably educated. The skill of note-taking would have been necessary for those who followed Jesus and desired to put his works and teachings into a written account. E. J. Goodspeed, *Matthew: Apostle and Evangelist* (Philadelphia: J. C. Winston, 1959). Regarding the date of the book, see Leon Morris, *The Gospel According to Matthew*, PNTC (Grand Rapids: Eerdmans, 1992), 11. Leon Morris summarizes, "Most modern scholars date it somewhere in the period from the 70s to the 90s, but there is good reason

emerging from within Judaism to follow Jesus, who was heralded as Israel's Messiah.[2]

Imagine being a Jewish person in the first century. You are familiar with the Old Testament and know there is the promise of a coming Messiah. Jesus comes and is heralded as the Messiah but many of your fellow Jews have rejected his messianic status. You still believe the Old Testament and that Jesus is the Messiah, yet many other Jews do not. This is the likely group to whom the Gospel of Matthew was written, a group of primarily Jewish Christians who were still clinging to the Old Testament and attempting to discern how to live a faithful Christian life in light of the new work that Jesus accomplished, but were rejected by many of their fellow Jews for doing so.[3] Thus, the Gospel of Matthew reveals to this group and to us how to live out a life of faithful discipleship based on Jesus's teaching. While it is true that the Gospels were written with a particular group in mind, the message is applicable to all Christians.[4]

---

for seeing it as appearing before A.D. 70, perhaps the late 50s or early 60s. We can scarcely be more definite."

[2] Graham Stanton, *A Gospel for a New People* (Louisville: John Knox/Westminster), 99. Graham Stanton argues that Matthew's community is one that has created a separate identity over against their parent body. Within the Gospel, there is a clear separation of two groups. This conflict and separation have been brought about by intense conflict. Stanton says, "A conflict is more passionate and more radical when it arises out of close relationships. The coexistence of union and opposition in such relationships makes for the peculiar sharpness of the conflict. Enmity calls forth deeper and more violent reactions, the greater the involvement of the parties among whom it originates."

[3] Ulrich Luz, *Matthew*, vol. 1, trans. James E. Crouch (Minneapolis: Fortress, 2007), 54. The Gospel of Matthew records increasingly strained relations between the two communities (Matt 10:17; 16:18; 28:15). Ulrich Luz also supports this position of separation of Matthew's community. He says, "In my opinion the Matthean community, whose mission in the land of Israel has come to an end, no longer belongs to the Jewish synagogue. The evangelists speak emphatically of 'their' or 'your' synagogues and scribes (4:23; 7:29; 9:35; 13:54; 23:34). That assumes that there are also our scribes (13:52; 23:34; cf. 23:8–10) and our assemblies, that is, that the institutionalization of independent Christian communities is well advanced."

[4] Richard Bauckham, ed., *A Gospel for All Christians* (Grand Rapids: Eerdmans, 1998), 3–4. Bauckham has challenged whether or not the attempt to discover the particular circumstances of a community may be off in the wrong direction. The commonly held assumption in scholarship has been that Gospels are written to address a particular community and particular community problems. Bauckham has suggested that Christian communities in early Christianity were not this isolated from one another. He says, "Since all the evidence we have for the early Christian movement shows it to have been a network of communities in constant, close communication with each other, and since all the evidence we have for early Christian leaders (the kind of people who might have written Gospels) shows them to have been typically people who traveled widely and worked in more than one

The writer of this Gospel understood both the uniqueness of being Jewish and the strain of being an outsider. Matthew, the tax collector from Capernaum, was an ideal writer to address a group of Jewish Christians who felt that they were marginalized within the Jewish community. Matthew's former life of collecting taxes from the Jewish people to give to the Romans certainly allowed Matthew to understand life from the perspective of being a marginalized Jew.

Theme and Key Passage

There are several major themes in the Gospel of Matthew. However, a major theme is "lived righteousness as critical to the discipleship mandate." This theme is revealed throughout the book, especially in Matt 22:36–40 and 28:18–20. Matthew 22:36–40 summarizes the intentions of God's Law as loving God and loving others as the true intention of God's commands to humanity. Matthew 28:18–20 presents that discipleship mandate with great clarity and simplicity. This call to disciple others is not merely a call to trust in Jesus but to teach others to embody his teachings.

Matthew 28:19–20 says: "Go, therefore, and make disciples of all nations, baptizing them in the name of the Father and of the Son and of the Holy Spirit, teaching them to observe everything I have commanded you. And remember, I am with you always, to the end of the age."

Purpose and Occasion

What is the essence of a true disciple? What is required to make disciples of those who do not know Jesus? The purpose of the Gospel of Matthew was to serve as a discipleship manual for the newly formed community to produce disciples who possessed an inside-out righteousness. Matthew informs the reader regarding the discipleship mandate by expressing the following ideas.

First, the disciple must understand who Jesus is. Jesus is the fulfillment of the Old Testament promises. All that Israel was unable to do, Jesus did through his life, death, and resurrection. He is not merely another great prophet of God, he is God himself in the flesh. Jesus draws together all

---

community at different times, the outlook and concerns of neither the early Christian communities nor their teachers would have been locally confined." If Bauckham is correct, then it logically follows that "since a Gospel does not address a specific community, we cannot expect to learn much from it about the evangelist's own community (even assuming he had only one, rather than a succession of very different ones), but in any case the enterprise of reconstructing such a community is hermeneutically irrelevant."

of the expectation of the Old Testament and brings it to a culmination.[5] Through his resurrection, Jesus shows himself to be King of the world. All earthly powers have lost their authority because Jesus has defeated humanity's greatest enemies.

Second, the disciple must understand the unique requirements of a disciple. There are so many paradoxical realities that a disciple of Jesus must understand and embody. He or she must understand that only those who realize their deep inability to please God or serve God in their own strength are actually those who are most able to serve God. God is pleased to give grace to those who understand their deep need for it. A disciple must have a new perspective on power. Power is not seen in dominating others for personal gain but in giving one's life for the gain of others. A disciple must realize his or her status in God's kingdom is not found in how high one can rise to positions of prominence in this life, but rather how low one can serve others. Only in learning and embodying these unique perspectives is one able to enter into the life of discipleship.

Third, the disciple must understand his or her mandate to make disciples. The disciple realizes that Jesus is truly King, and his unique kingdom will give life to all who will receive it. Disciples are a herald of this good news to the whole world. As people confess their need for Jesus, identify with Jesus's death and resurrection through baptism, and learn and embody Jesus's teaching, his kingdom is expanded and disciples are made until Jesus returns.

HIGHLIGHTS IN MATTHEW

The Birth Narrative (Matthew 1–2)

The Gospel of Matthew begins with the birth narrative of Jesus, which connects the story of Jesus to the Old Testament. In the first lines of his Gospel, Matthew gives Jesus's genealogy (i.e., his family tree). Jesus is declared to be in the family line of two of the greatest Old Testament characters, Abraham and David. Jesus is heralded as the one who would come to fulfill Israel's destiny. He is squarely revealed in the opening genealogy as the one

---

[5] Charles Quarles, *A Theology of Matthew* (Phillipsburg, NJ: P&R, 2013). Quarles reveals how Jesus is a new Moses, a new David, a new Abraham, and a new creation in Matthew.

who would sit on David's throne. While the genealogy is straightforward in this sense, the inclusion of five women in the genealogy appears odd. These women are Tamar, Rahab, Ruth, Bathsheba ("Uriah's wife"), and Mary. The first four of these women are Gentile in origin and are shrouded with some concern about their sexual behavior. In contrast with these women, Mary, the mother of Jesus, is initially shrouded in apparent sexual irregularity but is soon declared pure because the Holy Spirit is doing something new by her unique conception. The genealogies in the Bible are sections readers often skim over. However, in this opening genealogy these scandalous characters reveal the grace of God to use everyone in his kingdom work. Further, those whom the world is convinced are unusable by God are the very ones God is pleased to use.

The birth narrative is also punctuated with five Old Testament quotations that reveal the birth of Jesus as the fulfillment of Old Testament promises. Jesus is revealed as the virgin-born son who embodied the presence of God to his people (Isa 7:14; Matt 1:23). Jesus is born in Bethlehem as the fulfillment of the prophet Micah's prediction (Mic 5:2; Matt 2:1, 6). Jesus prefigures the story of Moses and Israel as he is forced into Egypt but emerges out of Egypt to fulfill his mission (Hos 11:1; Matt 2:15). The

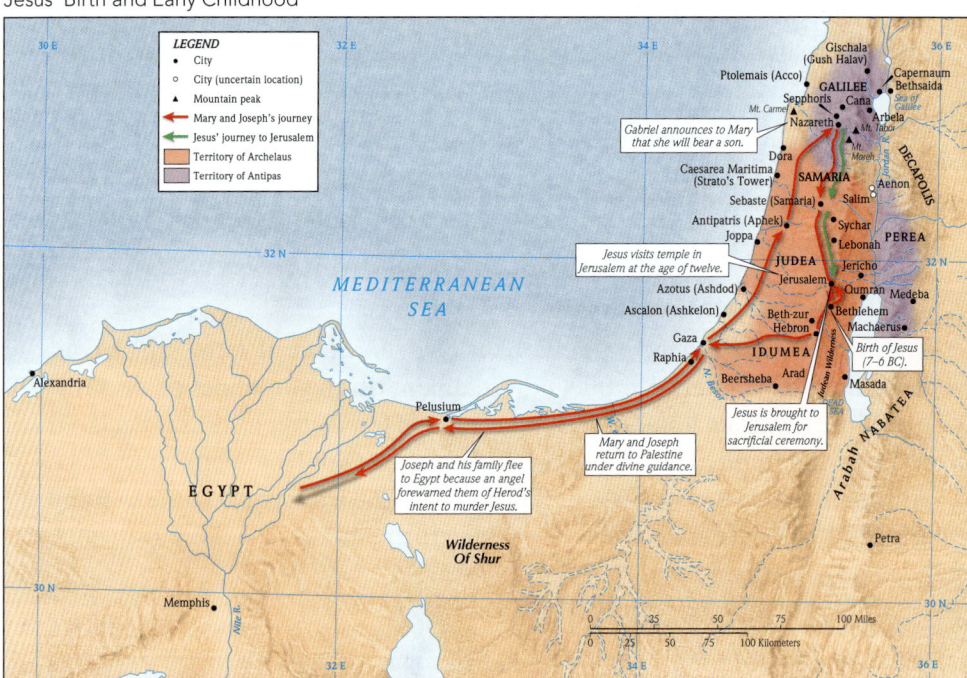

Jesus' Birth and Early Childhood

maneuvering of the magi to overcome the cunning of King Herod results in a Pharaoh-like killing of the babies (Exodus 1) and is reminiscent of weeping in times of past distress (Jer 31:15; Matt 2:18). However, just as with Moses under Pharaoh's reign of terror, God protects Jesus through Herod's rage. A foreshadowing of the glory of the humble Jesus is revealed when the magi, the mysterious men of the East, lay their treasures at Jesus's feet (Matt 2:11), foreshadowing the nations of the earth worshipping King Jesus. Jesus would settle in obscurity in Nazareth but would move out from there to the whole earth (Isa 11:1; Matt 2:23).

Strangely, on the pages of the New Testament the story of the Old Testament begins to reach its conclusion. Jesus is presented as the Savior from Israel who brings salvation to the whole world.

Jesus's Ministry Introduction and First Message: The Sermon on the Mount (Matthew 3–7)

John the Baptist called the nation of Israel to spiritual readiness in light of God's new work through Jesus. The people of Israel came to John the Baptist at the Jordan River to be baptized, to express their readiness for God's fresh action. The people expected God to come in power as the conquering King, and with him would come judgment. Thus, the beginning of Jesus's public ministry is one of identification versus condemnation. He came to the Jordan River and stood alongside the condemned, revealing his heart not to condemn the world, but to stand in the place of the condemned (Matt 3:13–17). The ministry of John the Baptist is a continual reminder of the need for spiritual readiness for what God is doing in the world.

In a manner reminiscent of wandering Israel, Jesus entered the wilderness to be tempted (Matt 4:1–12). However, in the wilderness, Jesus did not succumb to faithlessness and disbelief. Instead, he exhibited dependency upon God and his work against the attacks of the Devil. Jesus emerged out of the wilderness victorious over the Devil's schemes to foreshadow his ultimate victory over all powers. In this, Jesus provided for us an example of how to defeat temptation in our lives. We should want to imitate his faithfulness in the wilderness in contrast to the Israelites' rebellion. Jesus showed us how to persevere in temptation, lean upon God's Word, and wait for God's ultimate vindication in our lives.[6]

---

[6] While the point of the temptation of Jesus is to show him as the true and perfect second Adam, we can certainly apply his approach to temptation in our lives; thus, the

As John's ministry diminished, Jesus's ministry increased. Jesus made his home base in a fishing village near the Sea of Galilee called Capernaum. Among Jesus's first disciples were two brothers, Peter and Andrew, who made their living fishing from the Sea of Galilee. Jesus taught these fishermen to fish for people (Matt 4:19). In the region of Galilee, Jesus's ministry attracted more disciples as well as the curiosity of bystanders. The nature of his kingdom ministry focused on people. Jesus came into the world to seek out lost humanity and to win them to the gospel like a fisherman catches fish.

The image of Jesus as a great teacher is prominent in this Gospel. The reader can imagine sitting in the grass on a beautiful hillside in Galilee to hear Jesus's words. The region of Galilee is full of rolling hills, and Jesus would have taught often in this beautiful pastoral setting. He went up on a mountain, in a manner reminiscent of Moses, and delivered his most famous message, the Sermon on the Mount. Jesus taught his listeners not merely how to receive a blessing, but rather how one is to live in a blessed state.[7] He revealed that blessedness comes through surprising dispositions. Those who live in a state of divine blessedness have a poverty of spirit, mourn over their sin, possess gentleness, hunger for a righteous life, possess mercy, are genuine in their desire to see God, pursue peacemaking, and are willing to be persecuted for righteousness' sake. These dispositions are the keys to real blessedness (Matt 5:1–12). Jesus's disciples who possess these characteristics have a profound effect on the world. As these dispositions are lived out, his disciples are like salt into a decaying world and light on a lampstand in a dark room or a city on a hill! These dispositions produce in the lives of Jesus's disciples a new way of being and acting in the world so that those who observe the good works produced from these dispositions give glory to the Father in heaven (Matt 5:13–16).

The opening section of the Sermon of the Mount should challenge us. Many of us seek merely to be blessed by God, rather than to live continually in a state of blessedness. We attempt to live a good life and influence those around us. We may attempt to do this through education, position,

---

emphasis we are bringing out above is how, through the empowerment of the Spirit, we can walk in obedience and resist temptation (Gal 5:16; Jas 4:7).

[7] Jonathan T. Pennington, *The Sermon on the Mount and Human Flourishing: A Theological Commentary* (Grand Rapids: Baker, 2017), 19–136. Pennington describes the difficulty for many readers to understand the difference of living in a state of blessedness versus merely being a recipient of a blessing. Jesus calls his disciples to understand how to live in a state of divine blessedness.

or income. Jesus told us that blessedness is found in places we do not often pursue. The first step to living in blessedness is to admit one's spiritual bankruptcy and need for God. The unique dispositions set forth by Jesus are the real paths to blessedness. Further, a person's influence will be greater in God's kingdom. In his kingdom we realize that we do not need more material things, or to find our worth in our education or position in life. What is needed is utter dependence upon God for all things. For those who learn this, their lives will be like a city that is set on a hill.

The purpose of Jesus's teaching was not to do away with Old Testament teaching. Rather, it was to bring the teaching of the Old Testament to its completion and reveal God's ultimate intentions. Jesus communicated that real transformation happens in the hearts of his disciples, which produces obedience to God's commands. This new righteousness will be the result of an inside-out change that will be brought about by Jesus in the heart of his disciples (Matt 5:17–20). Mere external compliance with God's command is not his ultimate intention. A religion of the heart requires heart change, not just behavior changes. A disciple does not merely abstain from murder; a disciple does not harbor unjustified anger in his heart toward others. A disciple does not merely refrain from adultery but pursues purity in heart and mind. Jesus calls his disciples to keep their word without any form of deceptive tactics.

Most radically, Jesus calls for love of others, even our enemies (Matt 5:21–48). This type of inside-out change cannot be accomplished apart from God's intervention in a person's life. To achieve this inside-out transformation, a person must recognize his or her utter need for God and Jesus's adequate provision for that need. Since true religion is a religion of the heart, any form of religious externalism, where we simply want to be seen as "good" by others, is to be rejected. True religion requires a heart aligned with God in prayer where the disciple prays for God's will and kingdom to come (Matt 6:1–18).

A disciple's orientation does not focus on success among the kingdoms of the earth. He or she is to be reoriented to God's kingdom and trust God for daily provisions while storing up treasures in heaven (Matt 6:19–34). While Jesus's disciples do have different priorities and possess a deep heart change, prideful condescension is never part of their attitude. Jesus condemns a spirit of judgment. He warned his disciples not to judge the motive and hearts of others. No spirit of superiority can be maintained while possessing the poverty of spirit. However, in humility, disciples are to first self-judge. Then disciples can help others grow in righteousness

(Matt 7:1–6). This call to discipleship will require perseverance through difficulty, knowing God is good (Matt 7:7–12).

This journey of discipleship is not an easy or well-traveled road. The discipleship journey is like a narrow road, a fruit-yielding tree, and a wise man who builds his house on a rock. Jesus wants his disciples to have an inside-out transformation that will result in a lived righteousness (Matt 7:13–29). The Sermon on the Mount confronts us with many of the major themes of Jesus's teaching. The paradox of this message is Jesus's heavy demands for right living and God's gracious provision to change the human heart. Disciples hear Christ's commands only to realize the depth of their spiritual need. It is precisely this recognition of their own inability that stirs God to give them his divine ability to live out his commands.

Jesus's Ministry and Second Message: The Sermon on Mission and Martyrdom (Matt 8:1–11:1)

Jesus's ministry illustrates the message that he taught. Jesus revealed his authority over sickness, the forces of the natural world, and even the demonic. He takes our weakness and diseases upon himself, and through his power he heals them (Matt 8:1–17). We discover, not only about Jesus, but what it means to follow him. To follow Jesus, one must do as he does. Jesus did not have an easy life or worldly comforts. The cost of discipleship will require suffering while following the powerful Jesus. A disciple of Jesus will suffer because the disciple, like Jesus, sees the spiritual need and is willing to meet it even through suffering. Jesus calls his disciples to see the harvest of people and be sent out. One of those called and sent was this Gospel's author—Matthew, the tax collector. Matthew recounts his call to discipleship and his welcoming of other tax collectors and sinners like himself to benefit from Jesus's call (Matt 9:9–13). As disciples of Jesus, we should be moved to follow him wherever he sends us. This may require sacrifice on our behalf, but compassion for people compels the disciple to go.

Jesus gave instructions on mission and martyrdom as his second major teaching in the Gospel, which set the context for sending out his apostles (Matt 10:5–11:1). The initial mission of the first disciples (learners), now apostles (sent ones), was to offer salvation to the house of Israel first. Ultimately, it was God's plan that, because of Israel's rejection, salvation would be offered to the whole world. Power in weakness is seen in the ministry of Jesus's disciples, because they have power over the demonic and sick. They were to travel lightly, rely upon those who were willing to offer hospitality; and, if the people would not listen, move on to the next town. Further, Jesus's disciples would suffer persecution on the mission. To live out Jesus's mission mandate, his disciples would be like sheep being sent among wolves. However, they were not to be naive about the dangers and suffering that awaited them. They were to be harmless to all they encountered but shrewd about negotiating the mission. The context of suffering would sift out those who would bear the name of Jesus amid struggle. Those who acknowledged Christ and those who helped Christian missionaries would be rewarded by God himself (Matt 9:36–10:42).

Our thoughts about our own discipleship and mission should be challenged by Jesus's words. Discipleship should compel us not to shrink from suffering but to embrace it if the mission demands it. Further, Christian mission done correctly is a strange mixture of power and weakness. The mission is never to be flashy but humble and dependent upon God as we go. Yet, in the midst of this apparent weakness, the power of God is seen clearly in his action through our lives and the changed lives of others due to the power of the gospel.

Jesus's Ministry and Third Message: The Parables of the Kingdom (Matt 11:2–13:53)

Jesus's mission was misunderstood and did not meet the expectation of many. Even John the Baptist questioned whether Jesus was the One. Jesus pointed to his powerful acts of healing as validation of his messianic status. The powerful, yet suffering Messiah concept was difficult for the disciples to understand. Jesus praised John the Baptist and declared that he was the last great prophet announcing the coming Messiah. However, those who participated in what God was doing then

> ### The Kingdom of Heaven
>
> The phrase "the kingdom of heaven" sounds unfamiliar to us. However, the idea of God's rulership over his world is a concept most of us can grasp. The question many of us have is, When will God come down and straighten out the evils of the world? The startling message of the Gospels is that God will indeed come down and impose his kingdom upon the earth. The mystery of the gospel is this future kingdom has come in partial form through the life, death, and resurrection of Jesus. The events of Jesus's life have given clear indication that he is the King of the world before the end of human history. Jesus has come before the end of time to decisively defeat sin, death, and Satan. In a mysterious sense, the power of God's future kingdom has already been manifested. Thus, the kingdom of heaven discloses to us God's rule of the world. The kingdom of heaven reveals that God's kingdom is already established in heaven, awaiting its full revelation on earth in the future. So the disciple prays for God's kingdom to come on earth as it is in heaven. The disciple knows the power already demonstrated in Jesus and awaits the full display of his rule on the world.

would receive greater spiritual blessings than those of a previous era. The rejection of John the Baptist was soon met with the rejection of Jesus himself. Jesus pronounced judgment upon those who heard his message and saw his works and yet rejected him. In the midst of this rejection, Jesus would humbly and gently carry out his mission until he obtained the victory. The suffering Messiah would be the victorious one (Matt 11:2–12:50). The tone changes near the middle of Matthew's Gospel, when Jesus becomes misunderstood and thus his manner of teaching changes.

In an act of judgment and mercy, Jesus spoke in parables. The parables of Jesus are the third major message in this Gospel. Parables are true-to-life stories that convey a deeper spiritual truth. Jesus disclosed the nature of the kingdom of heaven in his parables.[8] These stories reveal the nature of God's kingdom, the message of the kingdom, the greatness of the kingdom, and the precious nature of finding the kingdom. The parables of Jesus are not for greater understanding, but for concealment from those listening (Matt 13:11–17). Jesus, like Isaiah, was given the task of speaking to a generation that would not listen. Jesus realized that the more he spoke, and the more revelation was given, the greater the condemnation of the listeners. In an act of judgment, Jesus concealed the message in story form so that only those who understood the elements of the story understood its meaning. The real meanings of Jesus's parables were disclosed by him only for those who continued to pursue him and inquired about their true meaning. In an act of mercy, Jesus shrouded the meaning of his words so that his words would not further condemn those who were not listening.

Russian icon, *St. John the Forerunner with His Life*, first half of sixteenth century, Arkhangelsk Regional Museum of Fine Arts

---

[8] See Jonathan T. Pennington, *Heaven and Earth in the Gospel of Matthew* (Grand Rapids: Baker, 2009). Jonathan Pennington has decisively refuted the idea that Matthew uses the phrase "kingdom of heaven" as reverential circumlocution for God.

While is it is often taught that Jesus gave easy-to-understand stories so people would understand him more, this is not why Jesus preached in parables. The parables should warn us about our lack of listening to him and misunderstanding his message. It is easy to listen to Jesus without really hearing him. The demands of the teaching of Jesus often cause us to filter out the sections that cause us discomfort. Jesus realized that many who were attracted to him were not ready to follow him. This should cause us to reflect upon our own desire to internalize his message. Are we merely attracted to the charismatic figure of Jesus, or are we truly willing to listen, internalize, and live the contents of his message?

Jesus's Ministry and Fourth Message: The Sermon on the New Jesus-Formed Community (Matt 13:54–19:1)

The martyrdom of John the Baptist by Herod Antipas serves as a foreshadowing of Jesus's ultimate destiny. Jesus continued to encourage the faith of his disciples to see who he was and to put their trust in him. Furthermore, Jesus began to have greater conflict with the religious leaders. This conflict continues to build as Matthew's Gospel progresses. Jesus instructed his disciples on his impending death and told them that their journey of discipleship would be one of suffering. The strange mix of Jesus's power and glory appear in this section of the Gospel. Jesus went up on the mountain again in a manner reminiscent of Moses, and Jesus was transformed. In doing so, Jesus revealed his glory to the disciples as the glorious beloved Son of the Father before his suffering.

As Jesus prepared for his departure, he gave instructions to his disciples that would result in the formation of a new community, the church. His instructions about the church are the fourth major section of his teaching. Jesus's new community was to be entered into with childlike faith. Those who joined his kingdom with childlike faith should not be offended by anyone. There would be a great judgment on those who offended them. Jesus's community was to be a community that sought out the lost with great diligence, as a shepherd looked for a lost sheep. Further, the new community was to be accountable and pure. Those who heard the call to discipleship must live out the righteousness that they claimed to possess. A habitual breach of ungodliness should result in disciplinary action that could result in the disciple being put out of the community. However, the goal of any accountability and discipline was for restoration. Once repentant, the disciple was to be forgiven and restored into a merciful community (Matt 17:22–19:1).

While much more will be said about the church in other New Testament books, here Jesus laid the groundwork for his church. Many want to hear Jesus's message as focused on individualized spirituality. Jesus rejected isolated spirituality for accountable community. He was clear that discipleship was to be worked out in encouraging, accountable community. Jesus's call to discipleship was a call to a discipleship community ultimately manifested in the church. A disciple of Jesus should resist any notion of discipleship in isolation.

Jesus's Ministry and Fifth Message: The Sermon on Last Things (Matt 19:2–26:1)

As Jesus's death drew near, Jesus continued to teach about the kingdom of heaven. He addressed the barriers to entering the kingdom and the posture necessary for kingdom participation. While Jesus taught the disciples, they fundamentally misunderstood the nature of his kingdom. The disciples were jockeying for positions of authority rather than understanding the humility and service required to be a disciple of Jesus (Matt 20:20–28).

The final week of Jesus's earthly life was about to begin. Jesus, in fulfillment of prophecy, rode into Jerusalem on Palm Sunday on a donkey.

This painting, titled *Christ on the Cross with Saints*, was likely produced in 1430.

The voices of the crowd were similar to Jesus's disciples. The crowds understood his uniqueness; however, they certainly did not understand the reality of his kingdom and the path of suffering and death that would soon befall him. On Monday of Holy Week, Jesus entered the temple complex and rebuked the religious leaders for turning God's house of prayer into a place of selling and deception. On Tuesday of Holy Week, Jesus cursed the fig tree to symbolize the fruitlessness of Israel. That same day Jesus squared off with the religious leaders. First, the chief priests and elders challenged his authority. Then the Pharisees and the Herodians attempted to show that Jesus was trying to subvert Caesar. And, finally, the Sadducees confronted Jesus with the teaching on the resurrection. Jesus was able to maneuver out of these traps and further infuriate the religious leaders. He announced a full condemnation upon Israel's religious leaders and their failure to lead the people to real righteousness.

> ### Discipleship
>
> Discipleship is a process of learning to obey the teaching and behaviors of Jesus. Discipleship begins through personal denial and a commitment to follow him. Jesus is able, through his completed work on the cross and resurrection, to effect a transformation of the heart. The changed heart of the disciple now desires to follow Jesus and learn from him. Discipleship is a process of growth within the new community, the church, where disciples learn and obediently live out the mandates of discipleship and call others to trust in Jesus and walk according to his ways.

Also on Tuesday, Jesus gave his final major message, the Olivet Discourse (Matt 23:1–25:46). This is the fifth major message in Matthew's Gospel. Jesus instructed his disciples on God's powerful acts to occur in the future. In the near term, the disciples would witness the destruction of the temple in Jerusalem in AD 70. Jesus predicted this unfathomable event. However, this destruction would prefigure a future, greater time of God's judgment in the future. As human history draws to a close, a great time of tribulation will occur. This time will be a time of persecution. During this time false teachers and false messiahs will be abundant. However, this time of great tribulation will conclude with the coming of the Son of Man to gather his children and judge the earth. In light of the coming Son of Man, the disciples of Jesus are to be alert for his coming and faithfully serve him until he comes. While Jesus possesses humility and endures suffering, the time for mercy will come to an end. God's grace is not to be taken for granted. There will be a day of judgment when every person will stand before God. Jesus warned his disciples to live faithfully in light of this coming day. This final message reminds us that Jesus's message is not only a message of mercy, but a message of judgment. God's time for mercy will end, and he will come as judge. Therefore, those who fail to receive the mercy of God will fall upon his judgment on judgment day.

Jesus's Crucifixion and Resurrection (Matt 26:2–28:20)

As Jesus's death drew near, he prepared to eat the Passover meal with his disciples. This meal commemorated God's liberation of the Hebrew slaves out of Egypt. Jesus announced that a greater liberation through his death, as the Lamb of God, would occur. He revealed that his body would be broken and his blood shed to inaugurate the new covenant and offer forgiveness of sin.

At the Passover meal, Jesus predicted that Judas would betray him, and Peter would deny him. After the meal, the disciples went to the garden of Gethsemane to pray. Jesus called his disciples to a time of spiritual preparation. The moment of testing would soon befall them all. Only Jesus was ready to meet the moment as he gave his will over to the will of his Father. As Good Friday started, Judas betrayed Jesus, and Jesus was taken into custody by the religious leaders. Good Friday contained a series of trials. The Jewish religious authorities were under the authority of Rome; so while Jesus would have initial trials among the Jewish religious leaders, ultimately he stood trial before Pontius Pilate. Pilate questioned Jesus and attempted to sway the crowds to release him. However, the crowds chose to release Barabbas and crucify Jesus. This was a sad moment in the life of the disciples. The time of preparation was ending, and they were not ready for what would befall them. The call to all future disciples is to understand what Jesus is doing and be spiritually alert in the situations where God has placed you so that you will be able to participate with him and not deny that you know him.

The final moments of Holy Week were horrific, as Jesus was hung on a cross between two criminals. Jesus quoted Psalm 22 from the cross to declare that God's suffering would ultimately be vindicated. The death of Jesus was surrounded by events that give meaning to this moment. As Jesus shouted from the cross—at the moment he breathed his last—the curtain in the temple was torn in two, tombs were opened, and people were raised from the dead. The death of Jesus offered new access to God and led to the resurrection of the dead. He was buried in a new tomb by a man named Joseph of Arimathea. The cross is so central to Christianity because the death that Jesus died was not his own. He died on a cross, alone, to forgive the sins of humanity. Every sin that has been or ever will be committed was able to be forgiven at the cross.

While the cross was tragic, this is not the end of the story. Very early on Sunday morning, women came to the tomb to finish the burial process. They were met by an angel who announced that Jesus had been resurrected! The women were instructed that Jesus would meet the disciples in Galilee. In the final scene of Matthew's Gospel, Jesus declared that through suffering, death, and resurrection he is the true King, King Jesus! In his authority and for his kingdom, the disciples were to go throughout the entire world and make disciples of every nation. Disciple-making requires the call to discipleship, baptism, and teaching future disciples to observe all that Jesus commanded. Jesus promised that as his disciples carried the gospel to the end of the earth, he would be present with them on the mission.

The Gospel of Matthew introduces us to the message and ministry of Jesus, only to call us to participate with it in the present because Jesus is alive! Now that you have heard from Jesus, will you follow him and call others to be his disciples?

BIBLIOGRAPHY

Bacon, B. W. *Studies in Matthew.* London: Constable, 1930.

Bauckham, Richard, ed. *A Gospel for All Christians.* Grand Rapids: Eerdmans, 1998.

Blomberg, Craig. *Matthew.* Nashville: B&H, 1992.

France, R. T. *The Gospel According to Matthew.* Grand Rapids: Eerdmans, 2007.

———. *Matthew: Evangelist and Teacher.* Downers Grove: InterVarsity Press, 1989.

Goodspeed, E. J. *Matthew: Apostle and Evangelist.* Philadelphia: J. C. Winston, 1959.

Gundry, Robert. *Matthew: A Commentary on His Handbook for a Mixed Church.* Second edition. Grand Rapids, Eerdmans, 1994.

Hagner, Donald. *Matthew 1–13.* Dallas: Word, 1993.

———. *Matthew 14–28.* Dallas: Word, 1995.

Kingsbury, Jack Dean. *Matthew as Story.* Philadelphia: Fortress, 1988.

Luz, Ulrich. *Matthew*, vol. 1. Translated by James E. Crouch. Minneapolis: Fortress, 2007.

Morris, Leon. *The Gospel According to Matthew*, PNTC. Grand Rapids: Eerdmans, 1992.

Nolland, John. *The Gospel of Matthew.* Grand Rapids: Eerdmans, 2005.

Pennington, Jonathan T. *Heaven and Earth in the Gospel of Matthew*. Grand Rapids: Baker, 2009.

Pennington, Jonathan T. *The Sermon on the Mount and Human Flourishing: A Theological Commentary.* Grand Rapids: Baker, 2017.

Quarles, Charles. *A Theology of Matthew.* Phillipsburg, NJ: P & R, 2013.

Schnackenburg, Rudolf. *The Gospel of Matthew.* Translated by Robert R. Barr. Grand Rapids: Eerdmans, 2002.

Stanton, Graham. *A Gospel for a New People: Studies in Matthew.* Louisville: John Knox/Westminster, 1992.

Wilkins, Michael. *Matthew*. Grand Rapids: Zondervan, 2004.

Witherington, Ben, III. *Matthew.* Macon, GA: Smyth and Helwys, 2006.

3

MARK

RUSSELL SMALL

CONNECTION POINT

What relevance does this first-century writing have for us today? Have you ever been in awe of a person? Some people seem to have it all together or are extraordinarily talented. They seem to know the right things to say, keep a robust schedule, have great relationships, and remain upbeat even in difficult circumstances. If we are honest, a hint of envy often exists when observing these people. We may wonder how they have been able to grow into such extraordinary people.

In a similar way, the Gospel of Mark draws us into the extraordinary person of Jesus. Jesus is truly larger than life. He is able to help, relentlessly healing and teaching all who are in need. Even the supernatural realm is easily overcome by Jesus. Mark reveals to us a Jesus who is able to overcome every obstacle and challenge. It is easy for us, like those in Jesus's day, to be enraptured by personalities that are larger than life. Jesus wants to press us on our need to adore and emulate big personalities. He is a powerful figure in Mark's Gospel, but his real power is actually found in another aspect of his life.

The world is so enamored by the powerful, the forceful, and the relentless. The confusion in Mark is why does the powerful person of Jesus run headlong into the cross? How is the powerful Messiah the Suffering One? Jesus says that real power is not found in the ability to take the lives of others but in the willingness to lay down one's life for another. Many readers may see the crucifixion of Jesus as an aberration of his power. However, Mark reveals that the power of Jesus is truly seen on the cross. The most powerful person is not one who is able to put down all their foes but the one who is willing to lay down his very life for his enemies. Jesus demonstrates real power, and the insightful reader will see and be transformed by this new perspective on power.

With this in mind, consider making this your prayer as you read and study this chapter:

Heavenly Father, grant me insight into the person and work of Jesus. May I understand his power and his suffering. Help me to follow him as his disciple. Allow me to not rely upon personal self-will, but to die to my sinful self and allow the Holy Spirit of God to transform me into the person that God desires for me to become, in Jesus's name. Amen.

SETTING

Recipients

John Mark (Acts 12:12, 25; 13:13; 15:37–39) seems to have written this Gospel as early as the AD 50s.[1] It is believed that this work was originally

---

[1] The authorship of the Gospel of Mark is a complex issue. There is a distinction between the person who wrote the Gospel and the source of its content. The name Mark apparently comes from a little-known figure in the New Testament named John Mark. John Mark is a friend of Barnabas and a brief traveling companion of Paul . John Mark is not an eyewitness of Jesus, which makes him an unlikely candidate to write a Gospel. However, church tradition states rather plainly that the source of the material in Mark comes from Simon Peter. Simon Peter orally delivers the Gospel of Mark. "And John the Presbyter also said this, Mark being the interpreter of Peter whatsoever he recorded he wrote with great accuracy but no however, in the order in which it was spoken or done by our Lord, for he neither heard nor followed our Lord, but as before said, he was in company with Peter, who gave him such instructions as was necessary, but not to give a history of our Lord's discourse: wherefore Mark has not erred in anything by writing some things as he

written in Rome. There, Simon Peter gave an oral address to a Roman audience.[2] In this context, Mark is traditionally understood as Peter's interpreter. Mark likely wrote down Peter's words in Rome. These two collaborated together to produce the Gospel of Mark. The style of writing in the form of a Greco-Roman biography seems to fit with this occasion.[3] While Mark's Gospel may have in view a Roman audience, it certainly has been written for wide distribution. Thus, it is pertinent to all Christians.[4]

Theme and Key Passage

A major theme in this Gospel is the discipleship call to follow the serving, suffering Savior (Mark 10:45). While Jesus is presented as a powerful Messiah, he is also revealed as the Suffering One. The theme of how suffering is the path to exaltation and how the cross plays a major role is critical to understanding Jesus and the call to follow him. A disciple of Jesus should take up their cross and follow him.[5]

Mark 10:45 tells us: "For even the Son of Man did not come to be served, but to serve, and to give his life as a ransom for many."

Purpose and Occasion

Christians in Rome would likely face persecution during Nero's reign (AD 54–68). Therefore, Mark's Gospel would reveal to them the glory of suffering. Suffering is not a mark of failure in the Christian life but likely the

---

has recorded them; for he was carefully attentive to one thing, not to pass by anything that he heard, or to state anything falsely in these accounts." Eusebius, *Ecclesiastical History*, upd. ed., ed. and trans. C. F. Cruse (Peabody, MA: Hendrickson, 1998), 104–5.

Simon Peter is an eyewitness and has a distinct perspective on the person and work of Jesus. While this Gospel bears the name Mark, it likely gives us information about Jesus from Simon Peter. The Gospel of Mark is dated by the majority of scholars as the earliest of the four Gospels. This is sometimes called Markan priority. This means Mark was written first and likely that Matthew and Luke take some of their content from this first Gospel. See David Dungan, *A History of the Synoptic Problem: The Canon, the Text, the Composition, and the Interpretation of the Gospels* (New York: Doubleday, 1999).

[2] See the argument for Roman destination by Robert Stein, *Mark*, BECNT (Grand Rapids: Baker, 2008), 63–78.

[3] See the classic argument for the Gospel being a form of Greco-Roman biography by Richard Burridge, *What Are the Gospels? A Comparison with Greco-Roman Biography*, 2nd ed. (Grand Rapids: Eerdmans, 2004).

[4] Richard Bauckham, ed., *The Gospels for All Christians: Rethinking the Gospel Audiences* (Grand Rapids: Eerdmans, 1997).

[5] The theme of the atonement in Mark has been developed by Peter Bolt, *The Cross from a Distance: Atonement in Mark's Gospel* (Downers Grove, IL: InterVarsity Press, 2004).

path of obedience and maturity. The portrait of the powerful, suffering Jesus would be a timely encouragement to Christians facing persecution.

HIGHLIGHTS IN MARK

The Gospel of the Kingdom—In Galilee (Mark 1:1–8:21)

The opening phrase of Mark gives insight into the nature of the document. This document is the beginning of the good news—the gospel. What is the good news about? The good news is about Jesus Christ, the Son of God. This good news has come in the person of Jesus of Nazareth. He is revealed as an extraordinary figure who ushers in the kingdom of God. Jesus receives the designation of Christ (or Messiah) and will further be identified as the Son of God. The term "Christ" reveals Jesus's unique status as the promised Messiah coming from Israel. The term "Son of God" addresses the unique parent/child relationship that Jesus will have with

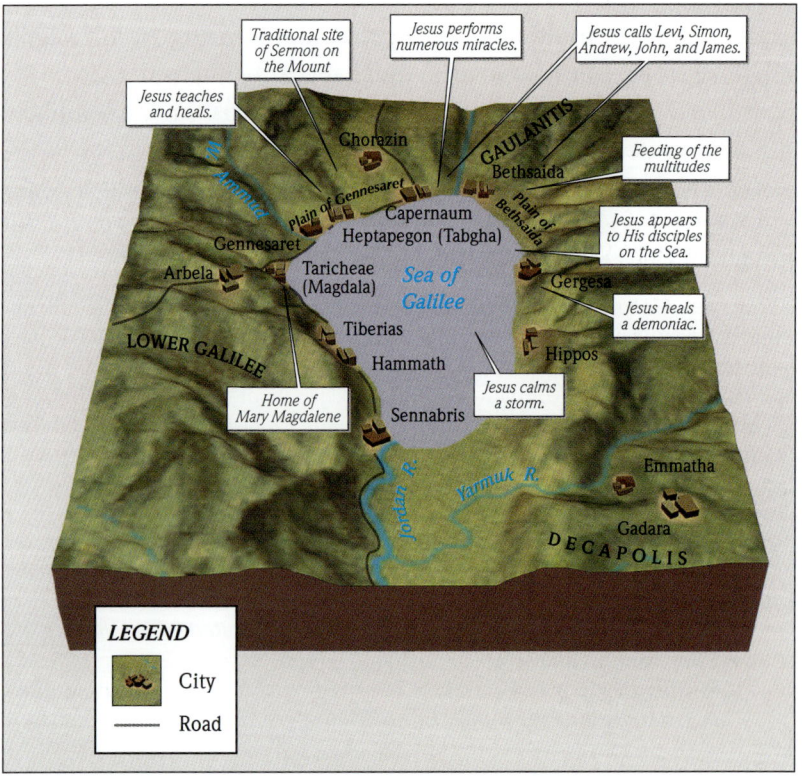

The Ministry of Jesus around the Sea of Galilee

God, the Father.[6] Further, the context of Mark is understood as the continuation of the Old Testament story where the promised messianic herald is preparing the way for Jesus and God's next fresh move in human history.

What stands out to the observant reader in these early sections is what is missing from Mark's description of Jesus's life and ministry. There is no genealogy, no birth story, and very little context given to a rather abrupt start of a dramatic story concerning Jesus. Mark is ready to describe the vigorous actions of Jesus. Additionally, the opening section of this Gospel is repeatedly punctuated with the word *immediately*. The reader encounters a tireless, powerful Jesus. The narrative records one mighty deed done after another. The reader is to be caught up in Jesus's dramatic and powerful personality.

One way to learn about Jesus is to understand the titles used to describe him. For example, the phrase "Son of God" reveals to us that Jesus has a family relationship with God the Father. Since Jesus has a relationship with God, and an ability to relate to humanity, he is able to bring us into a relationship with God the Father, through himself as the Son. He is the bridge.

Jesus declared that the time for a fresh inbreaking of God's kingdom had come. God's power would be seen. Jesus showed authority over Satan in the wilderness, was ministered to by angels, and had full authority over the sick and demon-possessed. Jesus's dramatic authority over unseen spirits and the demons' awareness of Jesus's power are clear signs that the powers of darkness are shaken at the presence of Jesus and the kingdom he brings. Jesus called others to participate in God's new act through repentance of their sins and to follow him in a process of discipleship. The opposition to God's new work was not only from supernatural agents of darkness but earthly opposition as well. The Pharisees were challenged and confounded by the powerful Jesus. His disregard for their traditions created tension between Jesus and the Pharisees that increases as the story unfolds. While the power of Jesus was on display, the foreshadowing of suffering was also present (Mark 3:6). The themes of power and suffering will punctate Mark's Gospel.

---

[6] The phrase "Son of God" also speaks to the divinity of Jesus. Jesus's self-attestation to God as his Father was seen as a statement of divinity whereby Jesus was making himself equal with God. This was another major reason the Jewish leaders were seeking to kill Jesus (John 5:18).

Jesus was truly bringing about God's kingdom on the earth. While God is in control of the world in a general sense, much that happens in the world is a result of living in a fallen, broken world. Jesus announced the kingdom of God and then visibly went about reversing the effects of sin and even supernatural bondage. The kingdom was coming, and that was really good news! Thus, the Christian is to be very hopeful about the power found through Jesus.

Because of the initial power displayed in Jesus's ministry, a lot of people gathered around him. These people sought Jesus with great intensity but limited understanding. They would soon be tested and thinned out by the things Jesus said and did. He did not come merely to make a display of power but to point to a deeper work that God was doing. Jesus did not come merely to attract a crowd but to deliver a message about God's fresh work in the world.

Jesus's own biological family did not understand his mission, and even attempted to gain control of him and subvert him from his mission (Mark 3:21). The scribes accused Jesus of being powerful because he was in league with the devil. The irony is that the powerful work and message of Jesus was constantly misunderstood by those who claimed to know the ways of God. Is the struggle of these original disciples to understand Jesus's mission any different from those who desire to follow him today? In other words, are believers often wowed by the power of Jesus without understanding his person or message? Many followers of Jesus are drawn to the benefits of Jesus without understanding the sacrifice and suffering often associated with following him.

When Jesus speaks, he discloses the mysteries of the kingdom of God. The parables were earthly stories with heavenly meanings (Mark 4). They were designed to be true-to-life stories that conveyed a deeper meaning. However, this meaning was not immediately obvious. In the parable of the sower, the message of the kingdom sown in the hearts of people and various responses occur with only a certain percent taking the message deep into their hearts and producing fruit (Mark 4:3–9, 13–20). The parables in Mark reveal that the kingdom of God was being sown in the world and in the hearts of people. Though the kingdom appeared small at the moment, the full effect of the kingdom would bring about universal blessings. However, some would internalize Jesus's message and be changed by it and others would quickly dismiss the message and not be transformed. The call of Jesus in this section is to see the small beginning in Jesus of God's great kingdom work.

Three episodes of restoration conclude this section: an exorcism, a physical healing, and a resurrection (Mark 5). These episodes reveal the unique power of Jesus. For those who are willing to have faith in him, his healing and deliverance are available. This section ends in Jesus's rejection (Mark 6). In the very place where he was raised, there was great unbelief. While Jesus performed a few miracles in Nazareth, his familial connection to the area created a spiritual barrier for people to see his true identity. The rejection of Jesus in Nazareth began the movement of Jesus beyond the region of Galilee.

Often, our interpretation of what Jesus is or should be doing clouds our vision of what he is actually doing. Jesus has come to liberate the world from all that holds it in bondage. As he attempts to communicate and demonstrate this, misunderstanding and rejection abound. This section of Mark calls us humbly to see what Jesus is doing and, as a good disciple, learn from him.

A unique mixture of power and weakness punctuates the mission of Jesus. He commissioned his disciples to spread the good news message. On one hand, the apostles had authority over unclean spirits and healing the sick. On the other hand, they would be vulnerable on the mission. The disciples could wear sandals and have a staff; other than that, they were to rely on God's provision. Further, there was great urgency to deliver the message of the kingdom. If the message was not readily received, then the disciples were to proceed to the next place as a sign of condemnation. Here, the mystery of Jesus's power was being embodied. The apostles were powerful, dependent disciples. They had power as long as they were dependent upon God's provision. If this dependency was lost, they had no power. So, strangely, the dependency was part of their power, not antithetical to it.

The death of John the Baptist made the prospect of death more likely for Jesus and his disciples. John's death occurred through a unique series of

> ### Missing the Obvious
>
> Mark introduces his Gospel by explaining his purpose to reveal the reality that Jesus is the Son of God. However, there is rich irony throughout the first seven chapters of his writing. Everyone seems to miss this reality of who Jesus is, despite the things he has done and said. He has proven himself time and time again. Here we are, seven chapters in, and the only ones who have recognized the divine nature of Jesus are the demons (Mark 5:6) and a Gentile woman (Mark 7:24–30). It is not until chapter 8 that the disciples begin to understand this reality.
>
> So, a question: are you missing the evidence of the glory of Jesus you have been given? The Jewish people to whom Jesus came missed it initially. Are you missing how Jesus is working around you and attributing that work to someone or something else?

The Ministry of Jesus beyond Galilee

events where Herod Antipas was influenced by his wife to murder John. This event echoes a similar event in the Old Testament where Jezebel influences her husband, Ahab, to commit evil against the prophet Elijah. Wicked people desired to kill God's prophets. Any sense of glamour the disciples thought would come by following the authoritative Jesus was quelled in John the Baptist's sobering martyrdom.

Despite what some might teach, this section reveals that following the powerful Jesus does not mean that we will be exempt from suffering or death. In actuality, this passage and other New Testament passages reveal that faithful servants of Christ should expect suffering (Phil 1:29; 1 Pet 4:19; 5:9–11). So, suffering may actually be a validation that one is following Jesus; rather than, as some teach, a reason for questioning.

While many struggled to fully grasp the identity of Jesus, others continued to resist him. The Pharisees saw Jesus as an affront to their authority. Jesus's violation of their traditions was a particularly egregious offense. For example, his disciples' lack of participation in ceremonial washings caused consternation (Mark 7:1–5). Jesus believed that the religion practiced by the Pharisees turned the intentions of God's law into ceremonial rites and rituals that entirely missed the spirit of God's commands. Jesus warned his disciples concerning the corrupting influences of such teaching. This opening section is a clear call to look again at the powerful, suffering Jesus and learn what it means to follow him. The disciple is to also recognize the dangers of false religion.

The Nature of Discipleship—On the Way to Jerusalem (Mark 8:22–10:52)

This section begins with the healing of a blind man in Bethsaida. The healing of this man was progressive. His eyes were opened, but he was only able to see blurry images of people. The second touch from Jesus enabled full clarity. This progressive miracle of sight serves as a paradigm for the disciples' progressive, albeit blurry, understanding of Jesus. Peter's great confession of Jesus's identity provides evidence that the disciples were gaining a clearer vision of Jesus as the Messiah (Mark 9:27–30).[7] The disciples had partial understanding of Jesus's messianic status. However, they missed that Jesus would also have to suffer. As a disciple of Jesus, we will likely have a progressive understanding of his full identity, even in spite of our bold confession of him. We should consciously deepen our awareness of who Jesus is.

Jesus's status as the Messiah is complex. While Jesus certainly revealed himself to all people, he knew that once the onlookers understood his claim of messianic status this would lead to his death. Strangely, the full recognition of Jesus would not lead people to worship but to desire to kill him. The authorities would not tolerate Jesus's messianic claim, so Jesus asked his disciples to not disclose his messianic status until the moment for his death was near. Jesus would not only be the powerful Messiah (Dan

---

[7] This confession is a central turning point to the entire Gospel. It is from this point Mark pushes his reader's attention to the cross.

7:13–14), but the suffering Messiah as well (Isa 53). Jesus told his disciples that he would be handed over and killed. The disciples did not comprehend the suffering aspect of the powerful Jesus. After Peter's great confession of Jesus's identity, he took Jesus aside and tried to rebuke his statement regarding his death. Even Jesus's disciples could be twisted into collaboration against him. Jesus called them to awareness of the drama of redemption that was being played out before them. It is easy for disciples of Jesus to think of the proclamation and reception of the gospel as a very human act.

Jesus set out the terms of genuine discipleship: Discipleship would not require his disciples to bear the cross that Jesus bore; his cross would be unique. Jesus would take upon himself the sin of the entire world. The disciple would need to take up his own cross. The mission of the disciple would have its own unique challenges and persecutions. The disciple was to reject self-will, give himself or herself to the mission, and follow Christ's path wherever it leads. Through this act of self-giving, the disciple might think that his or her life is lost; yet in light of God's kingdom, life is actually found. Clinging to life in a world of sin and death is losing. Giving one's life to God and spreading his message of life to the world is a means to find one's life. The full embrace of being a disciple of Jesus is not found in the willingness to bask in his power but in being willing to accept suffering for Jesus's name. The disciple who is willing to suffer for Jesus is actually disclosing that he or she is tapping into a deeper power that Jesus has given.

> **Discipleship**
>
> To be a disciple of Jesus, one must possess certain characteristics. Such characteristics include surrender to God's will, faith in God, prayer, awareness of one's sinful heart, humble service, forgiveness, withstanding temptation, and full confession of Christ to others. Through this deep dependency upon God his life is able to radiate out of the heart of the disciple.
>
> For more, see Hans F. Bayer, *A Theology of Mark: The Dynamic between Christology and Authentic Discipleship* (Philipsburg, NJ: P & R, 2012).

Strangely, through the suffering of Jesus, his power becomes more powerful. God's exaltation of Jesus was even more glorious because of his solidarity with sinful people. Jesus gave a glimpse of his current and future glory to the disciples. He took Peter, James, and John to a high mountain. There, Jesus revealed his glory to his disciples. Again, Jesus was attempting to imprint on the mind of his disciples that even in light of his upcoming suffering the glory of his person was still there. The suffering was not an absence of Jesus's power but a part of his power and glory.

The power and weakness of Jesus are not to be seen as contradictory, but complementary. Through Jesus's weakness and ultimate death his ultimate power will be revealed. For disciples to participate in this type of power, they, too, will need to humble themselves even to the point of suffering. In the crucible of suffering and deep dependency upon God the fullness of God's power will be realized in them.

As Jesus moved closer to Jerusalem, his movement was punctuated by predictions of his death. In Mark 9:30–32, Jesus predicted his death a second time. Even with this clarity and repetition, the disciples failed to grasp the significance of Jesus's words. In the presence of the self-giving, humble Jesus, the disciples still attempted to understand his kingdom and their roles in it. In human kingdoms, roles for high positions are jockeyed for and positions are gained after fierce competition. The disciples of Jesus fall into this same trap, but Jesus stated that his kingdom was an upside-down kingdom. The greatest is the least, and you move up in the kingdom by moving downward in servitude to others. A true disciple of Jesus should focus on moving down in service, rather than moving up in worldly rank. Disciples of Jesus are to rid themselves of dominant thinking. They should embody a heart of service and graciousness to others. Further, it will be those of childlike faith who will enter God's kingdom. Those who are willing to come to God with the simplicity and humility of a child are the ones who will participate in what God is doing.

In this context the demanding expectations of discipleship are being set forth through the rest of this section. We see the expectations of Jesus for his followers on display. He called them to live godly lives rooted in personal sacrifice and humility. Jesus calls us to submit every aspect of our lives in service and honor of God, whether it be our marriages or finances.

All too often, we seek to lean on the wisdom and rest in the structures of this world rather than living in anticipation of God's coming kingdom. The stripping away of earthly security is part of participation in God's kingdom. This point is evidenced as a rich young ruler desired to learn from Jesus about obtaining eternal life (Mark 10:17–22). The rich young ruler appeared to have the heart to follow God's commands, so Jesus pressed in. Unwittingly, money had become his god, despite the fact that the first command is a command to have no other gods in the place of God himself. It was not the money but the love of money and the idolatrous place it held in his life that was the problem. Jesus confronted this idolatrous area and called for radical change, but the man was not willing to follow Jesus at such a steep price and walked away.

We would be wise to heed this warning. Possessions and riches turn quickly into idols. These captivate the human heart to the degree that God is unable to have his rightful place. While riches and possessions are not inherently bad, they are quickly misused as objects of worship. Jesus communicated to his disciples that following him will require a choice between God and money. These two masters cannot be served at the same time. Glittering idols are so attractive to humanity. The disciple of Jesus is to turn from the luring temptations to follow him.

In Mark 10:33–34, Jesus predicted his death for the third time. He continued to communicate the nature of his mission and the cost of discipleship; yet again, there was confusion. Neither of these concepts was fully grasped by his disciples. The nature of God's kingdom was also misunderstood. In many earthly kingdoms the reigning king chooses a court or administration to share in the ruling functions. As Jesus's disciples awaited his kingdom, they continued to jockey for positions. To participate in

Rich Young Ruler: "This is Heinrich Hofmann's *Christ and the Rich Young Ruler*, 1889."

bringing in Jesus's kingdom requires joining with him in his suffering, but the disciples were only able to think about a possible position of honor. In the context of many misunderstandings of Jesus's words, a blind man did not ask Jesus for greater honor, but merely for mercy to be able to see again. Gracious Jesus, on the way to his own death, responded to the humble faith of the blind man and restored his sight. The clear application is that those who want to be exalted will be humbled, and those who are humble, God exalts.

The Centrality of the Cross—In Jerusalem (Mark 11:1–16:8)

As Jesus entered Jerusalem, a series of events and teaching surrounded the Jerusalem temple. As he made his appearance, he received an enthusiastic welcome from many within Jerusalem. The fickle crowd heralded him and celebrated him. Jesus quickly pronounced prophetic judgment against the corrupted religion of the religious leaders. He metaphorically cursed a fig tree representing fruitless Israel and then pronounced his judgment upon the corrupted religion in the temple. Rather than the temple being a place for all nations to encounter the living God, it had devolved into a place of buying, selling, and theft. Jesus's swift condemnation of the corrupted practices of the temple set off a series of conflicts. The religious leaders began to question Jesus's authority. As Jesus disrupted the religious establishment, there was a natural backlash from those in authority. Rather than welcoming what God was doing, they looked to persecute and kill anyone threatening their authority. Even though God's work was rejected by the Jerusalem religious establishment, the rejected Savior would still become the foundation for the salvation for all who would believe.

The Pharisees and Herodians questioned Jesus. Rather than attempting to point out the fact that Jesus was subverting the religious authorities, they attempted to point out that he was subverting the authority of the Romans. The Sadducees took a different approach at this stage. They questioned Jesus on the logical coherence of his teachings based on their misguided theology. If Jesus could not be convicted of subversion, the Sadducees would attempt to make his teaching seem incoherent.

Amid these confrontations some began to grasp Jesus's message. However, the destiny of the religious establishment and all earthly powers set against God were doomed to fall. Jesus predicted the destruction of the temple. In AD 70 the Romans would invade Jerusalem and tear down the temple. This historical act would mark the end of an era in Jerusalem. The Jewish religious establishment would be forever changed. Further, the destruction of the temple in Jerusalem serves as a symbol of the ultimate destruction that will occur at the end of time against all those who are against God's kingdom. The disciple of Jesus is to take hope that the Son of Man will come with power and great glory and bring an appropriate end to all things. In the meantime, the disciples were to be alert and aware of Jesus's return and faithfully serve him until he came. As the cross came into full view, Jesus's condemnation and rejection of all false religion was clearly seen. All that was wrong with false religion—including the need for power, money, and status—Jesus rejected and called his disciples to embrace his true form of religion.

In this final section of Mark, Jesus's death via crucifixion is central. Two responses reveal the various ways this moment is interpreted. First, a woman spontaneously anointed Jesus, which prefigures his upcoming burial. This lavish response was misunderstood by Jesus's disciples, yet the plan of God was moving forward. Second, in contrast to a woman who gave so much, we see Judas Iscariot, the betrayer. Judas was willing to sell Jesus out and set the plan of his betrayal in motion.

Jesus ate the Passover meal with his disciples. The Passover meal memorializes the liberation of the people of Israel from slavery in Egypt. Jesus used this meal to infuse it with greater meaning. He stated to his

The Last Supper: This mosaic from the thirteenth century, titled *Last Supper* is in Basilica di San Marco.

disciples that a greater salvation would occur than Israel's liberation out of Egypt. His death, represented in the bread and the wine, would be the basis of the ultimate salvation. The Passover meal revealed that God was about to enter into a new agreement with humanity (Jer 31:31–34). In this new agreement God would provide all that was needed for humanity's salvation, and they would only need to accept it. This agreement would be a one-sided covenant, in that God would pay the full debt for the sins of humanity.

After the Last Supper, Jesus led his disciples to pray in the garden of Gethsemane. The moment of preparation was ending. Jesus pleaded with his disciples to stay awake and pray to be spiritually ready for the moment that was about to come. The disciples fell asleep, which revealed they were not spiritually ready, but Jesus was ready to meet the moment with resolve. The plan of betrayal that Judas set in motion was now enacted. The religious leaders located Jesus in the garden, arrested him, and took him through a series of trials.

Jesus first stood before the Sanhedrin. The Sanhedrin questioned Jesus, especially regarding his messianic status. Jesus implied that he was the Messiah. This admission of his messianic status and identification as the Son of Man put the religious leaders on edge. Their resolve strengthened to put Jesus to death, while Peter's resolve to face this moment quickly diminished. Peter, in the context of conflict, denied Jesus three times. As a result, Jesus faced death without the support of his disciples. As we reflect on the failure of Jesus's followers, we are reminded that a disciple does not know when the moment will come when he or she will enter into a difficult test. The call for perpetual prayer and readiness is critical in the disciple's life. At the same time, knowing the end of the story, we are reminded of God's grace in restoring a repentant disciple to usefulness despite their past failures. Our God is a gracious and forgiving God.

Jesus was passed from the Sanhedrin to Pontius Pilate. Pilate questioned Jesus to understand the nature of his offense. Pilate was amazed by the accusations of the crowd against Jesus; but nevertheless, Pilate succumbed to the will of the mob and handed Jesus over to be crucified. Jesus was led to Golgotha, where he was crucified. His dramatic life was now met by an unexpected and dramatic death. The powerful Jesus was dead on a cross!

The cross has been contextualized so the reader can understand that Jesus did not die for his own sin, but the sins of the world. The cross is the judgment that should be ours, but Jesus lovingly took it upon himself, revealing his deep love and self-giving sacrifice on behalf of humanity. The cross was not Jesus's end, but actually the place of a new beginning.

The drama of the Gospel of Mark is not over. When the women approached the tomb to finalize the burial process, they did not find Jesus's corpse, but an empty tomb. The women entered the tomb to encounter a man dressed in white who proclaimed that Jesus was not there because he had risen! The women were told to go and tell the disciples about this astounding event. However, the women were overwhelmed and said nothing because of their fear.

Mark's Gospel leaves us with a risen Jesus and so many questions. What does the resurrection mean? Has Jesus defeated death; has he conquered sin? Has Jesus brought in God's kingdom? Is he now able to forgive humanity of their sins? Mark leaves the reader in suspense to think through all the profound implications that Jesus's life, death, and resurrection now mean. The Gospel concludes and still beckons for the disciple to continue the process of understanding Jesus and conforming his or her life to his discipleship call.

The Longer Ending of Mark (Mark 16:9–20)

The cliffhanger ending of the Gospel of Mark leaves some readers confused. Why does this Gospel end so abruptly? Reading the other Gospels gives a fuller picture of what happened following Jesus's resurrection. In an apparent attempt to fill in the gaps left open by the ending of Mark, multiple endings have been added. These endings appear to not be written by Mark and should not be considered original. The supplemental endings have been placed in some early English translations and could be in your current English translation. However, in most newer translations, a note is added stating these endings are likely not part of the original text.[8]

BIBLIOGRAPHY

Bauckham, Richard, ed. *The Gospels for All Christians: Rethinking the Gospel Audiences*. Grand Rapids: Eerdmans, 1997.

Bayer, Hans. *A Theology of Mark: The Dynamic Between Christology and Authentic Discipleship*. Phillipsburg, NJ: P&R, 2012.

Black, David, ed. *Perspectives on the Ending of Mark: 4 Views*. Nashville: B&H, 2008.

---

[8] There are various reasons given for the ending of Mark. For further study, see David Black, ed., *Perspectives on the Ending of Mark: 4 Views* (Nashville: B&H, 2008).

Brooks, James. *Mark*. Nashville: B&H, 1991.

Bolt, Peter. *The Cross from a Distance*. Downers Grove, IL: InterVarsity, 2004.

Burridge, Richard. *What Are the Gospels? A Comparison with Greco-Roman Biography*. 2nd ed. Grand Rapids: Eerdmans, 2004.

Dungan, David. *A History of the Synoptic Problem: The Canon, the Text, the Composition, and the Interpretation of the Gospels*. New York: Doubleday, 1999.

Eusebius. *Ecclesiastical History*. New Updated Edition. Translated by C. F. Cruse. Peabody, MA: Hendrickson, 1998.

France, R. T. *The Gospel of Mark*. Grand Rapids: Eerdmans, 2002.

Garland, David. *A Theology of Mark's Gospel: Good New about Jesus the Messiah, the Son of God*. Grand Rapids: Zondervan, 2015.

———. *Mark*. Grand Rapids: Zondervan, 1996.

Rhoads, David, Joanna Dewey, and Donald Michie. *Mark as Story*. Minneapolis: Fortress, 2012.

Stein, Robert. *Mark*. BECNT. Grand Rapids: Baker, 2008.

Strauss, Mark. *Mark: Exegetical Commentary on the New Testament*. Grand Rapids: Zondervan, 2014.

4

LUKE

DOTTIE RHOADS

CONNECTION POINT

What relevance does this first-century writing have for us today? You may flip through the New Testament and wonder how Luke's Gospel is distinguished from the other three. Does this often-neglected Gospel account offer a unique perspective on the familiar story of Jesus? Does it speak to the relevance of the gospel message for each individual? Luke presents the gospel of Jesus Christ as a direct answer to these questions. In Luke, the God of Israel has come in the person of Jesus to redeem, rescue, and restore his sinful, lost, and broken people. The gospel is for all people, and in Luke, it is the forgotten who realize and experience it.

If you wonder whether God really does see you, and ultimately, whether he is willing and able to help you, consider the gospel as Luke tells it. Read Luke, and become a witness to the extravagant ways in which the Creator has become the Redeemer and personally made it possible for the helpless to be made whole. Open Luke, and become like one of the characters in this story who finds that Jesus stops at nothing to make possible the salvation of all willing people. You will find that God can be trusted to keep his promises.

With this in mind, consider making this your prayer as you read and study this chapter:

> *Lord, thank you that throughout history, you have proven yourself to be faithful, powerful, and merciful. You not only made me, but in Jesus, you gave your life for me so that I could be saved from my sin and reconciled to you. Please empower me to walk closely with you and to respond to you in faith, so that I experience your living and life-changing presence. In Jesus's name, amen.*

SETTING

Recipients

Luke was likely writing in the mid-60s AD to a man he identified as Theophilus.[1] Theophilus, a common name at the time, means "lover of God"

---

[1] See Robert H. Stein, *Luke*, vol. 24, NAC (Nashville: B&H, 1992), 21. Though the Gospel is anonymous, the earliest records in church history reflect a unanimous position on authorship. The Muratorian Canon (ca. 170–180) names the physician Luke as the author of the Third Gospel, and the testimonies of church fathers, including Justin Martyr, Irenaeus, Clement of Alexandria, Origin, Eusebius, Jerome, and Tertullian, agree. Luke's authorship was accepted, without a hint of dispute or debate, until the nineteenth century. Considering that Luke was a minor character in the New Testament, being neither an apostle nor an eyewitness of Jesus's ministry, the unanimous testimony of church history is that much more convincing. While not much is known about Luke the man, phrases in Acts and Paul's own letters provide some clarity. The prologue of the Gospel reveals that the author was not an eyewitness to the events themselves (Luke 1:1–2), but according to the "we" passages of Acts, he was a traveling companion of Paul (Acts 16:10–17; 20:5–15; 21:1–18; 27:1–28:16). In his letter to the Colossians, Paul names Luke as one of the individuals who periodically joined him as a co-laborer and travel companion (Col 4:10–11, 14). It is likely that the Luke who church history names as author of the Gospel is the same Luke that Paul identifies as the Gentile doctor who played a part in the spread of Christianity and the growth of the church in its earliest stage. Even so, the message of the Gospel is not contingent upon the identity of an author. Given that he chose anonymity, what Luke is most concerned with was not identifying himself, but rather identifying his audience and clearly stating his thesis; he sets out to accomplish a particular purpose, and it is imperative that his intention is heard.

With regard to the date of the book, those who assign Luke a later dating, around AD 80–90, commonly do so as a result of reading Luke's eschatological discourses (Luke 19:41–44; 21:20–24) as references to the fall of Jerusalem in AD 70. There are several essential

in Greek. Though this meaning has sparked suggestions that Theophilus metaphorically represents Luke's ideal reader, there are several reasons to assume that Luke's Theophilus was a literal individual. It was customary for an author to dedicate his written work to the patron who financially contributed to its publication and circulation, and Luke's designation of Theophilus as "most excellent" implies that as a person of unique rank, wealth, and status, he was able to fund this project (Luke 1:3 NASB1995).

Given the care that Luke takes in articulating his apologetic (Luke 1:1–4), and given that dedicating a written work to an imaginary reader is an unknown practice of the time, it can be safely assumed that Luke wrote with a literal Theophilus in mind. While it is likely that Theophilus was Luke's patron, and his immediate reader, he was not Luke's only intended reader. As a historiographical narrative, Luke's Gospel is a carefully composed account of recent historical events. It was certainly Luke's intention that his work disseminate to a wider audience, assuring each individual to be certain that the dynamic events of the life of Jesus of Nazareth happened as they were reported. It is through these events and in the mouths of these characters that the story is told. Through Jesus, God has accomplished the fulfillment of ancient salvific promises, and Luke is committed to carefully testifying to the truth of the gospel.

Theme and Key Passage

Luke seems to arrange his Gospel account around one dominating theme: Jesus accomplishes the fulfillment of God's salvific promises. According to his eternal plan, God personally visits humans and fulfills his promises to redeem, reconcile, and restore them according to the salvation made available in Jesus. In his self-proclaimed mission statement, Jesus declares the form this mission will take.

Luke 4:18–19 says: "The Spirit of the Lord is on me, because he has anointed me to preach good news to the poor. He has sent me to proclaim

---

points to consider, though, that suggest an earlier dating. If it is granted that as God, Jesus possessed the ability to predict the future and make these statements prophetically rather than only retrospectively, a pre-AD 70 date is possible. The earlier dating seems not only possible but probable when it is considered that in Acts, Luke's sequel, the present tense is used for the temple that is still standing when Stephen is stoned (Acts 6:13–14). Having assumed Markan priority, Luke could not have been written before early to mid-60s. A mid-60s date is likely, given that Acts presents the Gentile mission in its developing stages and, most notably, does not mention the death of Paul (ca. late 60s). For a more thorough discussion of a mid-60s date, see Darrell L. Bock, *Luke 1:1–9:50,* BECNT (Grand Rapids: Baker Academic, 1994).

release to the captives and recovery of sight to the blind, to set free the oppressed, to proclaim the year of the Lord's favor.

In these verses, Jesus combines several texts from Isaiah and declares that God's promises to comfort the afflicted, heal the sick, and release the prisoners are fulfilled in him. With one eye on Israel's history and the other on Jesus's life, Luke draws a line of continuity between God's promises in the past and the unfolding events in the present. Luke's reader witnesses the dynamic ways in which Jesus brings about the whole-person restoration that characterizes his salvation. As promised, those held in physical and spiritual darkness and bondage experience the great reversal that Jesus brings.

Purpose and Occasion

Jesus's ministry took an unexpected form. Why does it look so countercultural? Should Luke's reader be surprised to find that Jesus included women in his inner circle, praised virtues of those demonized by society, and made a way for the least likely to be the greatest in God's kingdom? No, the reader familiar with God's nature, promises, and plan should expect it. The gospel message is good news for anyone who is willing to receive it; and in Luke's Gospel, it is most often those on the margins of society who are found ready.

Luke is the most intentional of the four Gospel writers to present the unfolding events as a continuation of humanity's history. He wrote to assure his readers that Jesus's life perfectly accomplished the eternal plan of God. Characters in the story are like actors in a grand drama; from their mouths and in the events of their lives the story of God-in-the-flesh is told. God has come, in the person of the Son, to fulfill his promises; and the reader of Luke's Gospel is confronted with the way that God's nature and plan are perfectly unchanged. The same God who worked mightily in Israel's history is at work again in an even greater way, and Luke is intent that his reader not miss it.

HIGHLIGHTS IN LUKE

Prologue; Promises Fulfilled in Jesus's Birth and Ministry Preparation (Luke 1:1–4:13)

The way Jesus came, the ones who rejoiced at his coming, and the source of their joy is a snapshot of what unfolds throughout the story. The God

Luke

Lorenzo Monaco painted this nativity scene, titled *Geburt Christi* in 1409.

of all glory was born humbly, among humble people who delighted in God. Luke's Gospel is heralded as one that is especially mindful of the plight of the downtrodden, and when this portrait of Jesus is held against the backdrop of the whole Bible, it is clear that Jesus gives flesh and breath the compassion of God (Exod 4:31; Pss 80:14; 106:4; 130:7–8).

Luke gives more detail about the birth of Jesus than any other Gospel writer. Those familiar with *A Charlie Brown Christmas* could perhaps join Linus in quoting Jesus's birth story. The familiarity of Luke's account, though, does not dilute its power. In the first three chapters, the Holy Spirit is active seven times. God is undoubtedly at work among these humble characters, and layers of Old Testament allusions indicate that he is keeping his promises in familiar ways (Luke 1:15, 35, 41, 67; 2:25–27; 3:16, 22).[2] Immediately, God begins fulfilling his promises to rescue the downtrodden and disenfranchised.

Fulfillment begins in the birth narrative. Both Mary and Zechariah hear God's plan from the mouths of angels, but Mary, the humble

---

[2] Jesus's and John's birth announcements are formulated like Old Testament birth announcements (Gen 16:11; Isa 7:14).

maidservant, is the ideal disciple who takes God at his word, while Zechariah, the priest, is slower to do so (Luke 1:5–38). The reader is struck by the realization that the single response God expects is faith. The theme of reversal continues. Angels announced God's birth to lowly shepherds; and God's glory, previously confined to the temple, "shone around them," in shocking demonstration that the Lord himself had become accessible to all men (Luke 2:9). Centuries earlier, God had promised that he would visit his people, redeem them from bondage, comfort them in weariness, and shine his light on all people (Isa 46:13; 49:6, 9; 51:4–5; 52:9; 60:1, 19). In Luke, unsuspecting figures rejoice at the fulfillment. Anna and Simeon, elderly representatives of faithful Israel, rejoice that this "consolation" and "redemption" had arrived in the child Jesus (Luke 2:25, 38). Though unremarkable by worldly standards, Anna and Simeon give a glimpse of the joy that belongs to all who see Jesus for who he is.

> **Disenfranchised**
>
> Luke presents the disenfranchised, rather than disqualified from God's kingdom, as honorable examples of faith. Luke's attention is most noticeable by comparison. For instance, Luke contains more material about women than any other New Testament writing, and twenty-three of his forty-two passages featuring women are unique to his Gospel. While Matthew's birth account is focused on Joseph, Luke's revolves around Mary's response of faith. Each of the Gospels names the twelve disciples, but Luke also names a group of women who traveled with and supported Jesus (Luke 8:1–3). A culture that placed lesser value on women would have found this odd, but Luke's reader and God's follower should not be surprised. God promised that "the glory of the Lord will appear/and all humanity together will see it" (Isa 40:5). In Luke, shepherds and priests, wealthy and poor, Jews and Gentiles, and men and women see God's glory in Jesus.

Whereas Matthew's account emphasizes the conflict brooding as the result of Jesus's birth, the characters in Luke's story burst forth with joy. Like musical breaks in a play, three praise hymns pause the movement of Luke's story and draw the reader in to watch themes develop.[3] Mary, Zechariah, and Simeon celebrate that God's salvation has arrived in the person of God himself, and they realize that the whole world is now being turned on its head.[4] Jesus was living proof that God had remembered to show mercy

---

[3] When taken together, these praise hymns sound like the next verse in Israel's song praising God for hearing, delivering and saving them (Exod 15:1–18; 1 Sam 2:1–10).

[4] The praise hymns of Mary (Luke 1:46–55), Zechariah (Luke 1:68–79), and Simeon (Luke 2:29–32) are known as the *Magnificat*, *Benedictus*, and *Nunc Dimittis*, respectively.

Galilee in the Time of Jesus

by saving and redeeming his people according to his promises (Luke 1:47, 50, 54–55, 68, 72–73, 77, 2:29–30).[5] In Jesus, God was visiting his people.

This visitation was for all people. Like Matthew, Luke anchors Jesus in his ancestry line, but he begins with Adam (Luke 3:38). The point is clear. Jesus is the second Adam, the representative of all humanity, and his perfect obedience in withstanding temptation in the wilderness indicates that where humanity fails, Jesus succeeds (Luke 4:1–13). He is the anointed, beloved Son and faithful Servant of God who will complete the purpose of humanity, rescue her from sin, and reconcile her to God (Ps 2:7; Isa 42:1). As God promised, this undiscriminating mission has a universal

---

[5] Joel B. Green, *The Gospel of Luke,* NICNT (Grand Rapids: Eerdmans, 1997), 117.

scope. Through Jesus, "all flesh will see God's salvation" (Isa 40:5; Luke 3:6), and Luke's story tells how.

Promises Fulfilled in Jesus's Active Ministry (Luke 4:14–9:50)

Though the characters at the beginning of the story rejoiced at the arrival of God's salvation, many would not. From the moment Jesus's ministry began, he faced rejection, even from his hometown. The theme of reversal is hard to miss. It is the least likely who will place faith in Jesus, receive salvation, and join his mission. Despite the rejection of many, Jesus was not swayed from his mission. He boldly announced that as Isaiah prophesied, he was anointed by the Spirit to proclaim the good news and restore and liberate the needy (Isa 58:6; 61:1–2). He knew he would be rejected by Israel, he knew, but as a result, his mission would expand to all people according to God's eternal plan (Luke 4:24–31). Humble faith is all that is required in response, but only the unsuspecting demonstrate it.

Immediately, Jesus's statements were proven true. In the face of rejection, he demonstrated his power to release the captives of illness, demonic forces, and sin, and he was declared Master and Lord. He was criticized for keeping company with notorious sinners, but he had come to call "sinners to repentance" (Luke 5:32). His good news meant whole-person restoration. Jesus's teaching and ministry addresses several questions about the unchanging nature of God and the salvation he offers. How far does God go to seek and save the lost; how effective is his power; and what does he expect in response?

Jesus demonstrated authority over the natural and supernatural alike by calming a storm (Luke 8:22–25), casting out demons (Luke 8:26–39), forgiving sins (Luke 5:20), healing the sick (Luke 7:1–10; 8:48), and raising the dead (Luke 7:14; 8:54). The God who spoke creation into existence and who breathes life into humans has shown his face in the person of Jesus. He proves

> **Luke's High Christology**
>
> What John states explicitly (John 1:1, 14), Luke reveals implicitly: Jesus was God in Israel's midst. The events of the story and the characters' confessions make this plain. Jesus is declared Savior, Redeemer of Israel, the Lord, and the Holy One of Israel—titles reserved for God alone. Centuries earlier, the prophet Isaiah promised that the Lord God would restore Israel and silence her enemies, and that all those opposing him shall be put to shame (Isa 45:16). Jesus forgives sin (Luke 5:21), subdues nature (Luke 8:22–25), and conquers supernatural forces with the power of God (Luke 8:26–39). He acts as only God can, and all those opposing him were put to shame (Luke 13:17). Luke reveals that humanity's enemies are cosmic, and ultimate suppression is spiritual. Jesus's power over them reveals that he is none other than God himself.

that there is no power, force, or problem that threatens his rule, nor is there a living soul outside of his care and beyond his reach. In return, he expects obedient faith, the result of seed falling on "good ground," taking root, and producing lasting fruit (Luke 8:15). What does this look like? Luke leads the reader out of the metaphorical classroom to encounter living visualizations of faith that persevere in testing because hope is anchored in Jesus (Luke 6:46–49; 8:18, 21).

Despite hearing Jesus's words and watching him work, his disciples and the crowd of Gerasenes traded faith for fear (Luke 8:22–25, 34–37). In two shocking reversals, a synagogue leader named Jairus and a woman with uncontrollable bleeding are leveled before God. Having both fallen at Jesus's feet (Luke 8:41, 47), they are paired to personify faith that neither withers in testing nor is choked by worries (Luke 8:13). Instead, their faith perseveres to "produce a crop" that Jesus commends and identifies as the marker of those in the family of God (Luke 8:15). Jesus reclaims those who death and destruction have held captive, restoring them not only to social and physical wholeness but to spiritual restoration within the family of God.

God's kingdom was advancing, but did the disciples understand what genuine faith meant and would ultimately require? Jesus knew that only personal commitments would endure, so in the quiet and away from the crowds, he looked at his disciples and asked them the ultimate question: "But you . . . who do you say that I am?" (Luke 9:20). With unflinching resolve, Jesus met Peter's confession, "God's Messiah" (Luke 9:20), with the declaration that as the Promised One he would be rejected, beaten, killed, and raised to life. Would their faith persevere?

Why would the Mighty God and Restorer of the helpless purposefully humble himself, succumb to the plots of evil men, and die on a cross? The disciples would all come to find that the promised Redeemer, Suffering Servant, reigning King, Son of Man, and Lord of all would walk in a path they could not foresee.

Yet all along, Jesus's ministry had been paving the path to his cross. The physical and societal wholeness Jesus offers is only a shadow of ultimate liberation and salvation. The good news of Jesus's rule is not only freedom from the effects of sin but freedom from sin itself (Luke 4:18–19). Without spiritual salvation, physical restoration is incomplete and temporary. The light and liberation of God's good news ultimately pierces through the darkness of the heart and sets humanity free from its most powerful enemy, sin and death (Luke 1:78–79). To accomplish it, the promise-keeping God would embody the paradox of his upside-down kingdom to an unfathomable degree by dying the death of the sinners he came to save.

Die to live, and give to gain. This is Jesus's way and the way of those who follow in his path. In giving up their lives, his disciples will gain their souls (Luke 9:23–25). Before they are able to process the magnitude of what Jesus predicts, the cost it will require, and the response it is to produce, they confront Jesus on a mountain, transfigured in majesty and glory (Luke 9:28–36). Flashes of white, the appearance of Israel's prophets, and a voice from heaven reveal that humiliation on the cross will not have the last word. Unendurable suffering is paving the path of unimaginable glory.

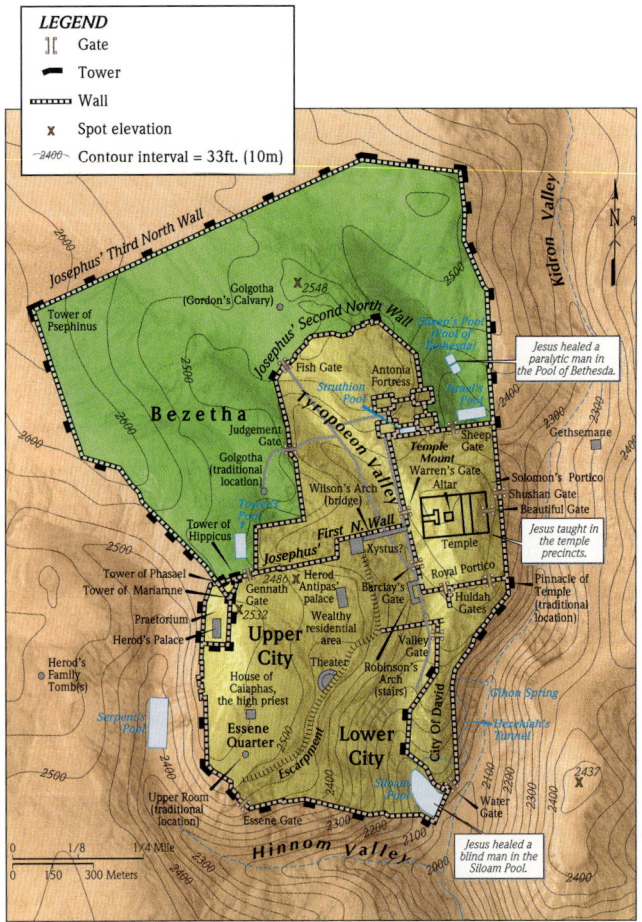

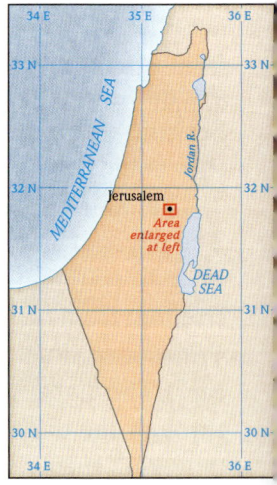

The Ministry of Jesus around the Sea of Galilee

Promises Fulfilled in Jesus's Journey to Jerusalem (Luke 9:51–19:44)

Luke's reader learns that things are not always how they seem. The reversal of Jesus's kingdom ultimately requires that the world's standard of greatness be flipped on its head (Luke 7:28; 9:48). Those who are great are those whose priorities align with God's, and to prove it, Luke highlights men and women whose surprising and unconventional actions were given Jesus's stamp of approval. Love God and love your neighbor, Jesus explained, and you will obey God's commands.[6] Obedience is practical, and often, greatness is surprising.

A despised Samaritan illustrates Jesus's command to "love your neighbor" (Luke 10:25–37), and an insignificant woman embodies what it means to "love the Lord your God" (Luke 10:27). After Israel's best, a priest and a Levite, forsake a dying man, a culturally despised Samaritan saves his life by practicing selfless and costly love (Luke 10:25–35). Love others sacrificially and love the Lord ultimately, Jesus teaches. Mary loves the Lord by feeding on Jesus's words (Luke 10:38–42). She sits at Jesus's feet like a disciple at the feet of a rabbi, but as a woman, her actions would be seen as presumptuous and culturally inappropriate.[7] Yet, rather than scolding her, Jesus praises her choice and legitimizes her position. Interestingly, no one else in Scripture, not even the disciples, is described as sitting at Jesus's feet. Mary is pictured as the disciple who gets it right. This woman is seen, welcomed, and loved by Jesus, and her response of love for the Lord is the priority guiding her behavior. An outsider and a woman embody God's commands because their values mirror his.

Jesus revealed the unusual faces of obedience, and he drew a shocking picture of God's family. Jesus not only restored individuals suffering from physical, social, and spiritual isolation, but he called them sons and daughters of Abraham, indicating that the true children of Israel are identified by their faith in Jesus (Luke 13:16; 19:9). His appeal is universal, but

---

[6] Biblical obedience is the result of heartfelt allegiance to God. The contrast between biblical obedience and obligatory obedience is personified when the characters of these passages are compared to the older son of Jesus's Lost Son parable. The bitter protest from the older son reveals that his participation in his father's work was born out of obligation rather than genuine love: "I have been slaving many years for you" (Luke 15:29). Obedience resulting from faith in the person of God is stripped of resentful compliance and infused with purpose.

[7] Paul alludes to this tradition in Acts 22:3. See Ben Witherington, *Women and the Genesis of Christianity* (Cambridge: Cambridge University Press, 1990), 206.

his way is narrow. Anyone who is willing is urged to follow Jesus because "the Son of Man has come to seek and to save the lost" (Luke 19:10). Salvation produces a shift in values (Luke 12:31; 14:27, 33) and a change in perspective (Luke 3:8; 18:14; 19:9; 22:26).

It is no wonder that in the face of this teaching, Israel's rejection of Jesus intensified. Though he mourned over Israel's stubborn unwillingness (Luke 13:34–35), Jesus's face was set on accomplishing his mission; he had the whole world in view (Isa 42:5–7). Through the complementary parables of the Lost Sheep, Lost Coin, and Lost Son, Luke lifts the eyes of the reader to a God who, in Jesus, is on mission to recover and restore what is lost (Ezekiel 34; Isa 49:22; Luke 15). Outsiders can be welcomed into God's family with joy, as people reclaimed from death, because God creates all people with immeasurable worth and desires that they be restored.

Being a member of this kingdom and participating in God's work certainly requires a reversal in values (Luke 16:15; 18:14). The faith of a widow, the humility of a tax collector, the simplicity of a child, and the persistence of a blind beggar are the surprising standards for God's kingdom people (Luke 18:1–8, 13–14, 17, 35–43). Be like them, Jesus said, because they are positioned to know, experience, and receive from God. They are on the margins of society, but they are at the center of God's plan. Their confidence is not in their own righteousness, their faith is not in their own means, and their salvation is not in their own will. They roll onto God the full weight of their burden, and they anchor their hope in his reliable and unchanging character (Luke 6:35–36; 11:1–13; 12:32). This God of mercy will respond, they believe; he has promised that he will, and in Jesus, he does. In God's economy, it is people with the faith of a desperate widow, and unwavering confidence in the knowable person of God, who can expect to receive his mercy and experience his salvation. Who else will trust God like this widow? Jesus asked. Those who do will find him eager to respond (Luke 18:7).

In the meantime, it looked as though things were going right for Jesus's mission, but under the surface, the conflict was only intensifying. In fulfillment of prophecy, Jesus peacefully entered Jerusalem on a donkey and was hailed as Israel's promised and victorious King (Zech 9:9–17). At Jesus's birth, the angels proclaimed, "Glory to God in the highest heaven, and peace on earth" (Luke 2:14), and now, the message was being understood by the crowds, who proclaimed, "Peace in heaven and glory in the highest heaven!" (Luke 19:38). The King was praised, his kingdom was advancing, and his peace was reigning from heaven to earth! Yet, it would all come at the highest cost. God would offer peace to all men, but he would pay the price with his own life.

Promises Fulfilled in Jesus's Suffering, Death, and Resurrection (Luke 19:45–24:53)

The peace of God's reign would not preclude judgment, Jesus warned. In fact, Jerusalem, the city of God's visitation, would be the epicenter of his judgment because, rather than believing and being saved, they had rejected their faithful God (Luke 21:5–36). Jesus marched into the temple, condemned the corruption of Israel's religious system, and aligned himself with the prophets who had been killed for preaching repentance as the path of peace. Suddenly, the plots of Jesus's enemies materialized, and their rejection took a wicked and violent form.

As Jesus predicted, he was betrayed and handed over to trial, beatings, and death. Six times during Jesus's trial and crucifixion, different characters in the story admitted his innocence, but the raging crowds would not hear it (Luke 23:4, 14–15, 22, 41, 47).

With condemned criminals on either side, Jesus was nailed to a cross. He had been born among the animals, and he was dying among criminals (Luke 2:16; 23:33). The Eternal and Almighty God stooped to a position unimaginable in order to save the lost; his mission culminated with Jesus in

This print, *Christ before Pilate*, is from 1845 and is currently held by the Library of Congress.

humanity's place. It was a place of shame, judgment, and transgression. The one who demonstrated unrivaled power, the power of life itself (Luke 23:43), was determined to endure this excruciating death. Any shred of hope that the plot would suddenly shift faded into obscurity as Jesus forgave his murderers, committed his spirit, and breathed his last (Luke 23:34, 46).

Through a "microcosm of reactions," Luke draws his reader in to this unbelievable moment played out in slow motion.[8] Jewish leaders mock, women weep, a thief believes, and the curtain closes. Light flees, and darkness falls, as creation bows its head and testifies that the King of Glory has been slain. The final act seems to have come to a horrific end.

Yet movement is seen behind the curtain. The tape rewinds, and Jesus's words are remembered: he would rise again (Luke 18:33). Light dawns on the third day, and the world awakens to the fulfilled promise that the Author of life has defeated death. Jesus is alive. God himself has come in mercy and power to fulfill his promises and fight for his people, and this glorious victory has come through the King's death and resurrection. Is this not what Jesus taught all along? Glory in suffering, and honor through shame. Luke's story is really his plea: be saved by the sacrificed life of this King, and experience the great reversal that characterizes his rule.

Of the four Gospel writers, Luke tells the most about the remarkable events of Jesus post-resurrection. After the tomb was found empty, first by the women and then by Peter, the resurrected Jesus appeared to two travelers on the road to Emmaus. Unable to recognize Jesus, the travelers lamented that hope in God's redemption had died with

> **New Creation Wholeness**
>
> Jesus reclaims the people of God and realigns them according to God's original intentions. Sin in the garden resulted in a humanity suffering from spiritual blindness, deafness, and death. The great reversal pictured throughout Luke's Gospel reaches its height when Jesus bears the punishment of a spiritually blind, deaf, and lifeless humanity and frees her to see, hear, and live (Luke 4:18). Celebrations that God's promised redemption come in Jesus bookend the Gospel (Luke 2:38; 24:21). Jesus seeks out women, the poor, Gentiles, children, and the cultural outcasts, and he restores them to places of honor by restoring them to himself. Luke brings the reader back to the design of creation, when men and women, made in God's image, walk in fellowship with him. Jesus has come to forgive men and women of their sins, free them from sin's effects, and give them a place in God's kingdom.

---

[8] Darrell Bock, *A Theology of Luke and Acts: God's Promised Program, Realized for All Nations*, Biblical Theology of the New Testament Series (Grand Rapids: Zondervan, 2012), 78.

Jesus on the cross. With his identity still undetected, Jesus started at the beginning of Scripture and explained how their hope in him was not misplaced (Luke 24:27). Finally, when Jesus broke bread for their meal, "their eyes were opened, and they recognized him" (Luke 24:31). The story of the Bible comes full circle. For the first Adam, eyes were opened to shame and death (Gen 3:7), but as a result of the last Adam, eyes are opened to resurrection and life. As prophesied by Isaiah, the risen Jesus brings the dead to life, frees the captives, and opens the eyes of the blind (Luke 4:18). God is at work fulfilling his promises.

BIBLIOGRAPHY

Bock, Darrell L. *Luke 1:1–9:50*. BECNT. Grand Rapids: Baker Academic, 1994.

_____. *A Theology of Luke and Acts: God's Promised Program, Realized for All Nations*. Biblical Theology of the New Testament series. Grand Rapids: Zondervan, 2012.

Green, Joel B. *The Gospel of Luke*. NICNT. Grand Rapids: Eerdmans, 1997.

Stein, Robert H. *Luke*. Vol. 24. NAC. Nashville: B&H, 1992.

Witherington, Ben. *Women and the Genesis of Christianity*. Cambridge: Cambridge University Press, 1990.

5

JOHN

CARA L. T. MURPHY

CONNECTION POINT

What relevance does this first-century writing have for us today? Can belief be distinguished between mental assent and a deeper trust? How does this kind of belief respond to disappointment, isolation, or confusion? These are some of the questions the author of the Gospel of John was seeking to answer in his account of the life of Jesus Christ. In this writing, John demonstrates how true belief in the God of the Scriptures changes the way we think, speak, and live. John's Gospel, unique and distinctive from the other three Gospel accounts, issues an invitation into *a life of belief in Jesus Christ*, both in the world that presently exists as well as the world to come.

Just as John's message was relevant to the first-century audience, it is equally relevant to us today. John's readers were much like us—living in a culture of doubt and misinformation regarding the true nature of God. Likewise, there was opposition to the growing New Testament church, both from within and without. John wrote to help his readers believe that Jesus is the Christ as well as to encourage those undergoing hardship for following Jesus. The Fourth Gospel shows the stark contrast of response between true belief and rejection of truth, between the kingdoms of light and darkness. In John's Gospel, knowing this "Word" that "became flesh and dwelt among us" (John 1:14) is more than mental assent—rather, it is a knowing trust that leads to greater life in and with God.

With this in mind, consider making this your prayer as you read and study this chapter:

> *Thank you, God, for giving us the revelation of your Son, the Word made flesh. Thank you that he walked among us, revealing to us the way to you, our Father. As we study John's account of the life of Jesus, would you quicken us by your Spirit, leading us into the true belief that leads to life? By walking with Jesus through the Gospel of John, may we know you deeply, trusting you with our lives. May you show us how our entire lives can be reordered to stay with you both in the day-to-day moments and the eternal life to come. Amen.*

SETTING

Recipients

John,[1] the son of Zebedee and disciple of Jesus, wrote around AD 80.[2] According to the almost-unanimous support of the early church fathers, John wrote from Ephesus.[3] Scholars point toward internal evidence that suggests John's audience to be Christians of the Diaspora, most likely Greek-speaking, Jewish believers.

---

[1] Relying on both internal and external evidence, most scholars identify the author of John's Gospel as John, the son of Zebedee and disciple of Jesus. See Andreas J. Köstenberger, *Encountering John*, 2nd ed, Encountering Biblical Studies (Grand Rapids: Baker, 2013), 6. The author of this Gospel does not name himself within the content, rather, self-identifying in John 21:20 as "the disciple Jesus loved." Both external evidence from early church tradition and internal evidence within the Gospel account suggest the author to be an eyewitness to the narratives recorded in the book of John.

[2] Köstenberger, *Encountering John*, 8.

[3] D. A. Carson, *The Gospel According to John*, PNTC (Grand Rapids: Eerdmans, 1991), 86.

Theme and Key Passage

Sources confirm that over 90 percent of the Gospel of John is unique from the Synoptic Gospels: Matthew, Mark, and Luke.[4] The array of items not included in John is noteworthy. There is a marked absence of narrative parables, an account of the birth of Jesus, a transfiguration account, the institution of the communion sacrament, and an account of the temptation of Jesus in the wilderness, among others.[5] Likewise, the concepts included in John's Gospel are different from Matthew, Mark, and Luke. For example, John's Gospel alone emphasizes that Jesus Christ is "*explicitly* identified with God."[6] The keywords in John demonstrate a notable transition in emphasis: light versus darkness, "life" (used thirty-six times), and "believe" (used ninety-eight times).[7] John is also particular about which sign-miracles (*semeia*) of Jesus to include in his account, choosing narratives that most effectively further his theme of Jesus as the Christ, one with God.[8] Likewise, only John includes the famous "I AM"[9] statements

> ### "I AM" in John
>
> Unique to John's Gospel is Jesus's use of the I AM statements. Drawing his audience toward Old Testament parallels of Yahweh's self-naming in Exod 3:14, Jesus aligns himself with this same divine nature. In John, we see Jesus responding with "I am," (4:26; 8:24, 28, 58; 13:13, 19; 18:5–6, 8), and seven more times he combines this declaration with a predicate-adjective qualifier: "I am the bread of life" (6:35), "I am the light of the world" (8:12; 9:5), "I am the gate" (10:9), "I am the good shepherd" (10:11, 14), "I am the resurrection and the life" (11:25), "I am the way, the truth, and the life" (14:6), and "I am the vine" (15:5). These statements invite the modern reader into a reflection of how they are walking in discipleship with Jesus, the great I AM, who through his incarnation has become "flesh and dwelt among us" (1:14).

---

[4] "Synoptic" is a term that woodenly means "from the same eye." It is a reference to how similarly Matthew, Mark, and Luke's Gospel accounts are. The term recognizes that these authors are writing from a similar perspective regarding the same subject, with a similar goal in mind for their respective audiences. In contrast, John's Gospel is substantively unique in every way. Thus, it is not considered as one of the Synoptic Gospels.

[5] For an extensive listing of these differences, see Carson, *Gospel According to John*, 21–22.

[6] Carson, *Gospel According to John*, 22.

[7] Elmer Towns, *John* (Chattanooga: AMG, 2002), xi.

[8] The presence of signs is of crucial importance to John's overall message. "All of Jesus's signs occur in the first part of John's gospel, which deals with Jesus's public ministry to the Jews. In human terms, this ministry turns out to be a failure, as John makes clear in his summary statement in 12:37: 'Even after Jesus had performed so many signs in their presence, they still would not believe in him.'" Köstenberger, *Encountering John*, 58.

[9] "When Jesus used the 'I AM' construction he was speaking in the style of deity . . . The overtones of deity that we find in its use in the Old Testament are not lost when move to the New." Leon Morris, *Jesus Is the Christ: Studies in the Theology of John* (Grand Rapids: Eerdmans, 1989), 107, 109.

of Jesus, as well as the only other designation of Jesus as "the Lamb of God" listed in the Gospels. John includes a great deal of Jesus's dialogue, inviting his readers to have a conversational look at who Jesus is and what he discussed with individuals.

The key verse in John conveys authorial intention toward an emphasis of intimate and confident belief that leads to the abundant life.

John 20:31 says, "But these are written so that you may believe that Jesus is the Messiah, the Son of God, and that by believing you may have life in his name."

Purpose and Occasion

With the destruction of the temple in AD 70, the Gospel of John is written partly as a response. John wrote with the intentional purpose of presenting the risen Jesus Christ as the solid answer to a discouraged Jewish Christianity. Likewise, many Jewish Christians were facing expulsion from local synagogues, alienation from their communities, and persecution for belief in Jesus Christ. John wrote with these circumstances in mind, reminding the downtrodden Jewish believers of the deity of Christ and their ability to trust him as the resurrected *Masiach*.[10] John's hope was that based on his eyewitness account all Jews would now place their belief in this Messiah,[11] with his Gospel pointing the way to Jesus as the hope of Jewish and Gentile Christians alike.[12]

HIGHLIGHTS IN JOHN

Prologue (1:1–18)

John begins his Gospel with a poetic hymn, a "hook" that draws the reader into the Christological beauty that threads its way throughout the entire

---

[10] That is, Messiah. Carson, *Gospel According to John*, 94–95.

[11] "The question of what would now become of Judaism was in everyone's mind John's answer is clear: he hopes to encourage diaspora Jews and proselytes to turn to Jesus, the Messiah who fulfilled the symbolism embodied in the temple and the Jewish festivals." Köstenberger, *Encountering John*, 10.

[12] For a good summary of this, see Kenneth O. Gangel, *John*, vol. 4, HNTC, ed. Max Anders (Nashville: B&H, 2012). "Luke wrote for an individual (Theophilus). Matthew and Mark targeted Jewish audiences with their record of Jesus's life and work. John wrote for the world, living as he did at the end of fifty years of church history, knowing that the gospel had already permeated the entire Mediterranean world." (2).

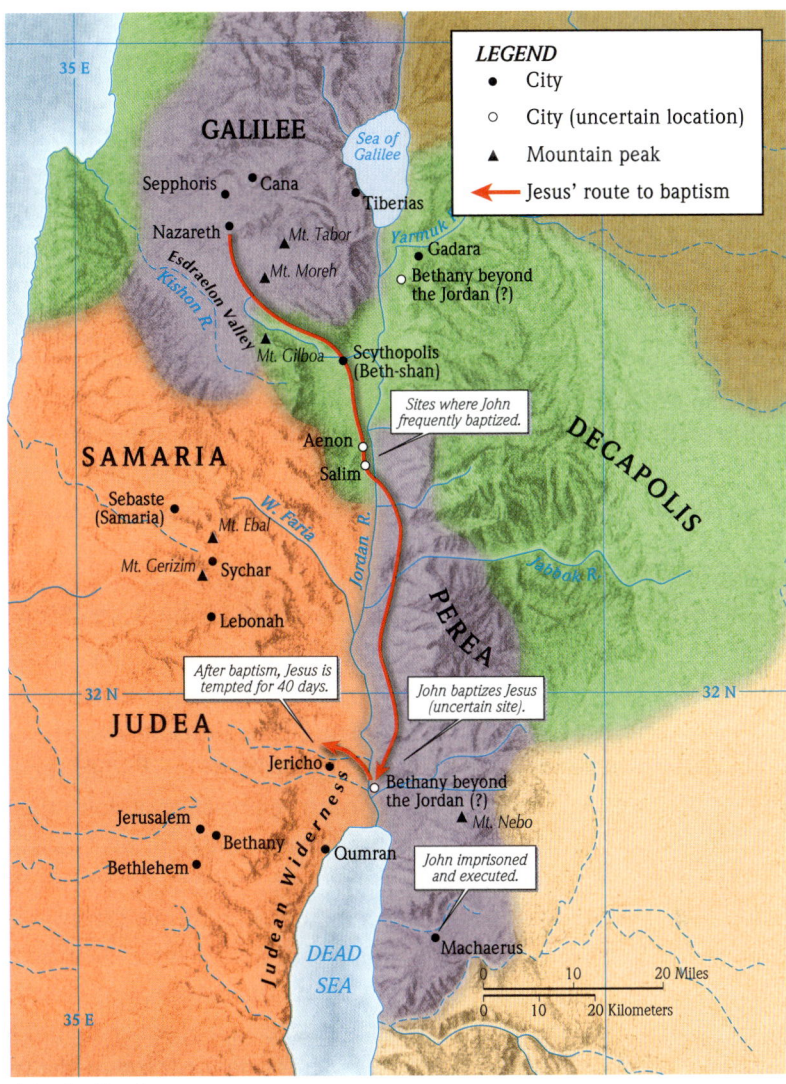

John the Baptizer

book.[13] With an intentional parallel to Gen 1:1, John introduces Jesus as "the Word," or *logos*, that "became flesh and dwelt among us" (John 1:14) and lives among us still.[14] This Word never loses his relevance, remaining the evergreen source of life needed for all generations—past, present, and

---

[13] For more information on the structure of John's Gospel, see Carson, *Gospel According to John*. I lean heavily on his breakdown of narrative structuring for this outline.

[14] Carson explains it this way: "God's 'Word' in the Old Testament is his powerful self-expression in creation, revelation, and salvation, and the personification of that 'Word'

future. The Prologue provides the thesis statement for John's Gospel, and the reader may observe that the succeeding content touches upon this theme continually.[15] Specifically, John paints a portrait of the deity of Jesus Christ: his presence as the Word before the origins of time, his participation in creation, and his union with the Godhead. This is the Christ, the one in whom all readers are invited to place their trust. Likewise, we are also introduced to John the Baptist as a primary witness to the deity of Jesus, showing through personal testimony the uniqueness and preeminent position of Jesus as "the light of men" (John 1:4).

John, the author, explains that this "light" was not welcome in the world to which he came. This dual theme of revelation and rejection is a common pattern throughout the book of John, leaving his audience with a poignant question: Will we receive or reject this Christ of whom John preaches? Each reader of the Gospel of John must come to this point of personal decision.

Jesus's Self-Revelation in Signs and Dialogue (John 1:19–10:42)

We begin the narrative portion of John's Gospel with a deeper introduction of who John the Baptist was—or more accurately, who he was not. He was the forerunner to the Christ, not the Christ himself. The placement of the Baptizer as a key witness to Jesus's deity helps to solidify the trustworthiness of Jesus's claims. In other words, the presence of John the Baptist helps each reader come to a deeper understanding of Jesus Christ, thus being able to enter into the belief, which John encourages his audience. Although the baptism of Jesus is not depicted, it is implied in this initial dialogue of the Baptizer (John 1:29–34). From here, we see the first disciples called into a life of following Jesus: first, the disciples of John; then Philip and Nathanael are introduced within the first chapter of the book (John 1:35–51). While John does not include a formal calling of the twelve as the Synoptics record (Matt 10:1–4; Mark 3:13–19; Luke 6:12–16), he does incorporate the narratives of this first chapter to transition the reader into the ministry of the Christ. We see a Christ who is deeply relational, one who calls and invites individually and specifically. We also see that Jesus named himself as "the Son of Man," (John 1:51), a mysterious reference to him as "God's messenger," a cryptic descriptor that may mean "his

---

makes it suitable for John to apply it as a title to God's ultimate self-disclosure, the person of his own Son." Carson, *Gospel According to John*, 116.

[15] Carson, *Gospel According to John*, 111.

hearers would need to listen to his message before coming to know who he was."[16] The Jesus of John's Gospel defied expectations and surprised many. This is a "hidden code," of sorts, in which each reader is invited to pay attention and see what is happening just below the surface.

After this introductory material, we see the beginning of what some scholars designate as the Cana Cycle. Seeing a pattern within the narrative blocks is helpful as we determine the author's original intent. We must remember that everything in John's Gospel is in service to one purpose: the belief that leads to life. We witness the unexpected first sign-miracle, or *semeia*, found in John's Gospel: the transformation of water to wine (John 2:1–12) at a wedding feast in the Galilean city of Cana. This is one demonstration in which Jesus shocked his early (and modern) readers out of our preconceived notions regarding who the Christ would be. Aspects of the relational dynamic between Mary, his mother, and Jesus himself are revealed in this brief but significant account. The text is careful to alert us that the disciples were present as witnesses to this extraordinary sign, another example of the validity of the witnesses in John. Scholars denote that the signs Jesus performed throughout John's Gospel have greater significance beyond simply demonstrating supernatural capability. These signs were included to express a deeper theological truth.[17] From this point forward, Jesus's fame will continue to grow in Galilee, even traveling through Samaria and into Judea, until it reaches its zenith before transitioning in the middle of John's Gospel.

The second half of chapter two (John 2:13–25) reveals an impassioned Jesus who cleansed Herod's temple of the corruption and commercialism that runs counter to true worship. Here we see Jesus make his first foreshadowing allusion to his death and resurrection (John 2:19), thus showing a Jesus who was not a victim of his death, but the orchestrator of his own crucifixion.[18] John then narrows his gaze, taking a microscopic focus on two individual conversations with Jesus: Nicodemus, the Pharisee (John 3:1–21) and the unnamed Samaritan woman at the well (John

---

[16] Elmer Towns and Ben Gutierrez, eds. *The Essence of the New Testament: A Survey*, 2nd ed. (Nashville: B&H Academic, 2016), 100.

[17] "When a miracle is designated by this term, it is seen as a happening that is not self-contained, not an end in itself. It has a meaning that is fulfilled elsewhere than in the miracle." Morris, *Jesus Is the Christ*, 2.

[18] These two events are closely linked in John's Gospel. Köstenberger explains it this way: "What the two events narrated in John 2 share is that they present Jesus as the restorer of Israel." (*Encountering John*, 58).

4:1–42). These two accounts are unique to John, and they are meant to demonstrate a contrast in response: true belief in Jesus produces a different life in the one who believes. John desires to emphasize this truth through the details of these two dialogues.

Entering chapter 5 we see the conclusion of the Cana Cycle and transition into the Festival Cycle of this Gospel. John next takes his readers into back-to-back healing narratives: the official's son (John 4:46–54) and a man by the pool of Bethesda (John 5:1–18). These two sign-miracles demonstrate the claims to deity that Jesus made in the preceding two chapters (John 3–4) as well as lead to an extensive dialogue of Jesus's authority (John 5:19–47). These two healings and the conversations inherent are used by John to point the reader back to belief in this compassionate and inquisitive Christ. John continues to ask and answer the question of Jesus of whether Jesus is worthy of a whole life's belief and commitment. Some may answer no. "The Jews," a term used frequently throughout John's Gospel to denote the religious Jewish establishment, became publicly hostile toward Jesus's healing on the Sabbath as well as to his reference of God as Father (John 5:18).

This discussion of authority transitions to the feeding of the 5,000, a narrative included in all four Gospels. Jesus not only fed this large crowd, estimated to be upwards of 20,000 men, women, and children, from only a few meager supplies; but he also used the occasion to identify himself with Yahweh, proclaiming, "I am the bread of life." Both this I AM statement and the sign-miracle served as a demonstration of messianic authority (John 6:1–15), concluding with the next sign-miracle of Jesus walking on the Sea of Galilee (John 6:16–21). Jesus did not, however, meet the volatile crowd's expectations of what the Messiah would be, and the scene ends with many followers abandoning him.

Chapters 7 and 8 of John's Gospel introduce more dialogue from Jesus, as well as an ever-increasing tension with the religious authorities. John shows the reader that many are beginning to question and form conclusions regarding

> ### Union with the Father
>
> When the Old Testament refers to God as Father, it is rare and often expresses God as Father corporately, over the nation of Israel, rather than as Father to the individual (Ps 89:26; Isa 64:8). More than any other Gospel, in John, Jesus identifies God as his Father and addresses him as such in prayer (John uses the term *Father* in his writings 137 times). The Gospel of John particularly identifies the theme of Jesus's oneness with the Father, which provides a further witness to his own divine nature. This also serves as an invitation to each reader who longs to enter a deeper union with our own Good Father.
>
> (See Morris, *Jesus Is the Christ*, 129–30.)

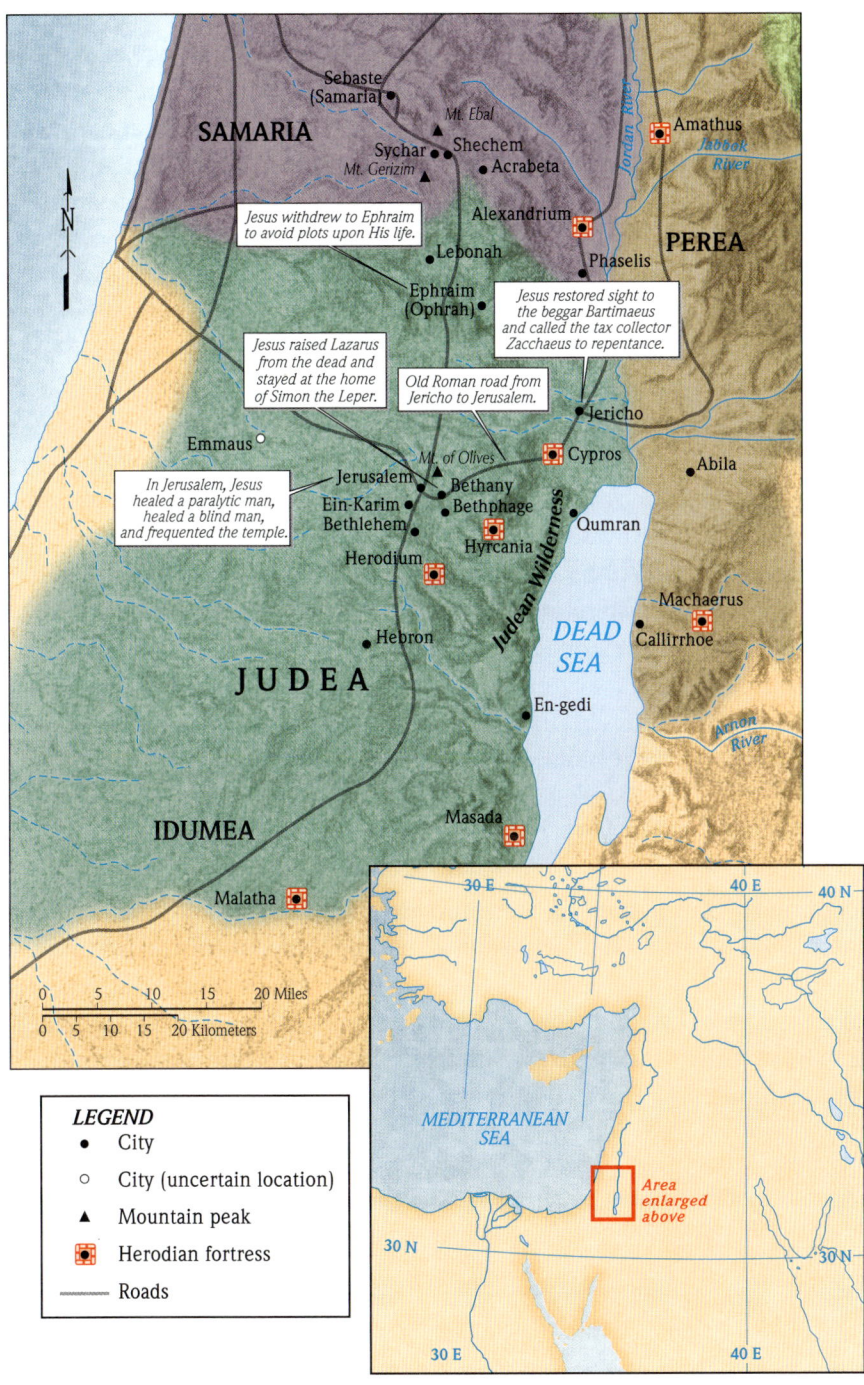

Jesus in Judea and Jerusalem

Jesus, including his own brothers (John 7:1–9). John does this to show that even those closest to Jesus misunderstood him, struggling with belief. Throughout these conversations, Jesus delivers two more I AM statements: "I am the light of the world" (John 8:12), given during the Feast of Tabernacles in Herod's temple, and the statement lacking a predicate-adjective: "Before Abraham was, I am" (John 8:58). This section concludes with the Jews' desire to stone Jesus.

In John 9, the author returns to a sign-miracle, giving his readers a vivid account of another Sabbath healing, dialogue, and the increasing confrontation with the Pharisees (John 9:1–41). This tension, begun early in the Gospel and carried throughout, increases the tension in every reader: we have a choice of whether we, too, will follow in the unbelieving footsteps of the Pharisees.

Finally, this section of self-revelation in the first half of John concludes with John 10, a lengthy discourse only found in John's Gospel. Jesus begins with two more assertions to deity, speaking, "I am the gate," (John 10:7) and "I am the good shepherd" (John 10:11, 14). The chapter ends with the Jews again wanting to stone him (John 10:31–39), providing a segue for the reader into the middle section of John—a transition in public opinion and narrative speed. Here, the reader must also begin to recognize the personal transition that John is building: What will *we* do with this Christ?

Transition: Life and Death, King and Suffering Servant (John 11:1–12:50)

Beginning with chapter 11 John moves his readers from what has been classically known as the "book of signs," encompassing the first half of John, to the "book of glory." Before the transition is complete, however, John wishes to introduce Jesus's last sign-miracle as well as signaling a movement from Jesus's earthly ministry to his last moments on incarnational mission.[19]

---

[19] Köstenberger's notes on John 11 provide great clarity on the importance of this inclusion: "The significance of the raising of Lazarus in John's narrative cannot be exaggerated. Most importantly, the event is the climactic, seventh sign selected by the evangelist to document Jesus's identity as 'the resurrection and the life' (11:25). Moreover, the raising of Lazarus is the sign that most closely foreshadows Jesus's own resurrection (even though Jesus's resurrection also plays a role in the symbolism of the second sign recorded in John, the temple clearing; see 2:20–22). Finally, the raising of Lazarus is the focus of Jesus's escalating conflict with the Jews, which we have tracked from the beginning of the gospel (esp. in chaps. 5–10)." *Encountering John*, 14.

John 11–12 focus on two key events that prepare the reader for the finale to come. First, we witness the raising of Lazarus, an event that foreshadows the coming resurrection of Jesus. During this narrative account, John records Jesus as saying, "I am the resurrection and the life" (John 11:25).[20] Second, we read of the anointing of Jesus by Mary, another clue that transitions the reader into the next act. With the triumph of Lazarus's rescue, and the honor of Jesus's anointing, the reader then enters into the peak of Jesus's public popularity: his triumphal entry into Jerusalem. The reader begins to hang on tightly as the narrative arc quickly jumps from crowd popularity to full rejection, and the hostility of the authorities also reaches a breaking point. What begins as a plot to kill the newly raised Lazarus culminates in a secretive plan to kill Jesus himself.

But John shows that none of this surprised Jesus (John 12:27–36). He was aware of the plots to take his life, and offered predictions in contrast to the people who had so recently applauded his triumphal entry. Those who believed, and John told us they are "many" (John 12:42), believed in secret, because they were justifiably afraid that they would be put out of the synagogue, the heart of Jewish community life (John 9:34). This is precisely the dilemma that early Jewish Christians faced for their own belief in Christ. We, the modern readers of John, also experience the alienation and isolation that can come from a life transformed by belief in Jesus.

The Questions of Jesus

Throughout the four Gospel accounts and Acts, Jesus asked over 350 questions of those he encountered. Five of the seven sign-miracles in John's Gospel include at least one question from Jesus. Likewise, the events and dialogue recorded between John 13 and 16 contain eight different inquiries from Jesus to his disciples. Why did he choose to utilize the Socratic method so often? The answers to this inquiry are varied, but at the center of his purpose is an invitation. He desired deep conversation with those he met, just as he continues to desire this with his disciples today. "It is with asking that he introduces himself to us." The questions of Jesus "speak into the chaotic, world-weary culture in which we live. They were relevant when first asked. They are still relevant today."

For a deeper discussion, see Cara L. T. Murphy, *The Inquisitive Christ*, 44.

Jesus's Self-Revelation in His Cross and Resurrection (John 13:1–20:31)

The final major section of content in the Gospel of John begins with the night before Jesus's crucifixion. The reader is invited to sit with the disciples for the

---

[20] Morris adds, "That he is the resurrection means that death, which to us appears so final, is no obstacle, and that he is the life means that the quality of life that he imparts to us here and now never ceases." *Jesus Is the Christ*, 117.

Last Supper between Jesus and his disciples, which was designated to celebrate the Jewish Passover feast. John does not include the traditional institution of this church ordinance, choosing instead to include (1) the only Gospel account of the disciples' foot washing from Jesus, (2) a prediction of his betrayal by Judas Iscariot, and (3) an in-depth dialogue with an inquisitive and prayerful Jesus. For John's audience, chapters 13–17 read as one long conversation, one on which readers are wholeheartedly invited to eavesdrop. In John, Jesus is the God who initiates conversation with his people, a conversation that is still needed today by all who continue to read this Gospel account.

John 13 commences with a kneeling, humble Jesus, practicing foot washing, an act normally designated to the lowest slaves in the household. In doing this, Jesus invited his disciples to also accept this posture of humility going forward. This, John tells us, is part of the posture of life-transforming belief for all disciples, both first-century and modern-day. It is important to note that Jesus washed the feet of his betrayer, Judas Iscariot. John tell us that as Jesus identified him, Judas left the table and "immediately left . . . it was night" (John 13:30).

With the betrayer gone, John 14–16 takes the reader deep into a dialogue between Jesus and his remaining disciples. The mood of these chapters holds tension, urgency, and poignant questions from both the disciples and their Teacher. Within the chapters, Jesus introduces two more I am statements: "I am the way, the truth, and the life" (John 14:6) and "I am the vine" (John 15:5). With these two proclamations, Jesus once again reinforces his message of deity using metaphor and vivid imagery, asking for the kind of belief that fosters intimate depth. Throughout these three chapters, Jesus uses his remaining hours to teach his disciples about the role of the Holy Spirit, a major emphasis in John's Gospel. The Holy Spirit is identified as the "Helper" (John 14:16 NASB1995), "the Spirit of truth" (14:17), "the Counselor," and the one who would "teach you all things and remind you of everything" (14:26). In this dialogue Jesus foreshadows how his presence will remain with each of us, despite the events of his death.

John 17 represents the longest prayer of Jesus in the Gospels, praying for himself, his disciples, and those who would later choose to become disciples. Through this prayer we identify Jesus as our Intercessor and High Priest, the one who presents his people before the throne of God.[21] This

---

[21] John 17 provides an incredibly unique look into the prayer life of Jesus Christ. Köstenberger adds, "Jesus's prayer in chapter 17 is unique to John's gospel. It is by far

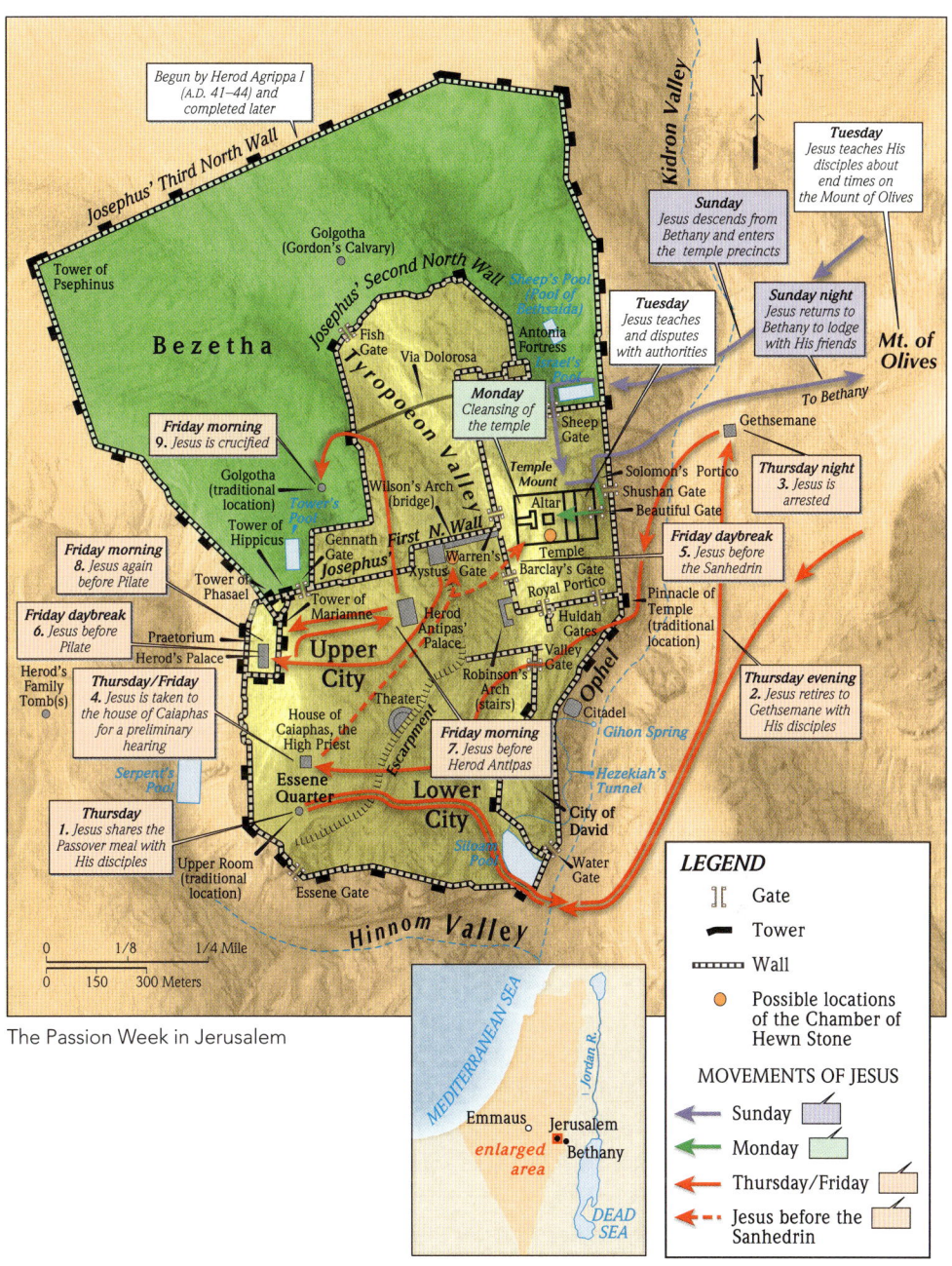

The Passion Week in Jerusalem

the longest prayer of Jesus recorded in any gospel and comes at a strategic point in Jesus's ministry, sandwiched between his final instructions to his closest followers and his passion. Jesus's 'high priestly prayer,' as it is sometimes called, affords us a rare glimpse into Jesus's consciousness and perspective on his imminent suffering" (*Encountering John*, 157).

Jesus has incredible relevance for us today, as we still desire a way into the presence of God. John shows us that Jesus is this way.

With the conclusion of Jesus's prayer, the reader is thrust rapidly into the rising action and intensifying narrative of his condemnation. John 18 and 19 present mounting tension for the reader as we see Jesus betrayed by Judas in the garden of Gethsemane. With his arrest, Jesus gives his final I AM declaration in John's Gospel, "I am he" (John 18:5), in response to the soldiers' and temple police officers' inquiry.[22] From here, we witness the arrest of Jesus. The remaining portion of John 18 jumps back and forth between Jesus's illegal trial before the Jewish Sanhedrin, his Roman trial before Pontius Pilate, and Peter's repeated denial of relationship to Jesus.[23] Chapter 18 concludes with Jesus's condemnation and sentencing to capital punishment.

The reader witnesses the events of Jesus's flogging, mockery, and crucifixion in John 19. The pace is quickened as we read, but the mood is heavy as John describes these events as only an eyewitness is able. In several areas, John makes clear to his Jewish audience that these events are in direct fulfillment of Old Testament messianic prophecy (cf. Pss 22:16; 34:20; 69:8, 21; Zech 12:10). Chapter 19 ends with the reappearance of Nicodemus, as he provides an embalming mixture for the body of Jesus as he is entombed.

John 20 dawns with hope, flooding the modern reader with joy and bringing to all who weep the revelation of the resurrected Christ. We begin with a surprise: the tomb is empty, and we discover this through the eyes of John and Peter. Bewildered, the two disciples leave the tomb to a weeping woman. From here, John shows us that the good news of a risen Jesus is given first to Mary, who then announces the message to the grieving disciples. Then Jesus appears to his hiding friends on two separate occasions: (1) giving them a mysterious God-breathed gift of the Holy Spirit, and (2) inspiring the famous conversation between Jesus and "doubting" Thomas. John 20 concludes with the overall purpose of John's Gospel being clearly stated:

> Jesus performed many other signs in the presence of his disciples that

---

[22] Towns summarizes the meaning behind this declaration of divinity: "Jesus responded in a momentary revelation of his divine glory. Jesus used the familiar title "I am" (Greek, *ego eimi*, 18:5), identifying Himself with the Old Testament name of Jehovah" (*John*, 180).

[23] Some have pinpointed over forty specific legal violations within Jesus's trial and condemnation. For a list of these, see Towns, *John*, 186.

are not written in this book. But these are written so that you may believe that Jesus is the Messiah, the Son of God, and that by believing you may have life in his name. (John 20:30–31)

Epilogue (John 21:1–25)

The Gospel of John concludes with a footnote to the Gospel, what many have called a "postscript" to the main body of work.[24] However, there are still a few things that remain to be said. In this final chapter, we need to see the humor of how Jesus approached his forlorn group of fishermen. Bringing forth an obvious parallel with their first meetings, Jesus once again interrupts their fishing procedures with a question and a suggestion to try a different method. Once the disciples recognize the man on the beach as Jesus, the chapter continues with two conversations: (1) the restoration of Simon Peter after his denial, and (2) the prediction of John's and Peter's manner of death. The book concludes with a final proclamation of the greatness of Jesus:

> And there are also many other things that Jesus did, which, if every one of them were written down, I suppose not even the world itself could contain the books that would be written. (John 21:25)

The readers of John's Gospel are left to decide for ourselves whether we can agree . . . and believe.

BIBLIOGRAPHY

Carson, D.A. *The Gospel According to John*. PNTC. Grand Rapids: Eerdmans, 1991.

Freeman, C. Hal, Jr. "John, Book of." In *Holman Illustrated Bible Dictionary*. Edited by Chad Brand, Charles Draper, and Archie England. Nashville: Holman Reference, 2003.

Gangel, Kenneth O. *John*. Vol. 4 of HNTC. Edited by Max Anders. Nashville: B&H Academic, 2012.

---

[24] For an in-depth treatment of chapter 21's placement in John, see Carson's commentary. He concludes, "If ch. 21 were added by the same hand, it must have been because the author thought the addition an improvement . . . The evidence in favour of an originally integral Gospel incorporating ch. 21 seems reasonably firm." *The Gospel According to John*, 668.

Köstenberger, Andreas J. *Encountering John*. 2nd ed. Encountering Biblical Studies. Grand Rapids: Baker, 2013.

Morris, Leon. *Jesus Is the Christ: Studies in the Theology of John*. Grand Rapids: Eerdmans, 1989.

Murphy, Cara L.T. *The Inquisitive Christ*. Nashville: FaithWords, 2020.

Strong, James. *The Exhaustive Concordance of the Bible*. Nashville: Abingdon, 1890.

Towns, Elmer, and Ben Gutierrez, eds. *The Essence of the New Testament: A Survey*. 2nd ed. Nashville: B&H Academic, 2016.

Towns, Elmer. *John: Believe and Live*. Twenty-First Century Biblical Commentary Series. Chattanooga, TN: AMG, 2002.

6

A CASE FOR THE RESURRECTION

GARY HABERMAS

Here's something that might surprise you: virtually all researchers, skeptics, liberals, moderates, and conservatives agree in recognizing a small but definite core of historical facts from the end of Jesus's life. And this core of facts reveals a lot about the reality of the resurrection.

THE MINIMAL FACTS ARGUMENT FOR THE RESURRECTION

This argument for the resurrection of Jesus is based on that small, "minimal" core of facts that all academically credible researchers agree on. Not too long ago I listed six of these events in a dialogue with an agnostic New Testament scholar. I used the historical facts that (1) Jesus died by crucifixion, (2) his early followers had experiences a short time later that they thought were appearances of Jesus, and (3) as a result, they were transformed to the point of being willing to die for this message. Further, two former unbelievers, (4) James the brother of Jesus and (5) Saul of Tarsus (later the apostle Paul), both similarly thought that they had seen the risen Jesus as well; and (6) this gospel message of the death and resurrection of Jesus Christ began to be taught very soon after these events.

Some might be surprised to hear that the agnostic scholar with whom I was dialoguing not only agreed with the historical nature of these six events, without exceptions, but he even added that each one was very well recognized.

How Do We Move from the Minimal Historical Facts to Jesus's Resurrection Appearances?

Using only the six facts about Jesus and his disciples listed above, backed up by the evidences that confirm them, we have a scenario that points very strongly to Jesus's appearing to his disciples after he died by crucifixion. Actually, we can boil the case down to those two ingredients. Did Jesus actually die on the cross? Then was he seen afterward having conversations with friends just as any of us might do? If Jesus was walking around and talking, seen by groups of witnesses (such as reported in the most scholarly tested text, 1 Cor 15:3–7), then his appearances are solid!

The result of it all is that we have six solid, agreed-upon facts, backed up with good historical reasoning. Rather incredibly, these six facts are enough to argue strongly against all of the major non-supernatural alternative hypotheses to Jesus's resurrection. This is the primary reason why only a minority of critical scholars today even attempt to argue these natural suppositions. But these six facts are also the strongest affirmative reasons for believing that Jesus appeared to his followers both individually and in groups after his death. That so many eyewitnesses reported these experiences is admitted by virtually all critical scholars. You would have to look hard to find very many dissenters.

Jesus's disciples were so sure of these facts that they were willing to die for this message, since it was the center of the gospel proclamation (as in Rom 10:9–10). True, many people down through the centuries have died willingly for a cause that they believed to be true as well as crucially important. But they are not willing to die for a view that they think is false.

Not only that, but we still have the conversions of the skeptics James the brother of Jesus and Paul. What changed them so radically? They were also willing to die for their new faith that they, too, had seen the risen Jesus. Both of them, among others, actually did die for their belief in Jesus's resurrection.

Last, the consensus view of even critical scholarship today is that the early resurrection message was preached right after the crucifixion by those who were involved in the experiences. Far from taking years or even decades to evolve and develop, the message burst forth from Jerusalem just a short time later and spread around the Mediterranean world.

CONCLUSION

The overall result has been an expansion of what we know about both the times in which Jesus lived and details from his own life. Hence, scholars have been pushed by the available evidence. Without question, the resurrection is a unique teaching in the history of religion. Those of us who believe that Jesus died and rose again are on solid ground indeed![25]

---

[25] For further reading, see Gary R. Habermas and Michael R. Licona, *The Case for the Resurrection of Jesus* (Grand Rapids: Kregel, 2004).

7

ACTS

ADAM MCCLENDON

CONNECTION POINT

What relevance does this first-century writing have for us today? Have you ever looked at the brokenness and evil of the world around you and wondered where God is? Have you ever felt left out, subpar, not good enough? Have you ever wondered how God could love you and if God could ever accept you? Such questions would have resonated with Luke's audience. After all, the Jews had been disillusioned by great leaders of the past. They waited for the Messiah to come and restore the throne of David; yet time and time again, they experienced failure and conquest. While the Jews felt hopeless and forgotten, the Gentiles felt left out. Many Jews misrepresented the kingdom promises as exclusive to the nation of Israel.[1] Much about the Jewish religious system shouted to those

---

[1] Genesis 12:3, Ps 67:1–4, the inclusion of Rahab in the genealogy of Jesus (Matt 1:5), the entire debate surrounding Acts 15, as well as many other passages all demonstrate that the inclusion of Gentiles is part of the great mystery previously hidden but now revealed (Rom 11:25; Eph 3:2–9; Col 1:25–27).

on the outside: "You're not welcome, and you're not good enough. You were not chosen; we were."

Simply because we do not always see God working does not mean he is not working. We also need to be careful not to let others, even churches, speak for God if what they say is contradictory to his Word. God is faithful to his promises and committed to redeeming his people and establishing his kingdom. There is room in God's family for you. Maybe you came from a broken home and have repeatedly experienced the disappointment of abandonment or broken promises. Throughout this book we see that God is faithful to fulfill his promises, push back the darkness, and equip his children to be faithful to the end as they anticipate a future, forever home with God their Father.

With this in mind, consider making this your prayer as you read and study this chapter:

> *You are a faithful and good God. Forgive me for all the times I've allowed others and my circumstances to shout louder than your Word and promises. You have provided salvation through Jesus, sent your Spirit to empower your children, and will send Jesus back again to complete the process and establish the fullness of your kingdom. Thank you. Now, just as you commissioned your people in Acts, help me to be a faithful witness of the good news found in Jesus to those I encounter in this life. Amen.*

SETTING

Recipients

Luke seems to have written before AD 70 to Theophilus.[2]

---

[2] Acts was written as a continuation of the Gospel of Luke. As Bock declares, "It is clear that the two volumes are the work of the same author." Darrell L. Bock, *Acts*, BECNT (Grand Rapids: Baker, 2007), 15. See the argument defending "Lukan" authorship in the "Luke" chapter of this book. While questions regarding Lukan authorship exists, we know the author is educated and, at least at times, a traveling companion of Paul. The vocabulary used by the author attests to his education. As Polhill observes, "His vocabulary is the largest of any New Testament writer and one that exceeds some secular Greek writings, such as those of Xenophon." John B. Polhill and Charles W. Draper, "Acts, Book of," *Holman Illustrated Bible Dictionary*, ed. Chad Brand, Charles Draper, and Archie England (Nashville: Holman Reference, 2003), 43. The "we" sections throughout

Theme and Key Passage

Acts is a book about God.[3] God is working and building his church despite opposition on all sides (Matt 16:18). The theme of Acts should be seen as three interrelated concepts: fulfillment of promise, experience of power, and expansion of the kingdom.

Acts 1:8 says, "But you will receive power when the Holy Spirit has come on you, and you will be my witnesses in Jerusalem, in all Judea and Samaria, and to the ends of the earth."

> **Martyr**
>
> The Greek word for "witnesses" in Acts 1:8 is *martus*, from which we derive our word *martyr*. While the Greek word means "someone who is a witness" or "someone who testifies," as a result of Christians being killed for their faith, the word *martyr* began to signify someone who is a faithful witness of Jesus while facing the punishment of death. The first martyr of the church was Stephen in Acts 7.

This theme is progressively played out in the book through the four Holy Spirit episodes where tongues are manifest.[4] Each episode represents a progressive unfolding of the theme as revealed in Acts 1:8, and each episode corresponds to one of the geographic markers presented there. Jesus's followers receive the power of the Holy Spirit, and as a result, they go to be his witnesses first in Jerusalem and Judea. Acts 2 presents the fulfillment

---

the book indicate his presence as a personal witness to many of the events presented in the work (Acts 16:10–17; 20:5–15; 21:1–18; 27:1–28:16).

Regarding the dating of this book, see chapter 4 for an explanation concerning who Theophilus most likely was.

[3] Bock agrees that "the apostolic band is not the central character of Acts. Rather, God's activity stands at the core of the account. Acts narrates God's work in establishing the church through Jesus's activity. Both Jews and Gentiles make up the church, the new people and community of Jesus. The work of Jesus and the establishment of this community of the Spirit represent the initial fulfillment of God's promises." Bock, *Acts*, 2.

[4] While maintaining the essential theme, Acts, as a book, can be broken down and understood in other ways as well. For example, versus focusing on the various Holy Spirit episodes, one can also read Acts through the ministry of different apostles. Early on in the book, the focus is on the ministry of the twelve apostles, then primarily Peter, but by the end of the book the focus is on Paul's ministry. Acts could also be divided up into the specific missionary journeys of Paul. Additionally, the book can be read as a transition from ministry primarily to the Jews to ministry primarily to the Gentiles; however, this last approach does not seem to be fully consistent with the message of the book. Throughout the book, and by the end of the book, the gospel is still being extended to the Jews (Acts 28:23–28), and Paul is welcoming anyone who wants to come and hear him talk about the gospel of the kingdom of God (Acts 28:30). Acts 28:30 again reiterates that narrative that everyone is welcome to hear and respond to the gospel through faith and repentance despite ethnic origin. That being said, it should be noted that the Jews are consistently described as rejecting Jesus as the Messiah while the Gentiles seem much more receptive.

of this prophecy and shows the expansive impact of gospel ministry in that region. Then, due to persecution, the gospel is received in Samaria (Acts 8) as evidenced by the presence of the Spirit and confirmed by the apostles. The last part of Acts 1:8, where "the ends of the earth" is mentioned, is fulfilled in two different places. A Gentile leader in Caesarea believes and receives the Spirit in Acts 10, showing that non-Jews can be saved and become citizens of God's kingdom (Phil 3:20) despite not being circumcised (Acts 15:1–35). Finally, we see the gospel going well outside of Israel deep into the Roman Empire. This Holy Spirit episode appears in Acts 19 in Ephesus where Paul leads some disciples of John the Baptist to faith in Jesus.

By the end of the book, we see the gospel of the kingdom flourishing far beyond its birthplace in Jerusalem. Paul is in prison in Rome, which is approximately 1,431 miles by air, and approximately 2,500 miles by land from Jerusalem. Certainly, in the first-century world, the gospel had gone well beyond Jerusalem as God was faithfully fulfilling his promises, empowering his people, and expanding his kingdom. Acts, ultimately, is about God.

Purpose and Occasion

Who is able to enter into a relationship with God, and where is this kingdom God promised? The audience to whom Luke wrote needed clarity. While Luke conveys many historical moments in this book, he is doing so with a purpose. He has been commissioned to write this document because confusion exists, in part, concerning whether Gentiles are able to be a part of God's family without being circumcised or converting to Judaism. Luke is expanding upon the Gospel he wrote and showing how the many promises Jesus made through his parables and teachings have come to life with amazing results.

As you read Acts, keep three thoughts in mind. First, notice the strong Jewish setting of the beginning of the book, such as the location, activities, and conversations (Acts 1–2). Contrast that setting with the end of the book. Acts ends with a Roman citizen in prison in Rome proclaiming the gospel of the kingdom of God to Gentiles in the heart of the empire (Acts 23:11; 28:11–31).

Second, remember that God's plan from the beginning has been to include the Gentiles in the kingdom of God. This truth is evidenced throughout the Old and New Testaments (Gen 12:1–3; Acts 15:6–18). Use the specific teaching moment from Jesus's life presented in Luke 13:22–30 as a lens to better understand what is happening in the book. In Luke 13:22, Jesus was teaching from town to town while traveling toward Jerusalem. Along the way, someone asked him a question about salvation. In response, Jesus did something remarkable. He actually proclaimed that non-Jews will be able to come through him to be welcomed at the feast table with Abraham, Isaac, and Jacob in the kingdom of God. The table was a place of acceptance and fellowship.[5] The table was for family. The table was a moment of connection in the first century. Eating together in the home was a significant moment, and Jesus used that picture to let the Jews know that while they had rejected him, many non-Jews would believe in him. Through faith in Jesus people are restored to God and become his children (John 1:12). No one is righteous based on heritage or adherence to the law. In actuality, those who try to keep the law are revealed as lawbreakers because they cannot do it. The way to forgiveness and redemption comes through faith in Jesus alone. Many Jews trusted in their covenantal heritage and rejected Jesus, missing him as the Messiah. The irony is that many non-Jews received him and are now part of the kingdom of God.

Third, notice the incredibly rapid growth of the early church. The church is a living glimpse of the kingdom of God and in part serves as a fulfillment of some of the parables Jesus spoke regarding the kingdom. Think of the parable of the mustard seed or the leaven (Luke 13:18–21). God designed his people to meet as a local "church gathering." These gatherings are more than a moment to learn about God; they are designed by God to engage one another as kingdom citizens and encourage one another to be faithful in anticipation of the return of the King (Heb 10:23–25). The picture of the church in Acts does not support the modern consumeristic approach to church; rather, we see in Acts a people gathering to participate and contribute to the worship of God and invest in one another's lives. The church gathering was not occasional and optional but regular and essential to these early believers.

---

[5] This idea is briefly alluded to in Polhill's commentary where he observes Luke's emphasis on the sharing of meals through his Gospel and Acts (*Acts*, 49).

HIGHLIGHTS IN ACTS

The Promised Spirit Empowers the Apostles (Acts 1:1–2:4)

Luke ends his Gospel somewhat abruptly, condensing a lot of details (Luke 24). The last chapter of Luke begins with the chaos surrounding the resurrection of Jesus. People are confused at first, but by the end of the chapter, they are confident and worshipping Jesus. What happened to bring about such transformation?

In Acts 1, Luke begins by providing a brief recap of how he ended his Gospel (the Gospel of Luke), but he does so by providing some details he previously left out. Jesus did not just come back to life, greet his followers, and ascend into heaven. He spent significant time with his followers over forty days proving to them that he had physically risen from the grave. The culture was a superstitious one in many respects.[6] Jesus's followers were initially terrified and confused. He spent time with them and convinced them that he was in fact alive. Additionally, during this time, Jesus taught them about the kingdom of God. A kingdom involves a ruler, a people ruled, and a region ruled. The kingdom of God is the rule and reign of God that begins in the hearts of his people now but comes to completion at the end of the age when a literal kingdom is established on earth (Rev 21–22) and all creation is brought into submission under God's rule (1 Cor 15:24–28). Unlike many of our local churches today, Jesus did not spend time talking about "heaven" in our traditional sense, but Jesus trained his disciples concerning the realities of the kingdom of God.

Consequently, after forty days, when Jesus promised to send the Holy Spirit and was about to ascend into heaven, the disciples asked him, "Lord, are you restoring the kingdom to Israel at this time?" (Acts 1:6). This question and the answer provide the foundation for everything else in Acts. Do not miss it. Jesus responded: "It is not for you to know times or periods that the Father has set by his own authority. But you will receive power when the Holy Spirit has come on you, and you will be my

---

[6] Acts 12:15 is one example of the supernatural and superstitious nature of this culture. When the slave girl reported that Peter was out of prison, standing at the gate, and wanting in, the people gathered dismissed her claim and decided it was his angel there instead. Matthew 14:26 is another example where the disciples thought Jesus was a ghost.

witnesses in Jerusalem, in all Judea and Samaria, and to the end of the earth" (Acts 1:7–8).

Jesus's followers wanted to know when the kingdom would be fully established, but Jesus told them that they were focused on the wrong thing. He does not want his people focused on when he will establish the fullness of the kingdom; Jesus wants his people focused on bringing others into the kingdom through the power of his Spirit. By the Spirit of God, Jesus's followers are to engage everyone with the message that he is the Messiah. "There is salvation in no one else, for there is no other name under heaven given to people by which we must be saved" (Acts 4:12). All who come to trust in Jesus as the Messiah are counted as part of God's family and *citizens* of his kingdom.

In response to Jesus's word and the angel's prompting, the apostles returned to Jerusalem and prepared for the ministry that awaited them. Finally, the waiting was over. The Spirit of Promise (John 14:16–17) came in a unique way, filling them and empowering them for the ministry God had for them.[7]

> **Speaking in Tongues in Acts**
>
> Much debate exists around what it means to "speak in tongues." A common belief is that tongues involves speaking in a heavenly or angelic prayer language. While a defense for this position can arguably be made from 1 Cor 13:1 and chapter 14, this use is not what Luke has in mind in Acts. Luke is using the word *tongues* interchangeably with *language* (Acts 2:3, 4, 6b, 8, 11b). Tongues in Acts is a gift whereby the Holy Spirit comes upon people and causes them to speak in a known language. Not only was the gift of tongues given to enable communication, but in Acts 2, each person was also hearing in their known language. For this reason, Pentecost should be seen, in part, as a reversal of the Tower of Babel.

The Promised Spirit Empowers and Expands the Church in Jerusalem and Judea (Acts 2:5–8:3)

The first significant Holy Spirit episode begins with the apostles in a house in Jerusalem, but immediately we see God's purposes and promises coming to life. The Spirit is sent to empower his people to share his message. What happens after the Spirit is received? A large sound is made, people begin to speak in various languages, and a crowd eventually gathers (Acts 2:1–6). Peter leveraged the unusual nature of the moment to preach the gospel of Jesus Christ with remarkable boldness and call people to repentance. As a

---

[7] Here are a few of the ways the Holy Spirit is referenced throughout the New Testament: Spirit of Christ (Rom 8:9), Counselor (John 14:16), eternal Spirit (Heb 9:14), Spirit of glory (1 Pet 4:14), Spirit of grace (Heb 10:29), and (John 14:17).

result, the church was born and grew rapidly. Jesus's disciples went from a small group of followers in a house to more than 3,000 people in a moment (Acts 2:41). The kingdom of God may have had a small beginning like a mustard seed (Luke 13:18–19), but it was growing fast and would soon outgrow what anyone would have naturally imagined.

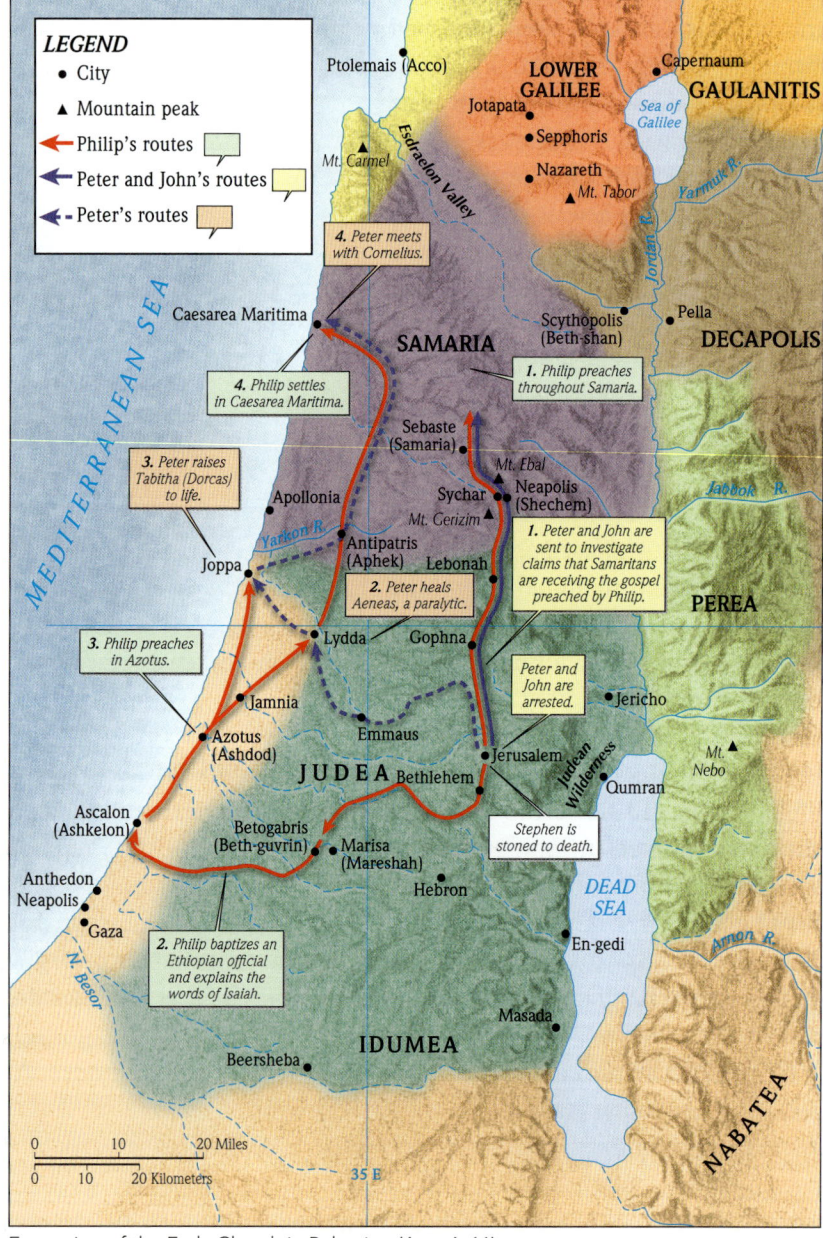

Expansion of the Early Church in Palestine (Acts 4–11)

This moment in Acts 2 sets the stage for the next several chapters. It is known as Pentecost. Pentecost, as a Jewish harvest festival, occurs fifty days after Passover (Lev 23:15–22). During this festival the Lord chose to pour out his Spirit upon his followers and began to build his church in fulfillment of his promise.

An important contrast needs to be made here. At Pentecost, a supernatural event happened. As a result of the Holy Spirit, people began speaking in languages previously unknown to them so that everyone could understand what was said in their own language. This moment created a gathering that allowed others to understand the gospel and be united in Jesus. Considering that, this passage should be read in contrast with the Tower of Babel moment in Gen 11:1–9. At Babel, people gathered in arrogance against God. God stooped down to see what they were doing. (Do not miss the irony that God had to come down to meet them at a tower they were trying to build up to the gods.) He brought judgment against them and divided up languages to create confusion and disunity so that they could not accomplish their purpose. In contrast, at Pentecost, God came down to bless his people. He brought his presence upon them to unite their languages so that the gospel could be understood and God's purpose accomplished.

> **Prayer**
>
> Take a moment and look at how the early church prayed in Acts 4:24–30. Notice four elements in their prayer:
> 1. They addressed God as he had revealed himself in the Old Testament.
> 2. They started with Scripture.
> 3. They submitted to God's sovereignty.
> 4. They asked for boldness to proclaim the gospel and reach the lost.*
>
> *McClendon and Lockhart make and develop these points in *Timeless Church*, 59–69.

As stated previously, Peter seized this opportunity with remarkable boldness by preaching a sermon. His sermon emphasized three points that should be considered in relationship to the rest of Acts. First, Pentecost was a fulfillment of prophecy. This event did not just happen. It was purposefully designed by God (Acts 2:16). Second, all were welcome. Even though it had not yet become evident in the book of Acts, from this first sermon we see God's plan that all were welcome in his kingdom regardless of their background and ethnic identity. Third, each person was responsible to respond to who Jesus was and accept him by faith as the Messiah in order to experience the benefits of salvation (Acts 2:38–40).

After this sermon, we see the message of the gospel blossom throughout Jerusalem and Judah. In response, persecution came against the church and the testimony regarding Jesus as the Messiah. The enemy did not want to see God's people and message flourish; however, ironically enough, the very persecution that was intent on stopping the gospel going forward was used by God to get the gospel to the Samaritans and beyond through powerful, Spirit-filled witnesses.

The Promised Spirit Empowers and Expands the Church in Jerusalem, Judea, and Samaria (Acts 8:4–9:43)

Saul, later known as Paul, was helping to lead the persecution against Christians (Acts 8:3). In response to this persecution, Christians began to flee Jerusalem into Samaria. What happened as a result? The gospel of Jesus spread and people in Samaria got saved. Wherever the people of God went, they continued to live out their mission to preach the gospel and make disciples. They were serving as God's witnesses everywhere. There are no accounts in Acts of believers going into a region and not making disciples there. The idea of a non-witnessing believer is unheard-of in Acts.

Another important idea is seen in this section. People, regardless of their background, were readily embraced and baptized into the church based upon their willingness to confess faith in Jesus.[8] However, once part of the church, actions or statements contrary to the ways of Jesus are grounds to question the authenticity of their faith. While this idea may be seen more clearly in Paul's epistles (1 Cor 5:1–5; 1 Tim 1:18–20; 4:1; 6:20–21; 2 Tim 2:17; Titus 1:16), it is also seen in Acts 8:9–25. Peter rebukes Simon, who has already made a

> **Was Saul's Name Changed to Paul?**
>
> A common misconception is that Saul's name was changed to Paul. This does not seem to be the case; rather, people during that time were often known by multiple names. Many pieces of evidence point to this, but perhaps none are stronger than these three. First, nowhere in Scripture is Saul said to have his name changed. Second, Saul is not called Paul at his conversion. Significant time passes after his conversion (Acts 9) before he is referenced as Paul (Acts 13:9). Verse 9 is evidence that "Paul" is an additional name, not a replacement. Finally, Paul is called Saul multiple times after his conversion, even by the Holy Spirit (Acts 9:19b–28; 11:25–30; 12:25; 13:1–9; 22:7, 13; 26:14). Since Paul saw the Gentiles as his primary audience (Acts 22:21), it makes sense that he would go primarily by Paul versus Saul in Acts and his letters.

---

[8] "Church," here, is used to designate the gathering of God's people. The word *church* can mean all believers in Jesus collectively. This use is known as the "universal church." "Church" can also refer to a specific gathering of believers, generally designated in a location. This use is known as the "local church." This last use is common throughout the New Testament. Many of Paul's letters are written to designated local churches. This use is also seen in the letters to the churches in Revelation 2–3.

profession of faith. He tells him to repent, which is a word normally associated with conversion in Acts. In other words, Peter challenges him in a way to determine whether Simon is going to submit his life to Jesus. The way Simon responds to this moment may well reveal the authenticity of his faith.

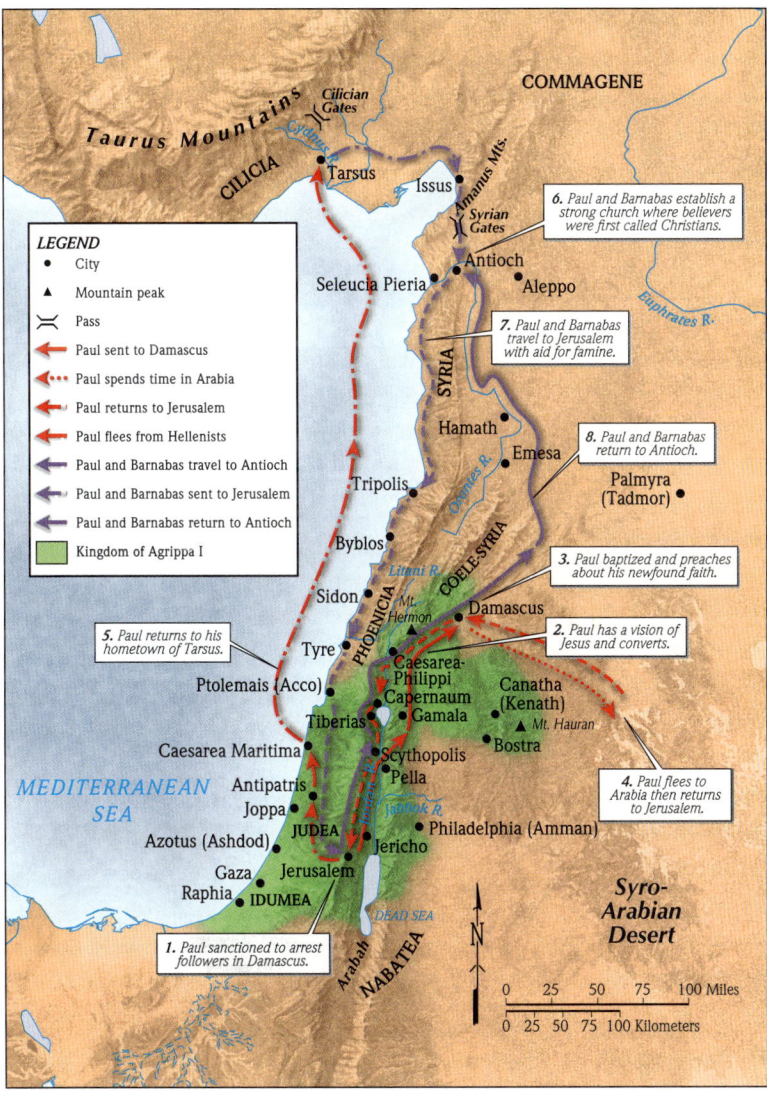

Paul's Conversion and Early Ministry

The Promised Spirit Empowers and Expands the Church throughout the Roman World (Acts 10:1–28:31)

The church continued to grow wildly. Even though Luke had set the stage from the beginning of the book that Gentiles had always been a part of God's plan, the church was birthed out of Judaism. As a result, many traditional thoughts persisted that contribute to confusion and concern within the Christian community as it related to the requirements of salvation. The first misconception Luke addresses has to do with whether or not Gentiles could be saved by faith in Jesus. The next Spirit episode answers this question while showing the continued fulfillment of Acts 1:8. In Acts 10, Cornelius, a Gentile Roman military leader, received a vision where he was told to reach out to Peter, who was staying at a tanner's house.[9] Peter came and preached Jesus to all those gathered in Cornelius's house, and they responded. Through this encounter, Peter witnessed the conversion of a group of Gentiles and their reception of the Holy Spirit. Accordingly, Peter was

> ### All Nations Gospel
>
> The "good news" concerning Jesus as the Messiah is not just good news for the Jew but for all. God desires all classes, genders, and races to know that he is merciful and gracious, abounding in love, and provides redemption for the sinner through Jesus, his Son (Ezek 33:11; 1 Tim 2:3–4).
>
> In the midst of the persecution of the early church, Philip was sent to an Ethiopian eunuch to explain the redemption that is found in Jesus, the light of the world. As a result, we see this man believe, be baptized, and continue on his journey, taking his newfound faith back to Africa.
>
> God desires his messengers to go. He desires all nations to know the truth, repent of their sins, and embrace Jesus as their Lord and Savior. Will you be sensitive to going wherever the Spirit leads to tell others about Jesus?

---

[9] A debate exists around this passage. Peter was staying at a tanner's house. A tanner dealt with dead animals. The question is whether a tanner was generally seen as ritually unclean in light of the law. If the tanner dealt with unclean animals, then the tanner would certainly be unclean by the standards of the law (Lev 11:24–25). If the tanner only dealt with clean animals, which seems likely in this context, it seems they would only be unclean if the animal died before being slaughtered, for example, by natural causes, disease, or killed by another animal (Lev 11:39–40). Some scholars argue that at least some Jews viewed tanners as unclean. David G. Peterson *The Acts of the Apostles*, PNTC (Grand Rapids: Eerdmans, 2009), 323. Others argue "it seems doubtful that [tanners] were regarded as unclean." Eckhard J. Schnabel, *Acts*, ZECNT (Grand Rapids: Zondervan, 2012), 471. While it is reasonable to conclude that tanners had an increased chance of being ritually defiled, there is not enough biblical or extrabiblical evidence to assume ritual uncleanliness based on that profession alone. Accordingly then, it is unlikely that Luke is drawing an ironic parallel between Peter's willingness to stay at a tanner's house while hesitant to engage Gentiles and see them saved.

Paul's Third Missionary Journey

convinced that God had indiscriminately opened salvation through faith in Jesus to the Gentiles (Acts 11:17; 15:7–11).

At this point in the book, an overlap exists where the focus shifts from Peter's ministry to Paul's. During this overlap, a second misconception is addressed. This second misconception, while related to the first, specifically answers the question of whether Gentile converts had to be circumcised to be saved (Acts 15:1). This question was considered by a group of apostles and elders in a meeting known as the Jerusalem Council. There it was determined that the answer was an emphatic no. Gentiles are saved by grace through faith in Jesus just as Jews are (Acts 15:11; Eph 2:8–9). Luke's point, reiterated through story after story, is that all are welcome into God's family. The only requirement is to believe in the Messiah Jesus (Acts 4:12; 14:1; 15:6–11; 16:31; 19:4; 28:23–24). This requirement for salvation does not mean that there are no other expectations. The Gentiles in conversion need to be considerate to their Jewish brothers and sisters as well as understand that coming to Jesus involves a submission to him as the messianic King (Acts 15:19–20). Gentiles, as a whole, were more accepting of a loose sexuality that allowed for self-indulgence and personal preference (1 Cor 5:1; 1 Thess 4:3–5; 1 Pet 1:14); nevertheless, Jesus required submission to God's standards of living (1 Cor 5:11; 6:13; Eph 5:3; Col 3:5–7; 1 Thess 4:3). All are welcome into the family of God through faith, yet all are equally expected to bring their lives into conformity to the standards of Christ as a result of their faith (Eph 2:10).

As mentioned above, this section shifts focus from Peter's ministry to Paul's. This shift makes sense in light of Luke's purpose in the book. He is showing the fulfillment of promise, experience of power, and expansion of the kingdom even to the Gentiles. He is showing how all the opposition in the world will not stop God's empowered witnesses from bringing all who are responsive into the kingdom. The gospel goes from a small group of Jewish believers huddled in a room (Acts 2:1) to the edge of the Roman Empire, affirming again that God's promises in part extend to the Gentiles. In case this point was missed in Acts 10, Luke reiterates it through the last Spirit episode in Acts 19:1–7. This time, Paul is well outside of Jerusalem and deep into the Roman Empire in Ephesus. The conversion of these Ephesians and his subsequent ministry in Ephesus resulted in the gospel of the kingdom being heard by "all the residents of Asia, both Jews and Greeks" (Acts 19:10).

In consideration of these things, Luke's shift in focus from Peter to Paul makes sense. Paul's ministry, while still including many Jewish converts, was uniquely focused on reaching the Gentiles with the message of the gospel (Acts 22:21; 23:11). Through faith in Jesus they are grafted in and part of God's family (John 1:12; Rom 8:15–17; Eph 2:19). This is why the book abruptly ends the way it does. Luke's purposes are fulfilled and his point has been made. Even imprisonment and death cannot stop the movement.

BIBLIOGRAPHY

Bock, Darrell L. *Acts*. BECNT. Grand Rapids: Baker, 2007.
Bruce, F. F. *The Book of Acts*. NICNT. Grand Rapids: Eerdmans, 1988.
McClendon, P. Adam, and Jared E. Lockhart. *Timeless Church: Five Lessons from Acts*. Nashville: B&H Academic, 2020.
Peterson, David G. *The Acts of the Apostles*. PNTC. Grand Rapids: Eerdmans, 2009.

Polhill, John B., and Charles W. Draper. "Acts, Book of." In *Holman Illustrated Bible Dictionary*. Edited by Chad Brand, Charles Draper, and Archie England. Nashville: Holman Reference, 2003.

Polhill, John B. *Acts*. Vol. 26. NAC. Nashville: Holman Reference, 1992.

Schnabel, Eckhard J. *Acts*. ZECNT. Grand Rapids: Zondervan, 2012.

8

ROMANS

A. CHADWICK THORNHILL

CONNECTION POINT

What relevance does this first-century writing have for us today? Romans is often approached as the great theology text of the New Testament, and for good reason. This work, however, has a context that must shape our understanding of how and why Paul says what he does. Paul was writing to a diverse ethnic body (Jews and Gentiles) of first-generation followers of a Jewish Messiah (i.e., King) living in the capital city of the Roman Empire. At the heart of the letter is the question of how the loyalty of these followers of King Jesus changes the way these two diverse bodies live together in unity as members of the kingdom of God. This concept of "enacted loyalty," or how this commitment to Jesus has life-altering effects, is what this letter is all about. When put in that light, it is perhaps easier for Western Christians to see the relevance Romans has for us today.

With this in mind, consider making this your prayer as you read and study this chapter:

Holy Father, you desire a people of every tribe, nation, and tongue living in harmony through their union in Christ. May you grant us grace to strive for unity despite our differences, knowing that you are seeking to unify all things under the Lordship of Jesus Christ. As we interact each day with a world often hostile to your purposes, may you equip us to do all things in love so that your kindness may be demonstrated to the world. We ask these things in the name of Jesus Christ our Lord, through the power of the Holy Spirit. Amen.

Ancient Rome

SETTING

Recipients

Paul was writing around AD 55.[1] The recipients of this letter were a group of Jewish and Gentile Christians struggling over what function the law of Moses should have in their community and how to attain unity amid this

---

[1] Romans belongs to Paul's "undisputed" letters, meaning there is little to no contention to the fact that the author of this letter was the apostle Paul. Indeed, it is often

divisive question. Much more will be said about this in what follows, but it is generally unquestioned that Paul's audience was mostly Gentile Christians, living in Rome. Though the majority of the population of Rome was Gentiles, there was a considerable Jewish minority present. Christians in both populations faced the challenge of living out their faith in a culture at odds with Christianity, including the pagan religions and the imperial cult.

Theme and Key Passage

The letter to the "saints" in Rome contains four major units (Rom 1:1–4:25; 5:1–8:39; 9:1–11:36; 12:1–16:27), which focus on a number of intertwined themes. Rightly hailed as a great theological letter, Romans, as most of Paul's letters, journeys from "what is true" to "what we should do." While the "what we should do" section of the letter (Rom 12:1–16:27) is often neglected in lieu of the dense theology and logic of the first three sections, Paul has clear practical goals in mind as he develops his theological arguments in the first three sections.

In Romans 1:16–17, Paul said: "For I am not ashamed of the gospel, because it is the power of God for salvation to everyone who believes, first to the Jew, and also to the Greek. For in it the righteousness of God is revealed from faith to faith, just as it is written: The righteous will live by faith."

Purpose and Occasion

Though Paul does not make his purpose explicit, several reasons likely prompted him to write this letter. The Gentile believers in Paul's audience had come to a point of conflict with either Jews or Jewish Christians in Rome. The emperor Claudius had forced the Jews to leave the city a few years earlier, and his edict expired around AD 55, allowing the Jews to return to the city. This may have been the origin of the controversy, since the Gentile Christians in Rome would have become accustomed to the lack of a Jewish presence. The questions in the letter concerning things such as food laws, circumcision, and other matters of the law likely arose as a result of Jewish or Jewish-Christian leaders returning to the city and expressing concerns over how these Gentiles were practicing the faith. Judaism and Christianity had not yet "parted ways," so Christians were seen as a sect of followers within Judaism. Paul wrote to unify this church, resolve these

---

considered to be Paul's most significant treatise. The letter is typically dated to the AD mid-50s, though some have argued for slightly earlier or later dates.

tensions, and give them a vision of the Christian life to sustain their God-given mission and fellowship.

At the time Paul wrote Romans, he was likely in the city of Corinth toward the end of his third missionary journey, preparing for a return voyage to Jerusalem to deliver a collection for the Jewish believers (Rom 15:25–28). Paul had arranged for a collection to be taken among the various churches in the Gentile world for the Jewish Christians suffering in Judea. He was hopeful that a generous and sacrificial gift from the Gentile believers for their Jewish brothers and sisters in Christ would go a long way in healing divisions within the body of Christ. Paul himself also desired to travel to Rome (Rom 15:23), and he may have intended his letter as a means of introducing himself to these followers of Jesus before his opportunity to visit in person.

HIGHLIGHTS IN ROMANS

Though many themes and passages abound in this rich book,[2] we will focus on four key elements of Paul's overall argument, which follows his chapter outline: Jewish and Gentile guilt before God and God's faithfulness and justice (Rom 1:1–4:25); sin and death defeated and new life secured (Rom 5:1–8:39); God's merciful plan for Jews and Gentiles to be united in Christ (Rom 9:1–11:36); and unity and faithfulness among God's people (Rom 12:1–16:27).

Jewish and Gentile Guilt; Divine Faithfulness and Justice (Rom 1:1–4:25)

Paul's introduction contains several important themes that set the stage for the message of Romans. First, Paul articulates the gospel as God's "good news, which was foretold through the Old Testament prophets. This news is that Jesus, the Son of God (Messiah) and Lord (i.e., divine ruler) fulfilled God's covenantal promises. These promises included the covenant with David (2 Sam 7:8–16; 1 Chr 17:7–14) for an eternal kingdom ruled by a Davidic heir (Rom 1:3); the new covenant, in which the Spirit of God (Rom 1:4) would be poured out on God's people (Jer 31:31–40; Ezek 36:24–38; Joel 2:28–32); and the Abrahamic covenant, in which

---

[2] On various contemporary approaches to interpreting Paul, see Michael F. Bird, ed., *Four Views on the Apostle Paul* (Grand Rapids: Zondervan, 2012).

God would bless the nations (Rom 1:5) through Abraham's seed (Genesis 12–17). The fulfillment of these promises in the incarnation, life, ministry, death, resurrection, ascension, and enthronement of Jesus is the heart of the New Testament gospel.

Paul desired to come personally to Rome, but until that could happen, his letter served as his presence to the churches there (Rom 1:8–15). He then reveals his thesis for the letter, which alerts the reader to its main themes.[3] Here, Paul lays out: (1) his complete commitment to the gospel; (2) the power of the gospel to save Jews, first in historical sequence but not "better," and Gentiles, second in historical sequence but not "lesser"; (3) the gospel as demonstrating God's "righteousness"; (4) God's righteousness as revealed "from faith to faith"; and (5) "faith" as the means of a righteous life. We will explore each of these ideas more fully below.

Paul's brief thesis statement occurs in Rom 1:16–17. Here, he lays out his unashamed commitment to the gospel, which he describes as having power to save Jew and Gentile. He also states that in this gospel the "righteousness of God" is revealed "from faith to faith," which is affirmed through his quotation of Hab 2:4, "The righteous one will live by his faith." Much debate has occurred over Paul's use of the phrase "righteousness of God," which could mean a number of different possibilities.[4] The terms *righteousness* and *faith* will occur numerous times through the letter, and the connection between them is important. By "righteousness," Paul likely refers to God's justice or "covenant faithfulness," meaning God has acted rightly in both his judgment and salvation of humanity and in keeping his promises. By "faith," Paul has in mind both the ideas of trust or commitment as well as the notion of faithfulness, as demonstrated by his quotation of Habakkuk.[5] Michael Gorman summarizes Paul's intent in 1:16–17 well: "In the gospel, God's saving covenant faithfulness is revealed through the faithfulness of Christ to generate faithfulness among those who hear it."[6] Through the course of the letter, Paul will argue that the

---

[3] In Greco-Roman rhetoric, this section would be called the *propositio*, or "proposition." Essentially, it is Paul's "thesis statement" for the entire letter that follows. See Ben Witherington III and Darlene Hyatt, *Paul's Letter to the Romans: A Socio-Rhetorical Commentary* (Grand Rapids: Eerdmans, 2004), 47–51.

[4] For example, righteousness "from God," as an "attribute" of God, or as an "activity" of God.

[5] See Matthew Bates, *Salvation by Allegiance Alone: Rethinking Faith, Works, and the Gospel of Jesus the King* (Grand Rapids: Baker, 2017).

[6] Michael J. Gorman, *Apostle of the Crucified Lord: A Theological Introduction to Paul and His Letters* (Grand Rapids: Eerdmans, 2017), 410.

covenant-making God has kept his promises dramatically and unexpectedly in the faithful life and death of Jesus, the divine Messiah, whom God raised from the dead in victorious approval. Jesus alone is capable of setting humans free from sin and death to live righteous lives by means of their being united to this victorious Christ.

Paul offers an accusation in Rom 1:18–32, which will be familiar to many readers. The language here is full of stock charges against Gentile sin and shares commonalities with some other passages from Jewish literature.[7] Paul declares that they have suppressed the truth of God's nature, leaving them without excuse before him because of their idolatry, sexual immorality, and disobedience (Rom 1:18–25). This resulted in God giving them over to their desires, which Paul says has left them "slanderers, God-haters, arrogant, proud, boastful, inventors of evil, disobedient to parents, senseless, untrustworthy, unloving, and unmerciful" (Rom 1:30). The human mind/heart is a damaged and ravaged place, one in which divine intervention is needed to make it healthy, vibrant, and whole.

The average Jewish listener at this point might shout a hearty "Amen!" at Paul's charge against Gentiles. To this, Paul adds, "You have no excuse, oh human, whoever you are, when you judge one another" (Rom 2:1, translation mine). Paul seems to confront now a specific dialogue partner.[8] Romans is structured as a "diatribe" between Paul and his "dialogue partner." This rhetorical strategy gives Paul the opportunity to confront head-on the false teachings addressed in the letter. Though not all humans are guilty of this entire list of sins, who can claim they have not acted in selfishness, anger, pride, or with a lack of mercy? Paul assures his readers that God's judgments are just and that his kindness intends to lead all to repentance (Rom 2:4). He warns those who do not repent that God's judgment will "repay each one according to his works" (Rom 2:6–8). This judgment is impartial, rewarding or condemning both Jews and Gentiles alike (Rom 2:11). Paul states "the doers of the law will be justified" (Rom 2:13). Paul is not offering a works-based salvation, and his comments must be set in the fuller context of what he has to say later about the work of Christ

---

[7] For example, the apocryphal book *Wisdom of Solomon*, 13–15. For more on Romans in its Second Temple Jewish context, see Ben C. Blackwell, John K. Goodrich, and Jason Maston, eds., *Reading Romans in Context: Paul and Second Temple Judaism* (Grand Rapids: Zondervan, 2015).

[8] Scholars debate the exact identity of this dialogue partner. The most likely options are a Christian Jew, a non-Christian Jew, or a Gentile convert to Judaism or Christianity. The issues at the heart of this are clearer, as will be discussed throughout this chapter.

and the Spirit, particularly in Romans 3–8. There he will make clear the proper source of the obedience he has in mind.

Paul concludes chapter 2, returning to the theme of partiality. He affirms that true circumcision is not outward, but inward: one whose heart has been transformed for good works through the Spirit of God (Deut 10:12–22; Jer 31:31–34; Ezek 36:24–32). Why does Paul mention circumcision? Some of Paul's opponents apparently taught that Gentiles needed to be circumcised, among other things, to be full members of the covenant-people of God. Much of Paul's purpose is to disentangle these Jewish expectations from the actual obligations placed upon Gentile followers of Jesus (Acts 15). This theme is a major focal point throughout the letter.

> **Faith and Works**
>
> The question of faith and works permeates several letters in the New Testament but especially Romans, Galatians, and James. Where James discusses faith and works as a way of contrasting mere belief in God without a faithful life, Paul's definition of faith includes the idea of faithful living, and he contrasts the faithfulness the believer finds in Jesus with what can be found in the "works of the law." Paul's does not discuss "faith" and "works" in general, but in the specific context of the Roman and Galatian situations, while James's discussion finds a slightly different context than Paul's. Both James and Paul agree that to have saving faith in Jesus means a trusting, total commitment to God through the work of Jesus Christ.

Paul's dialogue partner, whom he addresses in Rom 2:1, now chimes in with questions against Paul's proposal. Paul answers each question in turn; and thus, the portion of the letter reads much like a dialogue (or "diatribe" as it is often called), which is treated as such below.[9]

> Rom 3:1: *Paul's opponent*: "*So what advantage does the Jew have? Or what is the benefit of circumcision?*"
>
> *Paul*: The Jewish people were the recipients of God's covenants, promises, and God's Word! Those are some pretty great benefits!
>
> Rom 3:3: *Opponent*: "*What then? If some were unfaithful, will their unfaithfulness nullify God's faithfulness?*"
>
> *Paul*: Of course not! Our unfaithfulness does not mean God is unfaithful.

---

[9] On reading Romans as a diatribe, see Rafael Rodriguez, *If You Call Yourself a Jew: Reappraising Paul's Letter to the Romans* (Eugene, OR: Cascade Books, 2014).

Rom 3:5: *Opponent*: *"But if our unrighteousness highlights God's righteousness, what are we to say?"*

Paul: God is true and reliable, regardless of what humans do. He is the rightful Judge.

Rom 3:7: *Opponent*: *"But if by my lie God's truth abounds to his glory, why am I also still being judged as a sinner?"*

Paul: So should we sin as much as we want? That, of course, is absurd!

Rom 3:9: *Opponent*: *"What then? Are we any better off?"*

Paul: We are all under sin: Jews and Gentiles alike. We have all failed and fallen and succumbed to the power of sin, which our weak flesh on its own cannot resist. God's law reveals sin to us, and we all are ultimately powerless against sin without his help. Sin is too strong. The good news is that God's justice is not like ours. God has revealed his kind of justice in the death and resurrection of Jesus.[10] And Jesus's death and resurrection is a gift offered to free us and forgive us of our sins and give us new life. As when Moses led Israel out of slavery to Egypt, God leads humans out of slavery to sin through Jesus's faithful and sinless life, substitutionary death, and glorious resurrection!

Rom 3:27: *Opponent*: *"Where, then, is boasting? . . . By what kind of law? By one of works?"*

Paul: There is no boasting, except to boast in what Jesus has faithfully accomplished! Things such as circumcision have their place but are not what make us right with God. God is not only the God of the circumcised but the God of all!

Rom 3:31: *Opponent*: *"Do we then nullify the law through faith?"*

Paul: Not at all! In fact, this was the point of the law all along! The faithfulness of God's Messiah has the power to make us all right with God.

---

[10] Paul's use here of the Greek word *hilasterion* is debated. As Keener, however, recognizes, in the Old Testament, the term denotes the covering of the ark of the covenant, and thus Paul presents Jesus as "the place where forgiven humanity can meet God." Craig S. Keener, *Romans*, in *New Covenant Commentary Series* (Eugene, OR: Cascade, 2009), 60.

Rom 4:1–2: *Opponent*: *"What then will we say that Abraham, our forefather according to the flesh, has found?"*

Paul: I'm glad you mentioned that! The Scriptures say Abraham trusted God and was counted as righteous. His wholehearted trust in God meant he was in the right kind of relationship with God. And, he acted on his faith. All this happened, however, before Abraham was ever circumcised! So, if circumcision is necessary for reconciliation with God, how was Abraham reconciled before he was circumcised? You see, the law had not yet been given when God made his covenant with Abraham. Furthermore, God promised to bless the nations through Abraham as well. God's promises are for the whole world, not just the circumcised. Just as God brought life to Abraham and Sarah through Isaac when their bodies were in a sense "dead," he has brought the gift of eternal life to all people through the resurrection of Jesus from the dead!

> **The Law**
>
> For many Christians the law of Moses is an inherently negative idea, something done away with in Christ. The New Testament presents a more complicated picture of the law. Paul can call the law holy, righteous, and good, while also saying it brings with it a curse. As Jesus's teachings about the law (Matt 5–7) indicate, the law needed a fresh interpretation to reorient God's people to seeing its true purpose. Rather than burdening people with guilt, shame, frustration, or a sense of self-righteousness, the true intent of the law, according to Jesus, was to steer its readers to love God and to love their neighbors as themselves. It is this understanding of the law that Jesus, Paul, and James all uphold as of value for the new covenant community.

Death and Sin Defeated; New Life Secured (Rom 5:1–8:39)

Paul has backed his opponent into quite a corner! In chapter 5 Paul explains a bit further the significance of the death and resurrection of Jesus before his conversation partner chimes in again. Paul states that this new standing before God means we are now at peace with God through Jesus Christ (Rom 5:1). While we may not typically think of our "sin" as war against God, all of the spiritual forces of darkness hold captive those who have not yet been reconciled to him.[11] In Romans 6 Paul describes this as slavery or bondage to sin.

---

[11] As Paul describes them elsewhere, the "dominion of darkness" (Col 1:13), the rulers,

Sin is not just making a mistake or a brief lapse in moral judgment. Sin is a corrosive agent that bends and twists all things away from their God-intended purposes. Paul describes sin in this chapter as having "entered the world" when Adam sinned (Rom 5:12), bringing death along with it. Sin ultimately separates humans from the source of life itself—God. And sin multiplies itself throughout all humanity, establishing the reign of death over humans (Rom 5:16–17). Sin is an active and terrible force seeking to destroy God's creation.

Here is what is so "good" about this "good news," Paul proclaims: God *loves* sinners. Even while they are still sinners. God's love is not pre-conditioned. We do not have to have our act together before we come to God in faith. In fact, we cannot! In Rom 5:8 Paul wrote, "God proves his own love for us in that *while we were still sinners*, Christ died for us" (emphasis mine). God loved us while we were still sinners. His love does not rise and fall with our ups and downs. God loves us. Period. He loved us enough that the eternal person of the Son took on human flesh to break the generations-old cycles of sin and death and gave humanity a life of flourishing. Jesus, Conqueror of sin and death, through his obedience (Rom 5:19), has brought freedom and eternal, abundant life to humanity. And this love is now poured out in abundance to fill those who are God's children through their union with Jesus Christ. Paul's dialogue partner, however, still cannot quite wrap his head around this.

Ruins from the Colosseum in Rome

> Rom 6:1: *Opponent*: *"What should we say then? Should we continue in sin so that grace may multiply?"*
>
> *Paul*: Jesus does not offer mere forgiveness or a "get-out-of-hell-free card," but a new life. Baptism depicts this new life (Rom 6:1–5). Those who follow Christ join with him in his story. His story becomes their own. They are buried with him in their submersion

---

authorities, powers, and dominions (Eph 1:21), the "god of this age" (2 Cor 4:4), and the "rulers of this age" (1 Cor 2:8).

in the water, like being put into a grave and raised to new life, bursting forth from their casket, purified by Christ's resurrection. They exist now as new selves, new creatures (Rom 6:6). They have been freed from the captivity of sin and death, and assured eternal and abundant life (Rom 6:7–11).

As an aside, we need to note something at this point in the dialogue. Paul is aware of a tension in this reality. New Testament scholars sometimes refer to this as "inaugurated eschatology," the "already and not yet."[12] Though it is true that believers are already new creations, already united to Christ, already recipients of new life, and already raised with him, this reality has not yet been fully completed. There is still a struggle. Paul, thus, encourages the Roman church to not let sin reign; to no longer obey it (Rom 6:12). They cannot live with head turned backward toward their old prison cells. They are to offer themselves fully to God and his good purposes and no longer allow sin a place in their lives (Rom 6:13). Paul's opponent seems to miss this with his question in Rom 6:15.

> Rom 6:15: *Opponent*: *"What then? Should we sin because we are not under the law but under grace?"*
>
> *Paul*: We were slaves to sin, but we are no longer. Jesus Christ has freed us to live for God alone. Think of it this way: we are God's "slaves" now, committed solely to his purposes. Those enslaved to sin are rewarded only with death, but God has freed us from sin and death through Christ Jesus! And God will continue to work in our lives to make us more and more like Jesus, so that our lives are fit to fellowship with him forever (Rom 6:17–23).

As humans, we have to obey laws. If someone gets married, that person is legally bound to his or her spouse; but if the spouse dies, the person does not have to live as if he or she is still married, right? So, the way that sin used the law to keep us bound to death is not binding anymore, because we have died to that spouse. With Jesus, we are under a new kind of law—the law of the life of God's Spirit (Rom 7:1–6).

---

[12] For more on this, see Benjamin L. Gladd and Matthew S. Harmon, *Making All Things New: Inaugurated Eschatology for the Life of the Church* (Grand Rapids: Baker Academic, 2016).

Now, before continuing the dialogue, we need to make an observation. This next section brings us to another heavily debated section of Romans. The central question here is the identity of the "I" who now speaks. Numerous suggestions have been made, including that the "I" represents Adam, Israel, Paul's experience before being a Christian, or Paul's experience after being a Christian. One's approach must take into consideration that the "I" was once alive apart from the law (Rom 7:9); is fleshly and in slavery to sin (Rom 7:14); is not empowered to overcome the flesh and sin lives in them (Rom 7:15–20); needs to be rescued from their body of death and enslavement to sin (Rom 7:24–25). These things could be said of Adam, but not Israel, or Paul, either before or after his conversion (for when was Israel or Paul ever alive apart from the law; or did Paul still consider himself a slave to sin?). A proposal that appears to take them all into account is that Paul's dialogue partner is a Gentile who adheres to Jewish practices, and through this dialogue with Paul has now been convinced that the law is insufficient to rescue them from death.[13] We will follow this approach in the summary that follows while recognizing there are other possible interpretations.

> Rom 7:7–24: *Opponent*: The law has shown me what sin really is, and the desire to sin within me cannot be overcome by the law. Sin has sprung up, captured me, and made me a prisoner of death itself! Sin has taken God's good law and turned it against me. The law is holy, righteous, and good, but I am a prisoner to sin and death! Even with the knowledge of the law, sin's grip is not any looser. I am a prisoner to sin, unable to overcome my urges and keep God's commands. My flesh is weak and prone to the horrors sin craves. I want to live faithfully to God, but I cannot. Sin is too powerful and controls me. There is a darkness within me that I cannot tame. I see this now. Though I see the goodness of God's law, sin and death have imprisoned me. I am distressed, in misery! Will somebody save me from this bondage?!
>
> *Paul*: Do you now see? *Thanks be to God through Jesus Christ our Lord!* (Rom 7:25a).

---

[13] For defenses of this view, see Rodriguez, *If You Call Yourself a Jew* (Eugene, OR: Cascade Books, 2014); Rafael Rodriguez and Matthew Thiessen, *The So-Called Jew in Paul's Letter to the Romans* (Minneapolis: Fortress Press, 2016).

Rom 7:25b: *Opponent*: Yes, I am a servant of the law of God in my mind, but a captive of the law of sin in my flesh.

Paul's opponent has come to the realization that he is trapped in his bondage to sin, and the law is not capable of freeing him. The "law of sin and death" is the law overcome by sin, bringing death instead of life and flourishing. Paul answers with an incredible proclamation: "There is now no condemnation for those in Christ Jesus, because the law of the Spirit of life in Christ Jesus has set you free from the law of sin and death" (Rom 8:1–2). Paul is not "antinomian," (one who believes that the Christian life has no obligations). The law itself is transformed under the kingship of Jesus, something Paul will explain in chapters 12–16. He declares the law was not able to provide freedom because human flesh was too weak on its own. Jesus, the divine Son, has come in human flesh; but he overcame the power of sin through his obedient life and disarmed death through his resurrection (Rom 8:3–4). The law could not provide this victory because every human since Adam has succumbed to sin's power, but Christ did not. This life of Jesus is now provided to those who belong to him through faith, and Jesus's own faithfulness now becomes their identity through the transformative work of the Spirit of God. Paul explains that this new life comes with a new way of "being in the world," one full of life and peace (Rom 8:6). This Spirit-filled identity is true of all who belong to Christ now, but it will be fully completed in the future (Rom 8:11).

This new way of life means believers must walk by the Spirit and not by the flesh (Rom 8:4). They must "put to death" the deeds of the flesh as true children of God who are rebirthed by his Spirit (Rom 8:13). What a remarkable truth that those in Christ become God's beloved children, adopted into his family, and co-heirs with Christ! We share now in Jesus's victory and his inheritance. We have become siblings of the King, sharing in his victory, his inheritance, and his future rule and reign, all given without qualification. We do not earn this remarkable gift;[14] we receive it by our trust and commitment to Christ as Lord. This is why Paul can speak earlier in Romans of the overflowing nature of God's grace (Rom 5:17) and elsewhere of God's grace as abundant (1 Tim 1:14).[15]

---

[14] For the most recent and thorough study of Paul's understanding of grace, see John M. G. Barclay, *Paul and the Gift* (Grand Rapids: Eerdmans, 2015).

[15] Or as one lexicon defines, an "extraordinary abundance." William Arndt et al., *A Greek-English Lexicon of the New Testament and Other Early Christian Literature* (Chicago: University of Chicago Press, 2000), 1034.

Paul recognizes this marvelous gift is incomprehensible but notes the sufferings we temporarily endure now in our Spirit-empowered struggle against sin will pale in comparison to the glory that awaits us (Rom 8:18). All of creation will be freed from its decaying state and renewed for a glorious eternal future in which God and his children will once again dwell in joyful fellowship together (Rom 8:19–21). Imagine a future with no death, disease, sickness, fear, depression, pandemic, war, violence, suffering, or oppression. We are so accustomed to these realities that it is difficult to imagine life without them. But this is the promise that awaits God's beloved children. Paul refers to this future as one for which we "hope" (Rom 8:24). By this, Paul does not mean wishful thinking but rather a confident expectation that God will keep his promises in the future as he has already done in the past. This is why, with these glorious realities awaiting us, we, with all creation, "groan" in the present. We are waiting for this glorious future to take hold in the present (Rom 8:22–25).

In this context Paul assures us that we do not often know how to pray as we should. With such devastation surrounding us each day, we can become overwhelmed with despair. The Spirit, we are assured, knows our hearts and intercedes (pleads on our behalf) for God's help in our times of trouble. Further, all of this sorrow and suffering, Paul declares, is being bent by the mighty power of God toward good for his children (Rom 8:28). Though much debate about the doctrines of predestination and election has come from Paul's statements in Rom 8:28–30,[16] Paul's focus here is sometimes missed. His emphasis is on the future that awaits

> **Justification**
>
> While there is some agreement that Paul's understanding of the term *justification* entails the concepts of "justice," "righteousness," "faithfulness," and "acquittal," there is significant debate among scholars as to what exactly Paul meant. Some traditions focus on justification as a declaration of freedom or forgiveness, others the enabling of a righteous life, others still as an infusion of the righteousness of Christ into the believer. Though there is a spectrum of views on the doctrine, most Christian traditions view it as an important theological concept. A growing number of scholars see justification as a part of Paul's larger picture of salvation as "union with Christ."

---

[16] For various views on these matters, see Chad Brand, ed., *Perspectives on Election: Five Views* (Nashville: B&H Academic, 2006); David Basinger and Randall Basinger, eds., *Predestination and Free Will: Four Views of Divine Sovereignty and Human Freedom* (Downers Grove, IL: InterVarsity Press, 1986); Stanley N. Gundry and Dennis W. Jowers, eds. *Four Views on Divine Providence* (Grand Rapids: Zondervan Academic, 2011). For a corporate approach to Paul's teachings on election, see A. Chadwick Thornhill, *The Chosen People: Election, Paul, and Second Temple Judaism* (Downers Grove, IL: IVP Academic, 2015).

believers, that is, being "conformed to the image of his Son" (Rom 8:29). We often hear in Christian circles that "God has a wonderful plan for your life." Though sometimes misconstrued, when framed by Paul's comments here, it is wonderfully true. God has a wonderful plan for our lives—for us to be like Jesus! Christ, the firstborn, has preceded us in his justification (i.e., vindication by God through his resurrection) and his glorification at his ascension. These future realities for believers are assured to us because they are already true of Christ. What is true of him now will become our reality.

God is truly for us! It is easy for us at times to slip into thinking God is harsh, vindictive, and waiting on his heavenly throne for us to slip up so he can smite us, reject us, or punish us. Paul declares here that God is for us (Rom 8:31). And, if the God of the universe is seeking to bring about good for us, our fears, anxieties, and doubts in the present can be confidently given to him. Paul assures that no enemy, affliction, distress, persecution, famine, nakedness, danger, violence, death, life, angels, rulers, things present or to come, powers, heights, depths, or any created thing can separate us from God's love for us in Christ Jesus (Rom 8:37–39).

God's Merciful Plan: Jews and Gentiles United in Christ (Rom 9:1–11:36)

The book of Romans began with Paul arguing that Gentiles come to God on equal terms as Jews.[17] All are held captive by sin, and all are freed through trusting commitment to King Jesus. The question now reverses a bit, and Paul's interlocutor chimes in again as well. Paul now deals with this question: if Jesus is Israel's Messiah, why have so many Jews rejected him? Paul begins by recounting his sorrow over his fellow Israelites who are outside of the saving gift of Christ. He recounts the glorious privileges that belonged to Israel: adoption (Exod 4:22), the presence of the Lord's glory (Exod 40:34), the covenants (Gen 17:2; Deut 29:14; 2 Sam 7:1–29; Jer 31:31–40; Ezek 37:24–28), the Law (Deut 4:13–14), the temple (1 Kings 6), and the promises of God (Jer 32:42). Greatest of all, the gift of the Christ, "God over all," came from the lineage of Israel (Rom 9:5)

In spite of this, many of Paul's fellow Israelites had failed to recognize Jesus as their rightful King. His kingship was of a different form and fashion then many Israelites expected. The Messiah was supposed to free

---

[17] Much of this section is a summary of what I have developed elsewhere in Thornhill, *The Chosen People*.

Israel from their oppressors (i.e., Rome), and yet this Messiah died, and his followers claimed he was alive again. Paul does not see this rejection as a failure on the part of God's promises "because not all who are descended from Israel are Israel" (Rom 9:6). Paul makes this clear through several examples (Abraham, Isaac, Jacob, and Esau, etc.). His underlying point is that covenant membership in Israel has never been on the basis of ancestry alone (Rom 9:6–13). This causes Paul's dialogue partner to chime in again.

> Rom 9:14: *Opponent*: *"What should we say then? Is there injustice with God?"*
>
> *Paul:* God has not broken his promises to Israel (Rom 9:15–16). Just as he mercifully revealed himself to Moses (Exod 33:19), he has mercifully revealed himself to us in the present through his Son. If he can show his power through even Pharaoh, why can he not show his power through the Gentiles as well (Rom 9:17–18)? Israel's hardening does not mean God's unfaithfulness.
>
> Rom 9:19: *Opponent*: *"Why then does he still find fault? For who resists his will?"*
>
> *Paul:* Who are you to decide what God should do? God has never worked according to our expectations (think of Isaac [unlikely child], Jacob [usurper], Moses [weak in words], David [unfit warrior], etc.). Does the potter mold the clay, or does the clay mold the potter? God has patiently endured the disobedience of the Gentiles who were formerly his enemies, and they have become recipients of his mercy (Rom 9:22–23). The potter is making his people of both Jews and Gentiles, just as Hosea and Isaiah predicted (Rom 9:24–29).
>
> Rom 9:30–31: *Opponent*: *"What should we say then? Gentiles, who did not pursue righteousness, have obtained righteousness—namely the righteousness that comes from faith. But Israel, pursuing the law of righteousness, has not achieved the righteousness of the law. Why is that?"*
>
> *Paul:* Because they have not trusted in the faithful Messiah. They have tripped over Jesus instead of recognizing him as their Lord. Jesus is the stone Isaiah told us about (Isa 8:14; 28:16). I deeply desire their salvation (Rom 9:32–33). They do not know God as he has

been revealed in the Messiah (Rom 10:1–2). Jesus is the one to whom the law has been pointing, but they are still seeing the law as the destination and not as pointing to Christ (Rom 10:3–7). The message we proclaim is of the faithfulness of the Messiah, and if you yourself declare "Jesus is Lord" and trust that God raised him from the dead, you too will be saved (Rom 10:8–9). This is the same for Jews and Gentiles, and "everyone who calls on the name of the Lord will be saved" (Rom 10:13; cf. Joel 2:32).

Israel has already heard this beautiful good news, but they have not obeyed it by trusting in God's Messiah. This message has gone out through the whole world, and many Gentiles have received it, as Moses and Isaiah anticipated (Rom 10:14–20; cf. Deut 32:21; Isa 65:1). But much of Israel has rejected it (Rom 10:21).

Rom 11:1: *Opponent*: *"I ask, then, has God rejected his people?"*

Paul: Of course not! I am an Israelite, and there is a remnant of many others from Israel who have turned to God's Messiah in faith. This is the same as it was in the days of Elijah, when many in Israel worshipped other gods, but there was a faithful remnant (Rom 11:1–6; cf. 1 Kgs 19:18).

Rom 11:7: *Opponent*: *"What then? Israel did not find what it was looking for."*

Paul: Not the whole of Israel, but a remnant has (Rom 11:7). This is not so different from our ancestors, as Moses, Isaiah, and David attested (Deut 29:4; Ps 69:22–23; Isa 29:10). They spoke of many in Israel who did not understand or rejected God's way. They still do not see or understand Jesus for who he truly is (Rom 11:8–10).

Rom 11:11: *Opponent*: *"I ask, then, have they stumbled so as to fall?"*

Paul: Of course not! Just as many Gentiles, who were once disobedient enemies of God, have found mercy through Jesus the Messiah, so too Israel's rejection of Jesus is not final. There is still a chance for them to repent and confess Jesus as Lord (Rom 11:12–16). Think of God's people like a tree. If the tree is holy, so are all of its parts. Some of the natural branches (Israel) have been broken off because of their rejection of Jesus, and you, an unnatural branch (a Gentile) have been grafted in. The tree has grown from the seed of Abraham. You are a branch, not the root. Just as some of the natural branches (Israel) were broken off because they were dead (lacking faith in the Messiah), you must not be arrogant to think the same could not happen to you. You must stand firm in his love and mercy so as to not suffer the same fate. And, the natural branches (Israel) can also be grafted back in if they trust in God's Messiah (Rom 11:13–24). God is not done with Israel, and his mercy remains open to them, as it is to us today. His wisdom and goodness is deeper than any of us can conceive (Rom 11:25–36).

Unity and Faithfulness among God's People (Rom 12:1–16:27)

Paul's exchange with his dialogue partner ends here. He has argued that Jesus alone is the Conqueror of sin and death, the only one who can free humanity from their captivity. This salvation is offered freely, a gift from God, to all who declare Jesus as Lord and trust in his faithful work for their salvation. It comes with no preconditions or partiality; it is available to all—regardless of ethnicity, gender, or class—and regardless of how great their debt of sin. Jesus's death is capable of rescuing all humanity but is found only by those who give themselves to him and find their true identity in God's love.

Paul now moves from the "what is true" sections (Rom 1:1–4:25; 5:1–8:39; 9:1–11:36) to the "what we should do" section (12:1–16:27), as is the customary structure of his writings. He begins with the "indicative" statements (what is true) about what God has done for us in Christ (i.e., Romans 1–11). Once Paul has established these theological realities, his "imperative" section (what we should do) shows his readers how this impacts them in the here and now, revolutionizing their habits, commitments, and relationships.[18]

Paul begins his "what we should do" section with an overarching command to the Romans: to present their bodies as "a living sacrifice" to God (Rom 12:1). Having established the union of believers to Christ through his death and resurrection, Paul now moves beyond theological reality to practicality: the cross as a way of life. Those called by Jesus's name are also

---

[18] On this portion of the letter as its climax, see the excellent study by Scot McKnight, *Reading Romans Backwards: A Gospel of Peace in the Midst of Empire* (Waco: Baylor University Press, 2019).

A view from inside the Roman Colosseum

called to embody his ethic: a life of loved poured out for the good of others. Moving away from a self-centered life to a life open to others is the core of the Christian ethic. Everything else Paul commands flows from this reality.

This is summarized in the next portion where Paul instructs them not to "think of [themselves] more highly than [they] should think" because they belong to a "fellowship of differents."[19] There is diversity in the body of Christ, as the Romans themselves, with these ethnic tensions, well knew. Paul reminds them that the cross is the great equalizer, and differences do not create hierarchies. We are not all the same. There are differences in ethnicity, gender, class, and even gifting (Rom 12:5–8). We do all, however, possess equal and intrinsic worth because we are equally loved by God.

Paul reminds them of the essence of the Christian life: to live a life of love (Rom 12:9–21), meaning a commitment to seeking the good of others even at the cost of something to one's self. Leaders, servants, governing authorities (Rom 13:1–7), brothers, sisters, and even enemies (Rom 12:20)

---

[19] To borrow a phrase from Scot McKnight, *A Fellowship of Differents: Showing the World God's Design for Life Together* (Grand Rapids: Zondervan, 2015).

are all to be loved. The call of the Christian life is to love God, love others, and do good to all people as opportunities arise. Now, lest Paul be seen as an antinomian, one who thinks Christians have no "law" to obey, he understands that this is the essence of the Torah itself (Rom 13:8–10; cf. Lev 19:18; Deut 6:5). And, lest we count this as Paul's genius, his knowledge is demonstrated of Jesus's own teachings about the Law, which he summed up as "Love the Lord your God with all your heart, with all your soul, and with all your mind" (Matt 22:37), and "love your neighbor as yourself" (Matt 22:39). Rather than debates about circumcision or dietary restrictions, the law is fulfilled in love of God and love of neighbor. This is the law of the King (Gal 6:2), and thus, the law of the kingdom of God. Such a love seeks the good of others without judgment, knowing that God alone is the judge (Rom 14:1–23). This love lifts up the weak rather than condemns them for their weakness (Rom 15:1–6), so the people of God may worship in unity (Rom 15:7–13) and recognize that they are all worthy of love because they are each objects of God's own immeasurable love.

BIBLIOGRAPHY

Arndt, William, et al. *A Greek-English Lexicon of the New Testament and Other Early Christian Literature*. Chicago: University of Chicago Press, 2000.

Barclay, John M. G. *Paul and the Gift*. Grand Rapids: Eerdmans, 2015.

Basinger, David, and Randall Basinger, eds. *Predestination and Free Will: Four Views of Divine Sovereignty and Human Freedom*. Downers Grove, IL: InterVarsity, 1986.

Bates, Matthew. *Salvation by Allegiance Alone: Rethinking Faith, Works, and the Gospel of Jesus the King*. Grand Rapids: Baker, 2017.

Bird, Michael F., ed. *Four Views on the Apostle Paul*. Grand Rapids: Zondervan, 2012.

Blackwell, Ben C., John K. Goodrich, and Jason Maston, eds. *Reading Romans in Context: Paul and Second Temple Judaism*. Grand Rapids: Zondervan, 2015.

Brand, Chad, ed. *Perspectives on Election: Five Views*. Nashville: B&H Academic, 2006.

Gladd, Benjamin L., and Matthew S. Harmon. *Making All Things New: Inaugurated Eschatology for the Life of the Church*. Grand Rapids: Baker Academic, 2016.

Gorman, Michael J. *Apostle of the Crucified Lord: A Theological Introduction to Paul and His Letters*. Grand Rapids: Eerdmans, 2017.

Gundry, Stanley N., and Dennis W. Jowers, eds. *Four Views on Divine Providence*. Grand Rapids: Zondervan Academic, 2011.

Keener, Craig S. *Romans*. New Covenant Commentary Series. Eugene, OR: Cascade, 2009.

McKnight, Scot. *A Fellowship of Differents: Showing the World God's Design for Life Together*. Grand Rapids: Zondervan, 2015.

———. *Reading Romans Backwards: A Gospel of Peace in the Midst of Empire*. Waco: Baylor University Press, 2019.

Rodriguez, Rafael. *If You Call Yourself a Jew: Reappraising Paul's Letter to the Romans*. Eugene, OR: Cascade Books, 2014.

Rodriguez, Rafael and Matthew Thiessen. *The So-Called Jew in Paul's Letter to the Romans*. Minneapolis: Fortress Press, 2016.

Thornhill, A. Chadwick. *The Chosen People: Election, Paul, and Second Temple Judaism*. Downers Grove, IL: IVP Academic, 2015.

Witherington, Ben, III, and Darlene Hyatt. *Paul's Letter to the Romans: A Socio-Rhetorical Commentary*. Grand Rapids: Eerdmans, 2004.

9

1 CORINTHIANS

LEO PERCER

CONNECTION POINT

What relevance does this first-century writing have for us today? As you read through the New Testament, perhaps you get the distinct impression that you are reading mail intended for someone else. How does this letter from so long ago even relate to your current experience? Here is some good news: The material covered in Paul's letters to the Corinthians invokes images and ideas that are very familiar. In fact, these letters deal specifically with issues many people face today: subjects such as division, authority, authentic Christian living, and even controversies over sexual relationships, lawsuits, and worship.

In response to these subjects, Paul's answer is straightforward: when faced with controversy and division, life must be lived in a cross-shaped and selfless manner. Jesus is the model for how we are to live in a broken world. His model is revealed not by spectacular accomplishments or pride-fueled attempts to get ahead; rather, the model Paul provides in 1 Corinthians takes the values of the world and turns them upside down. As he responds to a number of concerns throughout this letter, Paul reminds his readers that Jesus's humble life, sacrificial death, and physical resurrection reveal the unique way Christians should live and the means by which they may accomplish such a life. If you wonder whether the Bible offers answers to real-life issues, and whether God has provided a means to live an authentically humble life of service, then 1 Corinthians is a great starting point.

With this in mind, consider making this your prayer as you read and study this chapter:

> *God, you keep your promises, and you make yourself known. Through your Son, Jesus, you reveal your goodness, grace, and mercy. Thank you for salvation through his life, death, and resurrection, and for his example of faithful love towards others. Thank you for your servant Paul, and for these words you provided through him to help us grow in your mercy and grace. Open the eyes of my heart to understand the truth of your Word, and empower me to live a life of courageous faith, obedience, and humble service to others. May my life reveal more of Jesus to others, until all know him. Amen.*

SETTING

Recipients

Both 1 and 2 Corinthians are universally acknowledged to have been written by the apostle Paul. The early church recognized both epistles as authentic, and this consensus has not been seriously challenged. Paul addresses his first epistle to "the church of God at Corinth, to those sanctified in Christ Jesus, called as saints, with all those in every place who call on the name of Jesus Christ our Lord" (1 Cor 1:2). Both epistles were written in the mid-50s of the first century during Paul's third missionary journey. The first epistle appears to have been written during Paul's lengthy stay in the city of Ephesus around AD 54–55 (1 Cor 16:8), while the second epistle was likely written by Paul around AD 55–56 from Macedonia after he was forced to abruptly depart Ephesus.

The Corinthians had a long history with Paul. To help us understand this history and these people, we must consider three subjects: (1) the history of Corinth, (2) the people of Corinth, and (3) Paul's interactions with

1 Corinthians

The Second Missionary Journey of Paul

the Corinthians. Corinth was a city of commerce, diversity, and division.[1] Ideally located on a narrow strip of land connecting the southern peninsula (known today as the Peloponnese) and the mainland of Greece, Corinth controlled the land route between the east and the west. It received goods in two harbors, Lechaeum (on the Adriatic Sea) and Cenchrea (on the Aegean Sea).[2] As a result, Corinth was well known as a destination for ships full of cargo and passengers.

---

[1] For more details on the history of Corinth, see Scott Hafemann, "Letters to the Corinthians," in *Dictionary of Paul and His Letters*, ed. Gerald Hawthorne, Ralph Martin, and Daniel Reid (Downers Grove, IL: IVP Academic, 1993), 164–73.

[2] William L. Lane, *Highlights of the Bible: New Testament* (Delight, AR: Gospel Light, 1981), 56; Bruce Longenecker and Todd Still, *Thinking Through Paul: An Introduction to His Life, Letters, and Theology* (Grand Rapids: Zondervan Academic, 2014), 109–10.

Ruins of the Temple of Aphrodite

An important commercial center to both the region and the greater Roman world (at one time Corinth was one of the largest cities in the Roman Empire), Corinth was known as a destination city.[3] The economy in Corinth was one selling point, but it was also known for its religious and ethnic diversity. As a prosperous hub for commerce and shipping, Corinth had a reputation for pleasure and vice, especially in the area of sexuality.[4] "To Corinthianize" was a term coined by Aristophanes to refer to the practice of immorality, and the term "Corinthian girl" was slang for "prostitute." A report even circulated that the temple of Aphrodite in Corinth

---

[3] When Paul entered Corinth in AD 50, the city had been part of the Roman Empire for less than a century. Destroyed in 146 BC for resisting Rome, the city was rebuilt by Julius Caesar as a Roman colony around 44 BC. It quickly grew in prominence to become the capital of the Roman province of Achaia and the administrative seat for southern Greece in the Roman Empire. See also Lane, *Highlights of the Bible*, 56–57; Longenecker and Still, *Thinking Through Paul*, 109–10.

[4] This reputation was stronger before the Roman occupation of Corinth, but some of the negative results of this sexual corruption apparently existed even in Paul's day. For additional information, see Lane, *Highlights of the Bible*, 56; Hafemann, "Letters to the Corinthians," 172–73.

housed around 1,000 prostitutes for use in worship.[5] While vice was one side of Corinth's reputation, the other part was religious. Corinth was home to many temples dedicated to a variety of Greek and Roman gods, and a significant Jewish population was also known to exist there. The confusing array of religions and "authorities" played a role in making Corinth a pluralistic melting pot of cultures, philosophies, and lifestyles.[6] These various religions also contributed to division in the city.

In a city of such diversity, the people regularly competed with each other for public recognition and honor, competition that often led to disagreement and conflict. With regard to the religious element of Corinthian society, the people would often seek recognition and honor for being connected to someone (divine or human) of great esteem. Much like some religious groups today, the connection to a particular divinity or temple became bragging points for why one group's religion was somehow better or more honorable than others. The people who first occupied Corinth after it was reestablished by the Romans did not come from elite backgrounds, so many of them were naturally hungry for recognition that derived from certain social, economic, or even religious connections. The idea of "honor" attached to a person's civil and religious connections became an area for boasting and competition in the city. To add to this spirit of competition, the city of Corinth was known for the Isthmian Games (which took place every two years and provided huge economic and social rewards for the winners). Large crowds from around the Roman Empire would flock to Corinth for the games in order to compete or participate in the commerce generated by the games. The presence of these games was an honor for Corinth and became one more reason for this pluralistic city to boast.[7]

Into this situation came Paul the missionary. He made his first contact with Corinth during his second missionary journey (Acts 18:1–11). After a brief stay in Athens, Paul traveled to Corinth where he spent eighteen months before returning to Antioch to prepare for his third missionary

---

[5] Lane, *Highlights of the Bible*, 56; Hafemann, "Letters to the Corinthians," 173; Thomas D. Lea and David Alan Black, *The New Testament: Its Background and Message*, 2nd ed. (Nashville: B&H Academic, 2003), 403.

[6] Lane, *Highlights of the Bible*, 56; Longenecker and Still, *Thinking Through Paul*, 110; Hafemann, "Letters to the Corinthians," 173; Lea and Black, *The New Testament*, 403.

[7] Longenecker and Still, *Thinking Through Paul*, 111; Lea and Black, *The New Testament*, 403; Hafemann, "Letters to the Corinthians," 173.

journey.[8] During his time in Corinth, Paul met Aquila and Priscilla (tentmakers like Paul) and worked with a number of believers in the city to bring the gospel to both Jews and Gentiles. Luke records that Paul "reasoned in the synagogue every Sabbath and tried to persuade both Jews and Greeks" (Acts 18:4). This attempt to proclaim Jesus in such a divisive and debauched city often led to significant resistance. In fact, after many of the local Jews resisted Paul's message, the Lord saw it necessary to encourage Paul in a vision to remain vigilant and to keep proclaiming the good news of Jesus (Acts 18:9–10).

While Paul experienced many hardships for faithfully proclaiming the gospel, the Lord was certainly active in establishing his church in the city. As Luke wrote, "Many of the Corinthians, when they heard, believed and were baptized" (Acts 18:8). Those who came to believe during Paul's stay in the city (some Jews and some Gentiles) established a Christian community to which Paul would address two of the letters contained in the New Testament. This group included people who came from a Jewish background and were thus familiar with synagogue worship as well as many others who were associated with the various pagan religions that were prominent in Corinth at the time. The diverse backgrounds of the members of the church in Corinth often made it difficult for the church to achieve unity and avoid competition and division.[9]

Themes and Key Passages

While division is one clear theme, Paul also addresses the topics of sexual immorality, lawsuits, proper worship practices, marriage, spiritual gifts, and the resurrection. Division arose over several of these topics, division that was often the result of either confusion or pride. In his response to these concerns, Paul emphasizes the need for unity by recognizing that true honor in God's economy comes not from amazing accomplishments but by learning to be humble and serve others selflessly. The selfish life that emphasizes personal success is contrasted with a life focused on Jesus and his sacrificial love. For Paul, a life of loving, humble service is the only proper way to receive true and meaningful honor—the honor that comes from God. To elevate the needs and interests of others above oneself and

---

[8] For a list of factors that may have led Paul to remain so long in Corinth, see Lane, *Highlights of the Bible*, 56–57.

[9] Paul categorizes the Christians in Corinth as Jews, Greeks, slaves, free, rich, and poor. See 1 Cor. 12:13 and Hafemann, "Letters to the Corinthians," 173.

lay down one's life in service to others is to live a life of true honor. In short, the imitation of Christ is the highest calling to which one could aspire. The following passages give evidence to this reality.

> 1 Cor 2:1–2: "When I came to you, brothers and sisters, announcing the mystery of God to you, I did not come with brilliance of speech or wisdom. I decided to know nothing among you except Jesus Christ and him crucified."
>
> 1 Cor 11:1: "Imitate me, as I also imitate Christ."
>
> 1 Cor 13:13: "Now these three remain: faith, hope, and love—but the greatest of these is love."

Paul also develops the idea of Christlike humble service while addressing the specific concerns of the church in Corinth. In addressing these issues, Paul provides instruction designed to provide clarity on matters that were misunderstood by the new Christians in Corinth and emphasizes the importance of pursuing unity by imitating the example of Christ. In the first four chapters, Paul challenges the Corinthians to find unity in the person of Jesus (especially his life, death, and resurrection) and not in the wisdom or ability of a human author. True unity flows from an understanding that all experience God's grace not on the basis of their human standing but only by means of the humble death of Jesus. Christians therefore are to recognize that they are servants of one another and not competitors when it comes to living out the Christian faith.

In chapters 5 and 6, Paul addresses issues surrounding sexual immorality and lawsuits among Christians by reminding them that Jesus's sacrificial death makes them members of one body. Their actions thus affect others (and even Jesus). Unity is found when we recognize the importance of treating each other not as objects for personal satisfaction but as people for whom Jesus died. Instead of competing with one another for recognition and using one another for our own ends, Christians must be willing to put the needs of others first. The idea of humble love and sacrifice will play out in a similar manner in later chapters that deal with subjects such as marriage, proper worship, spiritual gifts, and the resurrection. In his treatment of each of these issues, Paul emphasizes that the Christian standard should be humility and love.

Purpose and Occasion

Paul's relationship with the Corinthians was complicated and sometimes rocky. When he first visited, those who became Christians welcomed his leadership and advice. After he left Corinth, however, other leaders (like Apollos) came to the city to help train the new Christians. This soon led to division as the Christians in Corinth began taking sides based on favorite preachers. Divided by allegiance to a favorite viewpoint or by social and economic status, each side boasted that its approach to the Christian life was the best.[10] These divisions (coupled with some questions about doctrine and life in the church) prompted people from Chloe's household (1 Cor 1:11)[11] to report to Paul about the division and controversies taking place in the church. At the same time, another group in Corinth wrote a letter to Paul with specific questions about other concerns (1 Cor 7:1). The oral report Paul received from Chloe's household emphasized the disunity in the Corinthian church, while the letter asked questions dealing with several issues. Almost all of these involved self-centered attitudes or self-promotion in the church. There were also questions relating to doctrinal issues or worship practices. For example, prophesying and praying in the congregation is addressed in chapter 11, while spiritual gifts and their role in church worship occupies chapters 12–14. In addition, chapter 15 deals with the resurrection and may indicate sincere misconceptions in the congregation.

The visit by Chloe's group and the letter from the others prompted Paul to write 1 Corinthians during his third missionary journey while ministering in Ephesus (1 Cor 16:8). In this writing he attempts to deal with the problems that developed after his departure by reminding the believers that they were saved by Jesus's humble service and death and that they now follow his example by serving others. In every facet of life they must imitate his humility and life of love. As Paul's letter reveals, unity is found in being bound to one another in service to and for Jesus. Death to selfish ambition and a willingness to serve others create a strong community and allow God's people to be more effective in their proclamation of the gospel.

---

[10] Lane, *Highlights of the Bible*, 58–59; Longenecker and Still, *Thinking Through Paul*, 115–16; Hafemann, "Letters to the Corinthians," 174–75.

[11] Chloe may have been a leader in the Corinthian church or a group of Christians in Corinth may have gathered at her home.

HIGHLIGHTS IN 1 CORINTHIANS

Due to the topical nature of Paul's responses to the reports from Corinth, an outline of 1 Corinthians is not easy, but the progression of ideas and Paul's own language reveals some order. Chapters 1–4 are a response to reports from Chloe's delegation, and elsewhere Paul uses language such as "now in response to" or "now about" (1 Cor 7:1, 25; 8:1; 12:1; 16:1, 12) to indicate responses to the written report he received. What needs to be remembered as we read through 1 Corinthians is the central point: Jesus's humble service in his life, death, and resurrection is both the means by which we become God's people and the example we should all imitate as Christians. For Paul, salvation is both an individual reality and a corporate experience. Christians are not redeemed to be museum pieces; they are meant to be working models of God's intention for human life. To serve and to love requires others in the equation. One cannot practice service or love without someone to love or to serve. With that in mind, here are the highlights of 1 Corinthians.

A Corinthian street

Prologue: Opening Greeting and Thanksgiving (1 Cor 1:1–9)

As his greeting reveals, Paul reminded the Corinthians that their spiritual progress related to the work of God in their lives and, by implication, was not based upon their own merit, personal accomplishments, or giftedness.[12] Any spiritual gift or knowledge that the Corinthians received was due to God's gift of grace. It is, therefore, God's faithfulness, not human ability, that is the focus of Paul's expression of thanksgiving. Similarly, we should exhibit grace and mercy in our dealings with others in response to God's work in our lives. As God loved us, we should likewise love others. From this prologue, Paul begins to address specific issues that were of concern in the Corinthian church.

Divisions in the Church (1 Cor 1:10–4:21)

Paul began his discussion by addressing the divisions taking place among believers in Corinth (1 Cor 1:10–17). He explicitly designated this division as a form of "rivalry" that encouraged competition within the congregation rather than service to others. In its first-century context, to align with a particular "name" was to submit oneself to the authority of that person. In other words, to elevate a particular theologian or preacher as one's designation for honor or for prestige is to miss the point of the Christian life. No individual can meet your spiritual needs. People cannot do what Jesus alone can do. The Corinthians were using Paul or Apollos or Cephas as a way to make their own views on various matters appear more prestigious or credible. In response, Paul explained,

> ### Paul's Use of "Name" in 1 Corinthians
>
> Paul uses the word *name* at least six times in 1 Corinthians. "Name" is another way to say "authority" or to emphasize a position of honor or rule. Those who call upon the name of the Lord (1 Cor 1:2) are those who are his by yielding to his control. In most cases (see 1 Cor 1:2, 10, 13; 5:4; 6:11) Paul uses this language in reference to Jesus and our submission to him as our authority. In 1 Cor 1:15, however, Paul mentions that "no one can say you were baptized in my name." Paul reminds the Corinthians that he is not the one who saves. He is a servant, and their service and allegiance should belong primarily to Jesus. To make any human an "ideal authority" is to miss the point of salvation. We do not belong to Paul, Apollos, Peter, or to some other notable preacher; we belong to Jesus. He alone has the authority to save because of his service to God on our behalf.

---

[12] One unique aspect of this introduction is Paul referencing them as "the church of God" (1:2a). This reference is likely Paul's way of putting down this idea of divisions and factions within the church and reminding them that first and foremost they are God's church.

"The word of the cross is foolishness to those who are perishing" (1 Cor 1:18). In a society in which human pride and the pursuit of honor were common, Paul reminded the Corinthians that the gospel reveals that what may appear foolish to the world (e.g., Christ's humiliating death) is "the power of God to us who are being saved" (1 Cor 1:18).

To the Jews, the idea of a crucified Messiah was described as "a stumbling block" (1 Cor 1:23). From their perspective, the Messiah would come as a victorious conqueror, not one who would be humbled in defeat. The Gentiles also had reason to scoff at the Christian faith. In their view, divinity was not something that expressed itself in weakness. Gods were powerful and transcendent, they assumed, a belief that ran counter to the conviction that Jesus, a humble Jew from Galilee, was the resurrected Son of God. No wonder many of the Gentiles viewed the gospel message as "foolishness" (1 Cor 1:23).

In addition, the Corinthians subscribed to a worldly view of wisdom that was understood as the power to control or the power to succeed. Paul described God's power much differently, as something that could be humble and even "weak." The wisdom of the world says "the way up is to dominate." Paul's message is that God became a humble servant and died a humiliating death so that we could be his children. For Paul, God's wisdom is more powerful than the wisdom of the world because it recognizes a simple yet profound truth: God's weakness is stronger than any human strength (1 Cor 1:25). Through the humble work of Jesus, God is able to redeem a world that was lost because of arrogance. Contrary to common thought, Paul indicated that true honor, the honor that comes from God, is found in submission, service, humility, and even weakness. Because such honor comes from God rather than one's own accomplishments or merit, it allows one to boast in the work of God.

Paul's own preaching was not amazing from the world's perspective (1 Cor 2:1–5), and he came to Corinth "in weakness, in fear, and in much trembling" (1 Cor 2:3). His preaching apparently did not exude the eloquence highly praised in the Roman world but simply exhibited God's power—strength shown in humble service and weakness. Paul argued that this kind of preaching reveals God's wisdom (1 Cor 2:10–16) and that the superior type of wisdom is revealed by those willing to put others first. As God humbled himself by becoming human and dying by crucifixion, so also are Jesus's followers to exhibit a similar attitude to service. Many of the Corinthians had not reached that level. They saw the nature of ministry as a means of competition rather than as a call to service (1 Cor 3:1–4).

Paul noted that the famous ministers to whom they aligned were simply "servants" that God used to bring others to Jesus (1 Cor 3:5–9). They were not masters; their "names" could not save. Only Jesus is capable of saving, and he is the foundation laid by Paul and others (1 Cor 3:10–23). Their failure to understand these truths, Paul explained, was indicative of their immaturity.

Paul finished this section with a reminder that ministers to God's people are to acknowledge their role as servants. They are stewards who manage things that belong to someone else (in this case, God himself). The mission of servants is to make sure that the Master gets a return on his investment by faithfully engaging in the work to which they have been entrusted (1 Cor 4:1–13). In his stern address to the Corinthians, Paul hoped to motivate them to move away from pride and competition and to focus instead on how they might serve others in humility. He wanted them to grow in maturity as they served the One who humbly served and died for them. To that end, he planned to send Timothy to teach them (1 Cor 4:14–21). Paul then turned to some moral problems that were of concern in Corinth.

Dangerous Moral Problems: Sexual Sin and Pride (1 Cor 5:1–6:20)

Paul sandwiched his instruction pertaining to lawsuits among Christians between his discussion on sexual sins. The underlying issue in these chapters remains the problem of pride. In their arrogance, the church in Corinth had not responded well to these situations. Perhaps they thought that their own spiritual development or accomplishments made them superior to others and rendered them immune to moral issues. Perhaps the attitude of pride caused them to believe that they could adopt some morally dubious lifestyles without compromising God's grace or pleasure toward them. Paul refuted their pride, recognizing an arrogance that borders on death.[13]

Paul specifically addressed three issues: (1) incest (1 Cor 5:1–13), (2) lawsuits between believers (1 Cor 6:1–11), and (3) the consequences of sexual immorality (1 Cor 6:12–20). A young man in the church was evidently in a sexual relationship with his stepmother. This activity was shocking even to the non-Christians in Corinth, but the church allowed the behavior to continue without addressing it. Paul labeled their tolerance of this behavior as arrogant and misplaced "boasting." Could it be that they were bragging of their spiritual maturity and tolerance towards

---

[13] Longenecker and Still, *Thinking Through Paul*, 122–23.

"sinners"? We do not know, but Paul advised them to remove the young man from the fellowship. The goal for such discipline was to bring the sinner to repentance while protecting the church from their influence. He even reminded them that Christians should be careful to avoid fellowship with those who claim to follow Jesus but continue in sexual immorality, idolatry, greed, verbal abuse, drunkenness, and other sinful attitudes and actions. Paul admonished the church to remember that evil behavior in the church affected the whole congregation negatively. The safest route to ending this negative impact was to remove the sinful person and pray for repentance. This approach is based upon the reality that Jesus has equipped his people to make mature deliberations regarding sinful or immoral behavior in the church (Matt 18:15–20). Mature Christians are to seek sound and godly judgments between each other that encourage repentance and unity rather than arrogance and division.

With regard to Paul's instructions involving lawsuits between believers, it would appear that some in the Corinthian church were unable (or perhaps unwilling) to settle their differences in the church and resorted instead to going to court to get a civil judgment from outsiders. Paul argued that believers going to court against each other hinders the church's ability to proclaim the gospel effectively. Rather than taking advantage of each other, they should work together to show the kindness and mercy of God.

Paul concluded this section with a note concerning Christian freedom and a reminder to flee sexual sin. The salvation provided by Jesus puts us into a unique relationship with God and with each other. As members of the body of Christ, we are God's dwelling place, his temple. Therefore, what we do with our physical bodies has an impact on the church (the body of Christ).

Discussions on Marriage and Related Matters (1 Cor 7:1–40)

Having addressed the problem of sexual immorality, Paul transitioned to the related topic of marriage. Some ancient cultures admired celibacy as a high calling, and even Paul viewed it is a good and acceptable option.[14] Marriage, however, was a normal expectation in the first century (1 Cor 7:32–35). Paul advocated sexual relations in marriage as one way to combat sexual immorality. His instruction also makes clear that sexual expression is to be limited to the relationship between a woman and a man in marriage. All other forms of sexual expression are contrary to God's

---

[14] Lea and Black, *The New Testament*, 411.

design and amount to immorality. Paul urged those who were unmarried to remain single if called by God to do so, and he indicated that he was single himself (1 Cor 7:8–9).

Nonetheless, the church should show esteem to each person, regardless of marital status. Singleness has advantages for obeying and serving God (1 Cor 7:32–35), but marriage also has benefits both for serving God and serving others. The church needs to recognize this reality and find ways to encourage Christians to engage in faithful service to others, whether married or single. Married couples should not be pressured to separate to live celibate lives, and single people should not be pressured to marry unless called by God. In light of these discussions, Paul addressed issues related to separation and divorce (1 Cor 7:10–16).

In first-century Corinth, the likelihood of only one person in a marriage becoming a Christian was not unusual.[15] Paul spoke about how couples should handle these situations by reminding the Corinthians that their first obligation was to serve their marriage partners, whether they were believers or not. On the other hand, if a non-Christian left a Christian, Paul advocated remaining single and allowing the non-Christian to leave. The instruction in this section may seem difficult to understand in certain respects, but we must remember that Paul was answering questions from the Corinthians. Apparently, some Christian spouses struggled with how to relate to their non-Christian partners. Knowing what we do about the culture of Corinth, this type of situation was probably not uncommon. In these cases, Paul's admonition is clear: stay with them and serve them in the hopes that they, too, will come to know Jesus.[16]

Dinner or Demons? Meat Sacrificed to Idols and the Role of Personal Liberty (1 Cor 8:1–11:1)

This section may feel a bit odd to modern readers. Many of us do not deal with issues related to food sacrificed to idols, so the temptation may be to skip over some of this material and move on to the discussion about worship or spiritual gifts. Nonetheless, we would do well to listen to Paul's advice here, as it may be more applicable than at first sight.[17] While the particular circumstances that Christians confront may change somewhat from

---

[15] Longenecker and Still, *Thinking Through Paul*, 123; Lea and Black, *The New Testament*, 411.

[16] Longenecker and Still, 123.

[17] For more on the issues of meat sacrificed to idols, see Lea and Black, *The New Testament*, 411–12.

culture to culture, the principles behind Paul's instructions remain relevant even today. In the ancient world, meat leftover from being sacrificed to a deity was sometimes sold in the marketplace for a premium price because it represented the best cuts of meat. The question for the Corinthian believers was whether or not Christians should purchase or eat this meat. Two major viewpoints existed in the church on the issue. The "strong" seemed to think that eating this meat was permissible since an idol was nothing but an inanimate object with no spiritual authority. Eating the meat would have no spiritual consequence. The "weak," on the other hand, did not share the confidence of the "strong" and advocated from abstaining from the consumption of this meat or even meat in general.[18]

In theory, Paul seems to support the view of the "strong" group, but that is not the end of the matter. Since the "weak" have concerns over the food, Paul reminded the "strong" that they should defer to their fellow believers in humility. He indicated that Christians should never eat this meat if it would offend a fellow believer. He suggested that believers should willingly limit their own personal rights if exercising a freedom hinders the spread of the message of Jesus. Christians should be humble enough to avoid indulging in freedoms that may cause spiritual harm to others, even if their consciences are not violated.[19] The principle seems clear: humble service requires Christians to occasionally set aside their own rights in order to love or help others. Just as Jesus took on human flesh and willingly endured a humiliating death on the cross, so too must his followers be willing to lay aside their own freedom in order to bless others.[20]

In chapter 9 Paul offered himself as an example. He certainly had the right to receive economic support from the Corinthians while he served them. Nevertheless, he insisted on not receiving any funds, a right he gave up for their benefit.[21] During his time in Corinth, he made money through his tent-making business so that he would not be a financial burden to them (1 Cor 9:15–18). With regard to forfeiting rights, Paul did not expect any Christian to do less than his example. He believed that he was simply

---

[18] Longenecker and Still, *Thinking Through Paul*, 123–24; Lea and Black, *The New Testament*, 411–12.

[19] Paul discusses issues related to Christian liberty in greater detail with similar conclusions in Romans 14.

[20] Longenecker and Still, *Thinking Through Paul*, 124; Lea and Black, *The New Testament*, 412.

[21] Longenecker and Still, *Thinking Through Paul*, 124.

imitating Jesus in laying down his rights in order to serve others (1 Cor 10:31–11:1).[22]

But how does this relate today? We do not find ourselves in the grocery store wondering about whether the meat may or may not have been offered as a sacrifice to an idol, do we? While our culture is in many ways different, four principles are brought to our attention in Paul's instruction. First, we must remember that Christian freedom has exceptions (1 Cor 10:23–24). Christian freedom cannot be Christlike and also be selfish. It begins with the expectation of serving others. Second, regardless of the situation, Christians need to think relationally in their decision-making (1 Cor 10:25–27). This means that we need to reach out to others with the same grace God has given us and use our freedom to offer grace. Third, even though we are free, we are not free to be selfish. Instead, Christians must put others first (1 Cor 10:28–30). Fourth, we need to live in such a way that results in others seeing the character of Jesus in our lives (1 Cor 10:31–11:1). We are free to live humbly. We are free to seek the salvation of others. Not only are we free, we are obligated to do so. This freedom is what Paul expected of the Corinthian believers.

Disorders in Public Worship (1 Cor 11:2–34)

Paul then turned to two problems concerning worship in Corinth in which disunity and selfishness were evident. First, he addressed the proper decorum of women in corporate worship (1 Cor 11:2–16). Apparently, some women refused to cover their heads in defiance of custom. Paul originally instructed the Corinthian congregation that women should cover their heads in worship while Christian men were permitted to worship with uncovered heads.[23] Paul's chief interest in insisting on a veil for women and uncovered heads for men was to encourage the Corinthians to follow

---

[22] Longenecker and Still, 125.

[23] The nature of this head covering has been debated by scholars for some time. Some claim that it is the long hair of women. Others indicate that it was a veil of some sort that covered the head but not the face of a woman. Such a covering was customary in some Greek (and even Jewish) cultures in ancient times. In this particular case the head covering may have been a veil. For more information, see Leon Morris, *1 Corinthians,* TNTC, rev. ed. (Grand Rapids: Eerdmans, 1985), 150–51; Morna Hooker, "Authority on Her Head: An Examination of 1 Corinthian 11:10," *NTS* 10 (1963–64): 410–16; Craig Keener, "Man and Woman," in *Dictionary of Paul and His Letters,* ed. Gerald Hawthorne, Ralph Martin, and Daniel Reid (Downers Grove, IL: IVP Academic, 1993), 583–92; Ben Witherington III, *Conflict and Community in Corinth: A Socio-Rhetorical Commentary on 1 and 2 Corinthians* (Grand Rapids: Eerdmans, 1995), 234–35.

accepted traditions.[24] At the same time, Paul advocated for women to participate in and lead in corporate prayer and prophecy in the congregation (1 Cor 11:5, 13).

The second problem was unacceptable approaches to the Lord's Supper. In 1 Cor 11:17–34, Paul indicated that some of the rich members of the church were observing the Lord's Supper in a way that could cause distress or offense to those who were poor. We can certainly understand why this occurred. It was highly uncommon in the Greco-Roman world for those of different social classes to share meals with one another. However, by differentiating between rich and poor in the Lord's Supper, the people were creating disunity. A meal that was designed for the unity of the church was tragically used by the Corinthians to divide. As a result, Paul reminded the church to test themselves to make certain that no pride, division, or arrogance was fostered by how they treated each other. The Lord's Supper should be a reflection of the values of the gospel itself and an ongoing memorial for all time of the selfless death of Jesus for his people.[25] As such, the Lord's Supper should call believers to humility and to love toward each other in imitation of how Jesus treated them.

Communion

Dealing with Spiritual Gifts (1 Cor 12:1–14:40)

Another issue regarding worship occupied Paul's attention. Apparently, some in the Corinthian congregation viewed the use of spiritual gifts as a sign of honor in the church, and they began to argue over the respective values of their spiritual gifts. The lack of humility and love led many to think that the more spectacular gifts (such as tongues) were more valuable than other gifts given by God's Spirit.[26] Some Corinthians used their spiritual

---

[24] Lea and Black, *The New Testament*, 413; Longenecker and Still, *Thinking Through Paul*, 126.

[25] Longenecker and Still, 127.

[26] For background on the issue of tongues, see Longenecker and Still, 128–29; C. M. Robeck Jr., "Tongues," in *Dictionary of Paul and His Letters,* ed. Gerald Hawthorne, Ralph Martin, and Daniel Reid (Downers Grove, IL: IVP Academic, 1993), 939–43.

gifts to enhance their own status, which resulted in a competitive spirit and conflict in the congregation. By looking to spiritual gifts as a means for self-aggrandizement, these people violated the nature of the gift as something given to the entire body by God's grace. While God gave a diversity of gifts to the church (1 Cor 12:1–11), the intention was for these to be used for the common good and not for rivalry or personal status. Paul illustrated the interdependence of all believers by comparing the church to a body, an apt description given his previous description of them as the "body of Christ" (1 Cor 6:15; 12:12–31). Just as a human body relies on the cooperation and coordination of many different members, in similar fashion the church is to rely on the gifting of its individual members. To accomplish this cooperation, Paul reminded the Corinthians of the nature of love and its priority in fellowship (1 Cor 13:1–13). Love displaces envy and self-promotion.[27]

After laying the foundation of love in the use of spiritual gifts, Paul discussed the importance of prophecy in the congregation (1 Cor 14:1–40). Perhaps indicating a setting in which unbelievers would join in congregational worship, Paul reminded the Corinthians that tongues are edifying primarily for the speaker (and perhaps the interpreter).[28] Prophecy, on the other hand, encourages all in attendance, as it speaks a word from God in a common language. Prophecy promotes understanding and intelligent response to God's Word. Paul emphasized that believers should seek gifts for the purpose of mutual encouragement and growth rather than for personal or selfish reasons. He urged all believers to love one another and to use their gifts toward that end. Again, the priority of putting others first is a primary response to an issue of worship.

Discourse on Physical Resurrection (1 Cor 15:1–58)

Paul discussed issues related to the resurrection of Jesus and the future physical resurrection of Christians. Some in Corinth apparently denied that the dead would rise (1 Cor 15:12). For Paul, this denial was a direct betrayal of the identity of believers in Christ. Paul reminded the Corinthians of Jesus's resurrection, even recounting the fact that hundreds of eyewitnesses testified to this very real event (1 Cor 15:3–8). He also noted that belief in Jesus's resurrection was a foundational doctrine without which Christianity loses its reason to exist. This resurrection has significance beyond the historical event, as it is the first of many resurrections

---

[27] Longenecker and Still, *Thinking Through Paul*, 129.
[28] Longenecker and Still, 131.

to come when Christians will be raised in glory. Then death will be finally destroyed and placed under Jesus's feet (1 Cor 15:20–28). Simply put, no resurrection of Jesus means no future resurrection for his followers and no final defeat of death and the grave. The death and resurrection of Jesus are important parts of the ongoing drama of salvation history, ultimately shattering spiritual forces and enemies intent on destroying God's good creation.[29] Jesus's resurrection is the start of the new creation where God will put right all that has gone wrong (1 Cor 15:23–28).

Much of the second half of chapter 15 deals with Paul's discussion of how our mortal bodies will relate to our future resurrected bodies (1 Cor 15:29–58). While continuity exists between the physical bodies of Christians and the resurrected bodies they will receive, there is also discontinuity. Paul used the image of a seed to describe this difference. Like a seed placed in the ground gives way to a plant, so also the mortal body gives way to the immortal body. The point Paul made is that the resurrection will provide an imperishable body suited for life with God beyond this earthly life (1 Cor 15:35–49). Paul reemphasized Jesus's victory over death, and used that victory as an incentive for believers to continue to serve God and others. According to Paul, eternal life will have a physical component. We will not be disembodied spirits, but we will have resurrected bodies with which we can continue to serve God.[30] If we will serve him eternally in immortal bodies, how much more should we accept the challenge to serve him now? The fruit of such labor will be glory to God and service to others.

Directions on Giving and Some Final Thoughts (1 Cor 16:1–24)

Paul covered a number of issues in his conclusion. Four verses are dedicated to the collection of funds for poor Christians in Jerusalem (1 Cor 16:1–4), a collection that in many ways reflected the nature of the Christian life. Paul wanted the Corinthians to lay aside money each week so they could give to others, in this case, the poor Jewish believers who were part of their spiritual family. This action imitates the loving sacrifice and mercy of Jesus. In addition to his reference to the gift, Paul outlined his travel plans for another visit to Corinth (1 Cor 16:5–9). Unfortunately, these travel plans would change, and this change plays a role in Paul's interactions with the Corinthians in 2 Corinthians. In the meantime, he indicated his decision to send Timothy to them in order to continue "the

---

[29] Longenecker and Still, 132–33.
[30] Longenecker and Still, 133.

Lord's work" (1 Cor 16:10–11). Paul concluded with an encouragement to stand firm in the faith, to be courageous and strong, but most importantly to do everything in love (1 Cor 16:13). Having completed his is instructions, Paul blessed the congregation with the hope that they would learn to emulate Jesus's humble love and service.

BIBLIOGRAPHY

Ciampa, Roy E., and Brian S. Rosner. *The First Letter to the Corinthians*. PNTC. Grand Rapids: Eerdmans, 2010.

Fee, Gordon. *The First Epistle to the Corinthians*. Rev. ed. NICNT. Grand Rapids: Eerdmans, 2014.

Garland, David. *1 Corinthians*. BECNT. Grand Rapids: Baker Academic, 2003.

Hafemann, Scott. "Letters to the Corinthians." In *Dictionary of Paul and His Letters*. Edited by Gerald Hawthorne, Ralph Martin, and Daniel Reid, 164–73. Downers Grove, IL: IVP Academic, 1993.

Hooker, Morna. "Authority on Her Head: An Examination of 1 Corinthians 11:10." *NTS* 10 (1963–64).

Keener, Craig. "Man and Woman." In *Dictionary of Paul and His Letters,* edited by Gerald Hawthorne, Ralph Martin, and Daniel Reid, 583–92. Downers Grove, IL: IVP Academic, 1993.

Lane, William L. *Highlights of the Bible: New Testament.* Delight, AR: Gospel Light, 1981.

Lea, Thomas D., and David Alan Black. *The New Testament: Its Background and Message.* 2nd ed. Nashville: B&H Academic, 2003.

Longenecker, Bruce, and Todd Still. *Thinking Through Paul: An Introduction to His Life, Letters, and Theology.* Grand Rapids: Zondervan Academic, 2014.

Mitchell, Daniel. *The Book of 1 Corinthians: Christianity in a Hostile Culture.* Vol. 7 of Twenty-First Century Biblical Commentary Series. Chattanooga, TN: AMG, 2004.

Morris, Leon. *1 Corinthians.* TNTC. Rev. ed. Grand Rapids: Eerdmans, 1985.

Robeck, C. M., Jr. "Tongues." In *Dictionary of Paul and His Letters*, edited by Gerald Hawthorne, Ralph Martin, and Daniel Reid, 939–43. Downers Grove, IL: IVP Academic, 1993.

Taylor, Mark. *1 Corinthians: An Exegetical and Theological Exposition of Holy Scripture.* NAC. Nashville: Holman Reference, 2014.

Thiselton, Anthony C. *The First Epistle to the Corinthians: A Commentary on the Greek Text*. NIGTC. Grand Rapids: Eerdmans, 2000.

Witherington, Ben, III. *Conflict and Community in Corinth: A Socio-Rhetorical Commentary on 1 and 2 Corinthians.* Grand Rapids: Eerdmans, 1995.

10

2 CORINTHIANS

LEO PERCER

CONNECTION POINT

What relevance does this first-century writing have for us today? Conflicts arise in life. That may seem a simple statement, but we all recognize this reality. When was the last time you experienced conflict? What was it like? Did another person challenge your abilities or expertise? If so, how did you feel about that challenge? Paul was no stranger to conflict. Controversy seemed to follow him wherever he went. He often found himself being forced to defend his ministry and authority. The book we call 2 Corinthians is an example of this. It is one of the most personal letters written by Paul and provides one of the most powerful and most straightforward explanations of his view of ministry.

Throughout the epistle, Paul expressed a range of emotions such as grief, indignation, and even joy. In 2 Corinthians, we hear from one who has been wounded by the actions and attitudes of others but also the confidence of someone called by God to present the truth about Jesus despite opposition. Throughout this epistle, Paul defended himself against personal attacks and accusations, and, in the process, demonstrated for us the nature of authentic and Christlike ministry. For Paul, true ministry included victory and suffering, conflict and reconciliation, and occasionally even life and death. Second Corinthians opens a window for us to encounter Paul during a very difficult time in his life and ministry. There were signs that the church of Corinth, a church he had worked hard to build, was indifferent or dismissive of his ministry and authority. In contrast, his opponents seemed welcome in Corinth. If you want to see how a person called to the ministry of Jesus responds to rejection and seeks reconciliation with those who have inflicted harm, 2 Corinthians will provide an excellent model for you.

With this in mind, consider making this your prayer as you read and study this chapter:

> *God, even when the world seems to fall apart, you remain constant and faithful. Your Spirit comforts us, and your Son, Jesus, sets a standard for us when we face crisis. When things fall apart in our lives, you remind us that Jesus's suffering is a source of comfort and reconciliation. In the life, death, and resurrection of Jesus, you reveal the means by which we can be your children and be reconciled to you. In Jesus, you also show how we can be reconciled to each other. Thank you for Paul, your servant, and for the words you have provided through him to help us understand the ministry of reconciliation. Open our eyes to understand your Word, and empower us to live in faith, obedience, and humility even in times of crisis. May our lives reveal Jesus to others, until all know him. Amen.*

SETTING

Recipients

As discussed in the previous chapter, both 1 and 2 Corinthians are universally recognized as authentic epistles of the apostle Paul. Paul appears to have written this epistle to the Corinthians during this third missionary journey, shortly after departing the city of Ephesus around AD 55–56. During Paul's lengthy ministry in Ephesus, he remained in contact with the church of Corinth. Concerned about their spiritual well-being and their willingness to accept his previous instruction, Paul sent Titus to provide them with encouragement and to get an update on their status. During

A view of modern-day Corinth

Titus's journey, Paul was forced to abruptly leave Ephesus (Acts 19:23–41). Concerned about the believers in Corinth, Paul then set out for Macedonia with the hope of finding Titus on his return (2 Cor 2:13). While it is difficult to determine the precise location from which Paul composed this work, cities such as Philippi, Thessalonica, and Berea are possibilities. What is clear is that the epistle was written "To the church of God at Corinth, with all the saints who are throughout Achaia" (2 Cor 1:1).

To help us understand the background of 2 Corinthians in particular, there are two areas of interest that we should mention: (1) the nature of the church of Corinth, and (2) Paul's unique relationship with them. The people of Corinth may be described as a diverse and pluralistic group of individuals, a description that would also apply to the church. Composed of both Jews and Gentiles, the members of the Corinthian church came from a variety of religious and cultural backgrounds.[1] The Jewish Christians came to faith in Jesus from Judaism, and Paul would have been regarded by many of them as not only the founder of the Corinthian church but also as a Jewish teacher. The Gentiles, on the other hand, would

---

[1] Paul refers to the diverse makeup of the Corinthians throughout his letters (e.g., 1 Cor 12:13). For an overview of the history of Corinth, see Hafemann, "Letters to the Corinthians," 164–73 (see chap. 9, n. 1).

have come from a variety of Greek or Roman backgrounds and would have formally worshipped a number of gods and/or goddesses.² Thus, one of the challenges for Paul and the other spiritual leaders in Corinth was developing a sense of unity among those who came to the faith from vastly different cultural, ethnic, and religious backgrounds.

Temple of Apollo, built ca. 540 BC in Corinth, Greece

Themes and Key Passages

Some important themes that are emphasized throughout this epistle include the following: the nature of Paul's apostolic authority and ministry, the centrality of the new covenant and its relationship to the old covenant, God's comfort to his people in times of suffering, the importance of giving, God's ministry of reconciliation, and the nature of faithful ministry. With regard to the final theme, Paul demonstrates throughout the epistle that regardless of the circumstances, the Lord calls us to invest our lives in meeting the needs of others—both physical and spiritual—as we follow Christ's example of humility.

> 2 Corinthians 1:4–5: "He comforts us in all our affliction, so that we may be able to comfort those who are in any kind of affliction, through the comfort we ourselves receive from God. For just as the sufferings of Christ overflow to us, so also through Christ our comfort overflows."

> 2 Corinthians 4:5, 7: "For we are not proclaiming ourselves but Jesus Christ as Lord, and ourselves as your servants for Jesus's sake. . . . Now we have this treasure in clay jars, so that this extraordinary power may be from God and not from us."

> 2 Corinthians 5:18–19: "Everything is from God, who has reconciled us to himself through Christ and has given us the ministry of reconciliation. That is, in Christ, God was reconciling the world to himself,

---

² For background on the religious world of the first century and the unique features of Christianity, see Larry Hurtado, *Destroyer of the Gods: Early Christian Distinctiveness in the Roman World* (Waco, TX: Baylor University Press, 2017).

not counting their trespasses against them, and he has committed the message of reconciliation to us."

2 Corinthians 8:9: "For you know the grace of our Lord Jesus Christ: Though he was rich, for your sake he became poor, so that by his poverty you might become rich."

When dealing with the issue of suffering, Paul reminded his readers that Jesus not only suffered but empathized with their situation. As we consider others who may be suffering, Paul reminds us of the importance of modeling the humility of Christ and comforting others as Christ has comforted us (1 Cor 1:3–7). Concerning reconciliation, Paul noted that reconciliation is not possible apart from the life, death, and resurrection of Jesus. God went to great lengths to reconcile humans, even allowing Jesus to suffer on our behalf. Similarly, Paul emphasized that we are to follow the example of Christ and learn to humble ourselves and to put the needs of others before our own needs. For Paul, such sacrificial and humble service was the mark of authentic ministry given by God. What some may consider weakness, Paul viewed as strength. In order to fulfill our calling as ministers of reconciliation (2 Cor 5:11–21), Paul encouraged us to willingly lay down our lives in humble service to others.

Purpose and Occasion

While Paul addresses several subjects throughout the letter, he wrote for three main reasons: (1) to express joy that the Corinthians had responded favorably to his recent attempts of reconciliation, (2) to defend his ministry as an apostle, a defense that may have been aimed at those Corinthians who had not yet reconciled with Paul, and (3) to request that the Corinthians participate in an offering he had organized for poor Christians in Jerusalem. Before discussing the high points of 2 Corinthians, a brief word regarding the first two major purposes is helpful.

With regard to the first purpose, we may observe that Paul wrote in order to celebrate his improved relationship with the Corinthians. As was discussed in the chapter on 1 Corinthians, Paul's relationship with the Corinthian church was often unsteady and at times even cold and strained. During his initial visit to Corinth (Acts 18), many Christians welcomed his leadership and advice. However, after his journeys took him to other locations and other teachers and preachers arrived, the Corinthians began aligning themselves with their favorite leaders. This shift naturally resulted in widespread division and disunity. It was during this time that the relationship between Paul and the Corinthians began to deteriorate. Some even began to question Paul's status as an apostle after observing the ministry of other prominent individuals who appear to have been quite eloquent and influential.[3] Paul's initial attempt to reach out to the Corinthians only served to make the situation worse.[4] Fortunately, the situation had improved by the time Paul composed 2 Corinthians. A short time before the epistle was written, he received a favorable report from Titus, who revealed to Paul that the Corinthians had warmly received his previous written correspondence (2 Cor 7:5–11). Second Corinthians was therefore written in part to express Paul's gratitude for their favorable reception of his recent attempts to reach out to them and to make further progress in mending what had once been an unstable relationship.

Throughout his letter, Paul explains the unique nature of his calling as an apostle and also defends himself against those who questioned his motivations. In light of these unique circumstances, 2 Corinthians provides a valuable portrayal of authentic Christian ministry and the power of reconciliation that is possible through the gospel.

Finally, Paul wrote to defend his apostolic status and his conduct as a

> ### Super-Apostles Versus Paul's View of Apostles
>
> The "super-apostles" (2 Cor 11:5; 12:11) apparently gained the confidence of the Corinthians and began to present a "modified" version of the gospel from Paul's version (2 Cor 11:4). They were skilled speakers, and the church in Corinth did not recognize the errors they introduced. Paul claimed that they taught "another Jesus . . . a different spirit . . . a different gospel" (2 Cor 11:4) from the one he preached, but the differences are not spelled out. Rather, Paul contrasted the actions and attitudes of the "super-apostles" with his own:
> 1. The super-apostles considered themselves to be superior, while Paul saw himself as the least (2 Cor 11:5–8).
> 2. The super-apostles were eloquent, speakers, while Paul failed to impress (2 Cor 11:5).
> 3. The super-apostles apparently thought that leaders should not suffer, while Paul believed that suffering is a mark of true apostleship (2 Cor 11:16–33).
> 4. The super-apostles placed a high value on visions, while Paul placed his value on weakness and humility (2 Cor 12:1–13).
>
> In spite of these differences, the Corinthians embraced the flash and pride of the super-apostles to the point of allowing them to take advantage of the church. Paul admonished them to repent and to realize that true ministry is in humble service rather than in the pursuit of notoriety. Service, not prestige or power, marks a true minister of the gospel.

---

[3] Longenecker and Still, *Thinking Through Paul*, 141 (see chap. 9, n. 2).
[4] Lea and Black, *The New Testament: Its Background and Message*, 406–7 (see chap. 9, n. 5); Longenecker and Still, *Thinking Through Paul*, 141–45.

minister of the gospel. This defense was needed because of the influence of his opponents, the so-called super-apostles, who questioned his apostolic authority and the validity of his teaching. These individuals, coupled with some misunderstandings between Paul and the Corinthians, led to stressful and painful interactions. The problems in Corinth were not all the result of misunderstandings, of course. Some of the tension between Paul and the Corinthians could be attributed to self-centered and self-promoting attitudes within the church. While 2 Corinthians reveals that some of these issues had been recently resolved, the problem of the "super-apostles" was not fully resolved. Paul thus spends roughly three chapters (2 Cor 10:1–13:10) addressing this problem. He offers a personal defense of his ministry and encourages the pursuit of reconciliation in 2 Cor 1:12–7:16; and he emphasizes the need for sacrificial giving in 2 Cor 8:1–9:15. In his treatment of these subjects, Paul reminds the believers that they were saved by the humble service and death of Jesus and that they now belong to him as servants. They should thus imitate his humility in their own lives and their relationships with others.

HIGHLIGHTS IN 2 CORINTHIANS

Before considering the highlights of 2 Corinthians, a basic overview may be helpful.[5] The epistle may be divided into five basic sections: (1) the introduction (2 Cor 1:1–11), (2) Paul's clarification and confrontation regarding his ministry (2 Cor 1:12–7:16), (3) his call for a collection and sacrificial giving (2 Cor 8:1–9:15), (4) his confrontation with his opponents (2 Cor 10:1–13:10), and (5) his conclusion (2 Cor 13:11–13). As we work

---

[5] Noting the shift in tone, some scholars have suggested that the canonical form of 2 Corinthians is likely a combination of several shorter letters Paul originally sent to the Corinthians that relate in one way or another to the subject of reconciliation or repentance. Questions concerning the unity of 2 Corinthians tend to consider the issues of language and tone in 6:14–7:1 and chapters 10–13. Some scholars see 6:14–7:1 as a part of a previous letter mentioned in 1 Cor 5:9, but the evidence is not clear enough to support the idea. Another suggestion views chapters 10–13 as the "painful or severe letter" (2 Cor 2:4). While an intriguing hypothesis to some, there is no evidence that the material in this letter circulated as separate or independent letters. We will thus affirm the literary of 2 Corinthians and treat it a single letter in this chapter. For further background on the composite theory of 2 Corinthians, see Longenecker and Still, *Thinking Through Paul*, 145–49; Lea and Black, *The New Testament*, 418–19; and Chad Brand, Charles Draper, and Archie England, eds., *Holman Illustrated Bible Dictionary* (Nashville: Holman Reference, 2003).

our way through 2 Corinthians, remember Paul's central point: Jesus's humble service in his life, death, and resurrection is the means by which we are reconciled to God, and it is also the example we are to imitate in our own lives and ministry. If Jesus suffered to make reconciliation possible between us and God, then we are to likewise invest our lives to see others reconciled with God. Like Jesus, we can also expect that our "ministry of reconciliation" will result in personal suffering and conflict.

Introduction: Opening Greeting and God's Comfort (2 Cor 1:1–11)

Second Corinthians begins much like most of Paul's letters, with a greeting that mentions both the senders (Paul and Timothy) and the recipients (the believers in Corinth). In 2 Cor 1:3, Paul provided an overview of the encouragement and protection he received from God when he experienced hardships and personal pain.[6] He mentioned that he was "completely overwhelmed" to the point that he "despaired of life itself" (2 Cor 1:8). Some may certainly relate to Paul with their own troubles. Perhaps you have been overwhelmed with difficulties and the emotional pain that comes from damaged relationships. Paul was certainly no stranger to such pain and reminds us that there is hope during these times. He focused on God as a Comforter who encourages and strengthens Christians in their afflictions. While no one enjoys suffering, believers experience the comfort that only God can provide and are thus equipped to comfort others who are likewise suffering. As believers, we recognize that our relationship with God is possible only because Christ willingly suffered. Similarly, God can use our suffering to encourage and strengthen others. How reassuring it is to know that while pain is part of the human experience, God is there for us in our times of discouragement and suffering! He can use the pain we experience for our good.

Paul's Clarification and Confrontation regarding His Ministry (2 Cor 1:12–7:16)

In 2 Cor 1:12–2:13, Paul offered the first defense of his ministry. His opponents had apparently attacked his character, so he offered a defense of his integrity. Paul did not defend himself because of his ego. This was necessary because his credibility as an apostle could not be separated from the message that he proclaimed. Simply put, to attack Paul's authority

---

[6] Lea and Black, *The New Testament*, 419–20; Longenecker and Still, *Thinking Through Paul*, 154.

or integrity was to question his message. We learn that a change in Paul's travel plans prohibited him from going to Corinth right away, a change that his opponents used to label him as untrustworthy and unreliable.[7] While his opponents portrayed him as indecisive and fickle, Paul made it clear that these changes happened as a result of pressing needs of the moment and were not an indication of any indifference to the Corinthians or his inability to keep promises. Much prayer and thoughtfulness had gone into this decision, and Paul came to understand that keeping to the original plan would have resulted in unnecessary heartache (2 Cor 1:23–2:4).

His genuine concern for the Corinthians was evident in his handling of the subject, as was his willingness to forgive. What many considered to be an act of weakness, Paul explained, resulted in a blessing. By not coming as planned, a more heated conflict between the Corinthians and Paul was avoided. Despite the reasonable basis for his delay, his opponents used his change of plans to attack his character. When we are misrepresented, forgiveness may seem to be a weakness, but Paul reminds us that these actions are imitations of Christ and will often result in reconciliation.

Forgiveness is a major emphasis in the next few verses (2 Cor 2:5–13). Showing a bit of vulnerability, Paul explained that his spirit was restless because he was waiting to hear from Titus about the situation between him and the Corinthians. Even though he was in Troas enjoying a season of fruitful ministry, he was deeply troubled by the situation and determined to make his way to Corinth to find out how they had responded to his previous instruction (2 Cor 2:12–13). After describing the relief he experienced when he received the good news from Titus that the Corinthians had responded favorably to his previous instruction, Paul provided insight regarding the character of his ministry (2 Cor 2:14–6:10). He emphasized that the power of the gospel is not dependent on the abilities of those who bring the message. While no minister is really adequate to proclaim such a consequential and valuable message, God calls us to faithfully present the good news of salvation (2 Cor 2:15–17).

In chapter 3 Paul reminded the Corinthians that he did not need to commend himself since their changed lives already served as evidence that God approved Paul's ministry. They were the only "letters of recommendation" he needed (2 Cor 3:1–3). Rather than prominent endorsements, Paul pointed to the work of the Spirit in the Corinthians' lives

---

[7] Lea and Black, *The New Testament*, 420; Longenecker and Still, *Thinking Through Paul*, 154.

as evidence of God's work through him. Though Paul certainly had his own limitations and shortcomings, God used him in a mighty way to change the lives of others. He recognized that it is only the Spirit who can make someone an adequate minister of the gospel (2 Cor 3:4–6). In God's hands, our weaknesses can be transformed into sources of strength and we become living examples of Jesus's ministry to us. Furthermore, when we proclaim Christ, we proclaim a greater covenant between God and humanity. As Paul explained, God has established the new covenant through the work of Christ, a covenant that is inherently superior to the old covenant (2 Cor 3:7–18). The new covenant is superior, Paul explained, because unlike the old covenant, it offers the hope of spiritual transformation and spiritual freedom.

Paul further elaborated on his perspective as a minister of the gospel in chapter 4, explaining that we do not lose heart when faced with hardships and mistreatment because of the reality that God makes his glory known through us (2 Cor 4:1–6). Only Jesus can make reconciliation between God and humanity possible, Paul observed. As ministers of the gospel message, we are nothing more than "clay jars," vulnerable and weak instruments capable of being shattered. In the first century, valuable documents and other treasures were often placed in clay pottery. While the pottery was inexpensive and fragile, it would often contain items of great value. So it is with the gospel. God uses weak and fragile vessels (human ministers) to proclaim spiritual truths of immeasurable worth. The power of the gospel message does not derive from the weak and deficient servants who preach it, but from the mighty God who transforms lives through its proclamation (Rom 1:16). What some regard as weakness, God uses to show his own glory. In the weakness of humanity, God's power emerges as a force of reconciliation

Many Dead Sea scrolls were found rolled up inside specific jars. The jars were made locally, in the Dead Sea area, and had tightly fitting covers. These two are from Qumran (Khirbet Qumran or Wadi Qumran) near the Dead Sea.

and transformation (2 Cor 4:7–12). This should remind us that God the Son became human and died so that we could be reconciled to God and become part of his spiritual family. Similarly, Paul concluded that God can use even our afflictions for his glory (2 Cor 4:13–18).

Central to the Christian faith is the hope in the future resurrection, a hope that Paul expounds in 2 Cor 5:1–10. The hardships we endure as we proclaim Christ and the pain we endure in this present life will one day give way to a heavenly reality. Although we must endure many afflictions as we serve him, God has promised that through Jesus, we will ultimately be restored to God and experience the glory associated with a resurrected body. As Paul explained elsewhere (1 Cor 15:1–58; 1 Thess 4:13–18), those who are in Christ will receive a new body when he returns and will spend eternity with him. This is a great hope that we must not forget as we face the many challenges of this present life. As we await the Lord's return, our focus is to be, like Paul, on pleasing God by serving others. Rather than allowing our human limitations and shortcomings to prevent us from actively pursuing the Lord's calling in our lives, we are each called to serve him faithfully, recognizing the power of the message we proclaim does not come from ourselves.

Paul used an interesting description of those who share the good news of Christ. He explained that each believer has the privilege of serving as a representative of Christ, a calling that is described in 2 Cor 5:11–6:13. Much like an ambassador in a foreign country, each believer serves as Christ's representative in a fallen world. Our faith in Christ was never intended to be a private matter. When we became part of God's family, we became his representatives to the world and thus became part of God's work of restoring his relationship with fallen humanity. As Paul's life testifies, those who proclaim the gospel message will inevitably encounter resistance and personal attacks. What we learn from this epistle, however, is that God does not call us to be popular in society but to be faithful in our task of serving as ministers of reconciliation. While it can certainly be uncomfortable to share the good news of Christ with others, and may even come at a personal cost, there is nothing more satisfying or worthwhile than sharing the message of hope in a fallen world and playing a role in God's work of reconciling unbelievers to himself.

How might you follow Paul's example? Has the Lord put you in a situation to share the good news of Jesus with others? Do you have opportunities to interact with friends, family members, colleagues, neighbors, or classmates who have not committed their lives to Christ? If so, how might you share with them the hope that you enjoy as a believer?

In addition to recognizing the important calling each of us have to serve as ministers of reconciliation, we learn from Paul's personal example the importance of following Jesus's example of humble sacrifice rather than those who think that "strength" or "ability" are superior characteristics. It is only natural for us to view our human limitations as liabilities that hinder us from serving the Lord. This perspective can be difficult for us to overcome in our social-media age. Each day we are confronted with the achievements and accomplishments of others and can quite easily become convinced that our lives are insignificant or that we will never measure up to the expectations of society. As Paul reminded us, however, God uses human weakness to draw the lost to himself. How reassuring it is to realize that that God accomplishes his work in this world not through those who are self-reliant but through those who faithfully proclaim the gospel and live with integrity, both of which were modeled for us by Paul in 2 Cor 7:1–16.

Paul's Call for a Collection and Sacrificial Giving (2 Cor 8:1–9:15)

In chapters 8 and 9, Paul expressed complete confidence in the Corinthians' willingness to serve others and encouraged them to follow through with their initial promise to collect funds for poor Jewish Christians in Jerusalem (2 Cor 8:1–7).[8] We know from the book of Acts and various references in the Pauline Epistles that Paul sought to collect funds from a number of Gentile communities for the impoverished Jewish believers in Jerusalem. In addition to modeling the sacrificial ministry of Jesus, the offering was intended to encourage unity between Jewish and Gentile believers. In his encouragement to give, Paul reminded the Corinthians of the example of the Macedonians who gave of their resources, despite the fact that they had little, and he reminded them of Jesus, who humbly gave himself for the benefit of others (2 Cor 8:8–9). In short, how can we not generously give to those in need when God has been so generous to us?

---

[8] The primary passages in which Paul refers to the collection he has organized for the Jewish believers are Rom 15:14–32; 1 Cor 16:1–4; and 2 Cor 8:1–9:15. For helpful background on the collection, see David J. Downs, *The Offering of the Gentiles: Paul's Collection for Jerusalem in Its Chronological, Cultural, and Cultic Contexts* (Grand Rapids: Eerdmans, 2016).

The ruins of the ancient Fountain of Peirene in Corinth, Greece

Paul's Confrontation with Current Opponents (2 Cor 10:1–13:10)

At this point of the epistle, Paul's tone changed dramatically as he turned his attention to his opponents.[9] His response became more defensive, and he began to express concern that his readers would not respond appropriately. Apparently, a coalition of Corinthians had attempted to dispute Paul's credentials. Among those who were resistant to his leadership was a group Paul referred to as "super-apostles" (2 Cor 11:5), opponents of Paul who were persuaded that their methods and abilities were superior. They claimed that Paul's habit was to speak boldly in his absence (when he wrote letters) but that he was in reality weak or timid in person (2 Cor 10:10). Paul addressed these accusations by explaining that he appealed to others "by the meekness and gentleness of Christ" (2 Cor 10:1). If he seemed timid or gentle, he was simply following Jesus's example. Nonetheless, Paul expressed confidence in his ability to defend himself against those who attacked his preaching (2 Cor 10:2–11). As we consider Paul's interaction

---

[9] While Paul identifies his opponents as "super-apostles" (2 Cor 11:5; 12:11), the specific identity of these opponents continues to be discussed by scholars. For an overview of some views, see Hafemann, "Letters to the Corinthians," 177–78 (see chap. 9, n. 1).

with the Corinthians, we are reminded that people will often challenge our motivations, abilities, and the nature of our ministry to others. Rather than become discouraged, we must be careful to avoid embracing the world's perspective that self-reliance is a sign of strength. Faithful service to the Lord will often result in being misunderstood and unappreciated, as unpleasant as this may be.

In contrast to Paul, a number of individuals had infiltrated the ranks of the Corinthians who were more interested in the acquisition of power, prestige, and position than in serving others. While the desire for human recognition is strong, we are to be careful to avoid the deceitfulness of those who live in a manner that is contrary to the example of Christ (2 Cor 11:1–4). With regard to the "super-apostles," Paul did not consider himself inferior despite the fact that he refused the financial support of the Corinthians (2 Cor 11:5–11). Paul's habit of working to provide for his own needs was regarded by some of his opponents as evidence that he was an illegitimate apostle. (In those days, traveling philosophers and teachers were often supported by the wealthy members of a city.) Paul's refusal to accept financial support was therefore interpreted as evidence that he was an amateur who was unworthy of respect. In response, Paul explained that he determined to pay his own expenses so as not to be a burden or to have his motives questioned. Contrary to his opponents, Paul viewed his lifestyle as a sign of apostolic legitimacy, since he did not engage in his work for financial reasons (2 Cor 11:12–18). From Paul's example we learn that God has called us to minister to the needs of others and that this often involves personal sacrifice.

In 2 Cor 11:16–12:13, Paul engaged in what he playfully described as boastful language in order to emphasize that his ministry was not foolish. He contrasted his work with the Corinthians with that of the "super-apostles" and found the latter lacking in true authority and authenticity. In his personal reflections, he described his own background in Judaism, the sufferings he had endured for the sake of the gospel, visions and revelations he had experienced, and many miraculous works that God accomplished throughout his ministry. These amazing experiences, however, were not what defined his ministry, made him a legitimate apostle, or led to his success. As he explained, God demonstrates his power through human weakness instead of human pride. Just as Jesus humbled himself during his life, and especially in his death, Paul's ministry also demonstrated that God works through those who serve others humbly and selflessly.[10] Paul closed his "boasting" with an almost sarcastic appeal to the Corinthians to forgive him for not being a "burden" to them (2 Cor 12:13).

In the close of this section, Paul returned to the topic of his travel plans (2 Cor 12:14–13:10). He had no interest in money, material possessions, or honor, preferring instead to sacrifice these things for others (2 Cor 12:15). The language in this section is certainly strong and designed to help his readers understand their error and to reinforce their need for heeding his instruction. He insisted that he would come to them again and, if necessary, would offer an even stronger rebuke! Jesus was "crucified in weakness" (2 Cor 13:4), Paul wrote, but now lives by God's power. The implication for believers is clear: we experience this power by humbling ourselves and living to serve God and others. How will we respond? Will we serve in weakness instead of seeking prestige, power, or position? Will we point others to the humble life, death, and resurrection of Jesus that alone is able to transform sinners into the people of God?

Conclusion (2 Cor 13:11–13)

Paul's epistle concludes with a word of encouragement. He wanted the Corinthians to grow in their faith, be united as the people of God, and live in the love of God through Jesus Christ. These final verses remind us that unity is found in humble and selfless service. If we want to fully live as God intends, we must serve one another as Jesus served us. Any other approach is not representative of God's love as revealed in Jesus Christ. May we all live worthy of the love given us by sharing it with others!

BIBLIOGRAPHY

Downs, David J. *The Offering of the Gentiles: Paul's Collection for Jerusalem in Its Chronological, Cultural, and Cultic Contexts*. Grand Rapids: Eerdmans, 2016.

Garland, David. *2 Corinthians*. NAC. Nashville: Holman Reference, 1999.

Guthrie, George H. *2 Corinthians*. BECNT. Grand Rapids: Baker Academic, 2015.

Hafemann, Scott J. *2 Corinthians*. NIVAC. Grand Rapids: Zondervan, 2000.

---

[10] With regard to his own "weakness," Paul refers on one occasion to a "thorn in the flesh" that deeply troubled him. Scholars differ on the nature of Paul's affliction, some arguing that it was a physical ailment of some kind, while others have suggested that it related in some way to his background, emotional pain that he experienced, or the public ridicule that resulted from his apostolic ministry.

Hafemann, Scott. "Letters to the Corinthians." In *Dictionary of Paul and His Letters*, edited by Gerald Hawthorne, Ralph Martin, and Daniel Reid, 164–73. Downers Grove, IL: IVP Academic, 1993.

Harris, Murray J. *The Second Epistle to the Corinthians.* NIGTC. Grand Rapids: Eerdmans, 2013.

Hurtado, Larry. *Destroyer of the Gods: Early Christian Distinctiveness in the Roman World.* Waco, TX: Baylor University Press, 2017.

Lea, Thomas D., and David Alan Black. *The New Testament: Its Background and Message.* 2nd ed. Nashville: B&H Academic, 2003.

Longenecker, Bruce, and Todd Still, *Thinking Through Paul: An Introduction to His Life, Letters, and Theology.* Grand Rapids: Zondervan Academic, 2014.

Martin, Ralph P. *2 Corinthians*. WBC. Nashville: Thomas Nelson, 1986.

Mitchell, Daniel. *Second Corinthians: Grace Under Siege.* Chattanooga, TN: AMG Publishers, 2008.

11

GALATIANS

LEO PERCER

CONNECTION POINT

What relevance does this first-century writing have for us today? There are times when, despite our best efforts to steer someone towards the truth, the person still ends up going the other direction. Has this ever occurred to you? Have you ever spoken truth to a friend but later found him or her making poor decisions? What was that like? How did this situation make you feel? Situations like this can cause intense emotions and negatively impact relationships.

A similar situation occurred nearly 2,000 years ago between Paul and a number of his brothers and sisters in Christ. He wrote the letter to the Galatians shortly after learning that many of his fellow believers had embraced deeply mistaken teachings about the gospel. He was angry that the Christians in Galatia were intent on turning their backs on the gospel he proclaimed to them. They even seemed willing to turn their backs on Paul in order to embrace the false teaching they received! As a result of the serious nature of the situation, Paul found himself defending his ministry and clarifying his message. For Paul, his ministry was straightforward—he was called to present to others (and especially to Gentiles) that a saving relationship with God can only be found by fully trusting in what Jesus alone has accomplished; the addition of any other item to that foundation, Paul emphasized, is dangerous, as it undermines the work of Christ. In short, Paul's letter to the Galatians contains Paul's response to those who reject the message of salvation by faith in Jesus alone.

With this in mind, consider making this your prayer as you read and study this chapter:

God, when we are rejected for defending the gospel, you are with us. You remain faithful and true even when others turn their backs on the truth. Your Son, Jesus, remains the only sure foundation for our relationship with you and with others. You remind us that his life, death, and resurrection allow us to have a saving relationship with you. Your Spirit guides us into healthy relationships with others and in Jesus alone we are reconciled to you and to each other. Thank you for Paul and for the words you inspired him to write. Open our eyes to understand Scripture, and empower us by your Spirit to live out its truths in every circumstance. May the truth of Jesus and him alone be revealed in us. Until all know him, we pray in Jesus's name. Amen.

SETTING

Recipients

The apostle Paul wrote this letter "to the churches of Galatia" (Gal 1:2) in AD 49 or shortly thereafter.[1] While there is little dispute regarding the writing's authorship, scholars continue to debate the precise identity of those referred to by Paul as "Galatians." Some have identified the Galatians simply as those who lived in the Roman province of Galatia. This view is often referred to as the "South Galatian theory" because of the viewpoint that the epistle was addressed to the Christians who lived in the

---

[1] The Pauline authorship of Galatians has not been seriously challenged and is universally recognized by contemporary scholars. Early Christians unanimously regarded Paul as the author and the letter circulated exclusively as part of the Pauline letter corpus. Paul likely wrote the letter between the conclusion of his first missionary journey and the time of the Jerusalem Council that took place in AD 49 or shortly thereafter. If this theory is correct, Galatians would likely be the earliest letter of Paul.

cities of the province that were located in the southern region, the same area that Paul visited on each of his three missionary journeys. Those who affirm the South Galatian theory look to Luke's description of the first missionary journey (Acts 13–14) as historical background for Galatians.

The other perspective, the "North Galatian theory," argues that Paul wrote to those who were of a particular ethnic group that settled in the

The First Missionary Journey of Paul

more sparsely populated northern regions of the province of Galatia. Possibilities include those who migrated from Gaul or perhaps Celtic invaders.[2] Those who hold this perspective naturally date Galatians a bit later, the early to mid-50s being common suggestions. The reason for this later date is that the descriptions of Paul's missionary journeys in Acts precludes the possibility that he traveled to the northern regions of Galatia during his first missionary journey. The first opportunity he would have had to travel to this area would have been during his second missionary journey. While there are strong arguments for both major theories regarding the recipients of this epistle, this chapter will tentatively suggest that Paul addressed the Christians in the southern region of Galatia shortly after the conclusion of his first missionary journey when he received a report that they were quickly departing from the gospel they originally received.

According to Acts, Paul and Barnabas visited locations such as Antioch of Pisidia, Iconium, Lystra, and Derbe during the first missionary journey. The area was home to large Jewish, Greek, and Roman populations. Their ministry in these cities was certainly eventful. We read in Acts that they received an invitation to speak in a synagogue in Antioch where their message drew interest among the Jews of the city (Acts 13:14–15). When Paul spoke in the synagogue a week later, a number of Gentiles also came to hear him (Acts 13:42–45). Angered at the favorable reception Paul and Barnabas received, some of the Jewish leaders began to speak against them and their message (Acts 13:45). Jewish opposition to Paul and Barnabas and their missionary efforts were repeated throughout the region of Galatia (Acts 14:1–19).

The ministry of Paul and Barnabas in the cities of Galatia was anything but mundane. Luke records that Paul healed a crippled man in Lystra (Acts 14:8–10) and that the inhabitants of the city confused Paul and Barnabas with Greek gods Hermes and Zeus (Acts 14:11–18), respectively. The excitement of their arrival, however, quickly soured after their

---

[2] For a more thorough discussion on this issue, any good commentary on Galatians will offer an evaluation of the various views. The following resources also provide helpful background information relating to the letter: G. W. Hansen, "Galatians, Letter to the" in *Dictionary of Paul and His Letters* (Downers Grove, IL: IVP Academic, 1993), 323–27; Lea and Black, *The New Testament*, 366–69 (see chap. 9, n. 5); and Chad Brand, Charles W. Draper, and Archie England, eds., *The Holman Illustrated Bible Dictionary* (Nashville: Holman Reference, 2003), s.v. "Galatians, Letter to the," by C. Hal Freeman Jr. Regardless of the origin, the Romans set up Galatia as a province sometime around 25 BC, and the population consisted of Greeks, Romans, and Jews.

opponents arrived in the city. The opposition that ensued was so intense that Paul was stoned by his opponents and assumed to be dead (Acts 14:19–20). Nonetheless, Paul survived and continued faithfully preaching the gospel message throughout Galatia. Ultimately Paul and Barnabas were forced to leave, but by the time of their departure many of those in the area had accepted the message of salvation through faith in Jesus alone. After accepting Christ, these individuals began to gather together for worship and edification in cities throughout the region.

It would seem that after Paul and Barnabas left the area, the new converts who formed the churches in the region began to experience confusion regarding the basis of salvation and the role of the Mosaic law. While Paul was clear that salvation is the result of faith in Christ, his opponents began teaching that those who follow Christ are also obliged to follow the law of Moses. That is to say, many began to accept the belief that when Gentiles come to the faith, they are obliged to follow Jewish traditions, customs, and laws. Christians today might find it difficult to understand why this issue would have been so divisive. In the first century, however, many regarded the Jews as God's covenantal people. Gentiles may certainly have a relationship with God, but it was widely understood that they could do so only by converting to Judaism. For Paul, the idea that converting to Judaism and observing the law were necessary for salvation was dangerous, as it undermined the sufficiency of Christ. In response to this controversy, Paul wrote Galatians, a powerful epistle designed to clarify the nature of the gospel and the importance of trusting in Christ alone for salvation.

Theme and Key Passages

A major theme in Paul's letter to the Galatians is the theological concept of justification. Justification is the divine act by which God declares sinners to be in a right relationship with him.[3] For Paul, one enters into a saving relationship with God not by observing the law but on the basis of God's grace, a grace that is applied to those who trust in Christ alone for their salvation. Thus, justification is the act by which we become part of the family of God and the beneficiaries of the salvation he provides for his people. Paul reminds his readers that Jesus alone is the one who can save us from our sins (Gal 1:4)—anything we trust as the basis of our salvation other than Jesus will result in spiritual death (Gal 4:8–11), and it is through

---

[3] For additional background on the meaning of the term "justification," see the sidebar in chapter 8 (page 122).

him that the promises made to Abraham are fulfilled (Gal 3:7–9, 15–18). Regardless of one's ethnicity, those who trust in Christ alone become members of God's spiritual family.

The family of God, Paul argues, is composed not of those with a certain ancestry (i.e., the Jewish people) but of those who have embraced Christ (Gal 3:28). Paul expresses grave concern that his readers will forfeit the spiritual blessings made available to them by trusting in something other than Christ for their salvation (Gal 5:1–6). To regard any tradition or law such as circumcision or Sabbath-keeping as the basis of one's relationship with God is to deny the truth of the gospel. In short, Jesus died to provide sinners with the means by which they can enter a saving relationship with God. To trust in anything but the work of Christ for one's salvation contradicts this good news.

In addition to clarifying the nature of his message and the consequences of embracing "a gospel contrary to what [they] received" (Gal 1:9), Paul also defends the authenticity of his own ministry among them. He was no stranger to opposition, and the message he proclaimed did not always make him popular (Gal 1:10). Yet Paul understood that justification by grace alone and through faith alone is the only means of Christian freedom and a right relationship with God. These themes may be observed through Galatians in passages such as the following:

> Galatians 2:19–20: "For through the law I died to the law, so that I might live for God. I have been crucified with Christ, and I no longer live, but Christ lives in me. The life I now live in the body, I live by faith in the Son of God, who loved me and gave himself for me."

> Galatians 3:27–28: "For those of you who were baptized into Christ have been clothed with Christ. There is no Jew or Greek, slave or free, male and female; since you are all one in Christ Jesus."

Purpose and Occasion

Paul wrote Galatians to defend his ministry and, more important, his message. The letter indicates that teachers came to Galatia after Paul and Barnabas had departed and taught a "different gospel" (Gal 1:6), which disrupted the faith of many believers (Gal 1:6–9). The identity of these teachers is not explicitly stated, but they may have been Jewish Christians who insisted that Gentiles could not become members of God's people if they were not fully

Jewish.[4] From their perspective, a full conversion to Judaism was necessary in order to experience the spiritual blessings of God. This would entail circumcision and adherence to the wider body of commands found in the law (Gal 4:9–11). This type of teaching established an ethnic standard for salvation and undermined the unity that believers have in Christ (Gal 3:27–29).

Facing intense opposition and the prospect that his progress made in Galatia would soon be lost, Paul wrote a sharp message to the Galatians that was designed to defend his teaching and provide clarity regarding the nature of the gospel. The seriousness of the letter may be observed in the absence of a typical greeting that is found in his other writings. The tone of the epistle clearly reveals the deep grief and concern that the churches in Galatia had embraced a teaching that ultimately results in spiritual slavery rather than spiritual life and freedom.

Because modern culture praises diversity and the tolerance of others' beliefs, we may be tempted to think that Paul was overreacting to the situation in Galatia. One of the key truths we learn from Paul's epistle, however, is that our beliefs have serious consequences. What we believe about Jesus is no insignificant matter. In fact, it is the basis of our relationship with God. For Paul, what one believes about Jesus and the gospel message is not something merely theoretical or academic. To the contrary, our conviction about Jesus and the salvation he provides influences how we relate to God, what we prioritize in life, how we conduct ourselves, and how we relate to others.

In sum, Galatians has three main purposes: (1) to expose the opponents and their false teaching, (2) to call the Galatians back to the true gospel that offers grace and freedom, and (3) to respond to charges leveled against him by these teachers. Paul accomplished these purposes in three ways: (1) he defended his message and ministry, (2) he articulated the scriptural basis of his gospel message, and (3) he demonstrated how his gospel message relates to daily Christian life.

HIGHLIGHTS IN GALATIANS

Introduction: Opening Greeting and Paul's Gospel (Gal 1:1–9)

The opening contains two significant theological statements and sets Paul's tone for the remainder of the letter. The first theological statement has to

---

[4] Paul's Jewish opponents are often referred to as "Judaizers."

do with Paul's status as an apostle. Much more so than in several of his other writings, Paul placed great emphasis in Galatians on his apostleship, stressing that it did not derive from human agency nor human authority. He was called an apostle by Jesus the Messiah and by "God the Father who raised [Jesus] from the dead" (Gal 1:1). His claim of a divine commission as an apostle reappears in various ways throughout the epistle. Modern readers may not fully grasp why Paul emphasized his apostolic authority to the degree that he did. It should be recalled that an apostle was a representative. If Paul was truly Christ's representative, his message was authoritative. The second theological claim made by Paul in the opening is that Jesus is the only means by which humanity can be rescued from the present evil age, a claim that places Jesus's crucifixion at the center of his gospel (Gal 1:3–4).

Verses 6–9 expand the greeting but are conspicuous for what it does not contain. Paul offered no thanksgiving or word of praise for his recipients, as was his custom in his other writings. In fact, this is the only Pauline epistle that offers no clear statement of gratitude or expression of praise for the original readers. Instead, he rebuked them for "so quickly turning away" from the gospel they originally received (Gal 1:6). Paul's sense of urgency and degree of concern was clear. He was incensed that the Galatians were turning their backs on the gospel of freedom in Christ to pursue another (albeit distorted) gospel (Gal 1:7–8). As he makes clear even from the onset of his writing, anyone who preaches a gospel contrary to Paul's message, the message of salvation by faith in Christ alone, will be under a curse (Gal 1:9).

Paul's Ministry and Message Defended (Gal 1:10–2:21)

In Gal 1:10, Paul began the body of his letter by defending his ministry and message. He made the simple statement that his ministry was

Greek copy of the last page of the letter to the Ephesians (6:20–24) and the first page of Paul's letter to the Galatians (1:1–8), dated to about AD 150 to 250

aimed at serving God and not at gaining approval from humans. In addition, the gospel that he proclaimed is to be embraced because it originated from Jesus himself and not from any human source (Gal 1:11–12). When we receive a message that has cycled through several sources, we may rightly question its reliability. When it comes directly from its source to us, however, its content is more trustworthy and reliable. Similarly, Paul's message was not a secondhand message that had been influenced by several people. To the contrary, he was commissioned directly by Christ to proclaim the good news of salvation. Paul's defense continues with an autobiographical account of his life and call as a messenger of Jesus to Gentiles (Gal 1:13–17). As his reflections of prior experiences illustrate, his authority was not dependent on church leaders in Jerusalem or those who were apostles before him.[5] Even though his interactions with the leaders in Jerusalem were mostly positive (Gal 1:18–24), Paul fulfilled his call without reliance on their authority.

In Gal 2:1–10, Paul refers to a visit to Jerusalem in which he presented his message to James, Peter, and John.[6] Titus and Barnabas accompanied Paul (Gal 2:1–2), and yet Titus (a Gentile) was not required to be circumcised even though some "false brothers" tried to force him to do so (Gal 2:3–5). Paul understood that if circumcision was necessary, his preaching would be in error and his credibility as an apostle would be forever tarnished (Gal 2:6–10). Paul resolutely made his stand, defending not only his calling but also the message he courageously proclaimed. His

> ### Four Commands
>
> Paul gives four commands regarding the believers' response to the Holy Spirit:
>
> - Gal 5:16: "I say, then, walk by the Spirit and you will certainly not carry out the desire of the flesh."
> - Eph 4:30a: "And don't grieve God's Holy Spirit."
> - Eph 5:18b: "Be filled by the Spirit."
> - 1 Thess 5:19: "Don't stifle the Spirit."
>
> Two of the commands are stated positively (Gal 5:16; Eph 5:18b), and two of the commands are stated negatively (Eph 4:30a; 1 Thess 5:19). Each imperative gives us a different perspective of the same command to live increasingly greater submission to the Spirit of God. So, while the believer receives the fullness of the Spirit at conversion, he or she still needs to grow in understanding of and submission to that Spirit.
>
> See P. Adam McClendon, *Paul's Spirituality in Galatians: A Critique of Contemporary Christian Spiritualties* (Eugene, OR: Wipf & Stock, 2015), 56–60.

---

[5] This claim may be Paul's response to the idea that he was not an "original" disciple of Jesus nor one of the first twelve. His opponents may have claimed that Paul was dependent on the authority of others for his message, and Paul responded with the idea that he received his gospel directly from Jesus himself. No human intervention or addition needed.

[6] See note 2 for background information regarding this visit.

reference to the endorsement he received from the "pillars" in Jerusalem may seem incidental to modern readers, but it left his opponents in Galatia with a serious problem. How could Paul's critics claim that his authority and teaching were invalid if his authority and teaching were both endorsed by the apostles in Jerusalem? Apparently, his opponents were aware that there was disagreement between Paul and Peter and referred to this incident to question Paul's authority. If Peter disagreed with Paul's teaching, they argued, why should the Galatians accept it?

In response, Paul clarified that when Peter visited Antioch, he refused to eat with uncircumcised Gentiles even though he did so previously (Gal 2:11–12). The pressure was so great that even Paul's companion Barnabas joined Peter in this refusal. From Paul's perspective, this was no minor incident, as it undermined the gospel message. While he regarded Peter and the other apostles as dear brothers in Christ, this was a matter in which he could not compromise, even if it involved confrontation. Peter's refusal to eat with Gentiles was in effect a public announcement that Gentiles were not the true people of God (Gal 2:13–14). Paul's rebuke of Peter therefore served as a strong affirmation of his belief that Jesus alone is necessary for salvation. It is also important to note that Peter's humble acceptance of Paul's rebuke had the effect of confirming that Paul's apostolic calling did not originate from the apostles but was of divine origin.

When we take a stand for truth, we may stand alone. At times we may find ourselves standing against people who we greatly respect or who have helped us in some way during our lives. Paul was certainly not looking for a conflict, but he understood that at times one must defend the truth at all cost. What about us? Are we willing to compromise the gospel in order to find acceptance in society or among family, friends, and colleagues? Do we value the gospel enough to take a stand, even if it comes at a personal cost?

Following his defense of his apostolic authority, Paul begins to focus more intently on important theological truths that were misunderstood by his readers. In Gal 2:15–21, he makes the conclusion that justification is by faith in the Messiah, and that adherence to the laws delivered through Moses cannot replace or add to the completed work of Christ. The recognition that the "works of the law" are essential for believers falsely assumes that humans can add something to what Jesus has already accomplished (Gal 2:15–16).[7] While Paul states elsewhere that "the law is good"

---

[7] There has been significant debate regarding phrases such as "works of the law" and "faith in Jesus Christ" in passages such as Gal 2:16. In Greek the two phrases are genitive

(1 Tim 1:8) and often describes it in very favorable terms, he is emphatic that it cannot enhance or replace what Christ accomplished through his death and resurrection. The law served several purposes, but it was never designed to serve as the basis of one's salvation.[8] This is actually good news for us because none of us are capable of following the law completely. Rather than trusting in our own ability to observe the law, Paul reminds his readers that we must trust only in Christ as the means of our salvation from sin. While it is indeed the case that holiness is required for salvation (Heb 12:14), the good news of the gospel is that we can be saved through the faithfulness and holiness of Christ rather than on the basis of our own merit.

Paul's Gospel Defined (Gal 3:1–5:1)

For Paul, salvation was granted on the basis of grace alone through faith alone. This understanding of the gospel was not a novel invention of early Christians, Paul argued, but a truth that has been a reality since the time of Abraham. For his readers who were confused about the relationship between faith and the law, Paul provided further support from a variety of sources, most importantly, the Old Testament. In this section (Gal 3:1–5:1) he appeals to three areas: (1) the Galatians' own experiences (Gal 3:1–6; 4:8–20), (2) common human experience relating to wills and inheritances (Gal 3:10–4:7), and (3) the experience of the patriarch Abraham (Gal 3:15–18; 4:21–5:1). His language in this section is very direct, and his exasperation is obvious. How could they leave his gospel for some other message? In a rhetorical flourish, Paul wondered aloud if someone had "cast a spell" on them. Have you ever felt that way about others? Has there been a time in your life when a friend, family member, or another acquaintance rejected the truth of God's Word for "another gospel"?

---

constructions. Typically, genitives indicate possession or origin, such as the possessive in English (i.e., "the book of the student" or "the student's book"). In light of this, it is possible to translate phrases translated in the CSB as "works of law" and "faith in Jesus Christ" as something like "the law's works" and "the faithfulness of Jesus Christ" (or "Jesus Christ's faithful acts"). Understood in this sense, these verses would seem to suggest that Paul was comparing what the law accomplishes to what is accomplished through Jesus.

[8] Generally, the law can be broken down into three broad categories: moral, civil, and ceremonial laws. While there is much overlap and this distinction is imperfect, it provides a good starting point to understanding various categories of the law. Additionally, the law served several purposes. While much has been written on the purposes of the law, it is sufficient to see four primary purposes. The law (1) reveals an ethic of God, (2) reveals the holiness of God, (3) reveals the sinfulness of humanity, and (4) reveals our need for a Savior.

In response to those who were convinced that salvation is based, at least in part, on the merits of the individual, Paul reminded his readers about their initial experience of salvation (Gal 3:2–6). He reminded them that they received Abraham's blessing on the basis of Jesus's actions rather than through their own efforts. Tragically, their actions had begun to contradict their past experience. Rather than continuing to trust in Christ alone, they were relying upon their own abilities and accomplishments. In other words, they were confusing what they regarded as external signs of God's people with the basis of their salvation. As discussed previously, many of the original readers of this epistle began to believe that those who are part of the family could be identified by their adherence to the law. This would be most apparent with regard to the laws that separated Jews from Gentiles (e.g., circumcision, Sabbath keeping, and dietary laws). In response, Paul was clear that God's people are not those of a particular ethnicity; that is, those who follow the law, but those who are marked by their faith in Christ.

A third-century Galatian plate

While you may not feel compelled to follow Jewish traditions, perhaps you have at one point or another assumed that you are in a right relationship with God because of your own religious "works." Perhaps you have assumed that God is pleased with you because of your morality, your family's Christian heritage, church attendance, or some other aspect of your life that would identify you as a Christian. To be clear, the gospel will naturally have a transforming effect upon a person's life. It would be a mistake, however, to confuse the outward manifestation of our faith with the basis of our salvation.

The great patriarch Abraham found himself in a right relationship with God not because of his own achievements but because he trusted in God's promises. As we learn from his example, the sign of a saving relationship with God is faith, not circumcision or other works of the law (Gal 3:7–9). Paul quoted from Gen 12:3 and 18:18 on this occasion to emphasize that God's people are not to be identified as an ethnic group but as those characterized by faith. Instead of acknowledging this truth, a truth revealed in the Old Testament, Paul's Jewish opponents misled the Galatians into thinking that they could be God's people by observing the works of the law. In response, Paul pointed out that those who try to keep the law are actually cursed because they are destined to fail (Gal 3:10–11). Rather than seeking a right relationship to God through the observance of the law, Paul quoted from the prophet Habakkuk to emphasize that those whom God declares righteous are those who "live by faith" (Hab 2:4). While it may at first seem discouraging to know that we are incapable of satisfying God's demands of holiness, it is liberating to discover that our salvation is not based upon our own ability to be perfectly faithful to God's commands but is based instead on the faithfulness of the one who was in fact perfect. The great truth of the gospel is that all humans, both Jews and Gentiles, can participate in Abraham's promised blessing (Gal 3:28).

Paul's opponents apparently taught that the appearance of the law 430 years after God made the initial covenant with Abraham somehow added to the necessity of faith. Abraham may have been justified before God on the basis of his faith, the argument went; but since the law was given later, it must also be necessary for salvation. From Paul's perspective, this argument was inconsistent and failed to recognize the role and nature of the law. As an illustration, he pointed to human wills as a way to explain the relationship between faith and the law (Gal 3:15). When a will was made, it could not be amended or altered. Furthermore, Paul observed that God made promises to Abraham and his "seed," a term that, in some versions, appears in passages such as Gen 12:7; 13:15; and 24:7 in the singular rather than the plural form. Based on this observation, Paul explained that the promise of God was not fulfilled in a particular ethnic group, such as the Jews, but in one individual—Jesus the Messiah (Gal 3:16–18). In sum, those who receive the inheritance that was promised to Abraham are not his "seeds" (plural)—that is, his physical descendants (i.e., the Jewish people)—but those who are in Christ (Gal 3:29), the "seed" (singular).

An additional point that should be emphasized is that the law functioned as a barrier between Jews and Gentiles. After the Hebrew people departed from Egypt, God gave them the law to, among other things, ensure that they would remain a unique people. Laws regarding circumcision, clean and unclean foods, clothing, and the Sabbath (just to name a few examples) made it difficult for them to assimilate into other cultures. The problem that Paul encountered was that Jesus had made salvation possible for both Jews and Gentiles, but the law was being used to divide the two peoples. No wonder that Paul was so angered! His opponents were not only looking to the law rather than Christ as the basis of salvation, they were also dividing the people of God on the basis of ethnic distinctions. For Paul, one's ethnicity or family background was irrelevant when it came to membership in God's family. A person did not need to become Jewish, he insisted, in order to be made right with God and to experience the fulfillment of the promises God made to Abraham. That could only be experienced through faith in Christ. This leads to an important question: if faith has always been the basis of a right relationship with God (as it was for Abraham), why was the law given in the first place? Stated negatively, the law was given "for the sake of transgressions" (Gal 3:19). Through the law we discover God's holiness as well as our inability to live according to his righteous demands. Positively, the law points us to Christ (Gal 3:20–26). As Paul stated, "Christ is the end of the law for righteousness to everyone who believes" (Rom 10:4). Now that Christ has completed his work, the law no longer serves as a "guardian" (Gal 3:24–25),[9] a role that was always intended to be temporary.

Paul continued his emphasis on the centrality of faith throughout chapter 4 by referring to inheritance and adoption practices. A will was often written in the Roman world to legalize an adoption. Once written, it could not be changed. In the same way, God made a promise to Abraham, which entailed a blessing for all nations, a promise that would not change (Gal 3:17). The promise came first, but the law was given to help humans see their need for spiritual help while they waited for the fulfillment of God's promises through the Messiah. Even though the promise includes an inheritance, heirs do not receive it until the time set by the father (Gal 4:1–2). As Paul explained, our redemption became possible and the promise was realized when Jesus came (Gal 4:3–7).

In the midst of his theological treatment regarding the relationship between the law and the promise of salvation, Paul paused to make some pastoral reflections (Gal 4:8–20). He was concerned that the Galatians had abandoned the gospel of freedom and thereby submitted themselves to spiritual slavery (Gal 4:8–11). Upon this basis, he was concerned that his

---

[9] The term *guardian* refers to an individual in the Roman world, usually a male slave, who was tasked with caring for his master's children. Guardians assisted them in their day-to-day activities, made sure that they completed each of their tasks, and provided general guidance and oversight. They had the reputation for being very strict since they were ultimately accountable to their masters for the children's progress and success. Once the child was of age, the guardian's role ceased.

labor for them would be wasted (Gal 4:11). Paul was certainly one who experienced many highs and lows in ministry. He saw many people come to faith, but he also witnessed many people fall away or fail to remain faithful to the true gospel. We can learn several things from Paul's example. One thing that is especially plain in this epistle is the serious consequences of what we believe. While we certainly want to avoid self-righteousness or needless conflicts, there are times in which those in Christ must remind others of the truth of God's Word. Perhaps there is someone close to you who is trusting in something other than Christ for his or her salvation. How might you lovingly share your concerns and point him or her to Christ?

Paul concluded this major section of the epistle by discussing the birth of Abraham's sons (Gal 4:21–23). One son, Isaac, was the fulfillment of God's promise. The other, Ishmael, was the result of Abraham's doubts and is thus described as a son "of the flesh" (Gal 4:23). Allegorically, Paul explained, these two sons represent two covenants (Gal 4:24) that lead either to freedom or to slavery. The difference is the promise. Isaac represents the promise since he was born according to God's promise. Conversely, Ishmael represents slavery since he was born by a very human attempt to make God's promise a reality. Many of us can identify with Abraham. We may be aware that God has promised his people various spiritual blessings but have doubts that they will come to pass or that they are a present reality in our lives. As a result, we attempt to bring about these promises on our own rather than trusting in God to fulfill them. How foolish it would be if we sought to earn an earthly inheritance for ourselves rather than accepting it as a free gift. We could not do this even if we tried! Similarly, only those who trust in Jesus can inherit God's promise of salvation. A right relationship with God cannot be accomplished by our own efforts; it is something that can only be accomplished through Christ.

Paul's Gospel Applied (Gal 5:2–6:10)

For Paul, our identity in Christ has a transformative effect to how we relate to God and to others. As we continue to walk in faith, we are encouraged to remain mindful of the dangers of reverting back to spiritual slavery (Gal 5:2–12) and to use the spiritual freedom we enjoy for the benefit of others (Gal 5:13–15). Those who trust in Jesus are to love and serve others, not by their own power, but through the enabling of the Holy Spirit who empowers those who have experienced new life in Christ (Gal 5:16–18). In other words, rather than trusting in our own abilities to live in the manner that God has called us, we are to rely upon the work of the Spirit

(Gal 5:16–26). When we do so, there will be "fruit" that may be observed in our lives.

> ### Denying Fleshly Desires
>
> Paul revealed something interesting about the Christian life in Gal 5:16. Do not miss it. He wrote, "I say, then, walk by the Spirit and you will certainly not carry out the desire of the flesh." Paul was speaking to believers, telling them that they would have fleshly desires. Regardless of how mature we become in Christ, we will have desires that are contrary to the Spirit of God. Thus, the mark of a godly person is not necessarily exemption from fleshly desires; rather, the mark of godly people is those who, despite fleshly desires, submit their lives to the will of the Spirit over and against their own appetites. In other words, they choose godliness. They "walk by the Spirit," submitting to his influence in their lives.

Paul's instruction reveals that we cannot live in a way that pleases God if we are not in a right relationship with him. One of the blessings that God gives to his people is the indwelling of the Holy Spirit. Only those who have received the gift of the Holy Spirit can exhibit the fruit of the Spirit; that is, outward manifestations of the transformative work of God. Rather than identifying God's people as those who observe certain traditions and laws, God's people may be identified by the way they live and treat others. While the ministry of the Holy Spirit is essential to living the transformed life to which God calls us, we should not view the Christian life as a passive experience. As we rely upon the Holy Spirit, we are instructed to proactively "walk by the Spirit" (Gal 5:16); that is, to live our lives in a manner that is consistent with the Holy Spirit's ministry in our lives. Finally, Paul emphasizes that as followers of Christ, our love should extend to those who fall (Gal 6:1–5) as well as those who faithfully serve the Lord and walk in faith (Gal 6:6, 10).

Conclusion: Paul's Signature and Suffering (Gal 6:11–17)

Beyond Paul's written autograph (Gal 6:11), his life revealed the signature of Jesus—the life of a person who suffered to make Jesus known to the Gentiles (Gal 6:17). Between his personal signature and the reminder of his own suffering, Paul reiterated his main point: selfish ambition and reliance on human ability will not produce spiritual freedom; this can only be accomplished through the completed work of Christ (Gal 6:11–16). Faith in Jesus alone was Paul's gospel of freedom. May we all live worthy of that love by sharing it with others!

BIBLIOGRAPHY

deSilva, David. *The Letter to the Galatians*. NICNT. Grand Rapids: Eerdmans, 2018.

Dunn, James D. G. *The Epistle to the Galatians.* Black's New Testament Commentary. Grand Rapids: Baker Academic, 2011.

Draper, Charles W., Chad Brand, and Archie England eds. *The Holman Illustrated Bible Dictionary*. Nashville: Holman Reference, 2003.

Hansen, G. W. "Galatians, Letter to the." In *Dictionary of Paul and His Letters.* Downers Grove, IL: IVP Academic, 1993.

Keener, Craig. *Galatians: A Commentary.* Grand Rapids: Baker Academic, 2019.

Lewis, C. S. *Mere Christianity*. New York: Touchstone, 1996.

McClendon, P. Adam. *Paul's Spirituality in Galatians: A Critique of Contemporary Christian Spiritualties*. Eugene, OR: Wipf & Stock, 2015.

McKnight, Scot. *Galatians*. NIVAC. Grand Rapids: Zondervan Academic, 1995.

Moo, Douglas. *Galatians.* BECNT. Grand Rapids: Baker Academic, 2013.

Schreiner, Thomas. *Galatians*. ZECNT. Grand Rapids: Zondervan Academic, 2010.

12

EPHESIANS

BENJAMIN LAIRD

CONNECTION POINT

What relevance does this first-century writing have for us today? Despite the numerous advancements and accomplishments that have taken place in society over the last century, anxiety and even despair remain common around the world. The spread of disease, the future of the economy, and the possibility of military conflict all remain enduring concerns. In addition to these more universal concerns, many individuals struggle with personal challenges such as broken relationships, personal tragedies, financial debt, and addictions. The challenges and hardships we face both individually and as a society often feel out of our control or beyond our power to influence or address. As we face the various challenges of life and contemplate the uncertainties of the future, it is natural for us to feel, at least on occasion, overwhelmed and discouraged.

While there is undoubtedly much in this fallen world that may cause us to experience periods of anxiety and even hopelessness, the apostle Paul reminds us in his letter to the Ephesians that we have every reason to rejoice as a result of the many spiritual blessings that have been given to us through Christ. Many of us recognize that our salvation is possible because of Christ's redemptive work some 2,000 years ago. What we often overlook and do not fully comprehend, however, are the many ways in which our salvation provides us with hope and joy, even in the midst of difficult circumstances. It is important to realize that for Paul, salvation is not a mere theoretical concept or something that will only benefit us in the future. Rather, it is a present reality that allows us to experience God's blessings even as we anticipate the final redemption of our fallen world (Rom 8:18–25). Although pain and suffering are a reality in the present age (John 16:33), Scripture reminds us that our salvation provides us with peace, joy, and comfort as we wait for the Lord's return. In light of this reality, we can join with Paul who exclaimed, "Blessed is the God and Father of our Lord Jesus Christ, who has blessed us with every spiritual blessing in the heavens in Christ" (Eph 1:3).

With this in mind, consider making this your prayer as you read and study this chapter:

Almighty God, enlighten the eyes of my heart in order that I may know the hope to which you have called me, the riches of your glorious inheritance you have given me along with your holy people, and your incomparably great power for those who believe. This great power is the same as the mighty strength you exerted when you raised Christ from the dead and seated him at your right hand in the heavenly realms, far above all rule and authority, power and dominion, and every name that is invoked, not only in the present age but also in the one to come [Eph 1:18–21]. In Jesus's name, amen.

SETTING

Recipients

Paul wrote, "To the faithful saints in Christ Jesus at Ephesus" (Eph 1:1) around AD 60–62.[1] Given its large population and influence, it is certainly

---

[1] Although the authenticity of Ephesians was not seriously questioned in the early church, many contemporary scholars reject the Pauline authorship of Ephesians and conclude that it was written by one or more unknown writers during the late first century. Some have concluded that the letter was written by a devotee of Paul who sought to enhance or preserve the apostle's legacy, or perhaps by a "Pauline school"; that is, a small group of

Ruins of the ancient Celsus Library in the ancient city of Ephesus

Paul's associates or followers who composed the letter in order to address contemporary issues in a manner that they believed was consistent with Paul's previous teaching. In many cases, those who challenge Pauline authorship assert that the style and vocabulary of Ephesians is dissimilar to the recognized Pauline Epistles and that the content of the letter is more general in nature than what might be expected in a letter of Paul to a specific congregation. These observations, however, can be accounted for without rejecting the authenticity of Ephesians. In addition to the explicit claim of authorship in Eph 1:1, the letter was quickly embraced as a Pauline writing in the early church. It should also be understood that the language of a writing is conditioned on a number of factors such as the themes and subjects it addresses, the possible use of a scribe, and the intended recipients. For a defense of the authenticity of Ephesians, see Gregory MaGee, *Portrait of an Apostle: A Case for Paul's Authorship of Colossians and Ephesians* (Eugene, OR: Pickwick Publications, 2013).

Despite the reference to the city of Ephesus in the opening of the book, many scholars believe that the letter was not originally addressed to those in Ephesus. There are two major arguments for this conclusion: (1) the fact that some of the earliest Greek manuscripts of Ephesians do not include the words "in Ephesus" in Eph 1:1, and (2) the apparent lack of specific instruction and references that are typical in Paul's correspondence to those in a particular location. In response, it should be noted that the majority of early copies of Ephesians do in fact include the words "in Ephesus" and that the wording of the passage is unconventional, if not grammatically incoherent, without these words. In addition, the title "to the Ephesians" was nearly universally recognized very early and even appears on manuscripts that do not include the words "in Ephesus." It is indeed the case that Ephesians contains less content that would have been relevant to a specific audience, but this observation does not in and of itself preclude Ephesus as the original destination of the letter.

If the assumption that each of the Prison Epistles was written from Rome is correct, Ephesians would have likely been written during the period of AD 60–62, though a date in the late 50s is also possible.

understandable why Paul sought to establish a vibrant church in the city of Ephesus. As one who devoted much of his life to the advancement of the gospel, Paul recognized the strategic advantages of establishing healthy churches in major population centers. Cities such as Antioch of Syria, Corinth, Ephesus, and Rome offered opportunities for Paul and other Christians to reach large numbers of unbelievers with the gospel and to establish local churches that could support further missionary efforts.

During the first century, Ephesus was one of the largest cities in the Roman world and served as the capital of the Roman province of Asia, an area located in the westernmost portion of modern-day Turkey. Archaeologists estimate that the city was home to around 200,000–250,000 inhabitants during the first century, a population that was comprised primarily of Greeks and Romans, though there was a moderate Jewish population there as well (see Acts 19:8). Those who visit the ancient site today will find the remains of several ancient temples, monuments, homes, fountains, baths, an agora (marketplace), outdoor theaters (one of which is referred to in Acts 19:29–41 and could hold more than 20,000 spectators), and a large second-century library. As the remains of the city testify, Ephesus was clearly a city of great significance in the Roman world.

In addition to serving as a notable commercial center with a thriving port and access to major trading routes, Ephesus was an important center of worship. The most well-known religious site in the city was the Artemision, one of the seven wonders of the ancient world. The temple was dedicated to Artemis, a Greek goddess often associated with the Roman goddess Diana. Among other things, Artemis was believed to protect women in childbirth, a role she inherited as a result of the myth that she assisted in the birth of her twin brother Apollo when they were mere infants. Thousands of pilgrims visited the temple each year, bringing great wealth and notoriety to the city. Despite the significant cultural and religious opposition that Paul experienced here and elsewhere, he reminded the Ephesians that "our struggle is not against flesh and blood, but against the rulers, against the authorities, against the cosmic powers of this darkness, against evil, spiritual forces in the heavens" (Eph 6:12).

Theme and Key Passage

One of the most important truths that Paul conveyed in this letter is that our salvation is the work of God, and it is intended to produce "good works," what we might describe generally as acts of obedience, service, and love. As we learn in this letter, the manner in which we live does not serve

Ephesians

The ruins of the ancient temple of Hadrian in Ephesus

as the basis for our salvation, but it does provide evidence of God's work in our lives.

Ephesians 2:8–10 tells us: "For you are saved by grace through faith, and this is not from yourselves; it is God's gift—not from works, so that no one can boast. For we are his workmanship, created in Christ Jesus for good works, which God prepared ahead of time for us to do."

Purpose and Occasion

Both Acts and the Pauline Epistles serve as our primary sources of information for the circumstances facing Paul at the time he composed Ephesians and the factors that may have prompted him to write to the Ephesians. It is evident from the book of Acts that Paul was well–acquainted with the city of Ephesus and the Christian population in the area. After visiting the city briefly during his second missionary journey (Acts 18:19–21),[2] he

---

[2] While it is conventional to refer to three specific missionary journeys of Paul, it should be understood that Paul actually engaged in several years of missionary activity between the time of his conversion and the beginning of the three major missionary journeys recorded in the book of Acts. References to his early missionary endeavors in his letters and in Acts reveal that he spent three years in Arabia immediately following his

spent over two years ministering there during his third missionary journey before he was forced to abruptly depart as a result of strong opposition (Acts 19:23–20:1). Despite the significant resistance he experienced, many of the Ephesians accepted Jesus as their Lord and Savior during his time in the city (Acts 19:17–20).[3] At the conclusion of his third missionary journey, Paul returned to Jerusalem where his presence resulted in an uproar and his imprisonment in Caesarea and later in Rome (Acts 21:17–28:31).

Traditionally, it has been understood that Paul wrote four epistles (Ephesians, Philippians, Colossians, and Philemon) during his first Roman imprisonment, the same imprisonment described by Luke in the final chapter of Acts.[4] According to Luke, this "imprisonment" as we often describe it, was in reality a house arrest and lasted two full years (Acts 28:30).[5]

With regard to the occasion that prompted the composition of this writing, it may be the case that Paul's situation played a greater role than the immediate circumstances facing those in Ephesus. Because it had likely been somewhere between three to five years since he had last set foot in Ephesus, he may have simply determined to take the opportunity to provide instruction and encouragement to those living there and elsewhere. His inability to travel, uncertainties about his future, and confinement in a rented house would have provided an opportune occasion to write to those he loved so dearly.

As many scholars have observed, there is a noticeable lack of references to specific issues that would have been of unique relevance to the church in

---

conversion (Gal 1:17–18), followed by several years of ministry in the regions of Syria and Cilicia (Gal 1:21). Paul then relocated to Antioch of Syria where he served for some time with Barnabas before they embarked on the "first" missionary journey (Acts 13:1–3).

[3] In addition to extensive local ministry, Paul also composed the letter of 1 Corinthians during his stay in Ephesus.

[4] Many scholars believe that Paul was ultimately released from the imprisonment recorded in Acts 28 and then engaged in additional missionary work throughout the Roman world. It was during this time that he wrote 1 Timothy and Titus. He was then arrested during the mid-60s and imprisoned for a second time in Rome. During this second imprisonment, Paul penned 2 Timothy and was martyred shortly thereafter by the emperor Nero. This viewpoint is reflected in the writings of early Christian historians and theologians such as Eusebius and Jerome. See, for example, Eusebius, *Ecclesiastical History*, 2.22, 25; Jerome, *On Illustrious Men*, 5.

[5] The similar content of Ephesians and Colossians indicates they were likely written during a short period of one another. While each letter contains unique material, the two letters include similar treatments of several subjects, often contain similar language, and make similar references to specific individuals (e.g., Tychicus in Eph 6:21 and Col 4:7). This suggests that Paul wrote Ephesians and Colossians at approximately the same time (early 60s) and that he treated subjects that he considered pertinent to those in both locations.

Ephesus. While this conclusion is sometimes overstated—the emphasis on spiritual warfare (Eph 6:10–20) and several theological and cultural issues would have certainly been of interest to those in Ephesus[6]—it is certainly the case that Paul addressed a variety of theological and practical matters that would have been of relevance not only to those in Ephesus, but to the wider Christian world. It is reasonable to conclude, therefore, that this epistle was written with an eye for a wider audience.

HIGHLIGHTS IN EPHESIANS

The Blessings of Our Salvation in Christ (Eph 1:1–23)

Following a brief opening, which included basic information such as the author and recipient(s), letters in ancient Greek and Roman society often included a brief expression of gratitude and/or a wish for the reader's welfare.[7] In similar fashion, Paul began Ephesians with a reference to "the God and Father of our Lord Jesus Christ" before elaborating on several of the ways in which he "has blessed us with every spiritual blessing in the heavens in Christ" (Eph 1:3). In contrast to the customary practice of stating a wish for the recipient's general welfare, Paul expressed joy and gratitude for the spiritual blessings that are associated with our salvation.

Paul began his letter by reflecting on the reality that our salvation was not the result of chance or achieved on the basis of our personal effort. Rather, it was decreed by God in eternity past (Eph 1:4–5, 11), accomplished through the death and resurrection of his son (Eph 1:7, 20–23), and is guaranteed by

> **Redemption**
>
> In Eph 1:7, Paul refers to the "redemption" we have received through Christ's sacrifice. Modern readers may assume that the term (*apolutrósis* in the Greek) is simply a synonym of "salvation." There is a specific nuance to the term, however, that would have been apparent to the original readers. The term was often used in reference to the release of a slave or captive upon receipt of a ransom payment. As such, it became a fitting description of our salvation. Just as many slaves or captives could only gain freedom through the payment of the redemption price demanded by his or her master or captors, we can only experience freedom from our bondage to sin "through His blood" (1:7).

---

[6] Paul's promise that he would send Tychicus would seem ill-fitting if the letter was not originally written for a specific audience (Eph 6:21–22).

[7] Galatians is the only Pauline epistle to lack the customary thanksgiving section.

the Holy Spirit (Eph 1:13–14). In sum, our salvation is entirely the work of the triune God who has provided for our salvation in the past, continues to work in our lives in the present, and will complete the work of salvation in the future (Eph 1:14). While we should expect to experience hardships and difficulties in this life, we can live with the assurance that God is sovereign over all things and that through Christ he will ultimately "bring everything together . . . both things in heaven and things on earth" (Eph 1:10).

What are the specific spiritual blessings God has given to us that result in hope, joy, and peace? Among the many blessings associated with our salvation, Paul reminds us that as God's people we can rejoice because of the fact that we have been adopted as God's children (Eph 1:5); we are redeemed and forgiven of our sins (Eph 1:7); we can know God's eternal plan of salvation (Eph 1:9); we have been chosen by him through no merit of our own (Eph 1:11) and the Holy Spirit provides a guarantee of our salvation and future hope (Eph 1:13–14). Whenever we experience discouragement, discontentment, or anxiety about our present circumstances or what the future may hold, we must not overlook the richness of our salvation and the hope that we have in Christ. Rather than become fixated on our immediate circumstances and difficulties, Paul reminds us that our joy and hope will increase as we grow in our understanding and comprehension of the spiritual blessings that have been given to us through Christ (Eph 1:17–19).

The Purpose of Our Salvation in Christ (Eph 2:1–10)

As we consider the many spiritual blessings that relate to our salvation, we should not overlook the fact that there is a greater purpose to salvation than our personal well-being. Ultimately, the purpose of our salvation is to bring glory to God through a transformed life. It is not our mere change of status before God that brings him glory, but the "good works, which God prepared ahead of time for us to do" (Eph 2:10). As God cleanses our hearts, and as we obey him through the power of the Holy Spirit, we bring him honor and praise (this truth is also emphasized in Eph 1:6, 12, 14).

Only through the realization that we were once in a hopeless spiritual state can we appreciate the greatness of our salvation. Among other things, Paul states that before we were brought to faith, we "were dead in . . . trespasses and sins" (Eph 2:1), "walked according to the ways of the world" (Eph 2:2), and "were by nature children under wrath" (Eph 2:3). This sobering assessment of our life before Christ is consistent with what we find elsewhere in Scripture. For example, as Paul famously wrote to the Roman church, "all have sinned and fall short of the glory God" (Rom 3:23). The depiction of the human condition described throughout Scripture is clearly at odds with the common belief in modern society of the inherent goodness of humanity. To be clear, unbelievers are certainly capable of committing selfless and loving acts. As Jesus said, even those who are evil "know how to give good gifts to [their] children" (Matt 7:11). Despite occasional acts of goodness, Scripture teaches that those who have not experienced salvation are enslaved to sin (Rom 6). As Paul explained in Eph 2:2, the entire being of those who do not know Christ, both the mind and will, are in bondage to "the ruler of the power of the air."

In his reflections on humanity's hopeless state apart from Christ, Paul describes those who have not experienced salvation as spiritually dead (Eph 2:1). Just as one who is physically dead cannot recover voluntarily through personal effort, so too is it impossible for those who are spiritually dead to achieve salvation through personal effort. Salvation "is not from yourselves," Paul wrote (Eph 2:8), but is "God's gift." Because it is not something that can be earned by living what we might regard as a morally good life or by engaging in religious activities, we cannot take credit for the salvation that we enjoy. As Paul reminds us, "no one can boast" (Eph 2:9). In light of the fact that we were once dead in our sins and that we can experience salvation only by the grace of God, we are charged to live each day with the conviction that our salvation was granted to us by God and that it comes with a purpose. "We are his workmanship," Paul explained, "created in Christ Jesus for good works, which God prepared ahead of time for us to do" (Eph 2:10).

> ### "Adoption"
>
> In his description of our salvation, Paul wrote that we have been "adopted as sons through Jesus Christ for himself" (Eph 1:5). The Greek term *huiothesia* is used exclusively in the New Testament in reference to the status that Christians enjoy as adopted sons and daughters of God. Unlike today, wealthy Greeks and Romans with no suitable male heirs would often adopt a grown man who had demonstrated the capacity to effectively manage an estate. Once adopted, the son enjoyed the status of the father and ultimately the inheritance that he would leave behind. With the inheritance, however, often came the responsibility of maintaining the family's estate. Paul's reference to our adoption is noteworthy given that we were adopted by One with an unequalled inheritance, even though we were entirely unworthy of this status. In fact, God's plan to adopt us as his sons and daughters was "predestined" (Eph 1:5). Rather than simply enjoying our spiritual inheritance, God calls us to glorify Him through acts by producing good works (Eph 2:10).

The Cultural Implications of Our Salvation in Christ (Eph 2:11–3:21)

Before the establishment of the church, God's people were largely associated with a particular ethnic group; that is, the Jewish people. Because modern society typically regards religion as a private matter, the ethnic dimension of religion in ancient culture is often overlooked. In the book of Genesis, we read that God established a covenant with Abraham some 4,000 years ago and promised, among other things, to multiply his descendants, give his people a specific land, and establish his descendants as a great nation. (Gen 12:1–3).[8] From the time of Abraham to the time of Christ, Abraham's descendants were given many spiritual blessings and provisions so that through them, "all peoples on earth [would] be blessed" (Gen 12:3). What were the blessings given to the people of Israel? In his epistle to the Romans, Paul explained that to them belonged "the adoption, the glory, the covenants, the giving of the law, the temple service, and the promises" (Rom 9:4). Most importantly, "from them, by physical descent, came the Christ" (Rom 9:5).

The state of the Gentiles was not nearly as fortunate. According to Paul, they were at one time, "without Christ, excluded from the citizenship of Israel, and foreigners to the covenants of promise, without hope and without God in the world" (Eph 2:12). To say the least, this was a rather bleak assessment of the status of those who were not Abraham's descendants. The good news, of course, was that Jesus "came and proclaimed the good news of peace to you who were far away [i.e., the Gentiles] and peace to those who were near [i.e., the Jewish people]" (Eph 2:17). As a result of his death and resurrection, Gentiles were "brought near by the blood of Christ" (Eph 2:13). No longer is there a division between Jews and Gentiles with respect to spiritual blessings, as God "made both groups one and tore down the dividing wall of hostility" (Eph 2:14).[9]

What made the division between Jews and Gentiles most apparent to everyone was the Mosaic law. For the Jews, the law was regarded as the

---

[8] The terms of the covenant were recorded in Gen 12:1–3 and reiterated or alluded to in several subsequent passages in the Old Testament. In Genesis, the covenant is referenced in Genesis 15, 17, and 35:10–12.

[9] Many scholars understand the "dividing wall" as a reference to a stone wall in the temple complex that separated Jews from Gentiles. This partition was mentioned by Josephus, the first-century Jewish historian. See Josephus, *Jewish Antiquities* 8.71. Alternatively, some have suggested that the wall is simply a metaphorical reference to the law, given that it functioned in a figurative sense as a barrier between Jews and Gentiles.

means by which membership in God's covenantal community was established. While Gentiles could certainly experience forgiveness of sins and peace with God before the death and resurrection of Jesus, it was expected that they assimilate into Jewish culture and place themselves under the authority of the law. Rahab, for example, demonstrated the genuine nature of her faith when she hid the spies in Jericho (Jas 2:25). However, she later became a member of the covenant community of Israel and lived the remainder of her days under the law (Josh 6:25). Why was this expectation no longer the case? Scripture teaches that our relationship to the law has now changed as a consequence of Christ's redemptive work. According to Paul, "the law consisting of commands and expressed in regulations" (Eph 2:15) no longer functioned as the means by which God's people were identified or related to him. This was replaced by Christ. Consequently, there was no longer a division between Jew and Gentile as God's people were "built on the foundation of the apostles and prophets, with Christ Jesus himself as the cornerstone" (Eph 2:20). Interestingly, Paul described the

The ancient theatre in Ephesus is one of the largest in the region. It seated 25,000 spectaters and looked out over the valley.

truth that believing Jews and Gentiles would become one body in Christ as a "mystery"; that is, as something that was not revealed in times past (Eph 3:5).

With respect to his own calling, Paul was persuaded that God had appointed him "to proclaim to the Gentiles the incalculable riches of Christ" (Eph 3:8). Before encountering Christ, he was convinced that Christianity pointed to a false messiah and that those who were truly God's people were to carefully and faithfully adhere to the law. After encountering Christ, he understood that the means of salvation for both Jews and Gentiles was faith in Christ. In light of his conviction that Christ had fulfilled all that was anticipated by the law (cf. Rom 10:4), Paul faithfully and passionately proclaimed to Gentiles that through faith they were now "coheirs, members of the same body, and partners in the promise in Christ Jesus through the gospel" (Eph 3:6).

The Transformative Nature of Our Salvation in Christ (Eph 4:1–6:9)

Throughout the New Testament we find that Christian doctrine is not to be regarded as something merely theoretical or academic in nature. To the contrary, we learn that there is a direct correlation between how we live and what we believe about the nature of God, his relationship to us, and what he has done in this world. Those who recognize Jesus as their Lord and the One to whom they must give an account (cf. 2 Cor 5:10) will inevitably seek to walk in obedience to his commands and live in a manner that, as Paul stated elsewhere, is worthy of the gospel of Christ (Phil 1:27). On the other hand, those who embrace false teaching deny the lordship of Christ, or reject the promise of a future judgment, will naturally pursue earthly interests and demonstrate little concern for spiritual growth. It comes as a surprise to many readers of the New Testament that writers such as Peter, John, and Jude condemned false teachers not merely for what they taught but for living in a manner that was contrary to the gospel. Peter described false teachers, for example, as those who lead others to follow their "depraved ways" (2 Pet 2:2).

The inseparable connection between our theological beliefs and our behavior is evident in Paul's epistle to the Ephesians. After expounding on several theological topics such as the nature and purpose of our salvation, he offered a number of practical admonitions. At the beginning of the fourth chapter, Paul urged his readers "to walk worthy of the calling you have received, with all humility and gentleness, with patience, bearing with one another in love, making every effort to keep the unity of the

Spirit through the bond of peace" (Eph 4:1–3). In many ways, this passage nicely summarizes the content of the epistle as a whole. Having discussed the nature of our calling (Ephesians 1–3), Paul elaborated on some of the specific ways that we are to live in light of these truths (Ephesians 4–6). In response to the salvation that we have graciously received, Paul encouraged his readers to pursue unity in the body of Christ (Eph 4:1–6), the spiritual maturity of other believers (Eph 4:7–16), a lifestyle that reflects our calling as Christians (Eph 4:17–5:21), and God-honoring relationships that reflect the transformative work of the gospel (Eph 5:22–6:9).[10]

The Spiritual Power of Our Salvation in Christ (Eph 6:10–24)

Following a series of admonitions that largely pertain to the manner in which Christians are to relate to others in the church, home, and in greater society, Paul concluded his letter with a memorable allusion to Jewish texts such as Isa 11:5 and 59:17 and the non-canonical work *Wisdom of Solomon* (see especially, 5.16–20), which refer to God as a divine warrior. These vivid descriptions are designed to emphasize the truth that Christians are engaged in a spiritual battle, a battle that will continue to intensify as the day of the Lord's return approaches (Eph 6:13).[11] As Paul explained, "our struggle is not against flesh and blood, but against the rulers, against the authorities, against the

This statue demonstrates the traditional armor of a Roman soldier.

---

[10] This final section contains a series of "household codes," instructions that articulated the obligations of various members of a household to one other (e.g., slaves to their masters, children to their parents, wives to their husbands). Similar codes appear in Col 3:12–4:6, Titus 2:1–10, and 1 Pet 2:11–3:22. Unlike the codes in the wider Greco-Roman world, the New Testament authors emphasized the importance of treating others with love and respect and as members of one spiritual family.

[11] Paul's emphasis on spiritual warfare would have certainly resonated with his Ephesian readers. Luke recorded that before their acceptance of Christ, many of the Ephesians practiced sorcery and that there were attempts by some Jews to perform exorcisms (Acts 19:13–20).

cosmic powers of this darkness, against evil, spiritual forces in the heavens" (Eph 6:12).

As Christians strive to mature in their faith and to proclaim the gospel throughout the world, spiritual resistance will inevitably result. During these times it is vital that we "take up the full armor of God" (Eph 6:13); that is, that we make full use of the spiritual resources that God provides, recognizing that he is with us in the battle and will ultimately defeat the spiritual forces of this world that stand against him. Until that time, however, we must take our "stand against the schemes of the devil" (Eph 6:11), so that we do not become casualties in the spiritual battle.

BIBLIOGRAPHY

Arnold, Clinton. *Ephesians*. ZECNT. Grand Rapids: Zondervan Academic, 2010.
Barth, Markus. *Ephesians 1–3*. AYBC. New Haven, CT: Yale University Press, 1974.
_____. *Ephesians 4–6*. AYBC. New Haven, CT: Yale University Press, 1974.
Bock, Darrell L. *Ephesians*. TNTC. Downers Grove, IL: IVP Academic, 2019.
Bruce, F.F. *The Epistles to the Colossians, to Philemon, and to the Ephesians*. NICNT. Grand Rapids: Eerdmans, 1984.
Eusebius. *Ecclesiastical History* 2.22, 25.
Hoehner, Harold W. *Ephesians: An Exegetical Commentary*. Grand Rapids: Baker Academic, 2002.
Jerome. *On Illustrious Men*.
Josephus. *Jewish Antiquities* 11.5.7 §173. Translated by Flavius Josephus and William Whiston. *The Works of Josephus: Complete and Unabridged*. Peabody: Hendrickson, 1987.
Lincoln, Andrew T. *Ephesians*. WBC. Grand Rapids: Zondervan Academic, 2014.
MaGee, Gregory S. *Portrait of an Apostle: A Case for Paul's Authorship of Colossians and Ephesians*. Eugene, OR: Pickwick Publications, 2013.
Murphy-O'Connor, Jerome. *St. Paul's Ephesus: Texts and Archaeology*. Collegeville, MN: Liturgical Press, 2008.
Snodgrass, Klyne. *Ephesians*. NIVAC. Grand Rapids: Zondervan Academic, 1996.
Thielman, Frank. *Ephesians*. BECNT. Grand Rapids: Baker Academic, 2010.

13

PHILIPPIANS

A. CHADWICK THORNHILL

CONNECTION POINT

What relevance does this first-century writing have for us today? Paul's letter to the Philippians, though situated in its first-century setting, is a timeless exposition of the gospel. At the center of the letter is a dense theological reflection on the heart of the gospel, which Paul characterizes as the preexistence, incarnation, sacrificial life, death, victorious resurrection, exalted enthronement, and future judgment.[1] The rest of Paul's themes revolve around this, teaching us that at the center of the Christian life is sacrificial love.

It is easy today to get caught up in culture wars and become entrenched in our political parties, denominations, or social and ethnic identities. Paul shows us in this letter that the gospel rests on the foundation of Christ's sacrificial love, and that this love is to be embodied in the lives of his people. For the Christian, this means more listening, more serving, and more

---

[1] See also Matthew W. Bates, *Salvation by Allegiance Alone: Rethinking Faith, Works, and the Gospel of Jesus the King* (Grand Rapids: Baker Academic, 2017).

helping others flourish than infighting, insulting, or looking out for ourselves. It is not hard to imagine that Paul was deeply familiar with Jesus's own call to discipleship: to deny ourselves, take up our cross, and follow him. Philippians teaches us that this life of self-sacrificial love is the way forward for Christian unity, service, and ministry. In other words, Christians ought to be growing more like their Lord. So, reading this letter causes us to pause and ponder, How are we doing? Are we growing in self-sacrificial love and service, or do we live as if the world ought to revolve around us?

With this in mind, consider making this your prayer as you read and study this chapter:

> *Our Father, may you open my eyes to see how I can learn to more deeply love my neighbor through the words of this letter. Lord Jesus, thank you for your sacrificial love, which you call for us to inhabit in our daily lives. Holy Spirit, may you take the words of this letter to speak truth to my heart. May you meet with me as I reflect on the goodness of the gospel of Jesus Christ. Amen.*

The ruins of a sixth-century church in ancient Philippi

SETTING

Recipients

Paul wrote to the Philippians around AD 60.[2] From the book of Acts, we learn that Paul had visited the churches at Philippi on several occasions and that the city was a Roman colony that enjoyed a privileged status in the province of Macedonia (Acts 16:12; 20:6). It was thus a city where allegiance to Rome was considered paramount, and Roman culture, evidenced by the surviving inscriptions as well as what is known of the pagan worship practices of the city, permeated it.[3] The honor and shame culture of the ancient world, which privileged the elevation of one's public status, had firm roots in Philippi as well. The cultural expectation to elevate one's status and achievements in the public eye would have certainly been felt by the Christians of the city in addition to their pagan neighbors.[4]

Theme and Key Passage

Paul's letter to the Philippians is filled with a number of rich themes and theological concepts. The letter mixes the concepts of unity, joy, and suffering, all centrally linked to Paul's hymnic description of the incarnation, humiliation, and glorification of Jesus Christ. Paul demonstrated that the identity of the Philippian believers is grounded in

> **How Many Letters?**
>
> Some scholars have suggested that this letter to the Philippians may be a composite letter, made up of several letters pasted together. One major piece of evidence for this is that "Finally" that begins chapter 3 (KJV) is often seen as a concluding remark, but Paul continued for two more chapters after writing it. Much of the contents of chapter 3 also seem to be an abrupt departure from the themes Paul addressed in the first two chapters. In spite of this, considering there is no manuscript evidence that the letters were ever separated and there are rhetorical explanations for these elements (see especially Witherington, *Paul's Letter to the Philippians*, 15–17), more recent scholarship has increasingly come to see the letter as a whole.

---

[2] Paul's letter to the Philippians, though situated in its first-century setting, is a timeless exposition of the gospel. The dating of the letter is often tied to questions of its provenance, and range from the early to mid-50s to the early 60s AD.

[3] Gorman, *Apostle of the Crucified Lord*, 483–484 (see chap. 8, n. 6). This includes the imperial cult in which Roman emperors and their family members were venerated as gods. See Scot McKnight and Joseph B. Modica, eds., *Jesus Is Lord, Caesar Is Not: Evaluating Empire in New Testament Studies* (Downers Grove, IL: IVP Academic, 2013).

[4] See Joseph H. Hellerman, *Reconstructing Honor in Roman Philippi: Carmen Christi as Cursus Pudorum*, Society for New Testament Studies Monograph Series (Cambridge: Cambridge University Press, 2005), 109.

These are the ruins of the *Via Egnatia* road that went through Philippi. This road was constructed by the Romans in the second century BC. It allowed passage through much of what is modern-day Albania, North Macedonia, Greece, and European Turkey.

this reality: they belong to Christ, have identified with his death and resurrection, and thus actually participate in his identity. What exactly does that mean? As Michael Gorman has demonstrated, Paul understood the gospel not just as something to be believed, but something to become.[5] Through their union with Christ through faith, believers become identified with his likeness, share in both his sufferings and his victory, and thus both proclaim and embody the message of the cross in their lives. Nowhere is this clearer in Paul's letters than here in his letter to the Philippians.

Philippians 2:5 says: "Adopt the same attitude [i.e., "way of thinking"] as that of Christ Jesus."

Purpose and Occasion

Philippians is counted among Paul's "prison letters," as Paul referenced his imprisonment as early as Phil 1:7. Wherever Paul was being held, he references a nearby *praetorium* (Phil 1:13 DARBY). Traditionally it is held

---

[5] Michael J. Gorman, *Becoming the Gospel: Paul, Participation, and Mission* (Grand Rapids: Eerdmans, 2015).

that Paul wrote from his Roman imprisonment as he awaited trial before Caesar in the early AD 60s, though some contend that the letter was written from Ephesus or Caesarea Maritima.[6] In the midst of these challenging circumstances, Paul wrote to the Philippian church to encourage them in the midst of their own struggles, some personal and some collective, in order to show how the life of Jesus could both transform their way of living and offer deep and sustaining joy and peace in the midst of troubling circumstances. As Gorman summarized, "The purpose of the letter is to aid the Philippians in living out their 'citizenship.'"[7]

HIGHLIGHTS IN PHILIPPIANS

The Christ Hymn (Phil 2:5–11)

It may seem strange to start reading a letter in the middle, but the hub of Paul's letter to the Philippians is found in what is often called the "Christ hymn" of Phil 2:5–11.[8] Scholars debate whether this hymn is of Paul's own composing or if it was an early Christian tradition Paul inserted as a part of his letter.[9] Whatever the case, Paul endorsed the theology of the hymn by seeing it as both a theologically rich story (i.e., the gospel) and a pattern for the Christian life. Though full of difficult terms and grammatical constructions in the Greek text, what follows will attempt to explain the basic flow of thought of the hymn in its larger context.[10]

Philippians 2:6a: "who, existing in the form of God"

Paul, connecting back to Phil 2:5, speaks here of Jesus as "existing in the form of God." Does this mean Jesus only appeared to be God, was made God at some point, or is God in a lesser form? As we will see from the overall context of the passage, this is highly unlikely. Paul's word for

---

[6] See the discussion in Ben Witherington III, *Paul's Letter to the Philippians: A Socio-Rhetorical Commentary* (Grand Rapids: Eerdmans, 2011), 9–11.

[7] Gorman, *Apostle of the Crucified Lord*, 488.

[8] For echoes of Philippians 2:6–11 in the rest of the letter, see Gorman, *Apostle of the Crucified Lord*, 489–91.

[9] For a discussion, see Peter T. O'Brien, *The Epistle to the Philippians*, NIGTC (Grand Rapids: Eerdmans, 1991), 186–202.

[10] For detailed discussion of the key exegetical questions in this section, see O'Brien, 203–71.

"form" here (*morphē*) is defined by one lexicon as "the nature or character of something."[11] Jesus exists in the same nature as God, or as the Nicene Creed espouses, "Light from Light, true God from true God, begotten, not made; of the same essence as the Father." Though these are not Paul's words, in light of the contents of this Christ hymn, it is hard to imagine him disagreeing with them.

Philippians 2:6b, c: "did not consider equality with God as something to be exploited."

Here is another key that Paul did not have in mind that Jesus is neither a mere human made divine nor a lesser being trying to grasp at the divine nature. The eternal Son did not cling to the divine nature that he shared as a means to reject incarnation. Rather, in spite of his divinity, or perhaps even because of it, he willfully took on human flesh with all its limitations. Paul's phrase here is literally "to be equal with God."

Philippians 2:7a: "Instead he emptied himself"

The term used here by Paul (*kenoō*) of Jesus "emptying" has become a more formal theological term in Christian tradition (frequently as kenosis, or kenotic). The term is defined by one lexicon as "to take away the power or significance of something,"[12] which fits the meaning Paul had in mind here. Jesus did not lose his divine nature when he became incarnate, but he took on the limitations of human nature, living the full human experience.

Philippians 2:7b: "by assuming the form of a servant"

This is the first of three phrases in the Greek text that describe what Paul meant by the "emptying" in the previous clause. This phrase answers the question, "How did Jesus empty himself"; or "How did this emptying look?" First, Jesus took the form of a servant. Such was not a position of honor in the ancient world; it was the lowest position in society and was often entered into in desperation or by birth.[13] Lynn Cohick notes that the

---

[11] Johannes P. Louw and Eugene A. Nida, *Greek-English Lexicon of the New Testament: Based on Semantic Domains* (New York: United Bible Societies, 1996), 584.

[12] Louw and Nida, 682.

[13] See Joseph H. Hellerman, *Philippians*, Exegetical Guide to the Greek New Testament (Nashville: B&H Academic, 2015), 115.

hymn here may also be echoing the theology of the Suffering Servant of Isaiah 53 who also was described as suffering and experiencing humiliation.[14]

Philippians 2:7c: "taking on the likeness of humanity"

"Likeness" (*homoiōma*) here may reference back to Gen 1:26, where humanity is made in the image and likeness of God. In the incarnation, the eternal Son entered into the nature of human beings, living the life of a human, while also creating a "new humanity" in his death, resurrection, and glorification (1 Cor 15:12–58; Eph 2:15).

Philippians 2:7d: "And when he had come as a man"

Though seemingly a repetition of the previous phrase, a different term is used here, possibly describing the physical nature of Jesus as a man.

Philippians 2:8a: "he humbled himself"

As if the incarnation of the Son of God (trading the realm of heaven for that of fallen earth) were not enough, Jesus further humbled himself. The hymn specifies his humility as that of his death on the cross, but the Gospels also paint the life of Jesus as one of humble service, healing the sick (Matt 9:35), associating with outcasts (Luke 7:34; 15:1–2), and even washing the feet of his disciples (John 13:1–17).

Philippians 2:8b: "by becoming obedient to the point of death"

In creating a new humanity, Jesus, fully human, lived an obedient life to God, one surely empowered by God's Spirit in the fullest possible sense. His life of loving obedience came to an end in his ultimate sacrifice, dying on behalf of even those who put him to death. The crucifixion of Jesus is an event rich with meaning,[15] but Paul focused here on his radical obedience.

Philippians 2:8c: "even to death on a cross"

Crucifixion was both an intentionally excruciating means of death and a form of public humiliation. It proved a useful tool to Rome to suppress lawlessness and would-be revolutionaries. On this, Hellerman notes, "As a

---

[14] Lynn H. Cohick, *Philippians,* The Story of God Bible Commentary (Grand Rapids: Zondervan Academic), 117–18.

[15] See, for example, Joshua M. McNall, *The Mosaic of Atonement: An Integrated Approach to Christ's Work* (Grand Rapids: Zondervan Academic, 2019).

crucified slave, Christ has reached the utter nadir [i.e., depth] of his apparent descent into social oblivion."[16]

Philippians 2:9a: "For this reason God highly exalted him"

On the basis of his obedience even in the midst of a humiliating death, God "highly exalted" Jesus. The irony and "scandal" of the cross could not be more striking. Paul, writing to a Roman colony in which social status was paramount, lifted up the incarnate God-Man (a scandal in itself), who became a slave and offered his life on behalf of humanity through a publicly humiliating execution, as receiving high status and honor from God. Had you asked the average Roman citizen who was most honored by the gods, their last response would have been a crucified slave. This is why Paul wrote elsewhere that trusting in the cross as a means of salvation is perceived by the world as foolishness (1 Cor 1:18–31).

Philippians 2:9b: "and gave him the name"

The phrase "the name of the Lord" is repeated dozens of times throughout the Bible and calls to mind the name of God revealed to Moses at the burning bush ("I AM," or "Yahweh"; Exod 3:15–16).

Philippians 2:9c: "that is above every name"

That Jesus would be given the name above every name would be shocking to the average faithful Jew. Paul, before his encounter with Christ on the road to Damascus, would have likely considered it blasphemy and worthy of death. But the crucified and risen Jesus had now been revealed as the God of Israel incarnate.

Philippians 2:10a: "so that at the name of Jesus"

Paul did not intend for the name Jesus to replace the name Yahweh. Rather, Paul was, in a profound way, identifying Jesus as that same God. The doctrine of the Trinity is one that arises naturally from the words of Scripture itself, as this God whom Paul worshipped exists eternally as Father, Son, and Spirit.

---

[16] Hellerman, *Philippians*, 118.

Philippians 2:10b: *"every knee will bow"*

Paul here, and later in 2:11a ("and every tongue will confess that"), quotes from the text of Isa 45:23, which states, "Every knee will bow to me, / every tongue will swear allegiance." The one speaking in this text in the Old Testament is God himself, so Paul further strengthens his alignment of Jesus sharing in the nature and identity of Israel's God by connecting words about Jesus here with the words of Yahweh in Isaiah 45.

Philippians 2:10c: *"in heaven and on earth and under the earth"*

Paul was clear that Jesus holds supreme authority over all creation, humans, heavenly beings, and those in the underworld.

Philippians 2:11b: *"Jesus Christ is Lord"*

Here, Paul recited one of the central confessions of the Christian faith. Confessing Jesus as "Lord" both identifies him as the One God of the Bible (the Greek word for "Lord" [*kyrios*] is frequently used in the Greek translation of the Old Testament to represent the personal name of God) and recognizes his position as the rightful King of creation. Such a confession is thereby also a "pledge of allegiance" to living under the authority of this magnificent King.

Philippians 2:11c: *"to the glory of God the Father"*

God's glory is manifest in the humility of Jesus Christ. This trait, when found among God's people, brings further honor and praise to his name.

Returning to the line that links the hymn to Phil 2:1–4, Paul presented this hymn as both a model and a means for the Christian life:

Philippians 2:5: *"Adopt the same attitude as that of Christ Jesus."*

The Christian life is one of conforming to the sacrificial love exemplified in the cross of Jesus. The cross is not merely a means of forgiveness or atonement; it is the way of Jesus. As Mark 8:34 and Matt 16:24 attest, submitting to Jesus as Lord means denying oneself, taking up one's cross, and following him. Confessing Jesus as Lord is both a declaration and a way of life, directing all one's aims, activities, and habits to glorifying God in Christ.

Summarizing the import of this message for Paul's Philippian recipients, Hellerman concludes:

The ruins of the ancient theatre in Philippi

> God honors persons of high status in the *ekklesia* who view their power as a resource to be used in the service of others in the community of faith—even if this means renouncing their social status, or, rather, exchanging their privileges in the colony for the superior position of honor and status which they, like Jesus, will receive at the hands of God.[17]

In other words, Paul expected his Philippian faith-family to receive this message about Jesus not just as things to be believed but as a lifestyle to be embodied. Just as Jesus set aside his privileges for the sake of sacrificially serving others, so Paul called on the church to consider the needs of those around them and to meet those needs even if it meant some personal loss or sacrifice. To put it more bluntly, if the divine Son did not consider himself above a life of love, humility, service, and sacrifice, how could those who claim his name dare to do so?

---

[17] Hellerman, *Reconstructing Honor in Roman Philippi*, 166.

Sacrificial Ministry (Phil 1:3–30; 2:12–30; 3:1–11; 4:10–13)

As mentioned previously, everything else in this letter flows around the themes that arise from the hymn of Phil 2:6–11. Imprisoned during this writing, Paul was suffering "in chains" because of his commitment to and proclamation of the gospel (1:13 NIV). Paul considered this, however, a cause for rejoicing (1:18), because this had allowed the gospel to spread further, even to the "imperial guard" (1:13),[18] and had actually emboldened the witness of many other Christians who had heard of his situation (1:14). Though Paul was not thankful for the suffering itself, he saw how God was working in spite of it.[19] Paul hoped that his letter would likewise unify and embolden the Philippians against those who were opposing them in Philippi (1:27–30).[20]

Additionally, Paul commended two of his ministry partners (Timothy and Epaphroditus) for their sacrificial service in spreading the gospel and ministering to the saints (2:12–18). Timothy shows genuine concern for others, has served with Paul, and lives in such a way that prioritizes Christ and his kingdom (2:19–24). Epaphroditus likewise ministered to Paul even though he himself was sick almost to the point of death in doing so (Phil 2:25–30). Both of these men had represented what a life of cruciform-love should look like.

Paul similarly, in his encouragement to resist those who were pressuring the Philippian Gentiles to submit to Jewish marks of identity (Phil 3:1–3;

> **The Faith(fulness) of Jesus**
>
> The phrase Paul used in Phil 3:9 can be found in numerous places in his letters (e.g., Rom 3:22; Gal 2:16, 20; 3:22; Eph 3:12), and scholars debate the best translation. The Greek text is in the genitive case, which means the phrase could be translated as "faith *in* Jesus" (an objective genitive) or "faith" or "faithfulness of Jesus" (a subjective genitive). In Phil 3:9, the double mention of faith in the context probably indicates Paul had in mind Jesus's faithfulness (i.e., his faithful life and obedience to death), which believers then believe, trust, and commit themselves to (i.e., have "faith" in). In other words, Jesus's own faithfulness is the basis for ours, so being united with Christ means we share in, and thus can live in the power of, his obedience.

---

[18] This is likely a reference to the praetorian guards who served as the personal guard of the emperor in Rome or in the city at large. For a discussion, see O'Brien, *The Epistle to the Philippians*, 92–93.

[19] Cf. Rom 8:28; see also Cohick, *Philippians*, 40.

[20] Paul does not specify the nature of these opponents, but it seems best, in light of the social situation and the details in chapter 3, to conclude, as Cohick does, that they likely faced opposition from Jews and Gentile citizens of the city, though for differing reasons (Cohick, 19–21).

circumcision in particular) recounted his own status symbols. In Jewish circles, these would have no doubt elevated Paul's social standing considerably. Paul was circumcised on the eighth day according to Jewish customs, of the faithful tribe of Benjamin, a scrupulous follower of the law according to the traditions of the Pharisees, to the point of calling himself "blameless" (i.e., no one could accuse him of breaking the law; Phil 3:4–6). Yet all of these means of elevating his status he considered worthless. Here again we find echoes of Phil 2:6–11. Paul served a divine Son who humbled himself, became a slave, and died in public humiliation. Yet, because God glorified Jesus, Paul understood God does not show favoritism based on social standing, ethnicity, or any other factors. For Paul, knowing Christ was of greater value than any accomplishment, status, or rank he could obtain. For Paul, only the faithfulness of Christ (i.e., his obedient life and death; Phil 3:9) enables us to know and love God. So believers share both in "the power of his resurrection" (the gift of new life) and "the fellowship of his sufferings" (our self-denial, taking up our cross, and even facing suffering and persecution in his great name; cf. Phil. 3:10–11). Because of this, Paul can say in Phil 4:13 that he could do "all things" through the One who gave him strength. He could suffer or thrive, have plenty or nothing, be hungry or fed, because knowing Christ was enough![21]

> ### Joy and Anxiety
>
> Though the New Testament speaks only on occasion about "anxiety" (e.g., Matt 6:25–34; 1 Pet 5:7), Paul's words in Phil 4:6 are sometimes seen as a quick fix to those who tend toward anxiety disorders. "Don't be anxious, just pray" is sometimes offered as an easy solution. But those who have experienced anxiety, depression, or other mental health struggles know that there are often no quick fixes, and sometimes they are left, like Paul, with a "thorn in the flesh" (2 Cor 12:7–10). One useful tool, however, that cognitive-behavioral therapy has promoted, is listening to one's "self-talk" and replacing the lies anxiety can produce (often, what-ifs) with truth. This seems quite similar to the approach Paul commends here, to present our need to God, to express gratitude to God, and to concentrate our thoughts upon things that are true, honorable, just, pure, lovely, commendable, and excellent (Phil 4:6–9). This, however, is a daily struggle, not an easy solution, but God can equip those who struggle to persevere through these challenges.

The Cruciform Christian Life (Phil 2:1–4; 2:12–18; 3:12–21; 4:1–9)

Paul described his own experiences in cruciformity as well as those of his ministry partners. He also directed the Philippians to follow the way of

---

[21] A great resource in the spirit of Paul's words is Dallas Willard, *Life Without Lack: Living in the Fullness of Psalm 23* (Nashville: Thomas Nelson, 2018).

the cross. As mentioned previously, Paul framed the Christ hymn (Phil 2:6–11) with his call for the Philippians to forsake self-centered lifestyles and pursue unity in Christ through other-focused, self-sacrificial, love.[22] This would take effort on their part ("work out your own salvation," Phil 2:12), in addition to cooperating with the transformative work of the Holy Spirit in their lives and in their community. The unity of the local church, a "fellowship of differents" who come from different ethnic, economic, and cultural backgrounds, can indeed only be accomplished when a selfless spirit takes root.[23] This requires growing in maturity, putting the truth into practice, and embracing the ideals of the kingdom of heaven (cf. Phil 3:12–21),[24] not the empire of Caesar (i.e., the world and its empires).[25] It requires a rootedness and trust in the provisions of God so we do not see ourselves as threatened and at war with our neighbors, but see all we have as the provisions of God for us, which we must hold with open arms toward others.

BIBLIOGRAPHY

Bates, Matthew W. *Salvation by Allegiance Alone: Rethinking Faith, Works, and the Gospel of Jesus the King*. Grand Rapids: Baker Academic, 2017.

Cohick, Lynn H. *Philippians*. The Story of God Bible Commentary. Grand Rapids: Zondervan Academic, 2013.

Gorman, Michael J. *Apostle of the Crucified Lord: A Theological Introduction to Paul and His Letters*. Grand Rapids: Eerdmans, 2017.

―――. *Becoming the Gospel: Paul, Participation, and Mission*. Grand Rapids: Eerdmans, 2015.

Hellerman, Joseph H. *Philippians*. Exegetical Guide to the Greek New Testament. Nashville: B&H Academic, 2015.

―――. *Reconstructing Honor in Roman Philippi: Carmen Christi as Cursus Pudorum*. Society for New Testament Studies Monograph Series 132. Cambridge: Cambridge University Press, 2005.

Louw, Johannes P., and Eugene A. Nida. *Greek-English Lexicon of the New Testament: Based on Semantic Domains*. New York: United Bible Societies, 1996.

McKnight, Scot. *A Fellowship of Differents: Showing the World God's Design for Life Together*. Grand Rapids: Zondervan, 2015.

---

[22] Or as Cohick calls it, a "de-centering" of the self (Cohick, *Philippians*, 95).

[23] McKnight, *A Fellowship of Differents* (see chap. 8, n. 19).

[24] On the ideals of the kingdom, there is no better place to start than the Sermon on the Mount in Matthew 5–7, the charter of the kingdom of God; but also here in Phil 4:8.

[25] See Gorman, *Apostle of the Crucified Lord*, 485.

McKnight, Scot, and Joseph B. Modica, eds. *Jesus Is Lord, Caesar Is Not: Evaluating Empire in New Testament Studies.* Downers Grove: IVP Academic, 2013.

McNall, Joshua M. *The Mosaic of Atonement: An Integrated Approach to Christ's Work.* Grand Rapids: Zondervan Academic, 2019.

O'Brien, Peter T. *The Epistle to the Philippians.* NIGTC. Grand Rapids: Eerdmans, 1991.

Silva, Moisés. *Philippians.* BECNT. Grand Rapids: Baker Academic, 2005.

Thielman, Frank. *Philippians.* NIVAC. Grand Rapids: Zondervan Academic, 1995.

Willard, Dallas. *Life Without Lack: Living in the Fullness of Psalm 23.* Nashville: Thomas Nelson, 2018.

Witherington, Ben, III. *Paul's Letter to the Philippians: A Socio-Rhetorical Commentary.* Grand Rapids: Eerdmans, 2011.

14

COLOSSIANS

EUNICE J. CHUNG

CONNECTION POINT

What relevance does this first-century writing have for us today? Today, an increasing number of people are creating their own customized spirituality by selecting attractive elements from various religions and a myriad of other sources. This approach, built on individual interests and experiences, has wide appeal in our society that is often very suspect of organized religion or absolute truth. The result is that today's society is becoming more spiritual, but this spirituality is certainly not Christian.

In his letter to the Colossians, the apostle Paul declared a strikingly different message. He warned us against seeking a buffet of spiritual practices that appeals to personal preference, and to instead anchor our faith solely in Jesus Christ. The supremacy of Christ demands our complete and faithful worship, Paul wrote, and there are catastrophic consequences when we look to anything or anyone other than Christ as the source of our salvation or purpose in life.

Colossians reminds modern-day believers of the supremacy and majesty of Christ. This letter displays the glorious power and divinity of Jesus and calls us to faithful service to him. If we look to him, we will not lack anything of spiritual importance. What a hopeful message to proclaim in a world that is constantly looking everywhere for meaning and purpose! Jesus is indeed the one in whom "God was pleased to have all his fullness dwell" (Col 1:19).

With this in mind, consider making this your prayer as you read and study this chapter:

> *Lord, we pray that you would remind us of the centrality and glory of Christ. He is the image of the invisible God, through whose sacrifice we are now reconciled to you. As we study this letter, may our love and worship before you increase as we meditate on what you graciously have given and continue to supply. We pray that whatever we do, in word or deed, that we would do it all in the name of the Lord Jesus while giving thanks to God the Father through him. Amen.*

SETTING

Recipients

Paul[1] wrote to the Colossians from prison around AD 60–62.[2] Placing Colossae in its geographical and historical context reminds us that Paul

---

[1] Although debate surrounds whether or not Paul wrote this letter, we can safely assume that he is indeed the author. The unique language and vocabulary, stylistic difference, and an absence of certain prominent Pauline themes may bring Pauline authorship into question, but the style of Colossians parallels Ephesians, and its context aligns with Philemon. The uniqueness of language can be attributed to the uniqueness of the Colossian Heresy that Paul addresses and perhaps the use of a particular scribe. Furthermore, the early church universally accepted Colossians as an authentic Pauline writing. As Douglas Moo notes, "As an authentic letter of Paul (and so recognized by the earliest Christians), Colossians richly deserves its place in the Christian canon." Douglas J. Moo, *The Letters to the Colossians and to Philemon* (Grand Rapids: Eerdmans, 2008), 40. For a defense of the authenticity of Colossians, see Gregory S. MaGee, *Portrait of an Apostle: A Case for Paul's Authorship of Colossians and Ephesians* (Eugene, OR: Pickwick, 2013).

[2] Paul's location and the circumstances he faced when writing this letter are matters of debate among biblical scholars. The traditional viewpoint is that Paul wrote Colossians along with the three other Prison Epistles (Ephesians, Philippians, and Philemon) during his first Roman imprisonment during the early 60s of the first century. While this has been the predominant view throughout church history, some have suggested that Paul wrote earlier, perhaps from Ephesus or another Roman city that was located closer to the city of Colossae. For many, an earlier dating is attractive because of the close link between this

Remains of the ancient city of Colossae

wrote to real people in a real town to address real problems. The city of Colossae was nestled in the Lycus Valley, a mountainous and volcanic region in the Roman province of Asia (in modern-day Turkey). A fairly insignificant city in the first-century Roman world, it is unlikely that you would have ever heard of Colossae if Paul had not written this letter. For many years, the local economy was supported by an old highway from Ephesus that ran through the city. However, when the Romans built a new highway that bypassed them completely, Colossae's importance declined. By the time Paul wrote to the Colossians, the city was overshadowed by more important cities in the region such as Hierapolis and Laodicea, nearby cities that Paul references in his final greetings (Col 4:13).[3]

---

letter and the letter to Philemon. However, the overlapping similarities between Colossians and Ephesians enhance the traditional argument. The two letters address many of the same subjects, suggesting that they were written at the same time and from the same place. If Ephesians was written from Rome, as many have concluded, it can be suggested that Paul wrote Colossians during his first Roman imprisonment around the years AD 60–62.

[3] In Rev 3:14–22, the apostle John delivers a critique of Laodicea and uses a metaphor of hot and cold water. Laodicea relied on Colossae and its cold springs. This metaphor points out that although the Laodiceans viewed themselves as self-sufficient, they were not. It also highlights part of the spiritual significance of Colossae.

Whatever notoriety Colossae had at the time Paul wrote this letter quickly vanished a short time later. Ancient historians such as Tacitus and Eusebius both refer to an earthquake that ravished Colossae and other cities in the Lycus Valley in the early 60s of the first century.[4] Colossae was not immediately rebuilt, and its inhabitants quickly relocated.

We know little about the early history of the church in Colossae, but it was likely founded by Epaphras, who is addressed twice in the letter (Col 1:7; 4:12). Most likely, multiple house churches gathered in Colossae, one of which received Paul's letter to Philemon. Because the inhabitants of the city came from a variety of backgrounds—there were Romans, Jews, and local Phrygians living in the area—Colossian churches were also diverse, composed of both Jewish and Gentile Christians.

Little is known of Paul's relationship to the Colossians. Some have suggested that Paul never visited Colossae, but this is difficult to conclude with certainty. Located only 120 miles from Ephesus, it is entirely possible that Paul made at least one trip to the Lycus Valley during this three-year stay in Ephesus (Acts 19) or during one of his missionary journeys. Whatever the case, Paul had great affection for the Colossians and was deeply concerned about their spiritual progress.

Theme and Key Passage

The clear theme in Colossians is the supremacy and fullness of Christ. He is described in the letter as the Son of God, fully divine, supreme, sufficient, and above all things. Paul first declared Christ in his supreme glory (Col 1:1–2:3), defended his deity against false teaching (Col 2:4–23), then exhorted the church to live in the fullness of Christ (Colossians 3–4), a progression that moves from doctrinal and apologetic concerns to their practical implications. A key passage in Colossians that encapsulates these themes is found in 2:6–7:

> So then, just as you have received Christ Jesus as Lord, continue to walk in him, being rooted and built up in him and established in the faith, just as you were taught, and overflowing with gratitude.

---

[4] See Tacitus (*Ann.* 14:27) and Eusebius (*Chronica* 1.210).

Purpose and Occasion

Paul wrote Colossians in response to what was taking place in the region. Imagine this: Paul was imprisoned, and Epaphras visited him and provided him with updates on the Colossian church. Paul heard some troublingly news that false teaching was circulating among the local believers, so he wrote a firm but loving letter to correct the situation.

So, what was this wayward teaching that was of such concern to Paul? Often labeled the Colossian Heresy, Paul described it as a deceptive philosophy based on human tradition and the world, not on Christ (Col 2:8). It is difficult to pinpoint exactly what the false teaching entailed, because Paul was more concerned about dismantling the teaching than describing it. The teaching, however, undermined the purity of the gospel. Paul's references to holy days and dietary restrictions (Col 2:16) seems to suggest Jewish influence. His instruction also appears to counter pagan elements characterized by asceticism, mysticism (Col 2:17), or even early beliefs that later became associated with Gnosticism. The false teachers were advocating for a syncretistic teaching that blended Jewish and pagan elements, which came at the cost of worshipping Jesus as Christ and Lord.

Paul responded with a vivid and glorious description of the supremacy and fullness of Jesus Christ. He is the image of the invisible God (Col 1:15) who is above all things. He is Creator, Savior, Sanctifier, and our model of faithfulness. In him is all wisdom (Col 2:3) and knowledge (Col 2:2), and it was through him that God accomplished his saving work and peace (Col 1:20). The mystery of Christ is now fully revealed to the saints (Col 1:26) who are now one in him (Col 3:11). In light of the nature of Christ and the salvation that he has accomplished, Paul urged the Colossians to pursue the things that are above (Col 3:1), to live in a manner that reflected their devotion to Christ (Col 3:12–15), and to do all things in Christ's name, while always giving thanks to the Father (Col 3:17).

HIGHLIGHTS IN COLOSSIANS

Introduction (Col 1:1–2)

Paul greeted the Colossians with the phrase, "Grace to you" (Col 1:2), a common Roman greeting with a definitive Christian twist. Unlike the prevalent cultural understanding, the grace that Paul described is God's saving grace. As Robert Wall states, "Paul's vocabulary of God's salvation . . . underscores the stark contrast between God's saving grace and the secular forms of salvation offered by the ruling elites of the Roman world."[5] Even today, Christians understand the word *grace* in a much deeper manner than how it is perceived by the world.

> **Bearing Spiritual Fruit**
>
> Throughout the Bible the idea of being fruitful characterizes the believer's life. From the beginning, God commanded Adam and Eve to "be fruitful and multiply" (Gen 1:22 KJV). Jesus echoes this call to be fruitful by reminding his audience that he is the source of fruitfulness. He himself is the vine (John 15:1–8) and his followers are the branches. Paul lists other fruits of salvation in Colossians 1 and 3. Galatians 5:22–23 also famously lists the fruit of the Spirit, a beautiful description of the ongoing work of the Holy Spirit to guide the believer to continue to bear fruit in his or her life.

Paul's Prayer (Col 1:3–14)

Paul launched into a beautiful prayer for the Colossian church. The prayer is divided into two parts: thanksgiving for the Colossian saints (Col 1:3–8) and supplication for their maturity (Col 1:9–14). Paul based his thanksgiving on what he had heard about their faith in Christ and their love for one another (Col 1:4). He described the gospel as continuously bearing fruit not just in Colossae but all over the world (Col 1:6). He prayed that the Colossians would "be filled with the knowledge of his will in all wisdom and spiritual understanding" (Col 1:9).

Paul painted a vivid picture of salvation: God the Father has rescued believers from darkness into his beloved Son's kingdom of light (Col 1:13). The language used in this passage emphasizes that God's work of rescuing believers has already been completed, that the enemy has been defeated, and that believers are currently members of God's kingdom. Paul reminded the Colossians that God's work of salvation through Jesus was full and sufficient and that God had extended the invitation for saints to share in Christ's inheritance.

Throughout Colossians, Paul emphasized three important virtues, each of which were introduced in Paul's introductory prayer: wisdom, knowledge, and gratitude. What is the basis and foundation for these virtues? The answer is actually not a *what* but a *who*. Quite simply, it is Jesus. As Paul explained, the centrality of Christ plays a pivotal role in attaining wisdom, living out the knowledge with which one has been filled, and becomes the foundation for unending gratitude.

---

[5] Robert W. Wall, *Colossians and Philemon*, The IVP New Testament Commentary Series 12 (Downers Grove, IL: IVP Academic, 2010), 38.

The Centrality of Christ (Col 1:15–23)

Paul's beautiful and poetic description of Jesus is truly one of the great Christological passages of the New Testament. Although this section could be an excerpt from an early Christian hymn or confessional statement, it could also simply be Paul's hymnic response to the wonder of Christ's glory. Paul boldly asserted Jesus's deity, writing that he is the image of the invisible God (Col 1:15; cf. 1 Tim 1:17) in whom the entire fullness of God dwells bodily (Col 1:19). In sum, Jesus is fully God, the Creator and Sustainer (Col 1:15–17), and the reconciling Savior of the world (Col 1:18–20).

The reconciling work of Christ has accomplished peace and was made possible by his own blood (Col 1:20).

> **The Hypostatic Union**
>
> The *hypostatic union* is used to describe Jesus's nature as fully God and fully human. The hypostatic union teaches that both the divine and human nature are joined in the one person of Jesus. They are not mixed, but as the Chalcedonian Creed says, Jesus possessed these two natures "without confusion, without change, without division, without separation." Why is this important? God the Son in Jesus became human. As the God-Man, Jesus is the Mediator and Reconciler. He is the Great High Priest who went before God to offer the ultimate and final sacrifice for sin, himself (Heb 9:11–28). See John 1:1–18; Phil 2:6–11; and Heb 1:1–3 for other important texts that reveal who Jesus is.

Although once in opposition against God, believers now possess friendship, peace, and fellowship with him because of the blood of Jesus that was "shed on the cross." Though believers were once part of the domain of darkness, alienated and hostile to God (Col 1:21), and dead in sins and trespasses (Eph 2:5), they now enjoy reconciliation with God, a reconciliation that was accomplished by Christ in order for us to be presented as "holy, faultless, and blameless before him" (Col 1:22). In response, we are given a mandate to continue this ministry of reconciliation with others, further reflecting Christ's work of reconciliation within our own lives.[6]

In his prayer, Paul referred to Jesus as the firstborn on two occasions, once as firstborn over creation (Col 1:15) and again as firstborn from the dead (Col 1:18). To clarify, Paul's reference to Jesus as the firstborn over creation is not to be understood as a reference to his existence, for Christ is the eternal Son of God and uncreated. The term is used, rather, in reference to Jesus's supremacy and preeminence over all of creation (Ps 89:27).[7]

---

[6] See Paul's letter to Philemon as an example of Paul's ministry of reconciliation on behalf of a runaway slave, Onesimus.

[7] James D. G. Dunn further clarifies the proper understanding of Christ as firstborn. He writes, "That 'firstborn' must denote primacy over creation, and not just within creation, is

With regard to Paul's reference to Jesus as the firstborn from the dead (Rev 1:5), Paul reminds us that Jesus's physical resurrection is the basis of our own guarantee that believers will one day experience a bodily resurrection as well (1 Corinthians 15).

Paul's Ministry (Col 1:24–2:3)

Paul noted that his work completed "what [was] lacking in Christ's afflictions for his body, that is, the church" (Col 1:24). Paul was not saying that Christ's work is insufficient; rather, he asserted that Christ's work is incomplete in the sense that there is still work to be done to spread the gospel and grow the church. Paul understood his task as fulfilling Christ's call to strengthen the church, to proclaim the once hidden mystery (Col 1:26–27) revealed to both Jews and Gentiles, and to present all mature in Christ (Col 1:28).[8] Paul's commitment can be seen in his references to his suffering and tireless ministry (Col 1:24, 29; 2:1). The idea of suffering as Christian living might seem foreign to modern Western Christians, but the apostles embraced this calling to suffer for the name of Jesus Christ as an honor (Acts 5:41; Phil 1:29). Ultimately, Paul was willing to endure all things in order to "present everyone mature in Christ" (Col 1:28). Likewise, it was his desire for all Christians to "be encouraged and joined together in love, so that they [might] have all the riches of complete understanding and have the knowledge of God's mystery—Christ" (Col 2:2).

Note the rich language Paul used to describe Christ and being in him. The once hidden mystery is a "glorious wealth" (Col 1:27) in which are the "treasures of wisdom and knowledge" (Col 2:3) and through which the saints can receive the "riches of complete understanding" (Col 2:2). Similar to Jesus's parables of the hidden treasure and the pearl of great price,

---

indicated by the conjunction linking the two verses: he is 'firstborn of all creation *because* in him were created all things,' that is everything, the universe, the totally of created entities . . . Likewise in the final clause of the verse if 'everything was created and exist through him and for him,' that presumably also distances him from creation as creation's means and end." Dunn, *The Epistles to the Colossians and Philemon*, NIGTC (Grand Rapids: Eerdmans, 1996), 90–91.

[8] Christ gives a mandate in the Great Commission that the apostles in the book of Acts obey to spread the gospel to the nations. What Christ enacted, Paul continued and fulfilled with great joy and suffering. F. F. Bruce observes, "The present context rules out any suggestion that the reconciliation effected by the death of Christ needs to be supplemented." Bruce, *The Epistles to the Colossians, Philemon, and to the Ephesians*, NICNT (Grand Rapids: Eerdmans, 1984), 1541, Kindle.

The likely location of the Acropolis of the ancient city of Colossae

Paul utilized financial language to heighten the majesty and status of not only Jesus himself but the access a believer gains through faith.

Paul and the Colossian Heresy (Col 2:4–23)

Once Paul reflected on who Christ is and what he did, he directly addressed the Colossian Heresy. Paul was concerned that believers not be taken captive by worldly teaching that led them to needless division or detractions from the preeminence of Christ. Perhaps as somewhat of a surprise, Paul emphasized the importance of gratitude in this section. Rather than merely addressing the fine points of various theological positions, Paul observed that the overflow of gratitude for what Christ did helps to ensure that believers not fall prey to heresy (Col 2:7). Gratitude reminds believers of the spiritual circumcision they have received through the God-Man,[9] who has erased sin's debt and brought complete victory. In response, Paul encouraged the Colossians to worship God in a manner that is consistent with his character and nature and to be aware of deceptive teaching and

---

[9] Circumcision, a longstanding outward physical sign that demonstrated one's association with the people of Israel, is used in this passage in reference to the spiritual work of Christ, a work that is of greater significance (Ezek 44:9; Rom 2:29).

worldly philosophies (Col 2:8–15), such as legalistic attitude over food or holidays (Col 2:16–17), mystical practices that promoted visions and angel worship (Col 2:18–19),[10] or depriving the body (Col 2:20–23). How often do we look for a mystical or physical experience instead of focusing on the sufficiency of Christ? As Paul's words reveal, straying from the spiritual blessings found in Christ never enhances one's spiritual life but rather can bring great harm.

Paul invoked military language to highlight the larger spiritual reality of the Colossian Heresy. He rejoiced in the fact that they were "well ordered" (Col 2:5), a term that would have immediately invoked military imagery to a first-century audience. Here, the Greek word *taxis* was a military term used to describe soldiers standing shoulder-to-shoulder in an orderly formation. Paul built on this military imagery in Col 2:15, declaring that Christ's death and resurrection "disarmed the rulers and authorities and disgraced them publicly [and] triumphed over them in him." When a Roman legion returned from victory in the first century, they would have occasionally received a triumphal procession, a public parade as a sign of domination and conquest of the defeated enemy. What Christ did, Paul wrote, is even greater. Scot McKnight notes, "The ultimate paradox is now clear: the location to celebrate victory is not the Roman Forum or the public streets of Roman cities but instead the precise place where Rome thought it was dominant: the

A work by Marco Dente from 1527 entitled *A Roman Legion*

---

[10] The unique language of this verse has led to much debate and study. The false teachers may have been emphasizing either the worship of angels as spiritual beings or a practice in which angels were mediators or facilitators for worship. Those who uphold the latter viewpoint regarding Jewish mystical and apocalyptic literature, which describes worship-type experiences, allowed participants to worship alongside the angels before God (Moo, *Colossians and Philemon*, 227). While it is difficult to make strong assertions about the background of this passage, it is perhaps best to conclude that the Colossian Heresy took elements of both Jewish thought and pagan ideas and mixed them with Christianity to develop a method of living that, as Moo describes it, was "a syncretistic mix" (Moo, 229).

cross."[11] Christ attained eternal victory not on a physical battlefield but through his sacrificial work on the cross.

The Christian's New Identity (Col 3:1–17)

Having emphasized the preeminence of Christ and the dangers of looking to anything other than him for salvation or as the basis of faith, Paul transitioned to how these truths apply to his readers. First, Paul emphasized that believers have been raised with Christ, which serves as the foundation for their new life.[12] As a result of their relationship to him, believers are to put off the old self and its vices (Col 3:5–9) and instead put on the new self and its virtues (Col 3:12–15).[13]

This section of application reminds readers that Christian ethics and morality bear significant weight in the reality of the gospel in the life of a believer. Christian character matters a great deal. Christianity is not blind obedience to a set of rules but is transformative in nature. The daily renewal to become more like Christ is often referred to as the process of sanctification. Paul described this process as the putting off of sinful desires, thoughts, and behaviors and the putting on of all that reflects Christ. As chosen, holy, and dearly loved by God, believers cheerfully put on virtues and practices, even willingly forgiving others who may have wronged them. Above all, one must put on love. Love is foundational to all the other virtues; and as Paul emphasized, perfectly unifies believers not only to God but to one another in one body with Christ as the head (Col 1:18). In this body, there is no distinction in ethnicity, religious background, intellect, cultural awareness, or economic status, for Christ is all and in all.[14] As racial and economic divides persist in our culture today, Paul's words serve

---

[11] Scot McKnight, *The Letter to the Colossians*, NICNT (Grand Rapids: Eerdmans, 2018), 260.

[12] Colossians 3:1 begins with the phrase, "So if you have been raised with Christ." In the Greek, this phrase is classified as a first-class conditional, meaning that the premise or condition is assumed as fact. Believers being raised with Christ is a reality and not simply wishful thinking. The raising becomes the foundation for the subsequent application Paul exhorted the Colossians to embody in chapters 3–4.

[13] Throughout the New Testament, Paul compared and contrasted vices and virtues to highlight the vast difference of the individual before and after conversion. For examples, see Rom 1:18–32; 1 Cor 5:9–11; 6:9–10; Gal 5:19–21; Eph 5:3–6; 1 Thess 4:3–8; 1 Tim 1:9–10; 2 Tim 3:1–5; Titus 3:2–3.

[14] In Roman culture, the term *barbarian* was used as an insult to "uncultured" people who did not speak Greek. Scythians were viewed as dull people and mocked in Greek poetry as wild beasts (McKnight, *Letter to the Colossians*, 315). See Gal 3:28 and Eph 1:23 for similar statements by Paul.

as a powerful reminder that God's saving grace is not discriminatory and shows no favoritism. Paul ended this section with a powerful exhortation, "And whatever you do, in word or in deed, do everything in the name of the Lord Jesus, giving thanks to God the Father through him" (Col 3:17). Every facet of one's life is to be in grateful response to our God's great work.

The Christian House (Col 3:18–4:1)

Paul continued his treatment of the practical relevance of the gospel by referring to the manner in which believers should relate to one another in the home. Regardless of one's particular role in the home, the imperative in this section is to serve and love one another. Contrary to common thought and practice in the Roman world, Paul argued that mutual respect and honor must be evident among the members of a household.

Wives are called to voluntarily submit, not because of the husband's absolute authority or of some innate superiority, but as a Spirit-motivated response. Christ serves as the perfect example of submission—he is neither inferior nor unequal to God the Father but joyfully and obediently submitted to the Father's will (Phil 2:1–11). Similarly, Christ is the perfect example for husbands, as he gave his life as an act of selfless love. Both roles in a marriage involve selfless action and are based on a Spirit-filled life.

Paul instructed children to obey their parents, and fathers to not exasperate their children. Paul's address to children would have been highly unusual in the first-century world given that children were often viewed merely as the father's legal property, with a status barely higher than that of a slave. In the Roman world, the father controlled virtually all aspects of a child's life, from determining whether a newborn infant would live or die to choosing whom the child would marry. Thus, Paul's instruction to children and to fathers was countercultural.

Finally, understand that Paul was not condoning slavery when he instructed masters to treat their slaves "justly and fairly" (Col 4:1). On the contrary, he was encouraging masters to understand that they themselves "have a Master in heaven," a reminder that their treatment of others must be commensurate with their relationship with Christ.[15] While neither Paul

---

[15] Bruce notes, "The household codes did not set out to abolish or reshape existing social structures, but to Christianize them. As far as slavery was concerned, it took a long time for the essential incompatibility of the institution with the ethic of the gospel, or

nor the early church possessed the means to abolish the practice of slavery in Roman society, Paul's letter to Philemon, which again was written concurrently with Colossians, indicates that Paul viewed slavery as incompatible with the gospel message.

Conclusion (Col 4:2–18)

Paul concluded this letter with final instructions (Col 4:2–6) and final greetings (Col 4:7–18). Paul reminded the Colossians to be prayerful, thankful, and wise. Notice that Paul did not pray for an open prison door but an open door to share the gospel. When faced with suffering, our default prayer is often deliverance from suffering. However, Paul's practice was instead to use each occasion, no matter how difficult, as an opportunity to advance the gospel (Phil 1:12–14).

Paul sent greetings from Jewish co-laborers (Col 4:10–11) and Gentile co-laborers (Col 4:12–15), then concluded, as was his custom, with a handwritten greeting. Although it is easy to overlook a list of names, this list reminds us that the Bible is a compilation of real documents written to real people in a real time and place. They are part of the legacy of faith upon whose shoulders we stand, men and women of God who faithfully believed and vigorously defended the supremacy and fullness of Christ above all.

BIBLIOGRAPHY

Bruce, F. F. *The Epistles to the Colossians, Philemon, and to the Ephesians.* NICNT. Grand Rapids: Eerdmans, 1984.

Dunn, James D. G. *The Epistles to the Colossians and Philemon.* NIGTC. Grand Rapids: Eerdmans, 1996.

Eusebius. *Chronicle.* N.p.: Beloved, 2015.

Garland, David E. *Colossians, Philemon.* NIVAC. Grand Rapids: Zondervan Academic, 1998.

MaGee, Gregory S. *Portrait of an Apostle: A Case for Paul's Authorship of Colossians and Ephesians.* Eugene, OR: Pickwick, 2013.

McKnight, Scot. *The Letter to the Colossians.* NICNT. Grand Rapids: Eerdmans, 2018.

---

indeed with the biblical doctrine of creation, to be properly assimilated by the general Christian consciousness" (Bruce, *The Epistles to the Colossians, Philemon, and to the Ephesians*, 2770, Kindle).

Moo, Douglas J. *The Letters to the Colossians and to Philemon*. PNTC. Grand Rapids: Eerdmans, 2008.

Tacitus. *The Annals of Imperial Rome*. Translated by Alfred John Church and Williams Jackson Brodbribb. 1876; n.p. Pantianos Classics, 2017.

Wall, Robert W. *Colossians and Philemon*. The IVP New Testament Commentary Series. Downers Grove, IL: IVP Academic, 2010.

15

1 AND 2 THESSALONIANS

JEFFREY R. DICKSON

CONNECTION POINT

What relevance do these first-century writings have for us today? In a world that is culturally diverse and technologically advanced, it is only natural to question the modern relevance of the New Testament. As these ancient writings are read and studied, however, it quickly becomes apparent that while society has changed greatly over the last two millennia, modern Christians face several of the same challenges and share many of the same concerns as the first generations of Christians. It is not uncommon for modern Christians to ask questions such as, "Where do our friends and family go when they die?"; "How should we respond when our faith is opposed?"; "What are some ways that we can grow in our faith in Christ?"; and "What is God's will for our lives as Christians?" Although the world has changed in many ways since the first century, the instruction the apostle Paul provided in 1 and 2 Thessalonians remains a source of comfort, inspiration, and guidance for Christians today.

Living out the Christian faith is no easy task, even in ideal circumstances. Our natural desires are often contrary to the Spirit's direction in our lives (Gal 5:16–18), and we are frequently prone to spiritual weariness and indifference. In addition, many Christians around the world live in an environment in which opposition to the gospel is a common experience. Although Christian teaching was widely respected just decades ago, an increasing number of people in modern society regard it as radical and even dangerous. In sum, opposition to the Christian faith was not something particular to the first-century church. Christians around the world today experience many of the same hardships and challenges that faced the first-century church of Thessalonica.

In Paul's correspondence with the Thessalonians, he directly addressed the subject of growing in holiness in anticipation of the return of Jesus. Rather than assuring those going through difficult times that their troubles would soon vanish, Paul encouraged everyone, regardless of circumstances, to focus on their eternal hope. The various admonitions and instructions throughout his letters emphasize that in order to remain faithful to Christ and endure difficult times without losing hope, it is essential that we become aware of God's eternal plan and what he has promised believers. Only by living with an eternal perspective can we experience the peace that comes from God and live with a hope that is not shaken by life's circumstances.

With this in mind, consider making this your prayer as you read and study this chapter:

Father God, I am grateful that you are greater than our many questions and concerns. Thank you for making a way for me to be a part of your work on this earth. I ask that you would use this study of 1 and 2 Thessalonians to encourage me in my spiritual walk and that you would teach me how I should live and serve you in this broken and volatile world. Amen.

SETTING

Recipients

Both 1 and 2 Thessalonians are addressed "To the church of the Thessalonians" by the apostle Paul around AD 51–52 (1 Thess 1:1; 2 Thess 1:1).[1]

---

[1] Though Paul identified himself as the author of both 1 and 2 Thessalonians (1 Thess

Macedonia

The city of Thessalonica was the capital of Macedonia, an ancient Roman province in modern-day Greece. In Paul's day, Thessalonica was of great

---

1:1; 2:18; 2 Thess 1:1; 3:17), there is some question whether the apostle is responsible for writing both letters (especially 2 Thessalonians), given that they are so similar. While shared style and verbiage is typically counted as evidence for a common author, some have suggested that a later unknown writer attempted to imitate Paul's style and message in the composition of 2 Thessalonians. That said, is it very unlikely that the shared words, tone, and themes found in both these works is indicative of two different authors. The internal and external evidence suggests that both works were in fact written by Paul (as they both claim) and that the similarities point to a common author and the fact that they were written to the same audience during a short period of time of one another. For a more complete presentation of this debate, see D. Michael Martin, *1, 2 Thessalonians*, NAC (Nashville: Holman Reference, 1995), 25–29; and Jeffery D. A. Weima, *1–2 Thessalonians*, BECNT (Grand Rapids: Baker Academic, 2014), 40–53.

Though these letters are found near the end of the New Testament, the letters to the Thessalonians are among some of Paul's earliest works. Given that the contents of 1 Thessalonians appear to correspond to what was going on in and after what occurred in Acts 17, many scholars believe that this letter was written during Paul's second missionary journey. The contents of 2 Thessalonians leads many of these same thinkers to the conclusion that this second letter was written two months after the first. This would place the date of the writing of both these letters to around AD 51–52.

political and commercial significance and was home to a population of approximately 200,000 people. Located on one of Rome's important east-west trading routes (the *Via Egnatia*), this thriving city was visited by many travelers, including Paul, who first arrived in the city on his second missionary journey (Acts 17:1–9). It is clear from the narrative in Acts that the church that was founded in Thessalonica would have included a mixture of Jewish and Gentile Christians.

Theme and Key Passages

It is difficult to capture the essence of two different works even if they are written by the same author. That said, a two-part uniting theme that successfully describes the major contribution of both 1 and 2 Thessalonians is sanctification in view of the day of the Lord.

> 1 Thess 4:1: "Additionally then, brothers and sisters, we ask and encourage you in the Lord Jesus, that as you have received instruction from us on how you should live and please God—as you are doing—do this even more."
>
> 2 Thess 2:14–15: "He called you to this through our gospel, so that you might obtain the glory of our Lord Jesus Christ. So then, brothers and sisters, stand firm and hold to the traditions you were taught, whether by what we said or what we wrote."

Purpose and Occasion

Most scholars believe that Paul planted this church during his second missionary journey around AD 51–52 after preaching in a local synagogue and seeing "some" of the Jews and "a large number of God-fearing Greeks, as well as a number of the leading women" converted (Acts 17:4). This would have taken place shortly after God used a vision to instruct Paul to proclaim the gospel message in Macedonia (Acts 16:9). Paul heeded this instruction and preached in various cities and towns in Macedonia such as Philippi, Thessalonica, and Berea. While there were some who responded favorably to Paul's message, many of the Jews became incensed and formed a mob. Among other things, Paul was accused of crimes against the empire and was quickly forced out of the city. When the violent crowd failed in their attempt to apprehend Paul, they had Jason and several other believers arrested and brought before the local authorities. These men were released only after posting bond. Meanwhile, the Thessalonian believers "sent Paul and Silas away to Berea" (Acts 17:10).

Because Paul was unable to revisit Thessalonica in the weeks immediately following his initial visit to the city, he determined to pen two letters, both of which were probably written around AD 51–52.[2] It should be understood that in Paul's day, letter-writing was considered the best alternative when in-person fellowship was not an option. Letters were often used not simply to reveal information but as a means of encouragement, instruction, and even correction for those who were not able to be with their intended audience in person. Paul's written correspondence reveals that he had developed open lines of communication with the believers of the city and that he was deeply concerned about their spiritual growth.[3]

Considering these circumstances, Paul's letters provided much-needed encouragement and answered several questions that he could not address in person. In 1 Thessalonians, Paul sought to make at least three things very clear: (1) he wanted to address any misunderstandings the church

---

[2] This date is relatively certain given the content of the letter and the mapping of Paul's travels. After planting the church in Macedonia during his second missionary journey, Paul probably made his way to Corinth. During this process, he sent Timothy back to Thessalonica to encourage this new congregation. After Timothy returned with a report of what was going on in the new church, Paul probably wrote back to them on two separate occasions during his eighteen-month-long stay in Corinth. While in Corinth, Paul was forced to appear before the proconsul Gallio. According to an inscription discovered in Delphi, Gallio assumed the role of proconsul around the summer of AD 51 or possibly the summer of AD 52. This evidence is useful because it provides evidence that Paul's eighteen months in Corinth coincided with Gallio's tenure as the proconsul of the Roman province of Achaia. For further discussion, see Martin, *1, 2 Thessalonians*, 33–34.

[3] In addition to the question of authorship, there is some debate about whether the order of the letters in the New Testament is consistent with the order in which they were actually written. It should be recalled that the titles of the letters are not original and therefore do not settle the question of chronology. The chronology of the letters must therefore be determined by examining various clues from the content of the writings. Among others, Charles Wanamaker believes that a strong case can be made that 2 Thessalonians was actually written before 1 Thessalonians. Traditionally, it has been held that 1 Thessalonians was composed in Corinth several months after the founding of the church at Thessalonica. References in 2 Thess 2:2, 15; 3:17 to a previous letter have been cited as evidence for this hypothesis. However, Wanamaker and others believe that the concerned tone of 2 Thessalonians and the relatively positive tone of 1 Thessalonians indicate that Paul penned 2 Thessalonians first in response to various hardships and that 1 Thessalonians was written after the situation of the Thessalonians had improved. For further discussion, see Charles A. Wanamaker, *The Epistle to the Thessalonians*, NIGTC (Grand Rapids: Eerdmans, 1990), 53–63.

Ruins of an ancient forum in Thessalonica

may have had about his motivations, given that he left quickly after establishing the church (remember, he was run out of town by those who came against him); (2) he wanted to remind the church of the significance of their faith in Christ and how it should be applied in their everyday lives (1 Thess 4:1–12); and (3) he wanted to provide comfort to those who were troubled by providing clarity regarding theological questions that many in the church were voicing. Among the many concerns of the Thessalonian church was the ultimate fate of those who had previously died (1 Thess 4:13–5:11).[4]

Second Thessalonians was written for many of the same reasons as the first epistle. There is, however, a noticeable change in the tone and urgency from 1 Thessalonians, which may indicate that the church was experiencing a new wave of persecution. As the church continued to contend with

---

[4] For further insight pertaining to the threefold purpose of 1 Thessalonians, see D. A. Carson and Douglas J. Moo, *An Introduction to the New Testament*, 2nd ed. (Grand Rapids: Zondervan Academic, 2005), 544–46.

significant opposition, Paul placed great emphasis in 2 Thessalonians (especially in chapter 2) on the importance of living one's life in a manner that is consistent with the promise of the Lord's return. He offered instruction regarding the Lord's return in order to remind his readers of the certainty of God's eternal promises so that they might not live in discouragement (2 Thess 2:1–12) or fail to remain active in their service to the Lord (2 Thess 3:6–15). In sum, the Thessalonian letters emphasize that because the Lord will one day return and fulfill his promises, Christians have every reason to live with hope and to pursue godliness in their own spiritual walk.

HIGHLIGHTS IN 1 THESSALONIANS

Greeting (1 Thess 1:1)

First Thessalonians begins with a greeting that modern readers may find similar to a group text—"Paul, Silvanus, and Timothy."[5] The greeting indicates that the content of the letter was endorsed not only by Paul, but also by his close companions who had previously served with him in "the church of the Thessalonians," a new body of believers that was facing both theological confusion as well as opposition from those in the region. Before addressing these matters directly, Paul reminded his readers of their relationship to both "God the Father and the Lord Jesus Christ" and issued a blessing—"Grace to you and peace." This blessing helps establish the tone of this letter and draws the attention of his troubled readers to God's grace and the peace that comes only from him.

Paul's Relationship to the Church (1 Thess 1:2–3:13)

Paul began the body of his letter in a spirit of thanksgiving—"We always thank God for all of you" (1 Thess 1:2a). Despite all of the hardships that he had personally endured, Paul had reason to be thankful for what God was doing in Thessalonica. Many of those in the newly founded church

---

[5] In most letters Paul begins by identifying himself as an apostle (Rom 1:1; 1 Cor 1:1; 2 Cor 1:1; Gal 1:1) to establish his credibility and to emphasize the authority of his instruction. In other cases, he humbly referred to his subservience to Christ (Phil 1:1; Phlm 1) to emphasize the lordship of Christ. To the church at Thessalonica, reference to his apostolic status was deemed unnecessary, apparently because this was already made clear during his recent ministry in the region.

The ancient Arch of Galerius in Thessalonica

were faithfully engaged in service to the Lord, were willingly enduring harsh treatment and opposition, and were following the apostle's encouragement to pursue godliness. As a result, the church at Thessalonica stood out as an example to others in the region of how Christians were to serve one another and the Lord even during difficult circumstances (1 Thess 1:7–10). The example that was set by the Thessalonians serves as an important reminder for Christians today. In a society that places immense pressure on individuals to look, think, and behave a certain way, it can be very difficult to live in a manner that runs counter to cultural expectations. As Christians, we must remember that faithfulness to Christ often necessitates holding firm to beliefs that are unpopular, living in a manner that is considered by many to be foolish or strange, and pursuing godliness in a world that is increasingly hostile to the Christian faith.

After expressing gratitude for this special body of believers, Paul defended his own integrity by accounting for his absence and by emphasizing his own willingness to suffer for the sake of the gospel. Rather than seeking to avoid controversy and adversity, Paul reminded the Thessalonians that he had preached boldly and faithfully among them, his conduct in ministry was blameless, and his affection for the members of the church was beyond dispute—affection that was portrayed with analogies to both motherhood and fatherhood (1 Thess 2:7–12). These expressions of affection and love were offered to the Thessalonians in order to encourage them during a distressing period and to remind them of the partnership that he shared with them in Christ. Though Paul would have preferred to express his fondness and gratitude for the Thessalonians in person, he explained that Satan hindered him from a reunion (1 Thess 2:18),[6] and that Timothy had recently been sent back to serve the congregation in his place (1 Thess 3:2).

Paul ended this portion of his letter with a prayer for both himself and for the church. First, he prayed that the Lord might allow for them an opportunity to see each other again in person in order that they might be encouraged together and that he might have an opportunity to assist them in their spiritual journey (1 Thess 3:10–11). In addition to expressing his desire to meet with the Thessalonians face-to-face, Paul also prayed that the love that he had for this church would be evident among them. Finally, he prayed that the church would continue to remain steadfast in their faith and persevere until the Lord comes again (1 Thess 2:13). This final prayer provides a fitting transition to the next major section of the letter in which Paul responds to some of their questions pertaining to the events that will transpire at the end of the age.

Paul's Revelation of Things to Come (1 Thess 4:1–5:22)

As the church awaits the Lord's return and the events that will transpire as this day approaches, Paul encouraged his readers to live in a manner that reflects their commitment to Christ, particularly in the areas of sexual purity and brotherly love. By addressing these two areas, it may be assumed that sexual impurity and interpersonal conflict were especially problematic in Thessalonica (much as they are in the world today).[7] Unlike

---

[6] One translation of this verse reads "but Satan blocked our way" (NIV). Paul does not explain what this means, perhaps because he can rely on Timothy to explain recent developments to them in person or because his statement refers to the general opposition he experienced rather than a specific incident or source. Some have suggested that this refers to Jewish opposition to Paul's missionary efforts (1 Thess 2:15–16); others have speculated that Paul was alluding to an illness or other physical incapacity (based on passages like Gal 4:13; 2 Cor 12:7). Regardless of the specific form or source of opposition that is in view, Paul was clear in his assertion that his absence among them was justified and that it was the result of circumstances beyond his control.

[7] Marriages in the Greco-Roman world of the first century were concerned more with family arrangements than they were sexual monogamy. It was common and often even encouraged for married men to have multiple sexual partners. This attitude regarding sex

the many pagan religions of the first century, which called for external acts of worship while placing little or no emphasis on the transformation of one's character, Paul emphatically called attention to the importance of pursuing personal holiness and genuine love for others, emphases that remain pertinent today given our overly sexualized and increasingly hostile society. Rather than continue to engage in various forms of sexual immorality and promiscuity, Paul reminded the Thessalonians that it is incumbent upon each believer to control his or her sexual desires so that what was originally created as a blessing by God would not result in harm to others, the judgment of the Lord, or the inability to demonstrate to an unbelieving world the transformative power of the gospel (1 Thess 4:3–8). Furthermore, God calls us not just to remain sexually pure, but to exhibit genuine love to one another—something for which this church, as Paul recognized, was already making progress. In other words, God calls us not simply to avoid certain activities but to live in a manner that is consistent with one's devotion to Christ. While the church in Thessalonica had made observable progress, Paul regarded it necessary to emphasize the importance of living a quiet life, minding one's own business, and maintaining a strong work ethic (1 Thess 4:11). Such behaviors are appealing, even to those outside the faith, and often function as safeguards from other sins that detract from one's credibility and influence.

Following his exhortation to pursue personal holiness and brotherly love, Paul responded to some of the questions raised in the church about the timing of the Lord's return and the state of believers who had already died. Many expected Jesus to return quickly after his ascension. However, due to the long delay, several people had died in the period between the ascension (c. AD 33) and Paul's composition of the Thessalonian letters (c. AD 51–52). What happened to these people following their death? Were they somehow in the Lord's presence already? If not, did they miss the Lord's return? Paul answered these questions by providing his readers with insight pertaining to

---

and marriage is seen in the following comment given Cicero (106–43 BC), a Roman politician and philosopher: "If anyone thinks that young men should be forbidden to have affairs even with prostitutes, he is very strict indeed . . . for his view is contradictory not only to the law of the present age but even with the habits of our ancestors and with what they used to consider allowable. *Cael.* 48, in Cicero, *Pro Caelio. De Provinciis Consularibus. Pro Balbo,* trans. R. Gardner, Loeb Classical Library 447 (Cambridge, MA: Harvard University Press, 1958). Therefore, what Paul was encouraging the church in Thessalonica was countercultural, to say the least. Sexual holiness would have been one compelling way for the church to stand out in the first century world, and it remains one way to live conspicuously different today.

the hope of the Lord's return. While believers can be assured that there will one day be a physical resurrection of the dead (not simply an eternal spiritual existence), this resurrection will not occur before the Lord's coming. Furthermore, his return remains a future hope rather than an event that has already occurred in the past. The believers were not to be troubled, therefore, in thinking that the promise of resurrection was futile or that their loved ones were somehow bypassed when the Lord returns. Because of what Jesus accomplished on their behalf and the fact that his promise regarding his return remains, believers do not need to grieve as the rest of the world when experiencing the loss of a loved one (1 Thess 4:13) and can comfort each other during times of sorrow (1 Thess 4:18). One day, Jesus will return for believers, Paul asserted. The dead in Christ will rise, and those who are alive in Christ will be "caught up" together with them and remain with the Lord forever (1 Thess 4:14–17). The occasion in which believers are "caught up" to meet the Lord in the air is referred to by many as the rapture.

Paul comforted his readers by reminding them that while this future event will come unexpectedly,[8] believers can live with resolve and purpose, knowing that the Lord is sovereign over human history and that he will one day return. As "children of the day," (1 Thess 5:5) they should live as those who are ready for the coming of Christ and comfort each other as that day approaches (1 Thess 5:1–11). In addition to pursuing mutual encouragement, Paul provides practical instruction regarding four matters that should

> ### The Rapture of the Church
>
> The English term *rapture* derives from the Latin word *raptura*, a term that refers to the act of snatching or carrying something away ("caught up," 1 Thess 4:17). When used in reference to Christ's coming, it refers to the "snatching up" of God's people, an event that is described in 1 Thess 4:15–18 and awaits a future fulfillment. According to Paul, there will be a sequence of three events that take place at the rapture: (1) Jesus's personal descent, (2) the resurrection of the dead in Christ, and (3) the "catching up (Greek, *harpazó*)" of believers to meet the Lord in the clouds. Once believers meet the Lord, they will enjoy his presence forever. In 1 Cor 15:51–53, Paul explains that Christians who are alive on the earth when the rapture occurs will not "fall asleep" (die) and that their bodies will be instantly transformed. This event serves to spare those who are saved from experiencing the tribulation that will subsequently come to earth (1 Thess 5:9–10). The New Testament is clear that this future event is imminent; that is, it could happen at any moment, and its reality should inspire us to remain diligent in our service to him and in our proclamation of the gospel message.

---

[8] Additional passages that emphasize the imminent nature of Christ's return include Matt 24:36, 44; Mark 13:32; 1 Thess 5:2; and 2 Pet 3:10.

not be overlooked as believers await the Lord's return: (1) the honoring of church leaders (1 Thess 5:12–13); (2) the ministry to troubled church members (1 Thess 5:14–15); (3) the pursuit of God's will (1 Thess 5:16–18); and (4) the exercise of spiritual discernment (1 Thess 5:19–22). In light of the fact that the Lord's return awaits its future fulfillment, these admonitions should not be regarded as irrelevant or no longer pertinent. To the contrary, the giving of oneself to faithful service to the Lord is both necessary and profitable in light of the hope of the Lord's return. It should also be observed that Paul's admonitions are for the benefit not just of individuals but also the local church. Respecting leadership, helping those in need, encouraging and admonishing one another with biblical truth, and pursuing God's will as individuals and as a community of believers play an important role in the establishment of healthy and thriving local churches.

Conclusion (1 Thess 5:23–28)

Paul finished his first letter to the Thessalonians by pronouncing a blessing of peace in light of the coming of the Lord (1 Thess 5:23). The apostle then asked for prayer, encouraged the church to greet each other with a holy kiss,[9] requested that the letter be read to the entire church (1 Thess 5:25–27), and issues his familiar farewell—"The grace of our Lord Jesus Christ be with you" (1 Thess 5:28). His emphasis on God's grace is an especially fitting way to conclude the letter, as it is the grace of God that, as this letter demonstrates, provides redemption for God's people, fills them with hope, and inspires them to persevere as they await the return of their Savior.

HIGHLIGHTS IN 2 THESSALONIANS

Greeting (2 Thess 1:1–2)

The same "group chat" style of greeting that appears in 1 Thessalonians also appears in Paul's second letter to this church—"Paul, Silvanus, and Timothy: To the church of the Thessalonians" (2 Thess 1:1). Following an

---

[9] For additional references to this gesture, see Rom 16:16; 1 Cor 16:20; 2 Cor 13:12. Such kisses were a typical way in Paul's day to greet family members, close friends, or those to whom respect was given (think of it like a first-century version of the "side-hug"). Paul encourages the church to continue making use of this greeting for its intended purpose. For more on this custom, see the comment on Rom 16:16 in Craig Keener, *The IVP Bible Background Commentary*, 2nd ed. (Downers Grove, IL: IVP Academic, 2014), 457.

affirmation of this church's position in God and Christ, Paul offered a blessing of grace and peace before setting out to offer this beloved body of believers with additional instruction, guidance, and encouragement.

Perseverance in Affliction (2 Thess 1:3–12)

As in the first letter to this congregation, Paul began by expressing his personal gratitude, noting that the church was "flourishing" (2 Thess 1:3) and that they were following many of his instructions and admonitions. Like a proud father, Paul's joy was evident. He even said that he had bragged about their love for one another and remarkable perseverance in faith to the churches in other regions (2 Thess 1:4). Such boasting may have been perceived as a small consolation in comparison to the hardships and persecution that this church was facing. However, Paul reminded them that the troubles that they had endured and continued to experience were not overlooked. Those who were oppressing them and standing in the way of the gospel mission would eventually be judged with great severity. This would take place when God exercised rightful vengeance and condemned those who had opposed his own. In the meantime, Paul noted that it is his prayer that "our God will make you worthy of his calling" (2 Thess 1:11). Ultimately, Paul's desire was to see this church persevere, even in (or especially in) their struggle to glorify the "name of our Lord Jesus" (2 Thess 1:12).

> ### Eschatology
>
> The term *eschatology* is the theological term used to describe the study of "last things" or the "end times." This includes considerations of what happens when believers die, when Jesus will rapture the church, the period of tribulation and judgment of the world to follow, the second coming and ultimate victory of Christ, the resurrection of the saved, the millennial kingdom, the resurrection of the lost, and the reality of heaven (including the new heaven and the new earth) and hell. Although the study of eschatology is primarily concerned with future events, it is also of relevance to the study of Jesus, particularly the significance of his death and resurrection and the nature and purpose of his future coming.
>
> While much of the fascination associated with eschatology relates to cosmic battles, fantastic creatures, and indescribable phenomena described in writings such as Revelation, the Thessalonian letters remind believers that the reality of Jesus's future return is of significant practical relevance. Rather than providing insight merely aimed to satisfy our curiosity regarding future events, Paul sought to provide reassurance to troubled believers and to encourage them to live and order their lives in a manner that reflects their hope in the Lord's return (Titus 2:11–14). Ultimately, the fate of God's people does not involve perishing, but glory. In light of this hope, Paul admonished his readers to "stand firm," no matter what might come up against them (2 Thess 2:15–17).

The Last Judgment by Michelangelo (1541) in the Sistine Chapel, Rome

Perspectives on the Day of the Lord (2 Thess 2:1–17)

In 2 Thess 2:1–17, Paul encouraged the Thessalonians by providing further elaboration regarding the events that will one day transpire when the Lord returns. Though some in the congregation were of the understanding that the day of the Lord (the day of the Lord's return) had already passed, Paul explained that this had not yet occurred. The day will be unmistakable and impossible to miss, not something of little consequence that could be overlooked if one was not paying attention. According to Paul, the period leading up to the Lord's return would be characterized by a significant rise in apostasy and wickedness.[10] Leading the rebellion against God, his people, and his commands, will be a "man of lawlessness . . . doomed to destruction" who will claim to be God and demand to be worshipped (2 Thess 2:3–4).[11] This extremely influential and evil ruler who seeks the worship that belongs to God will be revealed, Paul explained, only when God in his sovereignty determines that it is the appropriate time. Once revealed, Jesus will swiftly and decisively destroy him. If this "man of lawlessness" was not around in Paul's day and has yet to be revealed, the people wondered, why were things in such disarray even now? The answer, according to Paul, is that Satan is actively working to prepare for the emergence of the man of lawlessness through a program of false miracles, signs and wonders, and "with every wicked deception" (2 Thess 2:9b–10). Satan's attempt to deceive will only increase as the day of the Lord's return approaches. Ultimately, those who refuse to submit themselves to the authority of Christ will fall victim to Satan's counterfeit efforts and will ultimately perish as a result.

The same deceptive forces that were at work in Paul's day are alive and active today as well. Thankfully, the same encouragement that the apostle offered to the church at Thessalonica is relevant even today. The church need not fear the rise of evil in the world or the events that will one day transpire, because Christ will be ultimately defeat evil and all enemies of the cross. What an encouragement! No matter what, the church must endure until the Lord returns. Victory is certain in the end.

---

[10] The noun *apostasy* in the original historical context referred to either political or military rebellion. In the ancient Jewish world, the term was also associated with forsaking the law of God. Given this background, the use of this word on this occasion likely refers to rebellion against God. Weima provides a robust definition of the word when he says, "It is the failure to receive the gospel of truth, which leads to salvation . . . instead accepting a false gospel . . . which leads to the worship of a pseudo god . . . and results in condemnation." Weima, *1–2 Thessalonians*, 510.

[11] For other biblical descriptions of this figure, see Dan 9:25–27; 11:29–32; 12:11; Matt 24:15; and Rev 13:14–15. This "man of lawlessness" is also known more popularly as the "antichrist." While the Bible teaches that the "spirit of antichrist" already exists and that it actively deceives people into denying that Jesus is the Christ (1 John 2:18–19, 22; 2 John v. 7), there will be a coming embodiment of this spirit in physical form in the future, resulting in the deception of many.

Prayers Offered and Requested (2 Thess 3:1–5)

Following Paul's instruction and encouragement regarding events that will occur in the future, he discussed some of the specific ways in which believers are to live as they await the Lord's return. Of first importance to Paul is prayer. Specifically, Paul requested prayer for the gospel to spread and that nothing would inhibit the mission of God (2 Thess 3:1–2). This call to prayer is offered with the assurance that God is faithful and will provide whatever is necessary for the church to persevere against the evil one (2 Thess 3:3). For Paul, few activities were more important and more necessary in the life of a believer and in the church than prayer. Perhaps this is why he encouraged prayer as an important practice for those who are growing in Christ in both of his letters to the Thessalonians (in addition to the present passage, see 1 Thess 5:17).

Protocols on Church Discipline (2 Thess 3:6–15)

After Paul's encouragement to pray actively, he instructed believers to avoid those in the church who were characterized by laziness and idleness: "Keep away from every brother or sister who is idle and does not live according to the tradition received from us" (2 Thess 3:6). This particular command may seem rather odd to modern ears. Why did Paul address this issue in the first place? It would seem that many individuals in Thessalonica were so concerned that the Lord's coming was near, or had already come, that they ceased working, choosing instead to live off the hospitality of others. Such behavior, Paul argued, was unbecoming for believers. Christ may indeed return at any time, but we must not wait in a state of idleness until this occurs. Rather, we are to follow Paul's own example by, as much as we are able, providing for our own needs and displaying a strong work ethic. Paul is not shy in directly confronting those who used their convictions about the Lord's return to justify an idle lifestyle. In fact, he even went so far as to instruct the church to not associate with such people. The urgency of the mission that God has given the church leaves no room for sluggishness! There is much to be done before Christ returns!

Conclusion (2 Thess 3:16–18)

Paul closed his letter with a prayer for peace and the Lord's presence for the church in Thessalonica. Because it was not uncommon for individuals to falsely attribute their works to more popular and well-known figures (2 Thess 2:2), Paul drew his attention to the fact that his letter was authentic.[12] As was customary during the time of Paul, most letters were composed by a scribe. Individuals would often pen the final words of their letters in their own hand, however, in order to assure the readers that the work was authentic and that they approved of the content the scribe had written on their behalf. The letter concludes with the same words that appear at the end of his first letter to this congregation: "The grace of our Lord Jesus Christ be with you all" (2 Thess 3:18). These words serve as a perpetual reminder to all believers that Christ is with us even as we await the day of his coming.

BIBLIOGRAPHY

Bruce, F. F. *1 and 2 Thessalonians*. WBC 45. Rev. ed. Grand Rapids: Zondervan Academic, 2015.

Carson, D. A., and Douglas J. Moo. *An Introduction to the New Testament*. 2nd ed. Grand Rapids: Zondervan Academic, 2005.

Cael. 48. In Cicero, *Pro Caelio. De Provinciis Consularibus. Pro Balbo*. Translated by R. Gardner, Loeb Classical Library 447. Cambridge, MA: Harvard University Press, 1958.

Fee, Gordon. *The First and Second Letters to the Thessalonians*. NICNT. Rev. ed. Grand Rapids: Eerdmans, 2009.

Keener, Craig. *The IVP Bible Background Commentary: New Testament*. 2nd ed. Downers Grove, IL: IVP Academic, 2014.

Longenecker, Richard N. "Ancient Amenuenses and the Pauline Epistles." In *New Dimensions in New Testament Study*, edited by Richard N. Longenecker and Merrill C. Tenney. Grand Rapids: Zondervan, 1974.

Martin, D. Michael. *1, 2 Thessalonians*. NAC. Nashville: Holman Reference, 1995.

Weima, Jeffrey A. D. *1–2 Thessalonians*. BECNT. Grand Rapids: Baker Academic, 2014.

Wanamaker, Charles A. *The Epistle to the Thessalonians*. NIGTC. Grand Rapids: Eerdmans, 1990.

---

[12] Paul had been known to use a secretary, called an amanuensis, to write letters on his behalf (see Rom 16:22). This was not uncommon, as professional writers were used for their skill in penmanship and their ability to take dictation. However, it was also not uncommon for an author to write a final word at the end of a work to validate the letter the amanuensis had written on his behalf. See Richard N. Longenecker, "Ancient Amenuenses and the Pauline Epistles," in *New Dimensions in New Testament Study*, ed. Richard N. Longenecker and Merrill C. Tenney (Grand Rapids: Zondervan, 1974), 281–97.

16

1 AND 2 TIMOTHY AND TITUS

MARK ALLEN AND JACK CARSON

CONNECTION POINT

What relevance do these first-century writings have for us today? The high-paced society of twenty-first-century America is markedly different than the contexts of 1 Timothy and Titus. When Paul wrote 2 Timothy, he was in prison awaiting execution. I doubt many of us can relate to that. First-century Christians, the original recipients of these letters, were trying to figure out what it meant to be a church, while we see churches all around us. They had to figure out how Christian slaves were to act, while we no longer have slavery as a sanctioned institution. They had to figure out how to feed the widows in their congregations, while due to modern systems of retirement, most churches today do not need to distribute food to widows. Many of the instructions throughout these letters can seem irrelevant to modern readers.

However, the themes and teachings of these letters have incredible significance for each of us. Have you ever wondered why churches exist? In the modern world, faith has become quite individualistic. If you have Jesus in your heart, the argument goes, why do you need to go to a church? Perhaps a friend has said something similar to you. First Timothy and Titus help us understand the importance of the church both as a community and an institution. These are letters about how Christians can "conduct themselves in God's household" (1 Tim 3:15), with a specific emphasis on sound doctrine (1 Tim 1:10; Titus 2:1) and good works (1 Tim 4:7; Titus 3:1).

While there are many instructions throughout these two letters about personal holiness, these letters primarily teach how the church should live as a community. Jesus taught that his followers should be the salt and light of the world. First Timothy and Titus help us understand how we do that together. Throughout these letters, we see two key themes that have direct relevance to our lives today.

First, these letters are full of references to "sound teaching" within the church. Modern society is an age of man-centered truth, and our neighbors and friends often view religious teaching as exclusively personal. Many of them will say, "Your faith in Jesus may be true for you, but I feel differently about that." Statements like that can be difficult and frustrating to hear, and it can be tempting to accept them as true. Why does it matter what other people believe?

These two "Pastoral Epistles" help us answer that question. Paul asserted throughout the letter that "sound teaching" in the church matters in very practical ways: Straying from sound teaching can lead to "envy, quarreling, slander, evil suspicions, and constant disagreement among people whose minds are depraved and deprived of the truth, who imagine that godliness is a way to material gain" (1 Tim 6:4–5). Further, sound teaching is a matter of life and death. Chasing after fruitless passions leads to "ruin and destruction" (1 Tim 6:9). Paul assured Titus that "sound doctrine" leads to a life of self-control, gentleness, and kindness (Titus 2:1; 3:1–2 NASB).

The second theme to pay attention to in these letters is "practical wisdom"—particularly in regard to living a godly and loving life. Paul's instructions are full of practical commands for the family of God. Paul explained how the church should pick leaders (1 Tim 3:1–13; Titus 1:5–9), relate to the culture (1 Tim 2:1–14; Titus 3:1–3), and take care of those who are vulnerable within the community (1 Tim 5:3–16; Titus 3:14). Undergirding all of this teaching is the idea that God has designed the world to work in certain ways. He created people to "pursue righteousness, godliness, faith, love, endurance, and gentleness" (1 Tim 6:11). Living according to this design is wise. When people do not live that way—when they operate rebellious to God's designs—it leads them toward a path of destruction. In our world we are constantly told that we can live however we like. "You do you" is the mantra of the twenty-first century. These letters help us see why our practical, everyday decisions matter.

While 1 Timothy and Titus emphasize the life of the church, 2 Timothy spends a great deal of time focusing on personal suffering and eternal hope. This gives 2 Timothy deep relevance for us today. In the modern world, people often experience overwhelming loneliness, depression, and suffering. Life can be difficult, and no one is immune to feeling pain and loss. The world we live in is broken. Eventually, we all experience the death of a loved one, and at the end of our days, we will face our own mortality.

Paul was facing his mortality when he wrote 2 Timothy (4:6). He was also suffering from betrayal (2 Tim 4:9–10, 14–15) and abandonment (2 Tim 4:16). Have you ever felt loneliness? Betrayal? Hopelessness? How do we deal with things that feel so wrong? First, we realize that they are wrong—suffering was never meant to be part of the human experience. Then, just like Paul, we place our hope in someone who will right every wrong (2 Tim 4:1) and welcome us into a new life (2 Tim 4:8). Even if we

Saint Paul Writing His Epistles by Valentin de Boulogne 1618–1620. The Museum of Fine Arts, Houston

suffer in this world—and we certainly will (2 Tim 3:12)—we can trust that there is a light at the end of the tunnel (2 Tim 4:18). What Paul taught in 2 Timothy is clear: we cannot endure suffering without hope, and our hope cannot be in this broken world.

With that in mind, consider making this your prayer as you read and study this chapter:

Father God, thank you for guiding the church—your family— through difficult issues, both in ancient times and today. Please open our hearts and minds to the significance that your gospel has on our daily lives. Help us to be people full of grace and kindness; help us to love our neighbors well. Please show us through these letters how we can live out the gospel in a broken and hurting world. Even if we suffer in this life, please help us hope in your eternal kingdom. Amen.

SETTING

Recipients

Paul likely wrote 1 Timothy sometime in AD 61–64.[1] He had two main recipients in mind throughout this letter. First, Paul was writing to

---

[1] The author of the Pastoral Epistles (PE) identifies himself as Paul. Many contemporary scholars have argued that these letters are pseudepigraphal in nature, and they were actually written by followers of Paul, perhaps in the second century. The rejection of Pauline authorship primarily comes from (1) the unique vocabulary used throughout the PE, (2) the unique style of the PE in regard to practical instructions and church structure, (3) the uniqueness of the heresy that both Timothy and Titus seem to be dealing with along with its supposed connection to second-century Gnosticism, and (4) the difficulty in placing the writing of the PE within the story of Acts. These are serious critiques, but they are ultimately unconvincing. Polycarp referenced the PE in *Pol. Phil* sometime around AD 135, and Irenaeus accepted Pauline authorship as early as AD 180. This places the writing of the PE at a very early point, and makes it difficult to imagine a scenario where pseudepigraphal writings would be accepted. The issues of style and vocabulary have multiple helpful solutions. First, Paul was likely older when he wrote the PE than when he wrote his other letters; this could result in a shift of emphasis and vocabulary. Second, the goals of the PE are obviously different than those of his other letters. These letters focus on the ministries of his disciples, the practical issues of running a church, and the shaping of future church leadership. It would be natural for these issues to become more prominent later in Paul's life. Third, these letters likely would have been written by a different scribe than Paul's other letters, and that could certainly contribute to the shift in style and vocabulary. It was normal for Paul to use a scribe in the composition of his letters (Rom 16:22), and he

Timothy, his "true son in the faith" (1 Tim 1:2). Timothy was the son of a Jewish woman and a Greek man, which caused some complexity for him as he began ministering with Paul. In fact, to satisfy those who still maintained a strong focus on Old Testament standards for Jewish people, Paul circumcised Timothy at the beginning of their ministry together (Acts 16:1–3). This demonstrates something significant about Paul, who spent much of his ministry arguing against the need to circumcise believers: Paul was willing to adjust himself (and Timothy) to further the work of the gospel in any given context.

---

did not add any statements in the PE about using his own hand (as he does in Gal 6:11; Col 4:18; 2 Thess 3:17). If Paul allowed the secretary to have a significant amount of editorial freedom, it could completely explain the shift in vocabulary that the PE exhibit. The charge of gnostic similarity within the heresy of the PE is, while not totally without merit, highly unconvincing. The similarities to the Judaizers are far more prominent. To assign a gnostic identity to the heresy identified in the PE demonstrates a predilection towards assuming a pseudepigraphal writing. However, the authenticity of the letters (particularly due to the early attestation) should be assumed unless compelling reasons arise. The practical nature of the letters can be ascribed to the very real need to establish orthopraxy after orthodoxy; the church needed to know how to organize itself after the death of the apostles, and Paul would likely have felt burdened to address that. Finally, it is likely that the PE do not fit into the storyline of Acts at all; they likely were written after Paul was released from his Acts 28 house arrest. No compelling reason exists to deny Paul's continued ministry post-Acts 28. For more on Pauline authorship, please see Philip H. Towner, *The Letters to Timothy and Titus*, NICNT (Grand Rapids: Eerdmans, 2006). Also see Gerald L. Bray, *The Pastoral Epistles*. International Theological Commentary (New York: T&T Clark, 2019) for an excellent defense of Pauline authorship of the PE.

The dating of the PE is directly related to the issue of authorship discussed above. A pseudepigraphal reading would need to place the date of authorship sometime between AD 64 (the burning of Rome and early dating for the execution of Paul) and AD 135, when *Pol. Phil* references the PE. The date would likely have to be between AD 70 (to allow for news of Paul's death to become widespread) and AD 120 (to allow the letters to become canonically recognized by the writing of *Pol. Phil*). This range of dates would prove difficult for a number of reasons. Foremost among them, Timothy and Titus would likely have been alive for a large portion of that time, and their disciples certainly would have been alive throughout the entire time frame available for pseudepigraphal authorship—not to mention the communal memory of the churches in both Crete and Ephesus. There would have been many people who could deny Pauline authorship throughout those dates. If Pauline authorship is believed, the best dates for the writing of the PE would be between AD 61–66. It is possible that Paul authored 1 Timothy and Titus as early as AD 61. He could have written shortly after the end of his house arrest. Taking an early (AD 59) date for Paul's house arrest, one could assume he would have been freed around AD 61. Since Paul was almost certainly killed around AD 65–66, 2 Timothy could be reasonably dated as early as AD 64 or as late as AD 66. For a helpful exploration of dating the PE, see Thomas D. Lea and Hayne P. Griffin Jr., *1, 2 Timothy, Titus*, NAC 34 (Nashville: Holman Reference, 1992), 275.

The ruins of the ancient Library of Celsus in Ephesus

The second recipient of 1 Timothy was the church in Ephesus.[2] While 1 Timothy is addressed to Timothy himself, it is important to also see the letter as a message to that church. Paul had left Timothy in Ephesus to guide the church as his representative, but false teachers (1 Tim 1:3–7), the complications of forming a church structure (1 Tim 2:8–3:16; 5:1–6:19), and Timothy's young age (1 Tim 4:12) all seemed to have complicated Timothy's mission. Paul wrote this letter to help demonstrate Timothy's authority to the broader church there in Ephesus. The core issue is, again, so that they would know "how people ought to conduct themselves in God's household, which is the church of the living God, the pillar and foundation of the truth" (1 Tim 3:15). (For background relating to Paul's ministry in this city, see the chapter on Ephesians.)

Paul likely wrote Titus near the time he wrote 1 Timothy. As you will see, these two letters have quite a bit in common, both thematically and

---

[2] Paul used the second-person singular throughout 1 Timothy until he arrived at the final verse. At the end of each PE, Paul switched to the second-person plural. He designed the letters to have the dual nature of both personal letter and ecclesial instruction.

stylistically. Titus, like 1 Timothy, was written with two audiences in mind. As a letter, it seems designed to accomplish goals quite similar to 1 Timothy. The first recipient of this letter is Titus—a Gentile believer who had joined Paul during his missionary work. Titus was with Paul during the Acts 15 Jerusalem Council (Gal 2:1). Titus also served Paul and the early church in several capacities—he was a representative of Paul's at the church in Corinth (2 Cor 8:16–17) before this letter was written; he was a leader at the church in Crete when this letter was written (Titus 1:5); and Paul sent him to evangelize Dalmatia after his time in Crete (2 Tim 4:10). During the Acts 15 Jerusalem Council, Titus would have had a front-row seat to the great controversy surrounding circumcision and the Judaizers. This is a significant fact to remember as you read the letter to Titus, and it likely gives some insight into why Titus was the one Paul sent to Crete.

The Mount Ida chain and the Messara plain in Crete, Greece

The second recipient of Paul's letter to Titus was the church in Crete. This letter addresses false teachings that were prevalent in the Cretan church, and Paul used the letter to rebuke those who were trying to take advantage of the young believers in Crete.[3] This letter is somewhat more

---

[3] Paul likely first visited the isle of Crete as a prisoner when he was en route to Rome

universal than 1 Timothy, and many of the teachings are laid out as broad principles instead of specific instructions. The universal nature of the instructions can make it particularly easy to apply the teachings of Titus to our churches today.

Paul almost certainly wrote 2 Timothy sometime in AD 65–66. This letter was written to Timothy, who was labeled Paul's "dearly loved son" (2 Tim 1:2). It is significantly more personal in content and tone than the other Pastoral Epistles. Paul spoke specifically about his situation at the time (2 Tim 1:11–12, 15–18; 2:10; 4:6–18) and personally about Timothy (2 Tim 1:3–8, 13–14; 2:1–3; 4:9, 19–21) throughout much of the letter. These personal notes seem to drive the theological discourse that happens between each personal reference. Paul still addressed false teachers in this letter (2 Tim 2:16–18), but it does not seem to take center stage as in the other Pastoral Epistles. Paul was sometime in-between his first legal defense (2 Tim 4:16) and his execution (2 Tim 4:6) when he wrote this personal plea to Timothy. He seemed particularly concerned about Timothy's development as a minister of the gospel (2 Tim 1:6–8, 13–14; 2:1–3; 4:1–5), and his advice can serve as a template for anyone looking to enter into ministry—he implored Timothy to pursue sound doctrine and godly living.

Theme and Key Passages

Paul developed several significant themes throughout 1 Timothy. We have already mentioned the key themes of sound teaching and practical wisdom. Church organization, the relationship between theology and practice, and the qualifications of leadership all serve as additional themes for this letter. Paul was essentially helping to provide the parameters and structure through which the church could fulfill its mission. In the process, he emphasized the need for the people of God to teach the truth, and he commanded them to live that truth out in their lives. This letter emphasizes that proper doctrine and proper living are dependent on each other. You cannot have one without the other.

---

in Acts 27, but it is clear that he did not stay there long enough to plant a church during that trip. Instead, it is fairly likely that he returned to Crete after the end of Acts, founding the Cretan church at that point. This would indicate that the church was quite young when Paul wrote this letter, and it explains a good deal of the false teaching that arose. Since the Jewish religion was well known, it makes sense that the new followers of Christ would have been tempted to adopt various aspects of Judaism.

1 Tim 3:15: "I have written so that you will know how people ought to conduct themselves in God's household, which is the church of the living God, the pillar and foundation of the truth."

Many of the themes found in 1 Timothy are repeated in Titus, but Paul uniquely emphasized two things in Titus. First, Paul repeatedly connected the teaching in Titus to the unfolding narrative of Scripture as a whole. He discussed how God planned from the beginning of time (Titus 1:2) to redeem a people for himself so that they could do good works (Titus 2:14) and inherit eternal life (Titus 3:7). This connection to the overarching story line of Scripture provides rich theological support for many of Paul's commands. These theological explanations help us as we attempt to apply these teachings in our modern churches. The second unique emphasis in Titus is Paul's insistence that believers should do good works for all people. While 1 Timothy emphasizes living a godly life, Titus puts the particular lens of "good works" into play numerous times.

Titus 2:11–14: "For the grace of God has appeared, bringing salvation for all people, instructing us to deny godlessness and worldly lusts and to live in a sensible, righteous, and godly way in the present age, while we wait for the blessed hope, the appearing of the glory of our great God and Savior, Jesus Christ. He gave himself for us to redeem us from all lawlessness and to cleanse for himself a people for his own possession, eager to do good works."

Interior of the Mamertine Prison in Rome. The stairs descend to a lower level called the Tullianum. According to tradition, this is the site where Paul may have been imprisoned in the weeks preceding his death. From here Paul would have written 2 Timothy.

There are two key themes in 2 Timothy that you should be aware of. First, Paul explained that gospel living leads to suffering (2 Tim 3:12). Throughout 1 Timothy and

Titus, Paul called the saints to prioritize godliness in their lives, but 2 Timothy explores an important aspect of that call. When we live with eternity in sight—prioritizing the gospel in all things—we will suffer for it. Paul's suffering was caused by his gospel living (2 Tim 1:11–12), and he continued to share the gospel—despite the suffering he experienced—so that others might experience eternal life (2 Tim 2:10–11).

This leads to the second key theme of this book. Why should we be willing to suffer for the gospel? Paul explained that God will redeem our suffering. Paul argued that we should embrace the suffering that we experience because of gospel living (2 Tim 1:8); he explained that the gospel is worth suffering for. We do not need to be afraid (2 Tim 1:7); Christ's death and resurrection will redeem our suffering (2 Tim 2:11–13). There will be a kingdom to come where all of our suffering will be made right (2 Tim 4:8).

> Remember Jesus Christ, risen from the dead and descended from David, according to my gospel, for which I suffer to the point of being bound like a criminal. But the word of God is not bound. This is why I endure all things for the elect: so that they also may obtain salvation, which is in Christ Jesus, with eternal glory. (2 Tim 2:8–10)

Purpose and Occasion

As we have already seen, Paul cared a lot about "sound teaching." It plays a prominent role in each of the Pastoral Epistles. Paul wrote 1 Timothy and Titus in response to false teachers who were troubling his mentees. Even in the more personal work of 2 Timothy, Paul explained that sound teaching was absolutely essential for any minister of the gospel.

As Paul wrote 1 Timothy, he was particularly concerned about some false teaching in Ephesus. Most likely, the false teaching that concerned Paul was not heresy, per se.[4] The false teachers did not seem to be denying

---

[4] It is quite impossible to reconstruct a full theology of the false teachers Paul confronted throughout the PE. In both 1 Timothy and Titus, there are only passing explanations of what they taught. It was clearly Jewish in origin (1 Tim 1:4; Titus 1:14), and it distracted people from godly living. It is likely that the teaching was a recapitulation of Old Testament law in a way that minimized the grace of Christ that should be the source of any believer's pursuit of godliness. The false teachers argued over specific words and controversies (1 Tim 1:4; Titus 1:14), and they seemed enamored by genealogies (1 Tim 1:4; Titus

Christ, the resurrection, or some other central Christian claim. Instead, they were focused on debating secondary issues, making them primary. Paul specifically said that they were pushing people to pay attention to "myths and endless genealogies" (1 Tim 1:4).

In Crete, something similar occurred. Deceptive teachers took advantage of the Cretan believers (Titus 1:10–11). These teachers were part of the circumcision party, which believed circumcision was a necessary part of salvation. Because they taught people to follow Jewish customs and laws (Titus 1:14), the believers in Crete were not focusing on good works and gospel living (Titus 1:16). Many of us only think of false teaching in terms of significant heresies. However, Paul was concerned about something subtler: he was worried that the people were taking small theological arguments and focusing on them too much. How often do we see this happen on social media today?

Paul wrote 2 Timothy to pass on what might have been his final advice. He loved Timothy (2 Tim 1:2), and throughout this letter, Paul provided a wealth of advice about being a minister of the gospel. He wanted to make sure Timothy was prepared to go on without him, and he wanted Timothy to come and be with him as he approached death (2 Tim 4:9).

HIGHLIGHTS IN 1 TIMOTHY

Greeting (1 Tim 1:1–2)

Paul's greeting in 1 Timothy is more elaborate than those found in many of his other letters.[5] He introduced himself as "an apostle of Christ Jesus by the command of God our Savior and of Christ Jesus our hope" (1 Tim 1:1). This introduction carries with it a great degree of authority, and it immediately establishes the source of Paul's authority. Much of this letter instructed the Ephesian church to organize themselves appropriately as the

---

3:9) and asceticism (1 Tim 4:1–5; Titus 1:15–16). The only major heresy that Paul directly named throughout the PE can be found in 2 Tim 2:17–18; the false teachers "Hymenaeus" and "Philetus" who claimed the resurrection had already passed. It is very unlikely that this teaching was in any way connected to Gnosticism or some other well documented heretical movement. These various teachings seem to be more related to the nature of a young church than that of an articulate and well-developed heresy.

[5] For an excellent discussion on Paul's greeting in 1 Timothy and the significance of his word choice, see Bray, *The Pastoral Epistles*, 1 Tim 1:1–2.

household of God. Paul wanted to be *very* sure that they understood the source of these commands was God himself. In verse 2, Paul addressed the letter to Timothy, his "true son in the faith." Such a title likely provided a great deal of authority for Timothy—authority that Timothy would need to carry out the directions and teachings Paul provided throughout this letter.

False Teachers, False Religion, and True Faith (1 Tim 1:3–20)

The body of Paul's letter begins by reminding Timothy of his mission—to "instruct certain people not to teach false doctrine or to pay attention to myths and endless genealogies" (1 Tim 1:3–4). Letters like this were read before the entire congregation, and since these false doctrines seem to have embroiled the entire church in debate and conflict, it is safe to assume that the whole congregation was aware of who these "certain people" were. Paul used this letter to publicly correct those leading the family of God astray.

Paul continued his rebuke of these "certain people" by explaining that their teaching leads to fruitless discussions. Although these people wanted to be teachers, Paul insisted that they were unfit to teach. While the exact teaching that these "certain people" were advocating is unknown, we can make a pretty good guess based on what Paul said to correct their teaching.

Paul then instructed the people that the aim of the Christian faith is "a pure heart, a good conscience, and a sincere faith" (1 Tim 1:5). He assured the readers that the law (meaning those rules and standards found throughout the Old Testament) was good.[6] However, just like anything else, the law could be misused and twisted. These "certain people" were misapplying the law.

The next section gives us some indication as to how these people were misusing the law. Paul explained that the law is for those who are unrighteous, not those who are righteous. Paul did not use the term "righteous" here to mean "sinless" or even to indicate some sort of standing before God. Based on his other letters, we know that he believed all people have sinned, and that makes them unrighteous before God (Rom 3:23). Instead, Paul is telling us something important about the nature of the law.

---

[6] Paul's view on the usefulness of the law is a hotly contested topic. The law (*nomos*) must be used lawfully (*nomimōs*) for it to be good. This play on words shows us clearly that the law was not at fault in this scenario; the false teachers were twisting the law due to their deficient views of grace. See Robert W. Yarbrough, *The Letters to Timothy and Titus*, PNTC (Grand Rapids: Eerdmans, 2018), 110–11.

The law is intended for the unrighteous; that is who it helps. It shows each of us that we are flawed, and it helps us recognize our flaws. Everyone who grew up in church knows how it feels to hear the pastor preach about a sin that you have recently committed. When someone points out the wrong that we have done, we feel convicted. The law helps the unrighteous see their unrighteousness.

But Paul said that the law is not for the righteous. Instead, he went on to point toward "mercy" and "grace" in his own life, "along with the faith and love that are in Christ Jesus" (1 Tim 1:13–14). Righteousness does not come through focusing on the law, Paul said. Righteousness comes through trusting in Christ's grace and meditating on his love for our lives. We cannot work our way toward a righteous life.

Moses with the Ten Commandments by Philippe de Champagne, 1648

This emphasis on grace—as opposed to a fixation on the law—should be quite familiar to us by now. This teaching is repeated throughout the entire New Testament. In 1 Timothy, Paul pointed toward grace as the motivation upon which good works should be done, but he emphasized the importance of doing good works throughout the entire book. Resting in grace must lead to godly living.

Holy Living and the Church (1 Tim 2:1–3:14)

This section carries forward the teaching and themes established in the first section. After informing the church that the law is not capable of producing right living, Paul provided them with an alternate strategy: a properly ordered and structured church centered on the gospel and its mission. Paul wanted the church in Ephesus to be a model of the Eschaton—a community of peace, holiness, and humility. The commands that he provided seem to be in direct contrast to the quarrelsome attitude that he corrected in the previous chapter. The church should be distinct and holy, not quarrelsome.

Paul began by telling the church to pray for all people, especially those in charge of the government. He did not want the believers to focus on arguing with those in charge of them; instead, he called them to live quiet lives filled with holiness. He based this command in the reality that God "wants everyone to be saved and to come to the knowledge of the truth" (1 Tim 2:4). Animosity and anger are not helpful in evangelism.

Paul went on to give specific instructions for the men and women of the congregation. Ironically, these instructions have been the source of a great deal of quarreling and debate within the church. It is, for that reason, one of the most important passages to understand within its literary and cultural context. The emphasis throughout this section is on living "a tranquil and quiet life" (1 Tim 2:2). In the spirit of that call, Paul commanded men to pray without anger or quarreling. We saw in the first section that the church was already prone to arguing, and Paul corrected the men of the congregation, who seem to have been inclined toward anger.[7]

Paul then corrected the women of the congregation (1 Tim 2:9–14). He directed them to wear modest clothing and avoid excessive jewelry. This instruction was in direct contrast to a cultural trend within Roman society that pushed women—particularly wealthy women—to live lives of promiscuity and sexual freedom. Paul did not want the women caught in this cultural trend, and he wanted them, just like the men, to live "tranquil and quiet [lives] in all godliness" (1 Tim 2:2).

Finally, Paul provided specific instructions about women teaching within the church. While a full exploration of this passage is beyond the scope of this introduction, it can be helpful to note that this passage is both universal in nature, as evidenced by Paul's use of the creation story in 1 Tim 2:13–14, as

> **The New Roman Woman**
>
> B. W. Winter convincingly argued that a movement among women, contemporary to the writing of the Pastoral Epistles, was gaining traction in Ephesus. This movement rejected traditional views on modesty and sexuality; it was a sort of "sexual revolution" among the wealthy women of Roman society, complete with the increased use of contraception and abortion to allow for sexual promiscuity. The movement emphasized a desire for public prominence, the pursuit of prestige, and a rejection of normative cultural standards. This particular cultural movement is likely what Paul warns the church against in 1 Timothy; he did not want the witness of the church harmed through an association with this movement.
>
> For more info on this movement, see Bruce W. Winter, *Roman Wives, Roman Widows: The Appearance of New Women and the Pauline Communities* (Grand Rapids: Eerdmans, 2003).

---

[7] See Lea and Griffin, *1, 2 Timothy, Titus*, 95, for a longer discussion on Paul's correction of the people's attitudes. See Yarbrough, *The Letters to Timothy and Titus*, 165, for notes on why this focused on males in the church.

An ancient theater in Ephesus

well as specific in its language and context. Paul was not saying that women are categorically forbidden to speak in church, since many of Paul's other writings would not support that interpretation. However, he was certainly saying something significant about the context in Ephesus as well as something significant about the roles of men and women in creation. Paul was clear throughout his writing that men have a particular spiritual responsibility for their families and the church. In this passage, Paul provided specific instructions for the context of Ephesus and the cultural transitions that were occurring there.[8]

---

[8] Perhaps no other verses in the PE can cause as much controversy as 1 Tim 2:11–12. Paul wrote, "A woman is to learn quietly with full submission. I do not allow a woman to teach or to have authority over a man; instead, she is to remain quiet." For the modern, Western reader, these verses can sound archaic and sexist. This verse has been interpreted in a number of ways throughout church history, with interpretations ranging from requiring all women in church to remain quiet at all times to a dismissal of the verses as purely contextual. Some have even attempted to argue that these words are not authoritative since Paul specifically said, "I do not allow" and not "God does not allow." However, a parallel passage in 1 Cor 14:34–35 makes this interpretation not only novel, but also highly difficult to maintain. Paul certainly maintained gender distinctives throughout his writing, but it is important to recognize a number of other passages when attempting to understand the relevance of this passage for today. Paul recognized the significance and contribution of women in ministry numerous times (Acts 18:26; Rom 16:1; Phil 4:3). Furthermore, Paul

Paul concluded this section by providing specific instructions for selecting leaders within the church, outlining the qualifications for elders

---

repeatedly pointed toward the unity that the church finds in Christ, arguing against the racial, sexual, and class divides that fill our world (1 Cor 12:13; Gal 3:28 ; Col 3:11). While there is not space in this introduction to explore a full theology of gender, there are three key points that are important to recognize in relation to the PE. First, Paul encouraged women to learn. While that may sound patronizing to you, it was actually a radical assertion of rights for women. Many cultures throughout the world have not allowed women to learn. Second, Paul told women to learn and not to teach, but the very command assumed that women have the capability to teach. Third, the command not to teach is certainly locked into the context of the church, and Paul encouraged women to teach younger women in other sections of the PE. This does beg the question: Why should women not teach in a church setting if they can teach in other settings? There are three possible explanations to consider. First, some propose that this command is limited in its scope, and Paul provided it in response to the specific heresy found in the church at Ephesus. This position finds unity with the parts of the Pauline Epistles that stress the equality of all people, but it fails to explain why this same command is found in 1 Cor 14:34–35. Second, some interpreters take their cue from Paul's theological explanation in 1 Timothy 2 and argue that women should not teach simply because they are more easily deceived than men are. This argument, beyond being recognizably false in our everyday lives, fails to account for the examples of female ministry laborers recorded in other parts of the New Testament. Third, the most convincing explanation begins with an important question: Did Paul consider teaching to be superior to learning? There seems to be very little evidence that he did. In fact, much of the modern rejection of these verses comes from negative views on learning and submissiveness. We see the learner as less significant than the teacher, and we see the one who submits as less significant than the one who leads. However, the entire corpus of the PE emphasizes that believers are called to submit to authorities, to live quiet and tranquil lives, and to serve others however they can. Paul saw each of these things as a good thing, noble and worthy of praise. While these verses can certainly still bother our modern conceptions of gender equality, it is absolutely necessary for us to understand them within the overarching theological and redemptive framework of Scripture—a framework that sees the first as last and the last as first. In context, while these verses do establish the significance of gender distinctives in ministry—notably partitioning, in some way, the public teaching ministry as a duty given to men—the PE as a whole serve as a master argument against the misogyny that many read into these particular verses. Paul repeatedly emphasized the command to love others and treat everyone with respect and kindness, and the demeaning or domineering attitudes that men have, at times throughout history, displayed toward women are fundamentally flawed and unfaithful. The Christian teaching on gender does indicate that there are distinctives for each gender; they are not interchangeable. Men are called to bear spiritual responsibility in some unique way; however, if this call is ever used to belittle or domineer women, it misses the mark entirely. There are two useful resources that you should explore if you are interested in this topic. For an excellent, conservative examination of this passage, see Andreas J. Köstenberger and Thomas R. Schreiner, eds., *Women in the Church: An Interpretation and Application of 1 Timothy 2:9–15*, 3rd ed. (Wheaton, IL: Crossway, 2016). For a theological engagement that attempts a mediating position, see Michelle Lee-Barnewall, *Neither Complementarian nor Egalitarian: A Kingdom Corrective to the Evangelical Gender Debate* (Grand Rapids: Baker Academic, 2016).

and deacons. The qualifications that he provided are in unity with the rest of the themes within 1 Timothy. He emphasized the need for godliness and temperance within both offices. If someone wants to lead God's household, he reasoned, they need to demonstrate that they can manage their own households well (1 Tim 3:1–13).

Keeping the Church Faithful (1 Tim 3:14–4:5)

Paul took a break from teaching about church structure in the following two sections. Instead, he paused to explain the significance of everything he was teaching. He wrote this entire letter so the Ephesian Christians would "know how people ought to conduct themselves in God's household, which is the church of the living God, the pillar and foundation of the truth" (1 Tim 3:15). Paul expressed the significance of the church in two ways here. First, he explained that the church is important relationally: it is the family of God. Second, the church is important functionally: it safeguards and protects truth.

Having established the significance of the church, Paul turned his attention back to the false teachers in Ephesus. He explained that false teachers will lead people away from the gospel (1 Tim 4:1–3). Paul, interestingly, explained that those who depart from the faith will "forbid marriage and demand abstinence from foods that God created to be received with gratitude" (1 Tim 4:3). This explanation provides more insight into how these "certain people" were misapplying the law by adding rules and laws onto the people of God that do not lead to holiness.

Timothy, Lead Virtuously (1 Tim 4:4–16)

This unique section directly addresses Timothy. Paul reminded Timothy not to be wrapped up in the "pointless and silly myths" (1 Tim 4:7) that were prevalent in the church. Furthermore, he encouraged Timothy to pursue godliness above physical training. In many ways, this section can be seen as a personal summation of the rest of the teaching within 1 Timothy; Paul was providing specific instruction on how Timothy could be a "good servant [or minister] of Christ Jesus" (1 Tim 4:6).

Paul went on to encourage Timothy in his position of leadership. He told Timothy not to let anyone "despise [his] youth" (1 Tim 4:11). In so doing, he supported Timothy's right to lead. It seems likely that many of the "certain people" in the congregation were critical of Timothy for his youth and inexperience, and they were using that as an excuse to ignore his authority. Paul responded to this critique by supporting Timothy's teaching and encouraging him to continue doing so (1 Tim 4:14–16).

Leading the Family of God (1 Tim 5:1–6:21)

Finally, Paul ended 1 Timothy with a series of instructions dealing with complex issues throughout the church. He directed Timothy to use wisdom in the way the church provided for widows and to be intentional in honoring the elders who led the church. He explained that slaves within the church should respect their masters, even if they were believers. These specialized instructions demonstrate that wisdom is sometimes necessary for running the household of God. Deciding which widows deserve financial support is not an easy or clear-cut issue, but it needed to be done. Paul provided a reasonable answer to the problem for Timothy, and in so doing, provides a model of wisdom for churches to follow even to this day.

As a closing note, Paul returned to correcting the false teachers within the church. He accused them of arrogance, a love of controversy, and fixation on financial gain (1 Tim 6:3–10). The implication is clear: these

---

Slavery

The Pastoral Epistles repeatedly encourage slaves to submit to their masters. This, for obvious reasons, can bother our modern consciences. We live with the looming evil of American, race-based chattel slavery in our minds. There were some who even abused these very texts to justify the institution of slavery in early America, and this has contributed to the ongoing racism that our world is struggling with today.

It is important to point out that the Bible in no way condones slavery. There are three things to understand about the relationship between these passages and modern-day slavery. First, slavery in the Ancient Near East and the Greco-Roman world was not the same as slavery in the antebellum South, despite the fact that we use the same word for both. Ancient slavery was not primarily racial; it was primarily economic. Many slaves held positions of prominence; some slaves owned other slaves. People would sometimes sell themselves into slavery for economic security. Second, Paul was not condoning even that form of slavery in these passages. Instead, he was teaching people how they should live within a system that was broken; slavery was a deeply ingrained part of ancient society. Christianity at the time had no power to address or overturn that institution, and Paul provided instructions on how they should "[make] the most of the time, because the days are evil" (Eph 5:16). Third, Paul's writing provided the intellectual and ethical framework to undermine the entire institution of slavery. He wrote that in the eyes of the Lord, slaves and masters were equal (1 Cor 7:22–23), and he denied the significance of class and racial distinctions among believers (Gal 3:27–28).

The gospel, rightly understood, leads to freedom. Ultimately, the New Testament and its teaching led to the abolition of slavery, even while still instructing people on how they should live in this broken world. For more information on how the New Testament led to the end of slavery as an accepted cultural practice, see Rodney Stark, *For the Glory of God: How Monotheism Led to Reformations, Science, Witch-Hunts, and the End of Slavery* (Princeton, NJ: Princeton University Press, 2004).

false teachers were leading people astray out of selfishness. Paul charged Timothy to flee from that sort of selfishness and to pursue righteousness instead. This personal charge reflects the whole teaching of 1 Timothy: the household of God must act with humility and righteousness, always loving others. The household of God cannot be a place of selfish gain, arrogant quarreling, or false teaching.

HIGHLIGHTS IN TITUS

Greeting (Titus 1:1–4)

Paul's greeting to Titus accomplishes two key things. First, he connected the church to the unfolding drama of redemptive history: Paul showed how the church is part of a plan that God formed before time even began. This establishes the importance of his message. Second, Paul explained his own connection to the unfolding narrative of redemptive history. As an apostle, he was a special leader appointed to help establish the church. This position gave him the responsibility to guide the church and showed that God had given him the authority to correct the church if it was in error. By greeting Titus as his true son in the faith (Titus 1:4), Paul shared his spiritual authority directly with him. The title of "son" was not primarily a title of subordination in the Greco-Roman world; instead, it was a title of inheritance.[9]

Titus's Mission: Elders, False Teachers, and Pastoral Concern (Titus 1:5–2:10)

Paul opened the body of this letter with three specific points. First, he explained that Titus was in Crete to establish proper church leadership. In the first century, believers did not have the advantages we have in modern churches. Seminaries did not exist to train pastors; there was no church history to use as a standard for decisions; and the Bible itself was not even compiled yet. This left room for a great deal of confusion, and that confusion allowed for numerous leaders to arise who were wholly unqualified. Titus, as an ambassador of Paul, was in Crete to help solve this problem.

---

[9] Paul certainly intended for this introduction to support Titus in his leadership of the Cretan church. As evidenced by Titus 2:15, Paul intended for Titus to have the authority to teach and instruct in contrast to the false teachers among them.

The second point that Paul emphasized is the dual qualification of a biblical leader. To be a leader in the church, someone must both live a godly life as well as hold sound doctrine with conviction. Paul repeated this double emphasis throughout the letter, an example of his skill in crafting effective and detailed arguments. If Titus was having issues leading the Cretan church (Titus 1:10), Paul's goal in writing this section was likely twofold. First, he needed to give Titus advice on choosing good leaders to help him run the church. This passage is effective in doing that. Second, Titus needed a way to identify and discredit poor leaders. The passage also accomplishes that. If a leader was arrogant, violent, or greedy, that person was automatically disqualified from leading the church. Greed as a disqualification for leadership plays a particularly significant role in the context of Titus. The false leaders and teachers in Crete were pursuing their roles specifically for financial gain (Titus 1:11). After establishing the list of qualifications for a leader, it was easy for Paul to point out the glaring disqualifications of the false leaders.[10]

> **Human Formation**
>
> The Pastoral Epistles emphasize the symbiotic relationship between faith and good works. Paul constantly fluctuated between theological truth and practical godliness and demonstrated that both are necessary for followers of Christ. This is because the gospel does not simply involve actions (which most of us understand by this point); however, the gospel is not just about belief. Scripture is clear that belief is the beginning of a believer's journey, but the gospel (sound doctrine) also leads to human formation. The gospel transforms the way we live.
>
> J. Dryden helps demonstrates the formative relationship between right teaching and right action, and he shows that the New Testament Epistles operate in *paraenetic* (virtue forming) ways. He explains, "For Paul, theological discourse reshapes convictions, desires and moral responsibilities" (J. de Waal Dryden, *A Hermeneutic of Wisdom: Recovering the Formative Agency of Scripture* [Grand Rapids: Baker Academic, 2018], 185–89).
>
> The Bible does not just inform our minds; it motivates and forms our lives.

---

[10] Paul was somewhat harsh toward the people of Crete, and he even quoted a negative saying about the Cretans in Titus 1:12. This saying was originally penned by Epimenides, a sixth-century BC Cretan philosopher. In addition to the obvious meaning of the quote, it is likely that Paul was referencing the original critique of Epimenides, who believed the Cretan people were teaching a false religion in his day. There was a common belief among Cretans that Zeus had died and his tomb was on Crete. Epimenides had critiqued them for their false teaching, since Zeus was supposed to be eternal and immortal. It appears that Paul is utilizing this saying to show how the Cretan people are prone towards believing in false religious teachings. For a more in-depth analysis of this quote, see Philip H. Towner, *1–2 Timothy and Titus*, The IVP New Testament Commentary Series 14 (Downers Grove, IL: IVP Academic, 1994), 51–53.

An ancient fresco found at the Cretan city of Knossos

This leads to the third point Paul addressed in this section. Paul encouraged Titus to teach godly living to the people, and he provided a series of specific commands based on the different people-groups in Crete—older men (Titus 2:2), older women (2:3), young women (2:4), young men (2:6), and slaves (2:9). A central theme throughout all of the instructions is the need to be self-controlled. Kindness, gentleness, and integrity all feature prominently as well. This is all connected to the concept of "sound teaching" (Titus 2:1).

Theological Foundations for Godly Living (Titus 2:11–3:15)

This section begins by looking at "sound teaching" that leads to godly living. Just as in 1 Timothy, the theological foundation of this letter is the gospel itself, with a particular emphasis on the unmerited grace believers have received from Christ. Paul, in particular, explored two key points of the gospel. First, he reminded the readers that Jesus died in order to redeem a people for himself. This redemption, however, is not merely an abstract spiritual redemption. Jesus did not die *just* to give people a way to avoid hell. Instead, Paul explained a second key aspect of the gospel: Christ died to purify a people who are zealous to do good works. That people, the church, are not only redeemed; they are also called to live in a completely new way.

If the Pastoral Epistles emphasize anything, it is this: At no point in the church's mission can we separate doctrine, or teaching from good works. Doctrine that is truly centered on the gospel will promote good works in the lives of those who hear it, and if any doctrine does not lead to good works, that doctrine is corrupt. Importantly, this call to good works did not primarily focus on avoiding sin, although that was certainly a piece of it. Instead, the call to godly living in Titus is inextricably linked to *doing* good things for other people. Modern Christians can sometimes focus so much on avoiding sin that we forget the very active call to do good. But godly living is not only about avoiding things. Yes, we should be concerned about our sexual purity and avoiding pride. However, those concerns should never be the only focus of a believer's spiritual life. Instead, believers also need to care for those in the most need throughout society (Titus 3:14).[11]

Since Christ showed grace to his people, the church, and gave himself up for them when they were evil, Paul argued that believers should give of themselves for all people as well. Paul charged the Cretan Christians to do good works and show gentleness to all (Titus 3:2). Further, Paul explained that they should take hope in the assurance of eternal life. Even if others wronged them or took advantage of them—as the false teachers had done—they could still hope in the promise of eternal life with Christ.

Finally, after thoroughly explaining the gospel and its connection to godly living, Paul turned his attention back to the false teachers who were the original inspiration of this letter. Everything that Paul wrote was certainly aimed at helping Titus discredit these teachers and protecting the church from them. Since Paul clearly indicated that these individuals were not paragons of godly living (Titus 1:10–11; 3:9–11), it stands to reason that this letter was very effective in discrediting them.

In our modern churches, we need to reflect on Paul's rebuke: Are the leaders in our churches truly godly leaders? Or do they just have persuasive personalities? After finishing his critique, Paul concluded his letter to Titus with a final exhortation: "Let our people learn to devote themselves to good works for pressing needs" (Titus 3:14).

---

[11] A good example of this is the emphasis that James puts on serving orphans and widows (Jas 1:27).

HIGHLIGHTS IN 2 TIMOTHY

Greeting (2 Tim 1:1–5)

Paul's introduction to 2 Timothy is uniquely personal in two key ways. First, he explained that he was an apostle "for the sake of the promise of life in Christ Jesus" (2 Tim 1:1). This source of motivation seems particularly significant in light of Paul's impending death (2 Tim 4:6); Paul was likely thinking of this "promise of life" regularly.[12] Second, Paul called Timothy his "dearly loved son" (2 Tim 1:2). If you received a note from someone who called you "dearly loved," you would likely read the entire note differently than a formal business note. The tone of a letter impacts the meaning of the words contained in that letter, and that is why it is so crucial to understand Paul's tone in this introduction.

Remember the Gospel and Remind Others of Its Truth (2 Tim 1:3–2:19)

Paul continued with personal notes and heartfelt expressions throughout this section. Paul said he prays for Timothy day and night (2 Tim 1:3), and he even remembers Timothy crying during their last farewell (2 Tim 1:4). Paul mentioned the faith of Timothy's mother and grandmother and then goes on to challenge Timothy to "rekindle the gift of God that is in you" (2 Tim 1:6). Whether Paul was rebuking Timothy for neglecting his gift or simply urging him to strengthen that gifting, the point is the same: Paul cared deeply about Timothy's spiritual health.[13]

The church has historically seen the relationship between Timothy and Paul as an excellent model of discipleship. This letter is a prime example of why. Paul spent a great deal of time encouraging Timothy in his spiritual journey. He challenged Timothy to trust the "sound teaching" that Paul

---

[12] The significance of this introduction for the entirety of 2 Timothy is profound. In fact, Towner argues that the main purpose of the entire letter can be summed up in this first verse: The gospel exists to produce new life, and it is this new life that motivates ministers of the gospel. See Towner, *1–2 Timothy and Titus*, 153–55.

[13] In Ben Witherington III, *Letters and Homilies for Hellenized Christians: A Socio-Rhetorical Commentary on Titus, 1–2 Timothy, and 1–3 John* (Downers Grove, IL; IVP Academic, 2006), 311–13, Witherington skillfully argues that Paul was trying to shame Timothy into actually practicing his gifting as a leader by mentioning the faith of his mother and grandmother. This is not wholly convincing, however. It is possible that Paul was simply urging Timothy to continue strengthening his gifting, especially after Paul's death, as Lea and Griffin, *1, 2 Timothy, Titus*, 187–88 suggest.

had given him (2 Tim 1:13), and he seemed to emphasize that teaching repeatedly (2 Tim 2:8). This does lead to a question: Why was Paul so concerned about Timothy's ongoing faith?

Rembrandt, *St. Paul in Prison*, 1627, Staatsgalerie Stuttgart

The text contains a few clues about Paul's concerns. First, he seemed to be worried that Timothy was be ashamed of Paul's imprisonment (2 Tim 1:8). Perhaps Paul was worried Timothy would not want to be associated with a convicted criminal. This may be why Paul went to great lengths throughout this letter to explain that the gospel is worth suffering for. He encouraged Timothy to share in suffering for the gospel (2 Tim 2:3). Paul may have been concerned that after he died Timothy would feel ashamed of his association with Paul and abandon preaching the gospel.

A second clue about Paul's motivations is found in his insistence that Timothy not be afraid (2 Tim 1:7). With Paul's impending execution, he was probably worried that his disciples would be scared into leaving the ministry. To guard against that, Paul encouraged Timothy to "be strong" (2 Tim 2:1) and "remember Jesus Christ" (2 Tim 2:8). In particular, Paul reminded Timothy that Jesus rose from the dead, and this was no doubt designed to strengthen Timothy's resolve.

Just as in the other Pastoral Epistles, Paul jumped quickly and intentionally between theology and practice, between sound doctrine and godly living. In doing this, he showed us that both our beliefs and actions matter; they both contribute to our formation as members of God's household. He drove this point home by critiquing two key false teachers, Hymenaeus and Philetus. He accused them of denying the resurrection (2 Tim 2:17–18) and leading people into ungodliness (2 Tim 2:16). The close association between false teaching and ungodly living is at the core of these letters.

What Does It Mean to Be Godly? (2 Tim 2:20–3:17)

Since Paul was encouraging Timothy to pursue godly living and right teaching, he spent some time in this section explaining what those things actually mean. Paul began with a dichotomy: some people are honorable; others are not. The difference between these two groups of people does not arise from their wealth, nationality, race, or intellect. Instead, Paul argued that honorable people *do* honorable things; they are kind to everyone, they patiently endure evil, and they correct others with gentleness (2 Tim 2:24). Honorable people pursue faith, love, and peace with a pure heart (2 Tim 2:22).

What about the dishonorable people? They indulge in youthful passions (2 Tim 2:22) and enjoy false teaching (2 Tim 2:23–24). Paul warned that there will be many of these people in the "last days."[14] Throughout the New Testament, the term "last days" can often mean the entire time between the death of Jesus and his second coming; as such, we are currently living in these "last days."[15] What will these dishonorable people be like? Paul provided a scathing list of vices; these people will be in love with themselves and money. They will be abusive, heartless, brutal, and obsessed with pleasure (2 Tim 3:2–5). Paul's description is both vivid and in complete contrast to the honorable people he described earlier.

Remember, Paul was connecting right teaching to the list of honorable virtues. He was saying that you have to have both in order to truly have either. If someone has memorized the Bible but does not love others well, then they really do not understand Scripture. The Pastoral Epistles teach us that there is more to right doctrine than simply head knowledge; to have the right teaching means connecting it to your life in the right way. Paul was worried about the mind's beliefs as well as the body's habits. You cannot know the text—truly, you cannot understand the Bible—unless you live out its teaching.

This brings us to perhaps the most well-known verse in all of 2 Timothy. Paul explained to Timothy that the way to become one of these honorable people is through Scripture: "All Scripture is inspired by God and is profitable for teaching, for rebuking, for correcting, for training

---

[14] The singular imperative *ginōske* is used here. It could be translated to say "Know!" or "Be aware!" as both a command and a warning.

[15] For more information on the use of "last days," see Bray, *The Pastoral Epistles*, 389–405. Also see George W. Knight III, *The Pastoral Epistles*, NIGTC (Grand Rapids: Eerdmans, 1992), 428–29.

in righteousness, so that the man of God may be complete, equipped for every good work" (2 Tim 3:16–17). This verse is often used to defend the inerrancy of Scripture; that is one of the theological implications of the text. However, that is not the main point of this passage. The primary teaching of Paul in this passage is that Scripture has a purpose. It makes "the man of God" (2 Tim 3:17) a better person. The Bible is true—of course—but even more than that, the Bible is *good*.

The Pastoral Charge (2 Tim 4:1–6)

Paul challenged Timothy to preach this *good* Scripture. If people would be led away by false teaching in the "last days"—and if being led away means becoming a horrible person—than the most loving thing Timothy could do is preach sound doctrine. In order to preach the gospel, however, Timothy would have to be willing to suffer.

Final Notes (2 Tim 4:6–22)

Paul, as a man approaching death, was well acquainted with the suffering that he was asking Timothy to face. However, Paul was confident that suffering for the gospel was worth it, and in his closing remarks he reminded Timothy of the eternal life to come for those who believe in Christ.

Paul concluded this letter to Timothy with a series of personal notes and warnings, and they show us how deeply Paul cared for Timothy. These personal notes also reveal a sad reality: Paul was alone. This great titan of the faith, who wrote roughly half of the New Testament, faced trials and death without any human beside him. A life in service of the gospel can be costly, but in the end, God brings those who love him "safely into his heavenly kingdom" (2 Tim 4:18).

BIBLIOGRAPHY

Bray, Gerald L. *The Pastoral Epistles I: 1 Timothy and 2 Timothy*. International Theological Commentary. New York: T&T Clark, 2019.

Dryden, J. de Waal. *A Hermeneutic of Wisdom: Recovering the Formative Agency of Scripture*. Grand Rapids: Baker Academic, 2018.

Knight, George W., III. *The Pastoral Epistles*. NIGTC. Grand Rapids: Eerdmans, 1992.

Köstenberger, Andreas J., and Thomas R. Schreiner, eds. *Women in the Church: An Interpretation and Application of 1 Timothy 2:9–15*. 3rd edition. Wheaton, IL: Crossway, 2016.

Lea, Thomas D., and Hayne P. Griffin Jr. *1, 2 Timothy, Titus*. NAC 34. Nashville: Holman Reference, 1992.

Lee-Barnewall, Michelle. *Neither Complementarian nor Egalitarian: A Kingdom Corrective to the Evangelical Gender Debate*. Grand Rapids: Baker Academic, 2016.

Marshall, I. Howard. *The Pastoral Epistles*. ICC. New York: T&T Clark, 2004.

Mounce, William D. *Pastoral Epistles*. WBC 46. Nashville: Thomas Nelson, 2009.

Ngewa, Samuel. *1 and 2 Timothy and Titus*. Africa Bible Commentary Series. Grand Rapids: Zondervan Academic, 2009.

Stark, Rodney. *For the Glory of God: How Monotheism Led to Reformations, Science, Witch-Hunts, and the End of Slavery*. Princeton, NJ: Princeton University Press, 2004.

Towner, Philip H. *1–2 Timothy and Titus*. The IVP New Testament Commentary Series 14. Downers Grove, IL: IVP Academic, 1994.

———. *The Goal of Our Instruction: The Structure of Theology and Ethics in the Pastoral Epistles*. New York: Bloomsbury Academic, 2015.

———. *The Letters to Timothy and Titus*. NICNT. Grand Rapids: Eerdmans, 2006.

Winter, Bruce W. *Roman Wives, Roman Widows: The Appearance of New Women and the Pauline Communities*. Grand Rapids: Eerdmans, 2003.

Witherington, Ben, III. *Letters and Homilies for Hellenized Christians: A Socio-Rhetorical Commentary on Titus, 1–2 Timothy, and 1–3 John*. Downers Grove, IL: IVP Academic, 2006.

Wright, N. T., and Michael F. Bird. *The New Testament in Its World: An Introduction to the History, Literature, and Theology of the First Christians*. Grand Rapids: Zondervan Academic, 2019.

Yarbrough, Robert W. *The Letters to Timothy and Titus*. PNTC. Grand Rapids: Eerdmans, 2018.

17

PHILEMON

JOHN CARTWRIGHT

CONNECTION POINT

What relevance does this tiny first-century letter have for us today? After all, not only was Philemon written nearly 2,000 years ago, it is also the third shortest book in the entire Bible (right behind 2 and 3 John). The answer is simple. Since the beginning of time, humanity has struggled in relational conflict with each other. It is as much a problem today as ever. In the millennia of observable human history, there have been constant improvements such as cures for diseases, modern transportation, inventions, and advancements in technology. Yet, despite all of those advancements, no one has been able to develop an easy remedy for resolving relational conflict.

Perhaps you have been hurt terribly by someone in your past and a deep root of bitterness has a hold of your heart. Or maybe you have considered hurting someone in return as a means of exacting revenge to even the score. Very often, when someone hurts or offends us, we consider them, in one way or another, in debt to us. In our eyes, they remain in a debtor's prison, unable to pay what we believe they owe us. Perhaps we even view that person as beneath us. And what about those of us who are neither the offender nor the offended? What might our role be in helping to resolve conflict? Modern wisdom would warn us against getting involved. "It's none of my business," or "Who am I to judge or get involved?"

In this short letter, we can observe a template for how to behave when seeking to resolve personal conflict. More specifically, Christians can learn about the theological basis for forgiveness. Additionally, we can learn that there is a major difference between biblical mediating and unbiblical meddling.

With this in mind, consider making this your prayer as you read and study this chapter:

God, you are just. You have given me your love and forgiveness without discrimination. Help me to do the same. Help me to see others the way that you do. Help me not to feel as though I can judge whether or not someone is worthy of my forgiveness, for how could I possibly think that I have the right to withhold something that even you do not withhold? I ask that you give me the faith both to learn how to forgive freely and also to intercede for those who need to reconcile with each other. Amen.

SETTING

Recipients

Paul wrote Philemon, along with Philippians, Ephesians, and Colossians, during his first Roman imprisonment, and as such this would likely make the date of writing to be sometime during AD 60–62.[1] The apostle Paul addressed the letter, "To Philemon our dear friend and coworker, to Apphia

---

[1] Richard R. Melick, *Philippians, Colossians, Philemon,* NAC 32 (Nashville: Holman Reference, 1991); Scot McKnight, *The Letter to Philemon,* NICNT (Grand Rapids: Eerdmans, 2017).

As these commentaries indicate, despite a brief period when it was questioned, nearly all scholars consider Paul to be the author of Philemon. Some authors make the case for an Ephesian imprisonment, however, which would make the date earlier. Nevertheless, the date of the writing will be the by-product of which prison Paul was in during this writing. Most argue for Roman imprisonment, which would favor AD 60–62.

The fertile Lycos valley, the region that contained the ancient city of Colossae.

our sister, to Archippus our fellow soldier, and to the church that meets in your home" (Phlm vv. 1–2). Although multiple people are listed as recipients, the rest of the letter makes it clear that Philemon was the primary recipient. It is important to point out that this letter is addressed to the church as well, and therefore would have been read publicly. In Paul's mind, the conflict he was addressing was not to remain a private matter.

One final thing to mention here is the connection between Colossians and Philemon. It is believed that Philemon lived in Colossae. This idea is supported, in part at least, by the fact that two prominent individuals mentioned in Philemon are also mentioned in the letter to the church at Colossae: Onesimus (Col 4:9) and Archippus (Col 4:17). For a good summary of the background of the city of Colossae and links for further study please review chapter 14.

Theme and Key Passage

The foundational theme of Philemon can be tied to two related words. In verse 6, Paul used the word *participation*, and in verse 17, Paul used the word *partner*. Both words are based on the Greek word from which we understand the concept of fellowship. The main characters of the letter to Philemon are of diverse backgrounds. We have the author of the letter, Paul, who was an apostle with a deep Jewish background. But we also have the subject of the letter, Onesimus, a runaway slave who was by the cultural standards of that day considered of little to no importance or social standing.[2]

Finally, we have the recipient of the letter, Philemon, a man of obvious prominence with a Gentile background. With such significantly different backgrounds, what could bind these three men together in such a way where Paul would use terms such as *participation* and *partner*, from which ideas such as fellowship, companionship, and mutual benefit are obvious extensions? The answer is simple: the gospel. Paul made the idea explicitly clear when he stated that in Christ "there is no Jew or Greek, slave or free, male and female; since you are all one in Christ Jesus" (Gal 3:28). Paul was not denying the physical reality of these distinctions; he was stating that these distinctions have no bearing on our equal standing in Jesus and how that reality should impact our standing with each other.

Consequently, Phlm v. 17 is the key verse of this brief book because it captures the essence of what Paul was asking of Philemon as well as providing the theological basis for that request.

Philemon v. 17 says, "So if you consider me a partner, welcome him as you would me."

Purpose and Occasion

Several factors must be considered as keys to understanding the background of Philemon. These factors revolve around the three key characters of this letter: Paul, Onesimus, and Philemon.

The first character is Paul. Paul was the author of the letter and utilized his role as an apostle to advocate on behalf of Onesimus. This imprisonment followed his third missionary journey and coincided with the final chapter of Acts. (For more on Paul's imprisonment, review chapter 12.)

The second character is Onesimus. Onesimus was a runaway slave of Philemon, who seems to have stolen from his master.[3] Although the details surrounding the circumstances are unclear, Onesimus connected with Paul in Rome during his imprisonment and became a follower of Christ (Phlm

---

[2] As a point of clarification, the Christian church has always been instructed to value every person as an image-bearer of God. In Christ, all believers are equal as children of God with all the rights thereunto regardless of the class in which they exist in that social system. However, Onesimus was a slave and viewed by those outside the church to be of a lower social standing than those in higher social classes. That is the simple reality of that day, and it factors into how Paul addressed this letter. Paul was working within a social system and trying to help bring a new realization in light of a Christian worldview.

[3] McKnight, *Letter to Philemon*, 38.

vv. 10–16). Onesimus accompanied Tychicus for the delivery of the letter to the Colossians (Col 4:7–9). This is believed to be the same time that the letter to Philemon was also delivered, which would mean that Onesimus would most likely have been present when the letter to Philemon was delivered and read.

The third key character for understanding the background of the letter to Philemon is, of course, Philemon himself. It is evident from the letter that in addition to Onesimus, Paul also converted Philemon to Christ (Phlm v. 19b). Exactly how and where Philemon was led to Christ is unclear, but it may have been while Paul was in Ephesus (Acts 19:10), since there is no record that Paul had a ministry where Philemon resided. Philemon had a close relationship with Paul (Phlm vv. 4–7). Philemon's role in this story was that he was quite obviously the master of Onesimus and the one to whom Paul addressed his appeal.

Paul's primary purpose in this brief letter to Philemon was to appeal to Philemon to receive Onesimus back. The basis for Paul's appeal was unity in Christ. Paul called on Philemon, a man whose love for others was well known (Phlm vv. 4–7), to exercise that love toward someone who was now also a brother in Christ, Onesimus. Paul acted as an advocate on Onesimus's behalf, not by coercing Philemon into action, but rather calling upon Philemon to act according to his understanding of the unity of all believers in Christ.

Does the Bible Promote Slavery?

Before there is an attempt to answer this question, it must be pointed out that there appears to be a great difference between most of the slavery we read about in the Bible and the slavery associated with the eighteenth and nineteenth centuries in America (as well as around the world). The Bible references slavery quite often. Slavery was very common. Some even estimate that as many as a third of the people during the first century of Christianity would have been slaves to one degree or another. Jewish law made protective provisions for slaves, and New Testament writers discuss the importance of fair treatment for slaves. In 1 Corinthians, Paul advises slaves to seek their freedom if possible. Paul also emphasizes that when it comes to one's relationship with Christ, there are no human distinctions such as "slave" or "free" (Gal 3:28). Slavery is even used, at times, as a positive metaphor for serving God. So while the Bible does not promote slavery, its existence is not ignored in Scripture. Sadly, Scripture has at times been abused and misused to justify slavery and view some races as less valuable than others. The reality is that the gospel message leaves no room for racism.

HIGHLIGHTS IN PHILEMON

Philemon's Public Testimony (Phlm vv. 4–7)

Paul let Philemon know that he was grateful for him because, even in a prison in Rome, he had heard of Philemon's acts of love toward fellow believers. In a time when technology such as email, text messages, or social media did not exist, it is quite profound that Philemon's behavior was noteworthy enough to come to Paul's attention while he was in prison or under house arrest. Paul not only recognized that others benefitted from Philemon's love, but he specifically noted that this behavior was a benefit to Paul himself (Phlm v. 7). It seems clear that Philemon was a man whose character was already in the right place for the biblical response to what Paul would request next.

Paul's Appeal to Philemon for Onesimus, Part 1 (Phlm vv. 8–16)

Paul began his appeal for Onesimus by informing Philemon that Onesimus was now a follower of Christ. Paul used a series of contrasts in this passage. He described Onesimus once as "useless" but now as "useful." He suggested that Onesimus was separated from Philemon briefly so that he could have him back permanently. He also asked that Philemon would have him back, not just as a slave, but as a brother. Each of these ideas

An ancient Roman mosaic from Dougga, Tunisia, showing two Roman slaves carrying wine jars and wearing typical slave clothing

contrasted who Onesimus was before (useless, earthly slave) against who Onesimus now was (useful brother in Christ, an eternal identity).

Another aspect of Paul's appeal for Onesimus was Paul's offering of perspective to Philemon. Paul wanted Philemon to consider the sovereignty of God in these circumstances (Phlm vv. 15–16), just as Joseph did in response to his brothers' evil against him (Gen 50:20).

Last, Paul's initial appeal to Philemon was in reference to their existing relationship. Paul referenced his authority in Philemon's life only to point out that he did not wish to order Philemon to obey him. Paul's appeal was based on love (Phlm vv. 8–9). Paul revisited this concept later, but for now, it was important to point out this incredible principle that we can learn from Paul. He did not make Philemon's response here a matter of obedience to himself. How often do leaders of Christ's church create confusion by calling the church to serve themselves instead of Jesus? However, despite this, Paul did not shrink away from pointing out that Philemon's choice to forgive Onesimus would be of great personal benefit to himself and that Paul's act of sending Onesimus to Philemon was like sending a part of himself (Phlm v. 12). This was not just sentiment, as we will see in the next section.

Paul's Appeal to Philemon for Onesimus, Part 2 (Phlm vv. 17–22)

Here Paul made his most direct appeal to Philemon. Philemon v. 17 would be considered the apex of the letter: "So if you consider me a partner, welcome him as you would me." Do not miss what Paul did here. Paul had already described the conversion of Onesimus to Christ as a direct result of his contact with Paul. Paul also implied the same in relationship to Philemon ("not to mention that you owe me even your very self" [v. 19]). Paul described himself as a brother to Philemon (vv. 7, 20). Paul also described Onesimus as a "dearly loved brother" v. 16).

Paul was making the case for forgiveness based on the biblical principle that regardless of earthly distinctions such as ethnicity, gender, or social class, we are all one in Christ (Gal 3:28). But Paul did this in a very powerful and convincing way. He called upon his relationship with Philemon ("if you consider me a partner" [v. 17]). Philemon would not argue against this truth. Paul's conclusion then was that based on the same truth that makes Paul and Philemon partners, Philemon should welcome Onesimus back.

Paul's argument was not purely sentimental; it's theological. He and Philemon are brothers, and Paul and Onesimus are brothers. Therefore, Philemon and Onesimus are brothers. Paul was making a countercultural argument here. The idea that, somehow, Onesimus—who was literally considered Philemon's property—could be considered as much of a partner to Philemon as the apostle Paul would have been radical.

But is this any more radical than the idea that God considers us his children and co-heirs with Christ? Forgiveness, then, should never be viewed as something that must be earned or only given to certain people because of their status. This is not how God forgives us, nor is it how he expects us to forgive others. As a leader, Paul mediated between Philemon and Onesimus and argued that no social classification could supersede the idea that we are one in Christ and therefore family.

One final item that is worth mentioning is Paul's utilization of his position. Paul utilized his leadership to speak up for someone who would not have had a voice. It is also worth noting that some would make the case that when Paul stated in Phlm v. 21, "I am writing to you, knowing that you will do even more than I say," he was referencing that Philemon might actually free Onesimus. Regardless, Paul neither ordered Philemon what to do by coercive "strong-arming," nor did he shrink away from being involved. He chose to act while making his case for action on biblical grounds. The implications for today's church, and its leaders, are numerous.

This chapter began with the question, "What relevance does this tiny first-century letter have for us today?" As long as sin remains, the issue of conflict and forgiveness will also remain, and this brief letter gives us a great picture of how believers can handle conflict in a God-glorifying way. What is important to note here is that forgiveness is not an option for the believer. Unforgiveness is not merely unkind; it ignores the reality of our equal standing as brothers and sisters in Christ, regardless of social standing. On the same basis from which Paul appealed to Philemon to reconcile, we must also obey. Additionally, observing believers should not choose to say, "It's none of my business" and allow conflict to go on without being willing to become involved. Like Paul, we can appropriately mediate the situation and urge believers to reconcile.

BIBLIOGRAPHY

McKnight, Scot. *The Letter to Philemon*. NICNT. Grand Rapids: Eerdmans, 2017.

Melick, Richard R. *Philippians, Colossians, Philemon*. NAC. Nashville: Holman Reference, 1991.

18

HEBREWS

MATTHEW KIMBROUGH

CONNECTION POINT

What relevance does this first-century writing have for us today? Since you have made it to this point in the book, you know the apostles taught, "Christ died for our sins according to the Scriptures" (1 Cor 15:3). The Gospels, Acts, and Paul's letters proclaim that the death of Jesus provides forgiveness to those who respond in faith. The conclusion of perhaps the most famous verse in the Bible, John 3:16, declares, "Everyone who believes in him will not perish but have eternal life." After reading well over half of the New Testament, though, you may still wonder, "Why?" Why does a man's death grant me forgiveness and life? Why did Jesus have to die? You may also wonder what Jesus is doing for the believer today. Is he merely playing heavenly golf right now, waiting for believers to arrive in paradise? Or might Christ's ministry to struggling humanity continue today?

If any of these questions resonate with you, Hebrews is the book for you. No New Testament writing offers a more robust explanation of the sacrificial death of Jesus and his current ministry to believers. No New

Testament writer more clearly links the crucifixion of Jesus to the Old Testament laws of sacrifice and priesthood (i.e., the Mosaic law or Torah). And no New Testament text offers harsher warnings to those who ultimately reject Christ.

The uniqueness of Hebrews demands careful study of this rich and challenging book. The student of Hebrews must keep one foot in the New Testament and one in the Old Testament, just as the theatergoer must understand the first act of the play in order to appreciate the second. Old Testament books like Leviticus and Deuteronomy come alive as we invest in Hebrews. And, prayerfully, our appreciation for the past and present ministry of Jesus will motivate our devotion to the Author and Perfecter of our faith, the Apostle and High Priest of our confession, the Son of God by whose blood the believer is forgiven.

With this in mind, consider making this your prayer as you read and study this chapter:

> *Father God, thank you for sending Jesus as the Great High Priest and sacrifice for sin. Please reveal the depth of his sacrifice to me as I study Hebrews. Grow my appreciation for all that Jesus did and all he continues to do for the children of God. As I learn, grow my faith and devotion to the Savior, who sympathizes with my weakness as a human. Thank you for the church he formed to protect those who struggle with their faith. Amen.*

SETTING

Recipients

Hebrews provides more questions than answers when it comes to the author, audience, and date. The book is anonymous and does not begin as a typical letter or end by greeting specific believers. Early church leaders suggested that Paul, Barnabas, or Luke might have penned the book; but Apollos holds sway among modern scholars.[1] Acts 18:24–28 paints

---

[1] Early church fathers who argued for Pauline authorship of Hebrews include Eusebius, Athanasius, Didymus the Blind, Epiphanius, Cyril of Jerusalem, Chrysostom, Jerome, Theodore of Mopsuestia, Augustine, Cyril of Alexandria, and John of Damascus. Even the KJV titles the book, "The Epistle of Paul the Apostle to the Hebrews." Not until 1522 did Martin Luther nominate Apollos as the author, becoming the first theologian to do

Apollos as a Jewish–Christian apologist known for his eloquence and comprehension of the Old Testament. Apollos was also an early church leader (1 Cor 1:12) and knew the apostle Paul (1 Cor 16:12). Likewise, the author of Hebrews (1) wrote advanced Greek with rhetorical skill, (2) was well-versed in the Old Testament, (3) knew Timothy, and (4) was a "second-generation" follower of Jesus—meaning that those who learned directly from Jesus taught the gospel to him and his audience (Heb 2:3). Paul would not describe himself as a second-generation Christian (Gal 1:11–12), but Apollos fit the mold in all categories.[2]

The title attached to the book at an early date reads, "To the Hebrews," suggesting that the audience was composed of Jewish Christians. The author closed the book, writing, "Those who are from Italy send you greetings" (Heb 13:24b). Most likely, expatriates from Italy sent their greeting back home to Italy, the location of the audience of Hebrews.[3]

Finally, the author wrote Hebrews sometime between AD 40–95, the latter

> **Septuagint**
>
> The Septuagint (abbreviated LXX) is the Greek translation of the Hebrew Scriptures (the Old Testament). The Septuagint often translates the Hebrew literally, but not always, as we see in Ps 40:6. The Hebrew reads, "You open my ears to listen," while the Septuagint says, "You prepared a body for me." The Septuagint translators apparently summarized the Hebrew rather than translating literally. Two practical implications arise. First, if you look up an Old Testament quotation in Hebrews, do not fear if it differs from your English Old Testament. Hebrews uses the Septuagint while your English Old Testament translates the original Hebrew. Second, the theology of Hebrews often depends on the distinct language of the Septuagint, such as the quotation of Ps 40:6 in Heb 10:5–7. Therefore, the Septuagint is worth studying as a theological resource in its own right since, like most today, the early church depended on a translation of Scripture.

---

so. Other potential authors include Clement of Rome, Epaphras, Mary (mother of Jesus), Philip, Peter, Priscilla, Silas, and Stephen, though the evidence does not support such proposals. See Herbert H. Bateman IV, Charts on the Book of Hebrews, Kregel Charts of the Bible (Grand Rapids: Kregel Publications, 2012), 19–25.

[2] Nevertheless, the inspired author, who was surely known to the audience, chose not to include his name. Given a robust theory of divine inspiration, identifying the author is not essential for a proper understanding of Hebrews. God did not inspire him to record his name, so we do not need him identified for exegesis. In addition, building exegesis upon an unproven author's identity is risky, so we must embrace the mystery. For an accessible introduction to the issues, see Karen H. Jobes, *Letters to the Church: A Survey of Hebrews and the General Epistles* (Grand Rapids: Zondervan Academic, 2011), 23–55.

[3] Another possibility is that the author wrote *from* Italy, possibly to Jerusalem or Alexandria. Alexandria, Egypt, was the home of Apollos, the birthplace of the Septuagint (the Greek translation of the Old Testament utilized consistently in Hebrews), and endured a time of persecution during the reign of Caligula (AD 37–41).

Objects are from ancient Israel, primarily artifacts from the eighth to seventh centuries BC. They give a brief glimpse into ancient Hebrew culture.

being the date of the first reference to Hebrews in post–New Testament literature.[4] Because of the destruction of the Jerusalem temple, AD 70 is also a watershed date. Hebrews 10:1–3 implies that priests were still offering sacrifices, implying that the Jewish temple was standing. If so, the author likely wrote between AD 50 and 70.[5]

Theme and Key Passage

Hebrews calls its audience to endure in faith in the enthroned Son, the better High Priest. Like 1 Peter, the persecuted audience of Hebrews needed the motivation to endure their circumstances at all costs, and faith was the foundation for endurance.[6] But what was to be the basis of their faith? In

---

[4] Read Hebrews 1 and compare 1 Clement 36:2–5, written approximately AD 95. For more on dating, see Thomas R. Schreiner, *Commentary on Hebrews*, Biblical Theology for Christian Proclamation 36 (Nashville: Holman Reference, 2015), 5–6.

[5] On the other hand, the author never refers to the "temple," only the "tabernacle." Likewise, the book of Acts never mentions Timothy's imprisonment (cf. Heb 13:23), opening the possibility that he was not jailed until after AD 70.

[6] The Greek *pistis* can refer to faith (i.e., belief) or faithfulness (i.e., deeds indicating

short, Jesus. He is better than any other foundation, even admirable ones like the angels, Moses, sacrificed animals, or faithful Old Testament saints. Of all the attributes highlighted in Hebrews, Christ's sonship and high priesthood make him the perfect mediator between struggling humans and the heavenly Father.

Hebrews 4:14–16 tells us: "Therefore, since we have a great high priest who has passed through the heavens—Jesus the Son of God—let us hold fast to our confession. For we do not have a high priest who is unable to sympathize with our weaknesses, but one who has been tempted in every way as we are, yet without sin. Therefore, let us approach the throne of grace with boldness, so that we may receive mercy and find grace to help us in time of need."

Purpose and Occasion

The author of Hebrews named only two problems troubling his audience members: apathy and persecution. First, the audience exhibited apathy in their growth as Christian thinkers and their participation in church life. In Heb 5:11–14, the author accused his audience, saying, "You have become too lazy to understand" (5:11b), and, "You need someone to teach you the basic principles of God's revelation again" (5:12b). Later, he warned them not to neglect gathering as believers, "as some are in the habit of doing" (Heb 10:25a). What, then, had produced such indifference among the audience members?

Persecution was the second problem the audience faced. According to Heb 10:32–34, they had survived "a hard struggle with sufferings," "taunts and afflictions," and even "the confiscation of your possessions." Such persecution may have contributed to the audience's apathy just as the once devoted apostle Peter abandoned Jesus after his arrest in the garden of Gethsemane. Therefore, the author wrote to assure his audience that Jesus deserves constant devotion. He was worthy of a life of suffering too, even demonstrating at his death how to suffer joyfully and obediently (Heb 5:7–8; 12:2).

Interpreters throughout Christian history have presupposed that the audience desired to leave Jesus behind and return to simple Jewish faith.

---

the activation of faith). The author of Hebrews intertwines these two senses throughout the book. For an advanced treatment, see Matthew C. Easter, *Faith and the Faithfulness of Jesus in Hebrews*, Society for New Testament Studies Monograph Series 160 (Cambridge: Cambridge University Press, 2014).

The title, "To the Hebrews," and abundance of Old Testament references suggest that the audience included Jewish Christians. More important are the numerous comparisons between Old Testament structures and Jesus, who was better. The implication was that audience members needed to hear that Jesus was better because they were pursuing the "lesser": Judaism apart from faith in Christ.[7]

On the other hand, the author never referred to the audience "returning" to Judaism.[8] Also, the "better thans" were almost entirely positive, comparing Jesus to something or someone great (at least in its era of history) in order to show that Jesus is even greater. By way of comparison, claiming that my pastor is kinder than Mother Teresa uplifts him because Mother Teresa was known as a selfless person. But the listener would mistake my intentions if he thought I was attacking Mother Teresa. Therefore, the author did not claim Jesus is "better" to devalue the "lesser," and the comparisons do not suggest the audience wanted to leave Jesus behind. We will treat apathy and persecution, then, as the primary occasions for Hebrews.

HIGHLIGHTS IN HEBREWS

Prologue (Heb 1:1–4)

The brief introduction to Hebrews sets the stage for the entire book. The author claimed that while God spoke in prior eras through prophets, he now spoke through his own Son. Who better represented what the Creator of the universe (Heb 1:2) wanted to say than a Son who is "the exact expression of his nature" (Heb 1:3)? In addition to the emphasis on God speaking that will continue throughout the first few chapters of Hebrews, the author introduced four major themes in the concise prologue. First, the arrival of Jesus marked a new era in which the end times have begun: "these last days" (Heb 1:2). The audience was already "receiving a kingdom" (Heb 12:28) and entering God's rest (Heb 4:3), but the full experience of these realities would only come in the future. Second, the author

---

[7] For a defense of this position, see Schreiner, *Commentary on Hebrews*, 7–8.

[8] Only in Heb 11:15 does the word *return* occur, referring to Abraham's ability to return to his homeland if he so chose. For a critique of the "return to Judaism" view, see Luke Timothy Johnson, *Hebrews: A Commentary*, The New Testament Library (Louisville: Westminster John Knox Press, 2006), 36–37.

treated Jesus as divine. Hebrews 1:2–3 claims that Jesus is the agent of creation who will inherit "all things." He is "the radiance of God's glory," just as heat and light radiate from the sun. Like a stamp that duplicates an original image perfectly, Jesus is the "imprint" or "expression" of God's divine nature. Third, Jesus is the High Priest who atones for sin (Heb 1:3c), the focal point of the central unit in Hebrews (4:14–10:39). His priesthood is effective since he has now sat down at the right hand of God (Heb 1:3). He is not merely a *different* agent of God but the ultimate representation of his Father.

> ### Rhetoric in Hebrews
>
> The Greco-Roman world valued rhetoric—the practice of effective argumentation. Two rhetorical skills dominate the argumentation of Hebrews, which is among the most advanced in the New Testament. First is *synkrisis*, the comparison between two people, events, or entities. *Synkrisis* stands behind many of the author's warnings and also the frequent "better thans" used to exalt Jesus. A second common device in Hebrews is the *Qal Wahomer* argument, where the author asks, "If the lesser is true, how much more is the greater true?" For example, if a lazy student passes the exam, how much more will a studious worker pass? Or in Hebrews, "For if the blood of goats and bulls . . . sanctify for the purification of the flesh, how much more will the blood of Christ . . . cleanse our consciences from dead works so that we can serve the living God?" (Heb 9:13–14).

Jesus: The Better Messenger (Heb 1:5–2:18)

The transition out of the prologue into the first unit of Hebrews may surprise the first-time reader. Of all the "better than's" in Hebrews, you may not expect the author to begin by proclaiming that Jesus is better than the angels. Why does he start here? Were they obsessed with angels? Did they think Jesus was an angel? Probably not. Instead, the author thought of angels as God's exalted messengers in order to show that Jesus was an even better messenger. What was clear to Greek readers is that the word *angel* (*angelos*) also means "messenger." Jewish tradition (*Jubilees* 1:27; 2:1, 26–27) holds that the angels mediated the Mosaic law, or, as Heb 2:2a expresses, "The message spoken through angels was legally binding." Jesus also speaks (Heb 2:3), but not as a mere angel. Angels are temporary ministers of God sent to serve humans (Heb 1:14); Jesus is the Son of God who will reign eternally. Whose message would you rather hear?

Chapter 2 turns to the problem of death and suffering in the world. The author answered a series of implied questions. If Jesus is better than the angels—crowned with glory and promised rule over all things—why did he suffer as a human? Why did his enemies still hold power? Even more, if Jesus is my Savior, seated at God's right hand, why am I suffering?

In response, the author's first shocking claim was that Jesus's death was a source of glory (Heb 2:9), not a reason for shame.[9] Second, the author redefines suffering, noting in Heb 2:10 that Jesus's trials made him "perfect." Later, the author clarified that Jesus faced all temptation without sin (Heb 4:15), so how could Jesus become "perfect"? The problem is that the English term *perfect* carries moral connotations, but the Greek can also mean "complete" or even "qualified."[10] What the author suggests, then, is that Jesus's suffering and death fully prepared him to function as a faithful brother who can identify with and help those who struggle. Just as the cancer survivor can more effectively minister in the oncology ward, so also Jesus can compassionately minister because he understands human weakness (Heb 2:11).

What about Jesus's enemies? The author had already claimed Jesus would one day crush his enemies (Heb 1:13; 2:8), but the future-oriented promise did not leave the believer helpless today. In Heb 2:14–15, the author explained, "Now since the children have flesh and blood in common, Jesus also shared in these, so that through his death he might destroy the one holding the power of death—that is, the devil—and free those who were held in slavery all their lives by the fear of death." The death of Jesus equips him to serve as humanity's High Priest and make atonement for sins (Heb 2:17). Furthermore, because of his brotherhood with humanity, "he is able to help those who are tempted" (Heb 2:18). In sum, Jesus has defeated the devil, revoked the fear of death, atoned for sins, and provided help for tempted believers. Thus, the suffering and death of Jesus do not prove he is unable to help today; rather, Jesus's weakness is the solution to all of our troubles.

Follow the Better Moses into God's Rest (Heb 3:1–4:13)

What most threatens churches today? Where do potential land mines lie? You might identify decreases in giving and attendance, moral failures among church leadership, or the church's poor reputation as the most considerable risks. For the author of Hebrews, however, the greatest threat to Christian communities was unbelief. To illustrate the point, the author pointed back to Moses and the Israelites at the time God brought them to the edge of the Promised Land. God had promised, in Genesis 12, to give

---

[9] Interestingly, the author waited to use the proper noun *Jesus* until this point in the letter, emphasizing that the person of Jesus was most clearly seen in his death.

[10] See Schreiner, *Commentary on Hebrews*, 96–97.

Abraham and his descendants a land of their own. This land promise featured prominently in Israel's hope. Therefore, when God brought Israel out of slavery in Egypt, they began a journey toward their new homeland—the land of promise. Unfortunately, ten out of twelve scouts returned from the land and warned that Israel could not defeat the giant inhabitants. The people did not trust God to protect them, so fear caused nearly all Israelites over the age of twenty to miss out on God's provision (Numbers 14). They died before reaching the "resting place" for the travel-weary Israelites. Speaking of the Promised Land, Moses later reflected, "Indeed, you have not yet come into the resting place and the inheritance the Lord your God is giving you" (Deut 12:9). We refer to the Israelites who died in the wilderness without entering the land of rest as "the wilderness generation."

An ancient folio of the Syriac Bible of Paris depicting Moses before Pharaoh.

In Heb 3:1–6, the author compared his audience to the wilderness generation by contrasting Moses and Jesus. Moses guided Israel as a faithful servant of God, but Jesus leads his household as a faithful Son. In Heb 3:7–11, the author quoted Ps 95:7–11 as a pointed warning to the audience of Hebrews not to harden their hearts like the Israelites whom God refused to allow into his "rest." God rescued Israel, and Moses led her out of Egypt. Even after seeing God's grace, though, they rebelled and disobeyed because they did not trust God. The author summarized in Heb 3:19, "So we see that they were unable to enter because of unbelief." The audience of Hebrews must avoid their infamous example.

The wilderness generation failed to enter the land of rest, but an even greater rest remains for believers today. In Heb 4:1–13, the author transitioned back to his own audience's situation, reminding them that the very "rest" God entered into on the seventh day of creation was open to the believer.[11] To make his point, the author quoted several Old Testament passages and frequently referred back to Psalm 95. It is no surprise, then, that he ended the unit with a warning that God still speaks and convicts through Scripture. God's Word cuts deep and strips all people naked, leaving no room to hide. The warning reveals the seriousness of unbelief because it cannot remain hidden. What, then, is the solution to the problem of unbelief? How does someone exploring Christianity avoid imitating the wilderness generation?

The author provided the answer in Heb 3:13, writing, "But encourage each other daily, while it is still called today, so that none of you is hardened by sin's deception." In the previous verse, the author recalled the sibling language of chapter 2, referring to his audience as "brothers and sisters." Christian siblings protect one another through daily attention and mutual encouragement. Notice, too, that the author did not merely expect a sermon on Sunday to prevent unbelief. All believers are responsible to minister to each other daily. The congregation bears this charge, "so that there won't be in any of you an evil, unbelieving heart that turns away from the living God" (Heb 3:12b). The author will continue to look to the Christian community throughout Hebrews as the solution to unbelief.

Do Not Neglect the Better High Priest (Heb 4:14–10:39)

The lengthy "central exposition" of Hebrews depicts Jesus as the Great High Priest and sacrifice for sin who inaugurates the new covenant. However, the author faced a serious hurdle: the problem of Jesus's lineage. The law of Moses stipulated that priests come only from the tribe of Levi, and only Aaron's descendants could serve as high priests.[12] Unlike a college student choosing a major, the average Israelite could not decide to become a priest because he felt called or gifted in that area. Therefore, the author could not argue that Jesus was a typical priest since he belonged to the tribe of Judah (Heb 7:14). Hebrews must take an unexpected route to establishing Jesus's priesthood.

The author clarified, "Christ did not exalt himself to become a high priest" (Heb 5:5). In other words, Jesus did not steal the priesthood for

---

[11] See the excursus "Sabbath Rest for Jewish Christians," in Ben Witherington III, *Letters and Homilies for Jewish Christians: A Socio-Rhetorical Commentary on Hebrews, James and Jude* (Downers Grove, IL: IVP Academic, 2007), 180–82.

[12] The distinction comes into view beginning in Exodus 28.

The Western Wall, a part of the ancient construction of and Dome of the Rock in the Old City of Jerusalem

himself or circumvent biblical norms. Only God can call a priest, and he did just that when, speaking to Jesus through Psalm 110, God said, "You are a priest forever / according to the order of Melchizedek" (quoted in Heb 5:6).

If you are unfamiliar with Melchizedek, you are in good company. His name only appears in two chapters of the Old Testament: Genesis 14 and Psalm 110. Melchizedek is an enigmatic figure who emerged after Abraham defeated an alliance of kings, winning back captives and resources for his partners. Genesis 14:18–20 describes Melchizedek as the king of Salem and priest of God who blessed Abraham. Abraham did not balk at this stranger but paid Melchizedek a tithe just as the Israelites would later tithe to the Levitical priests. After his brief appearance in Genesis 14, Melchizedek disappeared from the pages of Scripture until Psalm 110, where David anticipated a future priest like Melchizedek, who will sit at God's right hand as a conquering King.

Jesus could not become a Levitical priest, but he could serve as a priest like Melchizedek. The prophecy of Psalm 110 provides the crucial link in the author's theological chain. Through David, God promised long ago that another priest like Melchizedek would arise. "And this becomes clearer if another priest like Melchizedek appears, who did not become a priest based on a legal regulation about physical descent but based on the power of an indestructible life" (Heb 7:15–16). In essence, Jesus's earthly lineage no longer mattered because of his resurrection, making him a new kind of human and allowing him to serve like Melchizedek did in a pre-Levite era.[13]

With the problem of Jesus's lineage solved, the author moved on to explain how Jesus was a better priest with a better sacrifice, inaugurating a better covenant (Heb 7:23–10:18). First, Jesus is a better priest because the purification he provides will never end since he will never die again (7:23–25). Jesus now ministers in the heavenly tabernacle, the place of God's presence, where he continually intercedes on behalf of believers. Hebrews 7:25 says, "Therefore, he is able to save completely those who come to God through him, since he always lives to intercede for them." The result is that the believer enjoys unlimited access to God's presence through Jesus (4:16; 10:19–20).

Jesus is also a better sacrifice than bulls or goats. Before Christ came, animal sacrifices played a critical role, granting temporary purification for the sinner. In fact, when God gave the law to Moses, he instituted a system of atonement in which the sinful Israelite, and the nation as a whole, could offer a sacrifice as a substitute for sin (Lev 5:6). However, Hebrews claims such sacrifices could only help the body (Heb 9:9b–10, 13; 10:4), and their yearly repetition implied their ineffectiveness (9:25; 10:1–4, 11). We could compare the latter point to a wedding ceremony. If remaining married required a yearly wedding,

> ### The Warnings in Hebrews
>
> The most controversial passages in Hebrews are the warnings in 2:1–4; 3:7–4:13; 6:4–8; 10:26–39; 12:12–29. For centuries, theologians have mined these texts for implications regarding the doctrine of salvation. How do I know if I am truly saved? Can someone walk away from salvation? Is Jesus able to save me forever, or must I contribute something?
>
> As important as these questions are, the warnings in Hebrews serve a different purpose: to call the community to protect individual members who struggle with faith. The solution for spiritual doubt is a relationship with other believers who can encourage one another daily (Heb 3:12–13), bear fruit that benefits each other (6:7), minister to the persecuted (10:33), and strengthen the weak (12:12–13). Thus, audience members are most at risk when they neglect to gather with believers (10:25). On the other hand, the assurance of salvation grows by serving the saints (6:10).

---

[13] See Witherington, *Letters and Homilies for Jewish Christians: A Socio-Rhetorical Commentary on Hebrews, James and Jude,* 246.

we would not value the ceremony as much because of its temporary effect. It is the "once-for-all" nature of a wedding that makes it special. Likewise, Jesus only needed to die once (Heb 9:12, 15, 26–28) because his death cleanses the conscience once and for all (9:14). Hebrews 9:26b says, "But now he has appeared one time, at the end of the ages, for the removal of sin by the sacrifice of himself."

Finally, Jesus initiates a better covenant, the new covenant. The term *covenant* refers to an agreement between two parties, usually with stipulations for both.[14] In Hebrews 8, the author compared the old covenant mediated by Moses to the new covenant promised in Jeremiah 31.[15] The central new covenant promise is that God will remember the sins of his people no more. Believers experience God's forgiveness through Jesus's sacrifice alone. Forgiveness through Christ is the content of the gospel message, which all believers confess. Therefore, the author commands, "Let us hold on to the confession of our hope without wavering, since he who promised is faithful" (Heb 10:23).

Forgiveness and access to God's presence come through Jesus or not at all. Both the harsh warning in Heb 10:26–31 and the call to faith in Heb 10:32–39 motivate the audience to endure faithfully, looking to Jesus with hope no matter how bad circumstances look. "For you need endurance," the author reminded his audience in Heb 10:36, "so that after you have done God's will, you may receive what was promised." No matter how involved in a church they might be, those who devalue the sacrifice of Jesus have no hope, "but a terrifying expectation of judgment" (v. 27). Thankfully, the author was confident in his audience's future: "But we are not those who draw back and are destroyed, but those who have faith and are saved" (v. 39).

---

[14] In the early Israelite period, the word *covenant* usually referred to a treaty between a conquering nation and a defeated vassal nation. The conquerors would promise to protect and defend the vassal peoples, who would pledge allegiance to their former opponents. Either party's failure to live by these terms would break the covenant. Conversely, the Old Testament often emphasizes God's absolute faithfulness to the covenant. For a relatively brief but thorough introduction, see John H. Walton, *Covenant: God's Purpose, God's Plan* (Grand Rapids: Zondervan Academic, 1994).

[15] Hebrews 8:8–12 contains the longest Old Testament passage quoted in the New Testament.

Faithfully Endure, Waiting for the Better Future (Heb 11:1–12:29)
In light of all Jesus has done, the final main unit of Hebrews calls the audience to faithful endurance. Interpreters often refer to Hebrews 11 as the "Hall of Faith" because it tells a chronological story of Old Testament saints who maintained faith in God amid difficulty. The author first defined faith: "Now faith is the reality of what is hoped for, the proof of what is not seen. For by this our ancestors were approved" (vv. 1–2). Beginning in verse 3, the reader might expect tales of great successes, blessings, and times of joy, but Hebrews 11 emphasizes a different side of faith—confidence in God even when people did not receive what God promised: "These all died in faith, although they had not received the things that were promised. But they saw them from a distance, greeted them, and confessed that they were foreigners and temporary residents on the earth. Now those who say such things make it clear that they are seeking a homeland" (vv. 13–14). By not losing faith in God, these saints demonstrated that they were looking beyond this earthly life. God deserves their faith because "he has prepared a city for them" (Heb 11:16b).

The "Hall of Faith" does not end in Hebrews 11. In fact, the pinnacle of the author's list is Jesus himself, who faithfully endured both the cross and hostility from sinners (Heb 12:2–3). Believers, then, should run with endurance, looking to the examples of the "large cloud of witnesses" (12:1) and "keeping our eyes on Jesus (12:2). They must also realize that suffering may be a corrective measure God uses to produce "the peaceful fruit of righteousness to those who have been trained by it" (12:11b).

Later in chapter 12, the author also offered negative examples his audience should avoid. He depicted struggling congregation members as having spiritual disabilities that the church must heal (vv. 12–13). Another negative example is Esau, who sold his valuable inheritance for food (vv. 16–17). A final negative comes from the Israelites as they stood at the base of Mount Sinai. God warned them in Exodus 19 that if they touched the mountain, they would die. Therefore, they refused to hear the word of God, giving in to their fear and asking Moses to stand between God and Israel (Heb 12:18–21). Sinai became, for the author, a place of fearful separation from God, but his audience must see themselves on a mountain of fellowship: Mount Zion. There, the saints gather in the presence of God and his angels, confident they will never be shaken (12:22–29).

Letter Closing (Heb 13:1–25)

As the author began to close Hebrews, he issued a series of commands for community life. The first sums up all that the author hoped for his audience: "Let brotherly love continue" (Heb 13:1). If the church could live as a family, then hospitality, ministry to prisoners, marital purity, and even financial contentment would fall into place (13:2–6). Later, the author presented ministry to fellow believers as a sacrificial offering to God, writing, "Don't neglect to do what is good and to share, for God is pleased with such sacrifices" (13:16). Worship involves praise and gratitude, but brotherly love also honors God.

The closing benediction balances one of the most significant debates in theology: the relationship between God's sovereign work and humanity's responsibility. The apparent paradox appears throughout Hebrews. The command, "See to it that you do not reject the one who speaks" (Heb 12:25), appeals to the believer's responsibility. On the other hand, the author emphasized that God's will is to save through Jesus, writing, "By this will, we have been sanctified through the offering of the body of Jesus Christ once for all time" (10:10). Therefore, the author closed by reminding his audience to maintain theological perspective: "Now may the God of peace, who brought up from the dead our Lord Jesus—the great Shepherd of the sheep—through the blood of the everlasting covenant, equip you with everything good to do his will, working in us what is pleasing in his sight, through Jesus Christ, to whom be glory forever and ever. Amen" (13:20–21).

BIBLIOGRAPHY

Bateman, Herbert H., IV. *Charts on the Book of Hebrews*. Kregel Charts of the Bible. Grand Rapids: Kregel Publications, 2012.

Easter, Matthew C. *Faith and the Faithfulness of Jesus in Hebrews*. Society for New Testament Studies Monograph Series 160. Cambridge: Cambridge University Press, 2014.

Jobes, Karen H. *Letters to the Church: A Survey of Hebrews and the General Epistles*. Grand Rapids: Zondervan Academic, 2011. Johnson, Luke Timothy. *Hebrews: A Commentary*. The New Testament Library. Louisville: Westminster John Knox Press, 2006.

Schreiner, Thomas R. *Commentary on Hebrews*. Biblical Theology for Christian Proclamation 36. Nashville: Holman Reference, 2015.

Walton, John H. *Covenant: God's Purpose, God's Plan*. Grand Rapids: Zondervan Academic, 1994.

Witherington, Ben, III. *Letters and Homilies for Jewish Christians: A Socio-Rhetorical Commentary on Hebrews, James and Jude*. Downers Grove, IL: IVP Academic, 2007.

19

JAMES

A. CHADWICK THORNHILL AND EMILY C. PAGE

CONNECTION POINT

What relevance does this first-century writing have for us today? Do you ever read the Bible, or the teachings of Jesus, and say to yourself, "This is all well and good, but how do I make sense of this in my life?" If so, the book of James is here to help you. One of the important pieces of interpreting the Bible well is recognizing that it comes to us from different times, with its own sets of customs, characters, values, events, beliefs, and modes of communication. The Bible can seem a strange book at times, puzzling both familiar and new readers. This is where James, and specifically wisdom, comes to help. The Bible is not so much a list of dos and don'ts, or even "Basic Instructions Before Leaving Earth." The Bible is mostly a story, a narrative of God's interactions and interventions with his world.

Bible characters, for instance, are not always models of virtue. For example, we do not take our guidance from the life of David. Of course, the Bible does offer commands, but these commands are not always straightforward. When we get to commands on head coverings, meat sacrificed to idols, idolatry, or circumcision, for example, we often feel as if we are reading about a different world. That's because the world, over 2,000 years ago, *was* very different. Wisdom recognizes that life, just like the Bible, is not always black and white, not always easy to read, nor is it always clear what the "right" thing to do may be. Wisdom recognizes that life is messy, difficult, confusing, and at times downright hard. Wisdom does not leave us in despair, though. What James offers is a demonstration of how wisdom helps us see the teachings of the Lord "working" in everyday life. Jesus did not directly teach, for instance, about what to do when members of a congregation mistreat the poor and show favoritism to the wealthy, or how to deal with church leaders who misuse their words and position. But that does not mean Jesus had nothing to say on these matters. It is here that the book of James can show us the way: the way of wisdom.

With this in mind, consider making this your prayer as you read and study this chapter:

> *All-wise Father, as we meditate on the treasures of this letter, may our hearts be filled with your great love and our minds enabled to flourish from the truth we find within it. As we struggle to love you with all our being and to love our neighbor as ourselves in the midst of a changing and challenging world, we pray for your wisdom to guide us in each moment. Amen.*

SETTING

Recipients

James,[1] the brother of Jesus, is writing in the early AD 50s.[2] James's letter pulls important freight in the New Testament. It is a letter primarily to

---

[1] Though debate persists concerning the authorship of the letter, an entirely reasonable conclusion is that the James who penned it writes as an authoritative leader in the church and is quite familiar with Jesus's teachings. This James is indeed the same James who was the brother of the Lord Jesus Christ. See Peter H. Davids, *The Epistle of James,* NIGTC (Grand Rapids: Eerdmans, 1982), 2–22; Scot McKnight, *The Letter of James,* NICNT (Grand Rapids: Eerdmans, 2011), 13–38; Ben Witherington III, *Letters and Homilies for Jewish Christians: A Socio-Rhetorical Commentary on the New Testament* (Downers Grove, IL: IVP Academic, 2007), 395–400.

[2] Given the date typically assigned to James's martyrdom in the early to mid 60s, a date of the late to early 50s is reasonable for the letter (see McKnight, *Letter of James*, 38).

Jewish Christians rather than Gentiles. The central focus of the letter is reading the Sermon on the Mount through the lens of wisdom. Wisdom is that which brings truth to bear on the present realities of one's situation. Whereas law attempts to codify the right path forward, wisdom recognizes that legal guidelines cannot cover every life situation. Wisdom takes explicit guidelines and is able to apply them in situations that relate, even though explicit guidelines on those situations may not exist. The audience is identified as "the twelve tribes dispersed abroad" (Jas 1:1), which, along with references in the letter to the "synagogue" (Jas 2:2 ASV), and integration of numerous Jewish themes, likely indicates the letter was intended for Jewish Christians outside of the land of Judea (i.e., "diaspora" Jews).

Theme and Key Passage

As a wisdom text, James's flow of thought is not always easy to follow.[3] There are several key themes, however, that stand out from James's content. In this chapter we will examine four major themes: James's use of Jesus's Sermon on the Mount (which permeates the whole letter), his discussion of faith and works (Jas 2:1–25), his remarks about words and the tongue (Jas 3:1–4:17), and his comments on poverty, riches, and perseverance (Jas 5:1–12). James is a text with a practical heart. Its key message is that knowing God or the teachings of Jesus is not enough. Hearing without doing does a person as much good as buying healthy food without eating it. The nutrition does not lie in the acquisition, but in the digestion.

James 1:22 tells us: "But be doers of the word and not hearers only, deceiving yourselves."

Purpose and Occasion

Though James appears to have written this letter with the intention of it being widely circulated to Jewish Christians dispersed outside Israel,[4] two specific issues stand out in the letter: the treatment of the poor in the Jewish Christian community and the responsibilities of teachers for how they use their words and influence. It is not clear that James addresses a specific situation or locality in the letter, but it is quite possible that he had

---

[3] Witherington characterizes James's rhetoric as "enthymeme," meaning he does not always fully state his premises (Witherington, *Letters and Homilies: A Socio-Rhetorical Commentary on the New Testament*, 390). James at times expects his readers to read between the lines and connect the dots for themselves.

[4] Bauckham refers to the letter as a "paraenetic encyclical," or a "wisdom" letter intended to circulate broadly. Richard Bauckham, *James* (New York: Routledge, 1999), 13.

heard enough of these two issues arising within the Jerusalem church and outside of it that he sought to address with some detail how the Jewish Christian community ought to respond to them.

As Witherington notes, famines were not uncommon in the ancient world, and the issue of poverty and providing for the needs of the church family may be connected to such an event.[5] Since James was sensitive to these issues in his own community, he naturally sought to address them outside of Judea as well.[6] Concerning false teachers, it is evident as early as the events of Acts that some from inside and outside of the Christian community sought to take advantage of its growth (Acts 5:1–11; 8:9–25). While James could have had specific false teachers in mind, his familiarity with such figures in his own community may have again lent to his desire to address it to diaspora Christians as well.

The beautiful view from the Mount of Beatitudes, one of the likely locations for the Sermon of the Mount

---

[5] Witherington, *Letters and Homilies: A Socio-Rhetorical Commentary on the New Testament*, 402.

[6] Witherington, 402.

HIGHLIGHTS IN JAMES

James and the Sermon on the Mount (Jas 1:1–2:13)

The letter of James could be described as a meditation on the Sermon on the Mount. In the Gospel of Matthew, Jesus introduces the sermon as the fullness of the law (Matt 5:17–20). Essentially, Jesus said, "Do you want to know what God requires of you? Listen up." We thus might consider the Sermon on the Mount as the charter of the kingdom of God. In it, Jesus, the "greater Moses," unpacks the intent of the law, pointing at the kind of heart and actions God values. The kingdom ethic esteems the values and worth of others, even at the cost of something to one's self. One of the themes that runs throughout the sermon is that of sacrificial love, a virtue that Jesus himself embodied to the utmost.

What does this have to do with the letter of James? There are dozens of striking resemblances between James's letter and the Sermon on the Mount.[7] It is clear that the author was well acquainted with these teachings of Jesus. Consider the following parallels:

> **The Law**
>
> While many Christians often see the law as the "bad news," or perhaps as obsolete, this is not how either Jesus, or James, discussed it. Jesus told his followers in Matt 5:17–20 that he did not come to get rid of the law. The Sermon on the Mount, in fact, is Jesus's explanation about what the law really required. Jesus and James more reflect the attitude of the psalmist in Ps 119:97: "Oh, how I love your law! / I meditate on it all day long" (NIV). Though the law could not give the gift of new life, which only God through the work of Christ and the Spirit could provide (Romans 7–8), the law reveals the will and character of God to his people. When asked what the greatest commandment was, Jesus gave two: to love God (Deut 6:5) and to love your neighbor as yourself (Lev 19:18). According to Jesus, everything in the Law and the Prophets of the Old Testament "hangs" or "depends" upon these two commands. God is a God of love (1 John 4:8) who desires his people to be a people of love through his law of love.

- Have joy in trials (Matt 5:11–12; Jas 1:2)
- Be perfect/mature (Matt 5:48; Jas 1:4)
- Ask God for what is needed (Matt 7:7; Jas 1:5)
- God/Father gives good gifts (Matt 7:11; Jas 1:17)
- Be doers of the Word, not fools (Matt 7:24–26; Jas 1:22–23)
- The poor receive the kingdom (Matt 5:3; Jas 2:5)

---

[7] See Witherington, 393–95.

- The smallest matters of the law are important (Matt 5:18–19; Jas 2:10)
- The merciful are shown mercy (Matt 5:7; Jas 2:13)
- Know a tree by its fruits (Matt 7:16–18; Jas 3:12)
- Peacemakers are rewarded (Matt 5:9; Jas 3:18)
- You do not have because do not ask (Matt 7:7–8; Jas 4:2–3)
- One cannot serve two masters (Matt 6:24; Jas 4:4)
- The pure in heart are near to God (Matt 5:8; Jas 4:8)
- Those who mourn will be lifted up (Matt 5:4; Jas 4:9)
- Do not judge one another (Matt 7:1–2; Jas 4:11)
- Wealth rots and corrodes (Matt 6:19–21; Jas 5:2–3)
- Do not swear oaths (Matt 5:34–37; Jas 5:12)

James did not, however, simply reproduce the sermon. He was so well acquainted with the teachings of the Lord that he saw with clarity how they should impact the Jewish Christians to whom he wrote. We can see, as well, that James understood the teachings of Jesus and the law can be summarized in two commands: to love God with all of one's being, and to love one's neighbor as oneself (Matt 22:36–40). James referenced both the love of God, which must stand at the center of the life of the believer (Jas 1:12; 2:5), and the love of neighbor, which should flow from it (Jas 2:8). He referred to the latter as the "royal law," or in other words, the law of King Jesus, and referenced those who love God in Jas 2:5 as those who will inherit the kingdom. James had a kingdom vision of a glorious King who has given a royal law for his people to obey (Matt 28:19–20). This is the heart of James's letter.

This should be at the heart of the Christian life, as taught by Jesus and echoed here by James. How would our daily lives be transformed if they were shaped by these questions: Does this help grow my love for God? Is this a loving way to treat my neighbor? My children? My spouse? My enemies? Myself? Am I loving God and loving my neighbor as myself? If Christians miss this, they miss not only the heart of the letter of James, but the royal law of King Jesus himself.

Faith and Works (Jas 2:14–25)

When many think of the letter of James, they may think first of the controversy that surrounds it. In fact, it was this section of James that caused Martin Luther to write, "Therefore St. James' epistle is really an epistle of straw, compared to these others, for it has nothing of the nature of the gospel about it."[8] Harsh words! Luther, however, missed the mark on this matter, and what James wrote here finds harmony with the theology of the apostle Paul.

The heart of the controversy lies in what appear to be contradictory statements between these two leaders of the early church. Paul wrote, for example, in Rom 3:28 that "a person is justified by faith apart from the works of the law," while James wrote in Jas 2:24, "a person is justified by works and not by faith alone." Seems a pretty clear contradiction, does it not? And in the Greek text, Paul and James actually use the same words for "faith," "justified," and "works," so that does not solve the dilemma. This is why taking the context of a passage into consideration is crucial. To oversimplify a bit, Paul was writing to predominantly Gentile Christians who were being taught they needed to adopt certain Jewish practices such as circumcision or following certain dietary restrictions in order to fully be a part of God's kingdom family. Further, when Paul spoke of faith, he did not mean only something like "belief," but rather something like "total commitment" or "allegiance" (e.g., Rom 1:5; 2:13). James, on the other hand, was writing to predominantly Jewish Christians who were showing favoritism to the wealthy in their meetings to the neglect of the poor (Jas 2:1–13). In the context, James spoke of faith as mere belief or knowledge, something even the demons have (Jas 2:19). Both James and Paul agreed that the kind of "faith" that is pleasing to God is a faith in which one both believes that Jesus Christ is Lord (Rom 10:9; Jas 1:1; 2:1) and commits to offering his or her whole self to God through Christ (Rom 12:1). Faith for James and Paul was not simply "praying a prayer" or knowing the right things, or having the "right" doctrine. It was a trust and commitment to

> **The Gospel**
>
> The New Testament frequently speaks of the "good news of the kingdom" (Matt 4:23; 9:35; Mark 1:15; Luke 4:43; 8:1; 16:16; Acts 8:12). The gospel is not only that Christ died for our sins, though that is a central part of it. The gospel is the good news that God has kept his covenant promises of the Old Testament by coming to humanity through the incarnation of Jesus. Jesus's sacrificial death inaugurated the promised "new covenant" (Jeremiah 31; Ezekiel 36; Joel 2), and his resurrection began the divine restoration and reconciliation of all things (Col 1:20). When the New Testament authors discuss and describe this "good news," they talk about things such as Jesus's incarnation, life, death, resurrection, ascension, kingdom reign, and future return, and how those events fulfill God's promises. In other words, the gospel is the climax of the "big story" of Scripture about God and his love for the world.

---

[8] E. T. Bachmann, ed., *Luther's Works*, vol. 35 (Philadelphia: Muhlenberg, 1960), 362.

Jesus Christ as the risen Lord, evidenced by an obedience to his teachings. Remove any of those elements of belief, trust, or obedience, and you end up with a less than biblical view of faith.

The motivation that ultimately drove both Paul and James was to see the communities to which they were writing flourish through love of God and love of neighbor as one's self. Such a way of life unified their commitment to the good news of Jesus Christ as well as their commitment to love and serve those around them. Both the Roman church and James's audience had experienced divisions in their midst from ethnic and socioeconomic prejudices that had taken root.[9] James called his audience to examine their hearts and realize that their partiality to the rich and neglect of the poor was sin, pure and simple (Jas 2:9). They needed to repent and resurrect their dead faith (Jas 2:17) by changing their treatment of the vulnerable among them.

True Speech (Jas 3:1–4:17)

In connection with James's reflections on faith and works, he discussed the importance of "speech ethics" as a means for practicing true religion (Jas 2:14–26).[10] James used creative rhetoric to express his instruction to all believers, particularly leaders, that the tongue is one of the most powerful tools in the body, and it can be life giving or completely destructive. How a believer controls his or her speech is a strong indication of commitment to godly living.

James began his discussion of speech ethics by focusing on those who can do tremendous damage with their words: teachers (Jas 3:1). By "teachers," James was referring to the leaders of the Christian community who had great spiritual responsibility, especially since they were educated while most community members were not.[11] Just as Jesus taught that to whom much is given, much is required (Luke 12:48), James reminded his audience that leadership is not for the power hungry but is a role that must be undertaken with humility.[12]

---

[9] See Scot McKnight, *Reading Romans Backwards: A Gospel of Peace in the Midst of Empire* (see chap. 8, n. 18).

[10] Chris A. Vlachos, *James: Exegetical Guide to the Greek New Testament* (Nashville: B&H Academic, 2013), 104.

[11] For a further discussion of the status of teachers in the early Christian community, see McKnight, *Letter of James*, 270.

[12] McKnight, 271–72.

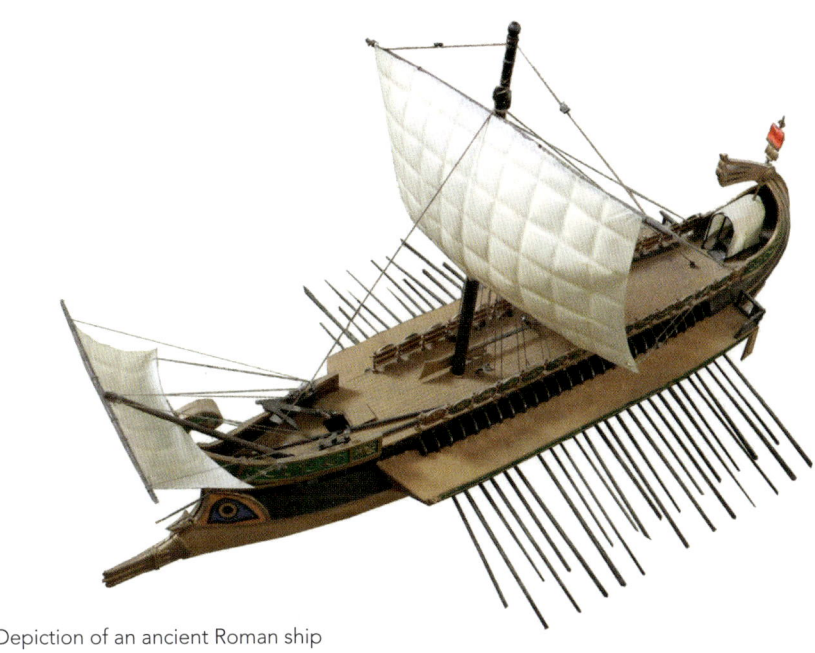

Depiction of an ancient Roman ship

The recognizable analogies of the horse and bit, ship and rudder, and spark and forest fire amplify the truth that in order to exemplify godly living, a person must escape the power of an untamed tongue (Jas 3:3–6). He described the person who can control his or her tongue as "perfect" (Jas 3:2 NIV), but if, as James said, "we all stumble in many ways" (Jas 3:2 NIV), how can anyone be perfect? Some interpreters argue that James was making a hypothetical point.[13] However, James wrote in Jas 1:27 that a person who does not control his or her tongue has worthless religion. It is evident that James saw controlling the tongue as a vital command, one that a believer *can* hope to obey—but through God's enablement.[14]

Godly wisdom is the means for living out true religion and controlling the tongue, and that wisdom both comes from and produces humility (Jas 3:13). James addressed the issue of those who act as though they have wisdom but live pridefully (Jas 3:14). His point was that having wisdom "from above" necessitates humility (Jas 3:17).[15] The measure of one's wisdom is

---

[13] Craig L. Blomberg and Mariam J. Kamell, *James*, ZECNT (Grand Rapids: Zondervan Academic, 2008), 153.
[14] Vlachos, *James*, 113–14.
[15] Blomberg and Kamell, *James*, 172.

revealed in the results; rather than producing strife and wickedness, godly wisdom produces peace, mercy, and good fruits (Jas 3:16–17).[16]

Often Christians are quick to point out Paul's instruction to speak the truth in love (Eph 4:15) when discussing James's instruction of true speech. A key aspect of James's teaching goes beyond knowing the wise thing to say (Jas 2:17). Wisdom leads believers to receive teaching just as much as it urges them to provide it where needed. It urges them to be "quick to listen, slow to speak" (Jas 1:19). It shows believers when to be wise by the works of our hands and when to sit in stillness (Jas 4:7–10).[17] Although a believer may sometimes want to speak, wisdom shows us at times godly speech means being silent.

In accord with James's commands to "submit [ourselves] to God" (Jas 4:7) and "humble [our]selves before the Lord" (Jas 4:10), he expounded what it would look like to live under God's authority. Genuine humility displays a willingness to submit to and position our lives under God's authority.[18] *Submission* is a controversial word in our culture, but it is a term that should be part of our daily mindset. Rather than making plans in our arrogance, sure we can make them happen (Jas 4:16), we must live according to the Lord's will, knowing he will prosper whatever he chooses (Jas 4:15). James ended this passage with the statement, "So it is sin to know the good and yet not do it" (Jas 4:17). The wisdom of a godly life does not just know the right thing to do, it does it in humility.

At the beginning of the passage, it seems as if James is giving us a reason to point the finger at our leaders for their failures (Jas 3:1). However, James reminded each one of us how "double-minded" we really are (Jas 4:8). If we slander those we see as unfit, we exemplify what James warns against: claiming ourselves righteous and appearing to worship God with a pure heart, but actually spewing bitterness from an equally bitter heart. James was not concerned with how Christians appear. Rather, he focused on the spiritual health of believers: on whether the wisdom of the Spirit or our selfish ambitions guides our thoughts and actions. Our moral "rudders" and "bits" can only lead us smoothly in one direction, otherwise we will be driven chaotically by a wayward heart.

---

[16] Blomberg and Kamell, 176.
[17] Witherington, *Letters and Homilies: A Socio-Rhetorical Commentary on the New Testament*, 504.
[18] Blomberg and Kamell, *James*, 193.

Poverty, Riches, and Perseverance (Jas 5:1–12)

In the midst of our cultural outcry against injustice, we are confronted daily with such extensive oppression that we at times become hopeless to see it end. James's letter reminds us that the Lord sees the oppression of the vulnerable, and he will rectify the injustices committed, in part here on earth, but fully at the coming of the Lord.[19] James expressed that the responsibility of the believer, both rich and poor, is to live justly and faithfully until the coming of the Lord (Jas 5:7–11).

An ancient Jewish half shekel

In James's world, the poor and the rich were not just the haves and have nots, but the poor were poor *because* the rich were rich. Resources were limited, and the wealth of one person was at the expense of the poverty of another.[20] The rich in James's day were guilty of unjust living, exploiting the poor, indulging their desires, and hoarding their gain (Jas 5:2–6).[21] James utilized the evocative image of the rich as fattened animals prepared for slaughter (Jas 5:5) to warn of the coming day of judgment for anyone who misuses their wealth. The corruption of the rich caused the continual suffering of the poor, and James warned that these actions would result in God's wrath.[22]

In Jas 5:7–8, James again used a pertinent analogy, this time of a farmer waiting for rain. Just as the farmer does not know when the rain will come, but knows it will, so the believer does not know when the Lord will come, but knows he will. Each appeal in Jas 5:7–11 is based on the imminent return of the Lord.[23] The exhortation for endurance echoes James's similar statement about steadfastness through trials at the opening of his letter (Jas 1:2–4, 12), and it also expands on James's discussion of wise living (Jas 3:13). Wisdom reminds believers that not only will the Lord return

---

[19] McKnight, *Letter of James*, 383.
[20] Witherington, *Letters and Homilies: A Socio-Rhetorical Commentary on the New Testament*, 511. For more on the economic context of James's letter, see Witherington, 526–27.
[21] Vlachos, *James*, 158.
[22] Witherington, *Letters and Homilies: A Socio-Rhetorical Commentary on the New Testament*, 528.
[23] Vlachos, *James*, 169.

and judge the wicked, but he will also judge us for being "double-minded" (Jas 5:9; 1:8). We cannot live naively, exclaiming, "Lord, come quickly!" without remembering that when he does, we will face his judgment just like the wicked who we wished to be spared from on earth.

James's letter is not a randomly constructed string of commands. He utilized impressive rhetoric to fluidly expound on the theme of righteous living, which is displayed by walking in the way of the wisdom that comes from above (Jas 3:17–18).[24] At the end of his letter, James reminds us that we are all answerable for rightly handling whatever God gives us, as little or much as it may be, and only godly wisdom may guide us to that end. James's encouragement focuses on the return of the Lord, which situates his commands to practice godly wisdom within the knowledge that God will soon, in his perfect timing, bring us up out of this life and into his presence.

BIBLIOGRAPHY

Bauckham, Richard. *James*. New York: Routledge, 1999.

Blomberg, Craig L., and Mariam J. Kamell. *James*. ZECNT. Grand Rapids: Zondervan Academic, 2008.

Davids, Peter H. *The Epistle of James*. NIGTC. Grand Rapids: Eerdmans, 1982.

Bachmann, E. T., ed. *Luther's Works*. Vol. 35. Philadelphia: Muhlenberg Press, 1960.

McKnight, Scot. *The Letter of James*. NICNT. Grand Rapids: Eerdmans, 2011.

———. *Reading Romans Backwards: A Gospel of Peace in the Midst of Empire*. Waco, TX: Baylor University Press, 2019.

Vlachos, Chris A. *James: Exegetical Guide to the Greek New Testament*. Nashville: B&H Academic, 2013.

Witherington, Ben, III. *Letters and Homilies for Jewish Christians: A Socio-Rhetorical Commentary on the New Testament*. Downers Grove, IL: IVP Academic, 2007.

---

[24] James's rhetoric is most noticeable in the Greek text but is also present in English.

20

1 PETER

ADAM MCCLENDON

CONNECTION POINT

What relevance does this first-century writing have for us today? Have you ever been afraid to speak up for your faith because of what people would think, say, or do? Have you ever felt dismissed or criticized on social media because you expressed your Christian worldview? Peter's audience understood the marginalization and attacks Christians experience. Christians throughout the world were regularly murdered because they refused to renounce their faith in Jesus. Such persecution is unjust, yet we often make the mistake of limiting persecution to such atrocities.

Social shunning, condescension, and slander are also serious aspects of persecution experienced by the church today, just as they were by the early church to which Peter wrote. Relational tensions are created when we choose the spiritual path of Jesus over the path preferred by our culture. While at times these paths are congruent, all too often they are at odds with one another. Those crossroads create tension.

Knowing that Jesus expected following him to bring strife in some of our closest human relationships (Matt 10:34–38), it should come as no surprise that following him can bring discomfort, criticism, and even hatred from the world at large. Taking a stand on the principles of Jesus as a result of our faith places a strain on relationships and brings criticism. When these difficulties arise, will you remain loyal to Jesus despite the consequences or will you compromise? Will you remember that your hope is in the world to come and not this present world, or will you despair?

If you seek to live out your faith, you will at times be socially shunned, patronized, and criticized. Now, certainly, throughout the world people and even entire villages are attacked because of their faith in Jesus. People are oppressed and persecuted. People have to leave their country and live as foreigners simply because they believe in Jesus, but persecution also takes on more subtle forms. Peter was addressing such persecution, and just as his message was relevant to his readers those many years ago, it is relevant to those of us who seek to faithfully follow Jesus today.

With this in mind, consider making this your prayer as you read and study this chapter:

Faithful Father, thank you for your promise that all who have placed their faith in Jesus's atoning work have a future inheritance in an eternal kingdom that can never be taken away. As I read, bring to mind areas in which my faith is weak, and strengthen my faith by your Spirit. Help me to trust in you and your promises more fully, and prepare my heart to be faithful despite what circumstances this life brings. Amen.

SETTING

Recipients

Peter seems to have been writing around AD 63.[1] His letter was addressed to "those chosen, living as exiles dispersed abroad in Pontus, Galatia,

---

[1] While debates about Petrine authorship exist, historical and internal evidence points to the apostle Peter as the author. Within the letter, the author claims to be Peter (1 Pet 1:1a), claims to have been present at "the sufferings of Christ" (1 Pet 5:1), and claims to be with Silvanus (1 Pet 5:12; cf. Acts 15:7, 22) and Mark (1 Pet 5:13; cf. Acts 12:12). For a more exhaustive discussion regarding the arguments for and against Petrine authorship, see Paul

1 Peter

J. Achtemeier, *1 Peter* (Minneapolis: Fortress Press, 1996), 1–43. Achtemeier concludes, "The best working hypothesis is anonymous authorship of a pseudonymous letter" (43). However, Michaels is correct when he declares, "The burden of proof still rests with those who choose the latter alternative [those who question Petrine authorship]; the traditional view that the living Peter was personally responsible for the letter as it stands has not been, and probably in the nature of the case cannot be, decisively shaken." J. Ramsey Michaels, *1 Peter*, WBC 49 (Nashville: Thomas Nelson, 1988), lxvi, lxvii. While Petrine authorship is favored, in the end, the setting and situation of the audience to whom the author wrote provides the greatest insight into the intended meaning of the letter.

The dating of the letter is dependent upon the conclusion regarding authorship. Since there is nothing explicit in the language or structure of the letter that would inherently tie the work to a specific period of time in the first century, other factors must be considered. If the use of "Babylon" in 1 Pet 5:13 is a reference to Rome, of particular interest is the lack of reference to the brutal persecution of Christians in Rome during Nero's reign. As a result, the letter is presumed to have been written before AD 64. If this dating is correct, it makes Peter's call to honor the emperor all the more startling and contrary to the natural human desire to rebel. For other arguments concerning an early dating of the letter, see Wayne A. Grudem, *1 Peter*, TNTC (Downers Grove, IL: IVP Academic, 1988), 36–38. Regardless of the precise date the book was written, Peter was writing to Christians living under the control and authority of the Roman Empire during the first century.

Cappadocia, Asia, and Bithynia" (1 Pet 1:1b). These cities were located in what is modern-day Turkey,[2] but the focus should not be as much on the location as on the description of these saints. They were on foreign soil. They were living as travelers longing for their homeland, and Peter was writing to them, reminding them that their ultimate homeland is heaven. He was encouraging them in the face of persistent persecution.

Considering this context, scholars frequently debate two critical questions. First, was this audience predominantly Jewish or Gentile?[3] This debate exists because several words and ideas in the letter would be more naturally understood by a Jewish reader (1 Pet 1:1–2, 10, 16, 18; 2:4, 5, 9, 12), while other words and ideas would be more naturally understood by a Gentile reader (1 Pet 1:14, 18; 2:10; 4:3–4). For that reason, and understanding the multicultural nature and development of the early church, the audience should be seen as a mix of Jewish and Gentile converts. Ultimately, knowing the spiritual corruption that was common to both, Karen Jobes wrote, "It makes little difference whether the original readers were Jews or Gentiles. Both spiritual systems were empty in that in themselves they offered no redemption, and both people groups were equally guilty in God's sight. Whether converts from paganism or Judaism, the letter's recipients needed to understand their new covenant relationship with God in Christ and the implications of that relationship for transformed living."[4]

Second, are these Christians literally foreigners or was Peter leveraging a spiritual metaphor? Again, both seem to be in play to some extent. It is reasonable, but certainly not absolute, that some believers displaced by the persecutions of the early church ended up in these cities in Asia Minor.[5]

---

[2] A reasonably detailed excursus discussing each of these areas is provided in Achtemeier, *1 Peter*, 83–85.

[3] For an argument for a predominately Gentile audience, see Thomas R. Schreiner, *1, 2 Peter, Jude*, NAC 37 (Nashville: Holman Reference, 2003), 38–41; and Michaels, *1 Peter*, xlv, xlvl. For an argument for a predominately Jewish audience, see Karen H. Jobes, *1 Peter*, BECNT (Grand Rapids: Baker Academic, 2005), 23–41.

[4] Jobes, *1 Peter*, 24.

[5] For a helpful elaboration of this position see Jobes, 23–44. This position is contingent upon a strong Jewish presence in the congregations. If the majority of the church gathering is Gentile and only a select group of Jews are present, the position that Peter is leveraging the reality of the diaspora for his introduction seems unlikely. However, if it is correct that due to the diaspora these churches received the gospel and started churches with a strong Jewish presence, this position is more likely. For those questioning how such a strong collection of churches were developed this early throughout Asia Minor, consider five factors. First, natives from some of the areas Peter mentions are present at Pentecost (Acts 2:8–10). Second, Paul has evangelized some of these areas. Third, through Paul's efforts, people

These believers were literally "exiles." Peter then leveraged this title in order to apply their physical situation to the broader spiritual reality of the church at large. In other words, all believers, regardless of nationality, are spiritually citizens of the kingdom of God (Eph 2:19–20; Phil 3:20), who because of their allegiance to Jesus fit somewhat awkwardly in the present age. Thus, Christians are of a different social order, and their allegiance to Jesus is contributing to social and political tension. Therefore, whether they were literally foreigners or not, they were, as we are, certainly spiritual foreigners.

Theme and Key Passage

Several thematic movements are seen and felt within 1 Peter,[6] but when looking at the book as a whole, a unifying theme seems to emerge: faithful endurance, future glory. We are to endure faithfully in this life in anticipation of the future glory that is ours in Christ Jesus.

First Peter 5:10–11 says: "The God of all grace, who called you to his eternal glory in Christ, will himself restore, establish, strengthen, and support you after you have suffered a little while. To him be dominion forever. Amen."

Purpose and Occasion

Imagine a suspenseful story being heard for the first time. The listener is filled with anxiety and anticipation. Now, the next time that story is heard, it is different. The story is still suspenseful. The story is still exciting; however, anxiety and anticipation are tempered. Why? Because the ending is already known. When the end of a matter is known, tension is relieved.

That's what 1 Peter is about. Peter was reminding believers living in the depressing and difficult circumstances of this fallen world that this world was not their home. A glorious future awaits all who have faith in Jesus,

---

traveling through other cities where Paul was preaching were hearing Paul, converting, and then taking Christianity on (Acts 19:9–10). Fourth, other Christians were evangelizing and traveling. Fifth, believers scattered due to persecution in Jerusalem traveled throughout the Roman Empire, which began by going throughout Judea and Samaria (Acts 8:4–5), but most likely eventually extended beyond those regions.

[6] Consider the following: Christ's sufferings (1 Pet 1:11, 19; 2:21–24; 3:18; 4:1, 12); heavenly hope (1 Pet 1:3–5, 7, 9, 13; 4:7; 5:10); living rightly in light of God's work in our lives (1 Pet 1:13–16, 22; 3:2, 13, 16–17; 4:2); prayer (1 Pet 3:7, 12; 4:7); relationship between fellow believers and the world (1 Pet 1:22; 2:1, 9, 12–20; 3:1–9, 13–17; 4:4–5, 8–11, 15–16; 5:2–5); salvation (1 Pet 1:2–3, 9, 12, 18–21, 25; 2:2, 7); sovereignty (1 Pet 1:1–3, 5, 20; 2:4, 8b–9); suffering (1 Pet 1:6–7, 11; 2:19–21, 23; 3:14–18; 4:1–2, 4, 12–19; 5:1, 9–10).

and because of that future, Christ followers can faithfully endure the most horrendous and oppressive circumstances. They must press on in light of the glory that will be revealed when they reign with Jesus in his eternal kingdom.

Peter was uniquely concerned with believers who were experiencing the oppressive weight of the world as a result of their allegiance to Jesus. These individuals were living under a pagan regime that was growing increasingly hostile toward Christianity. Peter's specific audience was experiencing tremendous pressure to conform to the cultural and cultic practices present in their local regions. This pressure came, not necessarily from Rome directly, but from local leaders and families specifically. Converting to Christianity came with a call to walk in holiness out of a heart committed to Jesus (1 Pet 1:13–16). Walking in holiness included abstaining from certain cultural practices that would bring compromise and confusion concerning faith in Jesus. These practices would include participation in certain parties, idol worship, corrupt social gatherings, and certain communal festivals and rituals in honor of the gods (1 Pet 4:3–4). The lack of participation in religious events might have even been viewed by some as an offense to the gods, which could remove favor or bring judgment. Additionally, as a result of their lack of involvement in some of these activities, others might begin to question converts' commitment to the community and the empire. Thus, loyalties were being questioned, and family and friendships were being strained under the weight of concern and suspicion.

Ironically enough, in the religious tolerance of the Roman Empire, anything perceived to undermine allegiance to the empire or the cohesion of the community was not tolerated. Subsequently, these believers were suffering trials that tested their faith and character (1 Pet 1:6). They were experiencing evil (1 Pet 3:9), insults (2:23; 3:9), slander (4:4), and ridicule (4:14). Others were trying to intimidate them (1 Pet 3:14) and making false accusations about them (3:16). Moreover, some of them may well have been experiencing the loss of personal property and physical abuse (1 Pet 2:19–20; 3:18; 4:1, 13). Under the weight of this persecution, Peter wanted to ensure that believers did not compromise their faith and lose heart. He wanted to remind them of the hope they had in Jesus: a hope not rooted in this world but in a glory yet to be revealed.

HIGHLIGHTS IN 1 PETER

Introduction (1 Pet 1:1–2)

Whether a news broadcast, a letter, or a phone call, the credibility of the contents of the communication are directly related to the credibility of the messenger. Peter wasted no time leveraging his authority as an apostle of Jesus Christ (1 Pet 1:1). As an apostle, he was eyewitness to the suffering Jesus endured (1 Pet 5:1), so what he said to these believers about enduring suffering in light of the eternal hope of heaven mattered.

While Peter's introduction follows the standard greeting form of a letter written during this time frame,[7] the content is significant, specifically in the terms with which he referenced the audience and the trinitarian certainty of their salvation. The Father, Son, and Spirit all work together in securing the Christian in faith for a glorious future.

> **Trinity**
>
> Is the term *Trinity* biblical? While the term is not explicitly found in the canon of Scripture, the concept certainly is (Isa 9:6; Matt 28:19–20; Luke 3:21–22; John 1:1–18; 10:30–36; 1 Cor 2:10–11; 8:6; 2 Cor 1:21–22; 13:14; Eph 4:4–6; Phil 2:5–6; Col 2:9; Titus 2:13; 3:5; 1 Pet 1:2; 2 Pet 1:21). So, why use the term? We use the term for the same reason that people who sew use terms such as "bullion knot stitch." Terms are created to serve as shorthand explanations to speed up communication. Versus explaining every movement in the stitch, two people who are familiar with various sewing techniques can simply say "Bullion Knot Stitch" and communication is complete. In the same way, Christians created the term *Trinity* to talk about a specific biblical truth. It serves as a quick way of explaining that God is one in essence, three in person (Father, Son, and Spirit).

Enduring in Light of Salvation (1 Pet 1:3–2:10)

After the introduction, Peter unveiled the theme of the letter. Like Paul, in his writings, Peter established some critical theological truths and then transitioned to show how those truths play out in their current cultural circumstances. He reminds his audience that while their salvation is certain, their suffering is purposeful and temporary (1 Pet 1:3–7). Despite the difficulties of this world, all who have faith in Jesus have an eternal hope that cannot be destroyed by the temporality of this life. Neither Satan, nor evil emperors, nor any power of this life can contaminate the eternal glory that

---

[7] A standard form can be seen in letters written during this time frame in this region, specifically Christian letters, as evidenced in many of Paul's writings. The standard introduction included the author, the recipient, and a greeting, blessing, or prayer.

awaits the children of God; therefore, persevere with expectant confidence (1 Pet 1:7; see also Rom 8:18, 31–39).

Considering this salvation, saints can have confidence while enduring persecution because they are eternally secure in Christ.[8] Peter pressed this point by using images familiar to the audience such gold and silver (1 Pet 1:7, 18) and seed,[9] grass, and flowers (1 Pet 1:23–25). He then leveraged those images to demonstrate the eternal quality and nature of faith in the gospel against the difficulties faith has to endure.

Because saints are secure in Christ, they should seek to live a life reflective of such a glorious salvation especially in the face of evil (1 Pet 1:13–16; Eph 4:1; Phil 1:27). Living this way involves an intentional mindset that is ready for the opposition that awaits. That's one reason Peter used the phrase "with your minds ready for action" (1 Pet 1:13). In the Greek language, this phrase is an idiom[10] that means "to gird up the loins of your mind." "Girding up one's loins" was something done when preparing for battle, running, or hard work. People in biblical times wore clothing—robes and tunics and such—that would flow around both legs at once. The image is similar to what you would envision in a modern-day, full-length skirt. This design made it difficult to move fast or run, so the people of that day would "gird up their loins," meaning they would reach down as if they were going to touch the ground in front of them. While remaining bent, they would reach and grab the back-most portion of the fabric closest to the ground and pull it forward. Then, standing, they would tuck it into their belt. Doing so resulted in makeshift pants allowing them a much better range of motion and securing any loose fabric that could impede movement. In light of that background, Peter literally told his audience to get their minds ready for intense action. The church has to remain mentally focused on the inheritance that awaits all those who are faithful in Christ Jesus.

Two specific points must be pressed from this foundational section. The first point involves the reality and the purposefulness of suffering.

---

[8] *Saint* is a term used throughout the New Testament for a believer. It emphasizes that through the atoning work of Jesus, and as a result of believers' union with Christ, Christians are now "saints," meaning "holy ones."

[9] The metaphor for "seed" in this context could refer to "procreation" or "plants." Due to the quote Peter provided from Isa 40:6–8, "plants" seem to be the source for the object lesson.

[10] Louw and Nida, *Greek-English Lexicon of the New Testament*, 332 (see chap. 13, n. 1).

While suffering should never be sought by the people of God, it should be expected. Peter acknowledged the reality and temporality of suffering, but he included a "so that" (1 Pet 1:7). These temporary moments of persecution that Christians face reveal the authenticity of their faith. Standing firm in the face of suffering has a way of putting a megaphone to one's faith. The world takes notice and tends to listen when a suffering child of God remains faithfully focused on Jesus with unwavering confidence in the future glory that awaits. Now, while the suffering Peter was specifically referencing was the persecution of Christians as a result following Jesus, many of these same principles apply and should apply to Christians when they are suffering in general as a result of living in a fallen world. This world is not home for Christians. Believers in Jesus have an eternal inheritance secure in Christ. That is where their hope is to resid; and. These truths regarding the eternal glory that awaits should sustain the faith of the children of God through bad medical reports, natural disasters, accidents, unemployment, and all other events connected to living in a fallen world, especially persecutio;.

The second point to be pressed involves the necessity of personal faith (1 Pet 1:21). "Faith" is synonymous with "belief."[11] To have faith is to "believe" in something. This point is made in 1 Pet 1:8–9. Peter wrote, "Though you have not seen him, you love him; though not seeing him now, you believe in him, and you rejoice with inexpressible and glorious joy, because you are receiving the goal of your faith, the salvation of your souls." While Peter was speaking to the collective group of saints gathered in each of the locations mentioned in the introduction, he was acknowledging the necessity of personal faith in Jesus, who

> ### Honor the Emperor
>
> Peter commanded believers, "Submit to every human authority because of the Lord, whether to the emperor as the supreme authority or to governors" (1 Pet 13:13–14a). Later in the same text, Peter pressed, "Honor the emperor" (1 Pet 2:17b). The Roman Empire during Peter's life was no friend of Christianity. That makes his comments remarkable enough, but consider that Nero may well have been the emperor at the time. Christians can voice opposition to governmental leaders especially in regards to policies that limit expressions of their faith; however, that opposition must be done in a godly manner regardless of the character of the leader. Christian expression directed towards governmental leaders should do three things: (1) rightly represent Christ; (2) show honor to the office being addressed; and (3) reflect a confidence that our ultimate hope is not in a worldly political system but in the future coming of Jesus.

---

[11] "Faith" and "belief" are different forms of the same word in Greek. "Faith" is a noun, and "belief" is the verbal form of that noun.

is the sacrificial lamb (1 Pet 1:18–21; Exodus 12; Isa 53:6–7; John 1:29; 1 Cor 5:7b). Salvation is only assured for those who have placed faih in the atoning work of Jesus on their behalf (Heb 9:11–15). The text explains that because these saints have believed in Jesus they are receiving the goal of their faith, which is "the salvation" of their souls (1 Pet 1:8–9). No hope or assurance exists apart from a personal profession of faith in Jesus (1 Pet 1:21).

Enduring within Social Structures (1 Pet 2:11–4:11)

The author then shifts to focus specifically on faithfully living for Jesus despite potentially oppressive social structures.[12] A significant idea permeates this section, as with all of this letter. Believers must consider their present response to this world in light of the future reality of the world to come (1 Pet 4:7). That theme propels Peter's instructions. The Lord will address the rights and wrongs of this world and the behavior of each individual (1 Pet 2:12; 4:5; 2 Cor 5:10). For the follower of Christ, the

This ancient race track, known as a "Stadion," demonstrates the kind of place used for early Greek Olympic race games.

---

[12] The use of "dear friends" (1 Pet 2:11) marks a notable transition in the book. The same transition appears in 1 Pet 4:12.

standard of living is the will of God (1 Pet 4:2, 19). They must not allow their conduct to be dictated by the ebbs and flows of their circumstances, but instead, use the gifts God has given them for kingdom purposes in service to God and one another (1 Pet 4:8–11). When believers forget about their future hope and become fixated on present trials, it is easy to fall back into worldly ways and compromise faith. For this reason, Peter begged readers not to be worn down under the weight of oppression and give in to fleshly desires (1 Pet 2:11).

Three social groups are uniquely featured: imperial subjects (1 Pet 2:13–17),[13] slaves (1 Pet 2:18–25), and wives (1 Pet 3:1–7).[14] Each group is given direction on how to live effectively for the gospel under authority, especially when that authority is ungodly. Remember, these people were trapped. They had little worldly hope. Peter was in no way affirming the oppression they were experiencing; rather, he was acknowledging the fact they had nowhere else to go, were oppressed, and needed hope. He gave them instructions on how to live despite their suffering and guided them on how to maximize their gospel witness while trapped in these circumstances. After all, where would these subjects flee? Where would these slaves go where they were not haunted by a similar situation? If a wife divorced her ungodly husband and left, she risked losing her children and becoming destitute. Peter selected the most oppressive general statuses in his audience and provided them with practical encouragement in light of their eternal hope. Christ followers, he wrote, must then expect suffering for doing the will of God and be faithful despite suffering (1 Pet 4:2). Peter continued to set the expectation of suffering more firmly as he prepared to transition to the last major section of the letter.

Enduring without Surprise (1 Pet 4:12–5:11)

Peter again challenged his audience not to allow circumstances to determine their faith in God. It is easy to presume that obedience to God's will guarantees comfortable circumstances, yet just as that was not true for Jesus, it is not true for his followers (1 Pet 4:1, 12–13). Difficulties were

---

[13] Why is the term *imperial subjects* used here versus *citizens*? Many who lived under Roman rule were not citizens but simply subjects. Though these people did not have the privileges of citizenship, they were still responsible for living in subjection to the rules of the empire.

[14] For a little background regarding each group, see Everett Ferguson, *Backgrounds of Early Christianity*, 3rd ed. (Grand Rapids: Eerdmans, 2003), 62–66 (imperial subjects); 59–61 (slaves); 72–79 (wives).

experienced by Jesus and should be expected by his disciples (1 Pet 4:13). Instead of despair, persecution for the sake of righteousness should result in rejoicing (Acts 5:41).

As agents of grace in this fallen world, God not only has a plan for how his children should engage the world but how they should engage one another as part of the family of God. Elders must not respond to those under their care in a manner representative of the world's leadership, which pursues power and self-interests.[15] Elders should focus on the glory that is to be revealed in order to motivate them to stay true to this divine perspective of leadership. Likewise, those under the care of the elders should follow in a way that reflects a life transformed by grace. Furthermore, all members of God's church should interact with one another in a way that demonstrates their hope is not in their world but in the world to come.

As an aside, we must not miss the connection that ties Peter's experience with Jesus to Peter's instructions to fellow elders (John 21:1–19). Though Peter had previously given in to the social persecution he experienced and denied his Savior, he was not dismissed or discarded;[16] rather, Jesus showed him tremendous grace. As Jesus ministered to Peter on the shore of the Sea of Tiberias (John 21:1), he tenderly cast a mighty vision for Peter and all who want to display a love for Jesus. A true love for Jesus should result not only in obedience (John 14:15) but also in a desire to "feed his sheep," that is, to care for his followers. Out of that experience

> **Peter's Death**
>
> In the same context where Jesus affirmed Peter's mission as a "feeder of God's sheep" (John 21:15–17), Jesus also prophesied that Peter would die as a martyr (John 21:18–19). Though uncertain and unverified, one church tradition believes Peter was crucified as a martyr upside down because he felt unworthy to be crucified in the same manner as his Lord.

---

[15] Does "elder" here refer to an "older person" or the "office of elder" as a church leader? While either could be in view, Peter provided responsibilities and described the office of elder role through the emphasis on "shepherding" the people of God; therefore, the office of elder is in view in this text (1 Pet 5:1–4). The use of "younger" in the text (1 Pet 5:5) then should be seen as a designation for everyone else in the congregation in contrast with "elder."

[16] See the sidebar titled "Peter's Death," above. Regarding that conversation, see A. B. Luter Jr., "Martyrdom," in *Dictionary of the Later New Testament and Its Developments*, ed. Ralph P. Martin and Peter H. Davids (Downers Grove, IL: IVP Academic, 1997), 719–22; J. K. Elliott, ed., "The Acts of Peter," in *The Apocryphal New Testament: A Collection of Apocryphal Christian Literature in an English Translation Based on M. R. James* (Oxford: Clarendon, 1993), 424–25; Daniel William O'Connor, "St. Peter the Apostle," *Encyclopædia Britannica*, accessed March 2, 2021, https://www.britannica.com/biography/Saint-Peter-the-Apostle.

A modern-day shepherd watching over his sheep

and conviction, Peter challenged his fellow elders to "shepherd God's flock" (1 Pet 5:2).

Conclusion (1 Pet 5:12–14)

Peter concluded with a brief customary benediction in which he mentioned that Mark and Silvanus (or, Silas) were present with him. These men seem to be the same ones mentioned in Acts with whom Peter and Paul had a relationship (Acts 12:12, 25; 15:22–41; 16:19–40; 17:1–15; 18:5; 2 Cor 1:19; Col 4:10; 1 Thess 1:1; 2 Thess 1:1; 2 Tim 4:11; Phlm v. 24).[17] Silvanus could have been the secretar to whom Peter dictated the letter;[18] however, it is more likely that Silvanus was simply the courier of the letter and the one who presented it to the churches.[19]

Regardless, the way Peter spoke of these men must not be overlooked. Notice the familial language with which they were referenced and the tenderness of his closing remarks. All these point to the deep familial ties

---

[17] While it is not certain, it seems that Silvanus and Silas mentioned in the New Testament are in fact the same person.

[18] The word *amanuensis* is often used to denote these secretaries. Such secretaries for letters were not uncommon.

[19] Jobes, *1 Peter*, 319–21; Schreiner, *1, 2, Peter, Jude*, 248–49.

experienced by the early church. Their newfound faith in Christ brought them into God's family and gave them a firm future hope of dwelling together in his kingdom.

BIBLIOGRAPHY

Achtemeier, Paul J. *1 Peter*. Minneapolis: Fortress Press, 1996.

Elliott, J. K., ed. "The Acts of Peter." In *The Apocryphal New Testament: A Collection of Apocryphal Christian Literature in an English Translation Based on M. R. James*, 424–25. Oxford: Clarendon, 1993.

Ferguson, Everett. *Backgrounds of Early Christianity*. 3rd ed. Grand Rapids: Eerdmans, 2003.

Grudem, Wayne A. *1 Peter*. TNTC. Downers Grove, IL: IVP Academic, 1988.

Jobes, Karen H. *1 Peter*. BECNT. Grand Rapids: Baker Academic, 2005.

Louw, Johannes P., and Eugene A. Nida. *Greek-English Lexicon of the New Testament: Based on Semantic Domains*. New York: United Bible Societies, 1996.

Luter, A. B., Jr. "Martyrdom." In *Dictionary of the Later New Testament and Its Developments*, edited by Ralph P. Martin and Peter H. Davids, 717–22. Downers Grove, IL: IVP Academic, 1997.

Michaels, J. Ramsey. *1 Peter*. WBC 49. Nashville: Thomas Nelson, 1988.

O'Connor, Daniel William. "St. Peter the Apostle." Encyclopædia Britannica Online. Accessed March 2, 2021, https://www.britannica.com/biography/Saint-Peter-the-Apostle.

Schreiner, Thomas R. *1, 2, Peter, Jude*. NAC 37. Nashville: Holman Reference, 2003.

21

2 PETER

CHRIS HULSHOF

CONNECTION POINT

What relevance does this first-century writing have for us today? The 2015 Disney–Pixar movie *Inside Out* gives us an animated glance into the way the mind and memory work in the life of an eleven-year-old girl named Riley. In the movie, memories are portrayed as bowling ball-like objects that are sorted by things such as emotion or importance. When a specific memory is recalled or something needs to be remembered, that previously created memory orb is brought into a projector-like place in the mind so that Riley remembers all that took place.

The book of 2 Peter also addresses memory. More specifically, Peter was writing to a group of believers whom he wanted to stir up by way of reminder (2 Pet 1:13). As false teachers were approaching, and Paul's death was imminent (2 Pet 1:14), there are three reminders that he wanted to communicate to these believers.

To use the *Inside Out* imagery, Peter had three memory orbs that he wanted to place in front of these believers so that they would be reminded of three important facets of growing in grace. These reminders point to the provisions of God, the approaching false teachers, and the return of Christ.

With this in mind, consider making this your prayer as you read and study this chapter:

> *Father, you have given us your holy Scriptures and everything we need for life and godliness. Help us to be students of your Word so that we can grow in grace, resist those whose message stands opposed to your grace, and live grace-filled lives as we actively wait for your return. Amen.*

SETTING

Recipients

"Simeon Peter" was writing as "a servant and an apostle of Jesus Christ" in the latter half of the first century.[1] There are a couple of good reasons why Peter might have chosen to use "Simeon Peter" rather than "Simon Peter" to identify himself at the outset of this letter. If Peter's audience was a mix of both Jews and Gentiles, a name like Simeon Peter that combined both his Hebrew and Greek names was much more audience-friendly. Additionally, the dual name of Simeon Peter highlighted both the name

---

[1] The opening verse of 2 Peter tells us that "Simeon Peter, a servant and an apostle of Jesus Christ" is the author of this letter (2 Pet 1:1). It is helpful to note that while this identify seems clear, it is the use of Simeon rather than Simon that has caused some to doubt Peter's authorship of this letter. Nevertheless, historical and internal evidence supports the apostle Peter as the author. See Schreiner, *1, 2 Peter, Jude*, 255–76 (see chap. 20, n. 3); "Authorship and Pseudonymity" in Richard J. Bauckham, *Jude, 2 Peter*, WBC 50 (Nashville: Word, 1983); "Authorship of 2 Peter" in Gene L. Green, *Jude and 2 Peter*, BECNT (Grand Rapids: Baker Academic, 2008); and "The Authorship and Canonicity of 2 Peter" in Curtis P. Giese, *2 Peter and Jude*, Concordia Commentary (St. Louis: Concordia, 2012).

Second Peter is often assigned a later date than its companion letter, 1 Peter, especially by those who dispute the Petrine authorship of the letter. The earliest copies of the letter are dated to the third and fourth centuries AD, and it is first referenced by name by Origen in the third century AD, though Kruger has argued that there are possible allusions and citations to 2 Peter already in the second century AD by Justin and Irenaeus and other sources (see Michael J. Kruger, "The Authenticity of 2 Peter," *JETS* 42 [1999]: 645–71). This evidence makes it reasonable to suggest a first century date for the letter, and thus within the realm of possibility that its origins are actually traced to the apostle Peter.

given to him by his parents (Simeon) and the name given to him by Jesus Christ (Peter).[2]

Peter described himself as "a servant and an apostle of Jesus Christ" (2 Pet 1:1). It is tempting to let prior understanding get the best of us when it comes to the term *servant*. A servant, or slave, of Christ "are those who represent Christ; they are active in the world as Christ's agents and wield his authority . . . the title slave of Christ carried authority by recalling the founding leader."[3] In describing himself as an apostle, Peter reminded his audience that he was a disciple of Jesus Christ and part of the group commissioned to take the gospel message from Jerusalem to Judea and Samaria and then to the ends of the earth (Acts 1:8).

The Calling of the Apostles Peter and Andrew, circa AD 1308, Duccio di Buoninsegna

There is little in these opening verses to describe Peter's audience by way of geography. However, 2 Pet 3:1 states, "This is now the second letter I have written to you." This would indicate that the audience of 2 Peter is the same audience as 1 Peter. Thus, Peter was writing "To those chosen, living as exiles dispersed abroad in Pontus, Galatia, Cappadocia, Asia, and Bithynia" (1 Pet 1:1b).

While nothing is directly stated geographically, there is a clear spiritual description of the letter's recipients. Peter described their spiritual experience by noting that they "have received a faith equal to ours" (2 Pet 1:1). He also described their spiritual position by indicating that their position was "through the righteousness of our God and Savior Jesus Christ" (2 Pet 1:1). Peter doubly identified himself, and now he has doubly identified the

---

[2] These are the two reasons for the double name that Peter uses as suggested by Giese. However, Giese also notes that Green gives various other reasons for Peter's use of this double name in his commentary on *2 Peter and Jude* (see Michael Green, *2 Peter and Jude*, TNTC [Downers Grove, IL: IVP Academic, 2007]) and provides a substantive interaction with arguments regarding authorship. Giese, *2 Peter and Jude*, 6–11.

[3] Ruth Anne Reese, *2 Peter and Jude*, The Two Horizons New Testament Commentary (Grand Rapids: Eerdmans, 2007), 130. Reese provides a helpful historical and cultural discussion on the term *servant* or *slave*. Her work here helps see these terms in light of the biblical context rather than an American historical context.

recipients of this letter. This dual identification reminded them that they had the righteousness of God, which is equal to Christ's because they are in him and, being in him, have all that he has and is.

Theme and Key Passage

We are all familiar with an abridged version of books or an evening sports highlight reel from the day's games. Both of these things are designed to give you an understanding of the whole by giving you only a part. In that same sense, 2 Pet 1:19 is an abridged version, or a highlight reel of sorts, for 2 Peter.

Second Peter 1:19 tells us: "We also have the prophetic word strongly confirmed, and you will do well to pay attention to it, as to a lamp shining in a dark place, until the day dawns and the morning star rises in your hearts."

If you break this one verse into three parts you will see the focus of the book by chapter. The first part of the verse draws your attention to God's provision of the Scriptures (2 Peter 1). The second section, with its focus on the dark place, calls your attention to the darkness of the coming false prophets (2 Peter 2), and the last part of the verse reminds the reader that Jesus Christ is returning (2 Peter 3).[4]

Purpose and Occasion

Peter marked out his purpose for writing when he stated, "I want to stir up your sincere understanding by way of reminder, so that you recall the words previously spoken by the holy prophets and the command of our Lord and Savior given through your apostles" (2 Pet 3:1–2).

The letter is a reminder designed to "stir up." This is a picturesque phrase. In fact, when we see it used in the Gospels, it is connected to the disciples waking Jesus before he calms the storm (Matt 8:23–25). Peter wanted to rouse his audience so that they were aware of the circumstances in which they found themselves.

What is the focus of these stirring reminders? The initial reminder is that of "the words previously spoken by the holy prophets" (2 Pet 3:2). In this context, Peter was reminding his audience of the message of the

---

[4] "Here is the book in microcosm, with emphasis on the reliable truth of the Bible's revelation, the need to cling to this truth as a way of avoiding error, and the eschatological focus on the return of Christ." Leland Ryken, Philip Ryken, and James Wilhoit, *Ryken's Bible Handbook: A Guide to Reading and Studying the Bible* (Wheaton, IL: Tyndale, 2005), 606.

Old Testament prophets as it relates to the "day of the LORD" (Isa 13:6–9; Amos 5:18; Joel 1:15). His second reminder is regarding "the command of our Lord and Savior given through your apostles" (2 Pet 3:2). This reminder also points to the second coming of Christ and the command to be prepared for that coming, proclaimed in the Olivet Discourse in Matt 24:42.

Taken together, there is unity between 2 Pet 2:1–2 and the contents of the book of 2 Peter. Michael Green writes, "What, then, was the command in which Old Testament prophets, New Testament apostles and the Lord himself concur? There can be no doubt that it is to live holy lives in the light of the Savior's return at the end of history."[5] Thus, the holy living of 2 Peter 1 (which stands counter to the lives led by the false prophets in 2 Peter 2) is preparation for the second coming of Christ.

The urgency of Peter's purpose is reflected in the occasion of the letter. Peter was nearing death and desired to leave final words of encouragement and warning to these churches in the northern half of Asia Minor (2 Pet 1:13). He wanted to remind them one more time of that which they already knew. In this sense, 2 Peter is to Peter's letters as 2 Timothy is to Paul's letters. They are both letters of last words.

Peter was not only motivated to write because of his imminent death; he was also prompted to write because of the encroaching false teachers. It was his desire to remind the believers of that which they had believed so that they would not be swayed by the teachings of the false teachers.

HIGHLIGHTS IN 2 PETER

A Reminder of God's Provisions (2 Pet 1:1–21)

Two major provisions are the focus of this opening chapter of 2 Peter. The first is God's provision for Christian living and the second of these provisions is the Scriptures. Peter opened this chapter on the provisions of God by noting, "His divine power has given us everything required for life and godliness through the knowledge of him who called us by his own glory and goodness" (2 Pet 1:3). In these verses Peter drew attention to the all-encompassing provision of God. He has provided everything we need

---

[5] Green, *2 Peter and Jude*, 147. Green provides a good summary showing how these two verses show the unified witness of the Old Testament, Jesus Christ, and the apostles.

for life and godliness. This indicates that whether the need is physical or spiritual, God is the one who provides for it. He provides for all things.

This need-meeting is the by-product of the knowledge of Jesus Christ. The knowledge that Peter had in mind here is more than just head knowledge; it is a personal and relational knowledge of Jesus Christ. The implication is that the more we come to know Jesus Christ, the more we come to understand that he the sole provider of all things. Consequently, we recognize that all of our physical and spiritual needs have been and are being met.

As Peter further elaborated on what God has provided, he connected this truth to the believer's calling and to the promises of God that these promises form the foundation of what it means to grow in grace so that we display both the nature and the character of God in the world around us (2 Pet 1:4).

The emphasis Peter placed on the provisions and promises of God leads to his next discussion on the how this all impacts present Christian living. In 2 Pet 1:5–11, Peter offered a picture of what growing as a Christian should look like. In the first half of these verses he explained how we are to take advantage of the promises of God by making every effort to add the seven specific character qualities of goodness, knowledge, self-control, endurance, godliness, brotherly affection, and love to the faith God has given us.

These qualities are not steps to be completed one at a time. Rather, they are things that ought to be continuously added to faith. There are two things that should be noted about this list. These character qualities stand in direct contrast to the character qualities of the false teachers Peter will describe in 2 Peter 2. Additionally, these character qualities correspond favorably to the fruit of the Spirit that Paul listed in Gal 5:22–23. Thus, while we are making "every effort to supplement," it is the power of the Holy Spirit at work in us that produces these character qualities or fruit of the Spirit (2 Pet 1:5–7). As Paul reminds us, "He who started a good work in you will carry it on to completion until the day of Christ Jesus" (Phil 1:6).

What is the result of this growing Christian life? Peter wrote that growing in the faith makes life meaningful ("They will keep you from being useless" [2 Pet 1:8a]), and it makes life fruitful ("They will keep you from being . . . unfruitful in the knowledge of our Lord Jesus Christ" [2 Pet 1:8b]). However, Peter also laid out the consequences for a faith that is devoid of this growth. He stated that this person is blind, shortsighted, and forgetful (2 Pet 1:9). In a sense, this sets Peter up for chapters 2 and 3, where this person is easy prey for the false teachers as well as susceptible to incorrect doctrinal beliefs: in this case, the doctrine of the second coming of Christ.

Peter ends this section on the provisions of God by reminding his audience of the trustworthiness of Scripture (2 Pet 1:16–21). It is trustworthy because it is not "cleverly contrived myths" (2 Pet 1:16). Instead, it is based on the eyewitness experience of the disciples. They saw and experienced firsthand the power, majesty, honor, and glory of Jesus Christ. The trustworthiness of the Scriptures is tied to the person of Jesus Christ. If Christ can be trusted, then so can the Scriptures.

Peter's reminder to them and for us is to "get growing." These provisions of God and the power of the Holy Spirit are all that we need to get started on this growth chart. Martin Luther put it this way: "But if you want to become pious, you must ask God to give you a genuine faith, and you must begin to desist from unbelief. When you receive faith, then good works will come automatically, and you will lead a pure and chaste life. Otherwise, you will preserve yourself by no other means. And even if you are able to conceal the knave in your heart for a while, yet he will finally emerge."[6]

A Reminder That False Teachers Are Coming (2 Pet 2:1–22)

If chapter 1 was Peter's encouragement to his audience, then chapter 2 serves as his stern warning to them. Peter reminded these believers that false teachers are coming (2 Pet 2:1–3) and that they will receive the same doom that previous false teachers have experienced

> **Can I Borrow That from You?**
>
> If you were to place the book of 2 Peter on top of the book of Jude, you would see some twenty-three places where the two books overlap. Both Peter and Jude used the Old Testament stories of Sodom and Gomorrah (2 Pet 2:6; Jude v. 7) and Balaam (2 Pet 2:15; Jude v. 11) in their arguments. They illustrated their points by writing about blemishes and feasts (2 Pet 2:13; Jude v. 12), slander and angels (2 Pet 2:11–12; Jude vv. 9–10), waterless things (2 Pet 2:17; Jude v. 12), deepest darkness (2 Pet 2:17; Jude v. 13), and irrational animals (2 Pet 2:12; Jude v. 10). Peter and Jude use similar imagery to describe the way the false teachers and interlopers have entered the community of faith (2 Pet 2:1; Jude v. 4), the way these imposters approach those within the community of faith (2 Pet 2:18; Jude v. 16) as well as their understanding of the condemnation these deceitful people face (2 Pet 2:3; Jude v. 4). Indeed, a large section of 2 Peter bears a striking resemblance to the book of Jude.

---

[6] Jaraslov Pelikan and Walter A. Hansen, eds., *Luther's Works: The Catholic Epistles*, vol. 30 (St. Louis: Concordia, 1967), 191.

(2 Pet 2:4–10a). Further, he vividly described both these false teachers (2 Pet 2:10b–17) as well as their victims (2 Pet 2:18–22).

Peter's reminder about the reality of the soon approaching false teachers recognizes their doctrinal errors ("They will bring in destructive heresies"

This is a Greek icon of the Second Coming. See how Christ is enthroned in the center, surrounded by the angels and saints. Made circa 1700.

[2 Pet 2:1]) and that these errors are centrally located on the person and work of Jesus Christ ("even denying the Master who bought them" [2:1]). These false teachers will bring destruction on themselves (2 Pet 2:1), and they will cause many others to follow them in living a depraved life (2 Pet 2:2). As a result of the false teachers and the unbelievers who believe their doctrine and follow their practice, the way of Christ will be run down.

Notice that there is a small shift between verses 2 and 3. In verse 2 Peter spoke specifically of the "many." However, verse 3 addresses "you." In other words, the "many" who follow these false teachers are unbelievers, while the "you" Peter addressed in verse 3 were believers. Thus, the false teachers will attempt to exploit believers because of their greed and through their "made-up stories" (2 Pet 2:3).[7]

Peter was essentially making the same argument that Jude made.[8] Lifestyle follows doctrine. When one wanders from the truth of the Scriptures it will negatively impact the way that he or she lives. Further, Peter pointed out that there would be collateral damage in the process. Some would follow and this would cause others to speak negatively of what they perceived Christianity to be. However, if we pay attention to what we hear and see, we will be able to avoid those who are looking to exploit both us and the faith for their own greed.

Peter moved on to pronounce the doom of the false teachers. He first announced that their judgment was certain (2 Pet 2:3). He followed that up by giving some Old Testament examples of judgment (2 Pet 2:4–9) and some illustrations of the false teachers (2 Pet 2:10–17). Finally, Peter also described those who fall victim to the false teachers (2 Pet 2:18–22). He pronounced the condemnation and destruction of the false teachers by connecting the condemnation and judgment of the angels who sinned with Satan, mankind during the days of Noah, and Sodom and Gomorrah as examples of God's condemnation and destruction on wickedness (2 Pet 2:3–6).

---

[7] In some sense, a literal translation of 2 Pet 2:2–3 is more graphic than our English translations. Peter was accusing the false teachers of using "plastic words" in order to "make merchandise" of the believers for their own personal greed. For more information on this literal translation see Peter H. Davids, *The Letters of 2 Peter and Jude*, PNTC (Grand Rapids: Eerdmans, 2006).

[8] For a more detailed list on the overlapping material in 2 Peter and Jude, see Mark Allen Powell, *Introducing the New Testament: A Historical, Literary, and Theological Survey* (Grand Rapids: Baker Academic, 2018).

Yet amid this message of judgment, Peter offered a message of hope. He pointed to the story of "righteous Lot" and the way in which God was able to rescue him during the condemnation and destruction of Sodom and Gomorrah (2 Pet 2:7–10). Peter was affirming God's ability to deliver the godly while at the same time administering justice on the ungodly in the day of judgment.

After comparing the condemnation and destruction of the false teachers to three specific Old Testament examples, Peter described the false teachers with a list of terms that placed them in direct contrast to the Christian growth chart in 2 Pet 1:5–7. Peter called them people who "follow the polluting desires of the flesh and despise authority. They are bold and arrogant people who are not afraid to slander angels. Further, these people are like irrational animals or spots and blemishes. They are children under a curse who love the wages of wickedness. They are "springs without water, mists driven by a storm. The gloom of darkness has been reserved for them (2:10–17). While all of these descriptions are informative, the last one is most revealing. It helps us see that these false teachers are not really believers who have made an honest mistake about their understanding of Christ. Instead, they are unbelievers. They know the truth, but they have rejected it and prefer to proclaim their own "made-up stories" (2:3).

The last section of the stern warning that Peter delivered in chapter 2 is for those who find themselves continually enticed by the false teachers or new believers who are doing the same (2 Pet 2:18–22). Peter warned them that the freedom they were seeking could not be found in the false teachers. Instead, they will only find bondage. When they self-exclude from growing in grace as is described in 2 Pet 1:5–7, they become easy targets for the empty words of the false teachers. In the end, Peter said, this is like preferring a meal of vomit over wholesome food.

What does all of this have to do with you and me? The reality is that false teachers are all around us today, and their message is just as alluring and damning as ever. Based on Peter's presentation on false teachers in this chapter, we can identify a false teacher by paying attention to two things. First, what is the foundation of their message? False teachers have stripped the Scriptures from their message and replaced that with their own stories (2 Pet 2:3). In turn, they have no room for Christ and the gospel (2:1). Second, instead, of Christ at the center, their life and doctrine are marked by empty promises of freedom that lead only to slavery and corruption (2:19).

A Reminder: Christ Jesus Is Returning (2 Pet 3:1–18)

The last of Peter's reminders is directed at the question of Christ's return. It seems that the false teachers had begun to proclaim that Christ was not coming back. To their assertion Peter described the day of the Lord (2 Pet 3:8–13) and then stated a series of duties for the believer as they waited for the soon-coming day of the Lord (2 Pet 3:14–18).

While it may seem that Peter is again in warning mode, he is actually back in encouragement mode. He reminded these believers that he was writing this reminder to stir up a sincere understanding (2 Pet 3:1). Peter began with the question that the scoffers or false teachers posed: "Where is his 'coming' that he promised?" (2 Pet 3:4a). To this question the scoffers offered this evidence: "Ever since our ancestors fell asleep, all things continue as they have been since the beginning of creation" (2 Pet 3:4b). In other words, these false teachers were intentionally and deliberately mocking God by saying something like "Jesus Christ is not coming back. Nothing's really ever changed since creation and that's not going to change."

Peter's response was quick and to the point. He described the ignorance of these scoffers by pointing out that they were deliberately overlooking the past history of the world, namely the flood (2 Pet 3:5b–6) and that they were ignorant of the future of the world (2 Pet 3:7). Peter's point is that things have changed at least once, and they will change again. Second, he drew attention to the fact that since God is eternal and outside of the bonds of time, his perspective of time is much different than ours (2 Pet 3:8). Not only is God's perspective different than ours, but so is his program. God is patiently building his church. He is "not wanting any to perish but all to come to repentance" (2 Pet 3:9). In other words, when it comes to time, God wants to make sure that there is plenty of it so that any who want to will turn to him in repentance.

Peter assured his readers that the day of the Lord would come and that it would "come like a thief" (2 Pet 3:10; see Matt 24:43; 1 Thess 5:2). It will be a time of destruction when the old heavens and earth will give way to a new heaven and earth. Because of this, believers should be people of holy conduct and godliness (2 Pet 3:10–13). Holy conduct and godliness are reflected in four duties. First, believers should be at peace and live a life without spot or blemish. Second, believers should remember that the patience of God has the salvation of others as its end. Third, believers have the duty to be on guard so that they are neither led away nor fall

(2 Pet 3:14–17). Finally, the believer is to "grow in the grace and knowledge of our Lord and Savior Jesus Christ" (2 Pet 3:18).

We would do well to remember Peter's reminder. Christ is coming back. Each day between today and when he comes back is a day of salvation. Therefore, we ought to be people who are ready to share the hope of the gospel. Since Christ is coming back, this ought to impact how we personally live as well. Our lives ought to be holy and godly, where we are actively growing in grace so that we are standing guard against those who would try to lead us astray or trip us up. Ultimately, this takes us back to where we started. We can live this kind of Christian life because "his divine power has given us everything required for life and godliness through the knowledge of him who called us by his own glory and goodness" (2 Pet 1:3).

BIBLIOGRAPHY

Bauckham, Richard J. *Jude, 2 Peter*. WBC 50. Nashville: Word, 1983.

Davids, Peter H. *The Letters of 2 Peter and Jude*. PNTC. Grand Rapids: Eerdmans, 2006.

Giese, Curtis P. *2 Peter and Jude*. Concordia Commentary. St. Louis: Concordia, 2012.

Green, Gene L. *Jude and 2 Peter*. BECNT. Grand Rapids: Baker Academic, 2008.

Green, Michael. *2 Peter and Jude*. TNTC. Downers Grove, IL: IVP Academic, 2007.

Kruger, Michael J. "The Authenticity of 2 Peter." *JETS* 42 (1999): 645–71.

Pelikan, J., and Hansen, W. A., eds. *Luther's Works: The Catholic Epistles*. Vol. 30. St. Louis: Concordia, 1967.

Powell, Mark Allen. *Introducing the New Testament: A Historical, Literary, and Theological Survey*. Grand Rapids: Baker Academic, 2018.

Reese, Ruth Anne. *2 Peter and Jude*. The Two Horizons New Testament Commentary. Grand Rapids: Eerdmans, 2007.

Ryken, Leland, Philip Ryken, and James Wilhoit. *Ryken's Bible Handbook: A Guide to Reading and Studying the Bible*. Wheaton, IL: Tyndale, 2005.

Schreiner, Thomas R. *1, 2, Peter, Jude*. NAC 37. Nashville: Holman Reference, 2003.

22

1, 2, AND 3 JOHN

MONTE SHANKS

CONNECTION POINT

What relevance do these first-century writings have for us today? Much, especially as it relates to answering the question, What is authentic Christianity? In a world that promotes "expressive individualism," is there really such a thing as authentic Christianity or do people simply make up their own "brand"? Institutional churches, media outlets, and social icons continually give opposing opinions of what "acceptable" Christianity looks like, so who can say what it is? Where does one search in order to discover it? The apostle John wrote three letters that provide answers to this important question.[1]

Authentic Christianity originated with the Lord Jesus Christ. It is based upon his life, teachings, death, resurrection, and ascension, as documented by his personal followers as well as their explanations concerning him and what he taught. One of those followers was John. That being said,

---

[1] Hereafter, all references to "John" are to the apostle John who was the "beloved disciple" of Jesus.

John wrote almost 2,000 years ago; consequently, some question whether anything written so long ago is still relevant. The answer is an emphatic yes! His letters are relevant because even though the world has advanced in some ways, people still struggle with the same things. They struggle with sin, shame, and guilt. They struggle with love and hate, lust and greed, truth and deception; and, most important, they struggle with finding God. Some things never change.

Nevertheless, Christianity is not some constantly changing brand seeking greater "market share." It is grounded in a personal relationship with the One who has conquered sin and the grave and offers eternal life to any who will receive him—and that's what John's letters are all about. They explain how authentic Christianity looks and how people can know whether they have been forever transformed by it.

With this in mind, consider making this your prayer as you read and study this chapter:

> *Heavenly Father, I thank you for loving me and for wanting me to know you even though I am sinful. I want to draw closer to you, and I am studying these letters with the hope that I can know what it means to have eternal life and be authentically Christian. Please guide me in understanding your truths and promises contained within them. Use this opportunity to change me, so that I will continually glorify you with all I am. Amen.*

SETTING

Recipients

John seems to have written these letters around AD 70–85.[2] Early Christians documented that John relocated to Ephesus around the time of the fall of Jerusalem (AD 70), and lived there until his death, around AD 100.[3] One should not presume that the designation "1 John" means that

---

[2] Estimating when these letters were written is a tenuous endeavor because historical data and internal clues are scarce. This estimate is a minority position; other scholars date their composition as occurring later.

[3] Eusebius, *Ecclesiastical History I*, trans. Kirsopp Lake, Loeb Classical Library 153 (Cambridge, MA: Harvard University Press, 1980), 3.1.1; 23.1–6.

it was the first letter John ever wrote.[4] It received this designation because the early church considered it the most significant of his letters. Likely, 2 and 3 John were likely written together, but since 2 John was written for a church, it was deemed more important than 3 John.

John, seeking to protect others from being associated with him, cryptically referred to himself as "the elder" in 2 and 3 John.[5] Some suggest that these two letters were written to accompany either John's Gospel or 1 John. Information contained in their endings, however, argues against this conclusion. Consequently, they were apparently written before 1 John and/or John's Gospel.[6] Third John was written to a pastor/elder named Gaius and 2 John for his church.[7] Soon afterward, he wrote 1 John, but not as an introduction to his Gospel;[8] instead, it is a letter written to introduce

---

[4] There is considerable debate over the authorship of works attributed to the apostle John. The earliest and most dependable Christian writings clearly assert that John wrote a Gospel, Revelation, and the three canonical letters traditionally attributed to him. The earliest known questioning concerning any of John's writings came from Dionysius of Alexandria (ca. AD 250), who doubted that John wrote Revelation. Dionysius speculated that a hitherto unknown "John" wrote Revelation; cf. Eusebius, *Ecclesiastical History II*, trans. J. E. L. Oulton, Loeb Classical Library 265 (Cambridge MA: Harvard University Press, 1980), VII.25–26.1. Eusebius, sharing the same beliefs, presented "evidence" for this other John from Papias's writings; cf. Eusebius, *Ecclesiastical History I*, III.39.1–7; and Monte A. Shanks, *Papias and the New Testaments* (Eugene, OR: Wipf & Stock, 2013), 137–57, 277–92. From these speculations, modern skeptics have perpetuated the notion by estranging John from Revelation, his Gospel, and his letters as well. The natural reading of Papias (who was a personal disciple of John) is that he referred to all of the apostles as "elders." He later differentiated the living apostles in his day from those no longer alive, where he again referred to John as "the elder John." Such a designation was not unusual, even Peter referred to himself as a "fellow elder" (cf. 1 Pet 5:1). Consequently, the non-apostolic figure commonly referred to as "elder John" is, quite frankly, a poorly defended myth. Others postulate that some of John's works were written by a mysterious group referred to as the "Johannine community." Nevertheless, the common vocabulary, themes, and concepts contained within the Gospel of John and these letters support the historically based and well-defended conclusion that they all were written by the apostle John. See Robert W. Yarbrough, *1–3 John*, BECNT (Grand Rapids: Baker Academic, 2008), 5–15 for the evolution of divorcing John from his writings.

[5] While John was certainly one of the older Christian leaders during this period, the adjectival title "elder" is not referring to his age. The early church used this title for those possessing apostolic authority; cf. Shanks, *Papias*, 137–47. Estimating John's birth circa AD 5 would make him between sixty-five and eighty years old when he wrote his letters.

[6] Marshall suggested that 2 John is older than 1 John. See I. Howard Marshall, *The Epistles of John*, NICNT (Grand Rapids: Eerdmans, 1978), 10.

[7] Gaius was a common Roman name. There are three other Gaiuses mentioned in the New Testament; however, it is unlikely that any of those received 3 John.

[8] Brown recognized that John did not quote Jesus from his Gospel in any of his letters. Raymond E. Brown, *The Epistles of John*, ABC (Garden City, NY: Doubleday, 1982), 33. This fact suggests that John's letters predated his Gospel. If John's Gospel did exist, then it

himself to churches in the region surrounding Ephesus, in present-day western Turkey.

Themes and Key Passage

All three of John's letters have two dominant themes: authentic Christianity is marked by (1) a dedication to the truth concerning the Lord Jesus Christ, as well as (2) a life devoted to genuinely loving other believers. Like the sides of a coin, these themes are tightly bound together, and their union cannot be overemphasized. If there is one verse that best summarizes his purposes for these letters, it may be 1 John 5:13:

> I have written these *instructions* to you *all* so that you might know that you possess eternal life, those believing in the name of the Son of God. (author's translation)

A bust of Nero, the ancient emperor of Rome who persecuted the Christian church

Purpose and Occasions

The church was in disarray after the Neronian persecutions (ca. AD 65–69). This period was difficult because persecution was still a threat. The Roman Empire viewed Christians as disloyal since they proclaimed that Jesus had conquered the grave and is God; thus, he is Lord of all—including Rome. Consequently, Christians were slandered with unspeakable labels and viewed as subversives. The church was dealing with internal conflicts as well. The seed beliefs of what would become Gnosticism and proto-Docetism were increasing their heretical influences.[9] Additionally, there were still Judaizers as well as other ethical

---

is hard to imagine that he would have avoided quoting the Lord from it (even Paul quoted Jesus; cf. 1 Cor 11:23–24 and possibly 1 Tim 5:18b, which is the verbatim of Luke 10:7). Instead, John appealed to what his audiences had heard from other apostles (e.g., Paul).

[9] Carson and Moo, *An Introduction to the New Testament*, 678–81 (see chap. 15, n. 4). Docetism was a doctrine that essentially rejected the incarnation of Christ by teaching that Jesus's body was not human but a manifestation or an "other-worldly" substance. Therefore, in this view, Jesus's suffering was not actual but perceived. John's emphasis in 1 John regarding the physical existence of Jesus may be intended to refute such teaching (1 John 1:1–2; 4:2; see also John 1:14).

issues such as antinomianism and legalism. False apostles, prophets, and teachers were also on the rise: all of whom were in ministry only for money, selfish pleasures, or fame.[10] Many churches were confused, apathetic, persecuted, and poverty-stricken. The church had witnessed the martyrdom of most of the apostles and early leaders. During this time, one of the last living apostles came to Ephesus and picked up the pieces of a battered church and brought renewal and a commitment to carrying out the Great Commission. He was the apostle John, and he came to restore the churches of Asia Minor to godly leadership, apostolic doctrines, and Christlike practices that were established "from the beginning" of the church's earliest days.[11]

HIGHLIGHTS IN 1 JOHN

First John is different from other New Testament writings because it is much more circular in its exhortations. Some characterize it as repetitive, even suggesting that its author suffered from advanced age. While John was in his later years, this letter is not affected by the onset of senility;[12] instead, it has a Spirit-inspired comprehensiveness that seamlessly cycles between theological declarations and pastoral applications.

Another feature is that John did not associate himself with this letter by name or title (e.g., "the elder"), and neither did he address any contemporary person or church within it. As a result, it has been aptly characterized as a circular sermon or treatise.

Additionally, 1 John's exhortations are delivered through generic and universal statements. For example, John did not name gnostics, Hellenists, or Jews as his opponents; rather, he described their assertions and behaviors. His approach demonstrates that this letter was not intended to be relevant to only a select group of people, but is applicable to anyone anywhere at all times. This letter has many repetitive themes, such as love and hate, light and darkness, and truth and deception. However, it has two main themes concerning authentic Christians, which are: (1) they *believe* the truth that Jesus's death is the only atoning sacrifice that provides for eternal life; and (2) they *demonstrate* their relationship with God by loving others.

---

[10] See Matt 7:15; Mark 13:21–23; Acts 20:28–31; 2 Tim 4:3–4; 2 Peter 2; Jude 11–16.
[11] John often used the term *beginning*; however, it does not always refer to the same point of origin.
[12] Brown, *Epistles of John*, 25.

An Apostolic Testimony (1 John 1:1–4)

John personally saw and physically touched the risen Lord (John 20:19–29; Luke 24:36–43). If a reader accepts only one assertion from this letter, it should be that John claimed to have witnessed the most amazing event in history—the resurrection of the Lord Jesus Christ. Regarding any questions about this event, John confidently asserted: "It's true!" He shamelessly proclaims its joyous news in this letter. One may believe or scoff at him, but it is a futile endeavor to suggest that John meant anything else.[13] Moreover, this experience provided him with the apostolic authority that is foundational for everything that follows.

The Solution for Sin (1 John 1:5–2:2)

John began by explaining why Jesus's death is so important, which is that his death is the only "atoning sacrifice" for the sins of "the whole world" (1 John 2:2)[14] However, this provision is only applied to those who believe. Sin is a nonnegotiable problem because, as 1 John 1:5 tells us, God is "light" (i.e., holiness, pure truth, and eternal life), within whom there is no darkness (i.e., sin, deception, and death). Therefore, when this world ends, God will not abide sin that has not been cleansed. One's sins must be atoned for in this life or they will be condemned in the next. Moreover, John declared that anyone claiming to be without sin is a godless "liar" (1 John 1:10). But, for those who have embraced Christ's sacrifice and confessed their sins, the "blood of Jesus" provides forgiveness and "cleanses" them from all unrighteousness.[15] A primary purpose for John's writing was to keep his "children"[16] from sinning; consequently, godly living is one of his main ambitions for this letter. Nevertheless, whenever believers sin, Christ's blood is the all-sufficient purifying solvent that washes away sin's stain, thus sustaining their relationship with God. Authentic Christians trust solely in Jesus for the forgiveness of sin.

---

[13] Brown, *Epistles of John*, 182.

[14] Yarbrough, *1–3 John*, 80. There is considerable debate over the terms *propitiation* and *expiation*. Expiation involves the cancellation, or removal, of sin via an appropriate sacrifice. Propitiation involves the appeasement of God's wrath. For an argument for propitiation, see Daniel L. Akin, *1,2,3 John*, NAC (Nashville: Holman Reference, 2001), 253–65.

[15] Jesus's death provides forgiveness for all intentional and unintentional sins.

[16] John affectionately referred to believers as "children" throughout his letters. Jesus described his followers in the same manner (Matt 18:3; Mark 10:24; Luke 18:16–17; John 13:33).

The Enduring Anointing (1 John 2:3–27)

This large section contains important themes that are interconnected with respect to a faith that endures and a faith that matures. These qualities are found in those who possess faith in Christ, and as a result, have received the anointing of the Holy Spirit. The second test of genuine faith is that anyone claiming to "know" him should keep his "commands" (1 John 2:3). Those who know him keep his word,[17] and those who disregard it are "liars" who are void of spiritual truth. Those who truly know the Lord show that their love for God has matured because their lives mimic Jesus's earthly life (1 John 2:4–6).

Next, John moves to a more specific test that involves loving other believers. This theme permeates 1 John. Anyone who does not love other believers lives in spiritual darkness. This darkness and the world's lusts are "passing away"; but the promise for those who live for the "will of God" is eternal life. Authentic Christians love other believers just as the Lord commanded (1 John 2:8, 17; see John 13:34–35).

While the world is passing way, its opposition to Christ is constantly increasing. Regrettably, some who had once associated with believers abandoned their churches and began publicly denying Christ, becoming "antichrists."[18] They denied that Jesus was the Christ (i.e., the Messiah). John explained that their abandonment of Christ indicated that their confessions were insincere, for if they were authentic believers, they would have endured in the faith and continued in Christian fellowship. This predicament reveals that the world is in its "last hour," within which the antichrist will appear.[19] Thus, those enduring in the faith can do so because they have an anointing from the "Holy One" (1 John 2:18–20). This anointing teaches believers spiritual truth, indicating John is referring to the Holy Spirit.[20]

---

[17] Although in the singular, the term *word* refers to all of Jesus's teachings.

[18] Scholars seek to identify these individuals as a specific type of "secessionists." Nevertheless, John provided a universal test for identifying any opponent(s) of Christ. Thus, any persons denying Jesus's divinity are "antichrists" regardless of what they call themselves.

[19] The "last hour" is a metaphor for "era" that refers to the final eschatological period of the world's history. John stated, "the antichrist *is coming*" (1 John 2:18), which should be translated as a future present verb from the Greek (Daniel B. Wallace, *Greek Grammar Beyond the Basics* [Grand Rapids: Zondervan Academic, 1997], 535–37). John is referring to the public appearance of a figure who will oppose the gospel (cf. 2 Thess 2:1–10; Revelation 13). D. Edmond Hiebert, *The Epistles of John* (Greenville, SC: Bob Jones University Press, 1991), 108–9.

[20] Regarding promises about the Holy Spirit, see Mark 1:8; John 14:16–17, 26; 15:26; 16:7; Acts 1:8.

The Hope of His Appearing (1 John 2:28–3:3)

With the disturbing news about the final antichrist's coming, John encouraged his audience with the promise of the Lord's second coming. The Lord's appearing refers to his abrupt visual return to establish his kingdom on earth.[21] Those abiding in him and hoping for his appearing can have confidence,[22] are purifying themselves, and will lack shame upon his arrival. John explained that while it is not clear as to what believers will be like at the Lord's appearing, they can take comfort because when he appears, they will be transformed and become "like him" (1 John 3:2). Authentic believers confidently hope for their Lord's second coming.

The Practice of Righteousness (1 John 3:4–24)

This section provides several characteristics of believers: they do what is "right" (1 John 3:7), love fellow believers, and keep God's commands. Some are troubled by verses in this section because they think they teach that Christians are incapable of sin (cf. 1 John 3:4, 6, 9); therefore, anyone who sins must not be saved. The problem with this interpretation is that it ignores what John has already written when he explained that believers confess their sins (1 John 1:8–2:1) and, consequently, receive forgiveness. John was not promoting Christian "perfectionism." He was, however, explaining that anyone habitually sinning did not "know him" (1 John 3:7). Therefore, anyone living a life of ongoing, unrepentant sin is "of the devil" (1 John 3:8) but anyone regularly rejecting sin is "born of God" (3:9).[23] John also identified another purpose for the Lord's first coming, which is to "destroy the devil's works" (1 John 3:8), thus acknowledging that Christians participate in a great spiritual struggle. More importantly, he explained that Jesus was revealed in order to take away all sin, and only he can do so because he was completely sinless.[24]

John moved from the general characteristic of believers to one that is more specific, which is that believers love one another. Using Cain as an illustration, John explained that believers should never hate other believers; instead, they should sacrificially love them. They can do so because the

---

[21] Akin, *1,2,3 John*, 130. On Jesus's promise to physically return, see Matt 24:37–44; 25:31–46.

[22] In reference to 1 John 2:28, the NASB1995's translation "abide" is preferred over CSB's "remain," simply because abiding carries the nuance of "harmoniously dwelling together" that is not obvious with "remain."

[23] Cf. John 3:3–7.

[24] On the sinless perfection of Jesus, see 2 Cor 5:21; Heb 4:15; 1 Pet 1:18–19.

Lord demonstrated that he sacrificially loves them through his death on the cross. John appropriately provided a practical application of what this type of love looks like, which is that Christians meet the real needs of other Christians (1 John 3:17). Finally, genuine Christians experience confidence before God because of the abiding presence of the Holy Spirit and because they keep his commands, which are twofold: they believe in God's Son, Jesus Christ, and they love one another.

The Absolute Test of Authenticity (1 John 4:1–6)

John returned to the preeminent test of Christian authenticity, which is whether one sincerely embraces the truth that Jesus Christ is God incarnate. John commanded believers not to accept everything naively, but regularly to "test" all things concerning spiritual matters (1 John 4:1). Those who "confess" that Jesus is the incarnate Christ are "from God" (1 John 4:2), but any who reject Jesus are not from God. They are guided by the "spirit of the antichrist" (1 John 4:3).[25] John explained that this type of examination was necessary because false prophets were throughout the world.[26] This mandate is particularly important given the previous section. Just because someone appears to do what is right or

> **Did John Promote Christian Perfectionism?**
>
> Some are troubled by 1 John 3:4, 6, 9 because they think these verses teach that Christians do not sin; therefore, anyone who sins must not be saved. The problem with interpreting these verses in such a grammatically isolated manner is that it ignores the observation John previously stated that believers confess their sins (1 John 1:8–2:1). Thus, John was not promoting Christian perfectionism (i.e., that Christians can attain a state of sinless human perfection). Instead, he was explaining that anyone habitually sinning without repentance does not know God. The exegetical key concerning this passage is found in 1 John 3:8, in which John explained that "from the beginning the devil *sins*" (literally translated). John meant that the devil is *always* sinning—in other words, he *habitually sins*. John did not mean that Satan occasionally sins, but because of his nature, he continually sins. Therefore, using the devil as the preeminent example, John was explaining that anyone who lives a life of habitual sin without concern or remorse has not been born again.

---

[25] Western culture depreciates spiritual realities while emphasizing the physical world and emotional subjectivism. John explains that it is the spiritual world that is the driving force within creation. People are greatly influenced by spirits, whether human or other, all of whom are ultimately influenced by either Satan or God. Jesus and Paul described Satan as the leader and influencer of this fallen world; cf. John 8:44–45; 16:11; 17:15; 2 Cor 4:4.

[26] Jesus warned about false prophets (Matt 7:15; Mark 13:21–23). John provides this test in the most universal manner; thus, it is relevant for all interactions with others regarding spiritual matters; Hiebert, *Epistles of John*, 180.

The Torches of Nero, by Henryk Siemiradzki (1878). According to Tacitus, Nero used Christians as human torches.

displays love for others does not mean that he or she knows God. Only those having trusted Christ and keep his commands actually know God. Consequently, there are only two types of people in this world: those deceived by the spirit of the antichrist and those who have conquered the spiritual forces of darkness by embracing Jesus Christ through the work of the Holy Spirit (1 John 4:4–6).

The Power of Love (1 John 4:7–5:3)

John returned to emphasizing love. Foremost, love begins with God, and it is only because God first loved humanity that anyone can love God. Twice John stated that "God is love" (1 John 4:8, 16). The objective proof of God's love is that he sent Jesus to be the "world's Savior" (1 John 4:14).[27] Consequently, by loving one another, Christians reveal that they are born of God. Furthermore, the believer's spiritual union with God is internally experienced because God's Spirit abides within them. Those maturing in their love for God and others replace fear with love.[28] Since no one can see

---

[27] "World's Savior" (1 John 4:14) references the fact that Jesus died for the world and his sacrifice is sufficient for all who will accept him. This term does not mean that his sacrifice is automatically applied to everyone, only that it is available to and sufficient for everyone.

[28] The word "complete" in 1 John 4:17 means "to bring to full measure, to accomplish"; in other words, to bring to maturity. Walter Bauer, *A Greek-English Lexicon of the New*

God, believers demonstrate that God indwells them by confessing Jesus is his Son and by loving one another.[29] No one can claim to love the unseen God and also hate God's creations, whom they can see. Thus, authentic Christians demonstrate their love for God by loving other believers and keeping God's commands. John says this is what it means to love God.

The Victory of "the" Faith (1 John 5:4–12)[30]

John informed believers that their faith in Christ has secured their inevitable victory over the demonic world.[31] Those who love God through Christ also experience the abiding presence of the Spirit. John explained that Jesus came by the Spirit, water, and blood, referring to his obedience, Spirit-filled life and ministry, baptism (i.e., water), and sacrificial death (i.e., blood).[32] Anyone rejecting Jesus makes God out to be a liar because God has testified to the truth about Jesus by providing eternal life within believers. Anyone not trusting in God's Son does not possess eternal life.

Testament, ed. and trans. William F. Arndt, F. Wilber Gingrich, and Fredrick W. Danker, 2nd ed. (Chicago: University of Chicago Press, 1979), s.v., *teleioō*.

[29] John's statement that no one has ever seen God refers to God the Father. Colin G. Kruse, *The Letters of John*, PNTC (Grand Rapids: Eerdmans, 2000), 161. John is not rejecting Christ's divinity. He means that no one has visibly seen and therefore understood God using human eyesight. Jesus taught that God is Spirit; therefore, he is invisible to the human eye (John 4:21–24; 5:37). Moreover, only he has seen the Father (John 6:46). Knowing this, John wrote in his Gospel that God the Father is only revealed by God the Son, who took on flesh in order to make the Father known (John 1:1–18). Consequently, while no one has seen the Father, some have witnessed God incarnate by "seeing" Jesus (1 John 1:1–4; 4:14).

[30] There is a famous textual issue involving 1 John 5:7–8 that is commonly referred to as the "Johannine Comma." The textual evidence argues against the longer reading. Bruce M. Metzger, *A Textual Commentary of the Greek New Testament*, 2nd ed. (New York: United Bible Societies, 1994), 647–49.

[31] John knows nothing of a Christianized "dualism" that promotes two equally competing powers (Akin, *1,2,3 John*, 174). Satan and this world are defeated because of Jesus's incarnation and resurrection. Although a spiritual battle still rages, the powers of darkness are already defeated.

[32] "Water" is not a metaphor referring to human birth (as mentioned by Hiebert, *Epistles of John*, 234), nor does it refer to the issue of water from Jesus side during his crucifixion (as mentioned by A. E. Brooke, *The Johannine Epistles*, ICC [Edinburgh: T&T Clark, 1957], 132). It refers to Jesus's baptism (not unlike the initiation ritual of the Jewish high priest; cf. Exod 29:4; Lev 8:6), which was a public declaration of his dedication to God's kingdom. "Blood" refers to his physical death as the atoning sacrifice for sin (1 John 1:7). See Marshall, *Epistles of John*, 232–34, for a discussion on the theological significance of these issues with respect to the early Gnosticism of John's day.

Our Confidence in Him (1 John 5:13–21)

First John concludes by discussing the confidence Christians can have concerning prayer. Believers can know that God works through their prayers as they pray according to his will. John moves from prayer in general to a practical pastoral concern, which is interceding on behalf of other believers engaged in sin.[33] Here John refers to the "sin that leads to death" (1 John 5:16), meaning one's willful rejection of God.[34] John reassured his audience that those born of God do not habitually sin because the One that is actually begotten of God (i.e., Jesus, cf. Luke 1:3–55; John 3:16) "keeps" them so that the "evil one" cannot "touch" them (1 John 5:18).[35] This Holy One also enables believers to understand that while the world is controlled by Satan, they possess eternal life and know the true God, who is Jesus Christ.[36] John assured believers they are preserved by the Lord Jesus Christ.[37]

HIGHLIGHTS IN 2 JOHN

Second John is the second shortest New Testament letter. It briefly provides apostolic directives to an unnamed church and informs it of John's future visit. He encouraged believers to abide in the truth concerning Christ while

---

[33] This issue involves known sins (e.g., fornication, substance addictions, etc.), not unseen sins or rumors.

[34] Understanding John's point concerning the praying for "ordinary" sins and not the sin "that leads to death" must be understood by the passage's greater context. The death in view is spiritual separation from God, not physical death (cf. 1 John 3:14; and Hiebert, *Epistles of John*, 262). The sin leading to spiritual death is progressively revealed in Scripture. It is introduced in the Old Testament as a person's willful rejection of God (e.g., Num 15:30–31). Jesus elaborated more fully on this sin, describing it as the "blasphemy against the Spirit," which is eternally unforgivable (Matt 12:31–32). John has explained that those who abandon the faith (1 John 2:18) or deny that Jesus is the Christ, or deny the Son and the Father (1 John 2:22) are committing the sin that inevitably leads to eternal death. Thus, the "sin that leads to death" is the willful rejection of the gospel, which results in eternal damnation (Marshall, *Epistles of John*, 247–48).

[35] The Greek word *aptō* in 1 John 5:18 is translated as "to touch." While acceptable, it is more appropriately translated as to "burn" or "harm" (s.v. "*aptō*," *Bauer-Danker Greek Lexicon of the New Testament*).

[36] First John 5:20 clearly affirms the deity of the Lord Jesus Christ.

[37] John's final command to guard against "idols" should not be undersold. Idolatry was systemic throughout the polytheistic Roman–Greco world. John was essentially commanding believers to reject this world's entire religious system. His command means nothing less than a rejection of the world's spirit of ecumenicalism out of loyalty to Christ alone.

exhibiting Christian love toward one another. John also commanded them to renounce those promoting any heresy that rejects the deity of Jesus Christ.

The Salutation (2 John vv. 1–3)

John referred to himself simply as "the elder," while also referring to this congregation as an "elect lady and her children." He personified this church as an esteemed woman. She is "elect" because God has sovereignly determined that the church constitutes his people; only it can fulfill his purposes in the world. It is possible that this congregation also met in the home of a great Christian matriarch.[38] He included himself within his blessings to this church, reassuring all believers that the triune God is the giver of grace, mercy, and peace, and that he administers his presence to them in truth and love.

A Commendation (2 John vv. 4–6)

John met others from this church, and described them as living faithfully for Christ. Their faithfulness was evident because they obeyed the command of the Father, which is to love one another and walk in obedience to God's commands.[39] Obedience to God's "commands" reveals authentic Christian love. Emphasizing this distinctly Christian ethic was essential given the directives that follow.

A Warning (2 John vv. 7–11)

Next John commanded his audience to reject anti-Christian "deceivers" and their message that Jesus—the Messiah—did not come "in the flesh."[40] He commanded his audience to "watch" themselves so that they might endure in the apostolic faith. Those that abandoned the teachings of Christ and accepted these new heresies proved they were not from God,

---

[38] Christians at Ephesus familiar with Paul's analogy of the church being Christ's wife (cf. Eph 5:23–24), or Jesus's Ten Virgins parable (Matt 25:1–13), would understand this metaphor (see also 2 Cor 11:2; 1 Pet 5:13). Some have suggested that John refers to an individual here who had a house church in her home.

[39] See Mark 9:7; John 6:40; 1 John 3:23; Kruse, *Letters of John*, 207.

[40] Akin, *1,2,3 John*, 228–29. Wallace interprets this phrase as "those confessing that Jesus Christ *has come* in the flesh." Wallace, *Greek Grammar Beyond the Basics*, 646. A wooden translation of the phrase in verse 7 is "the ones not confessing Jesus Christ coming in the flesh." The participles are present, which could mean that these antichrists reject the second coming of the Lord in the flesh. Most scholars, however, interpret this participle as meaning that they rejected Jesus's incarnation. The point is academic, for if they rejected Jesus's incarnation, then they would also reject his bodily second coming.

while those remaining faithful to the teachings of Christ would maintain the rewards of their faithfulness.

John also commanded adherence to what some consider to be an un-Christlike practice, which is withholding hospitality to heretics. Given his previous encouragement to love others, it is obvious he was not suggesting that Christians "hate" these deceivers but that they reject their false teachings.[41] Moreover, John was not calling believers to dissociate from other Christians because of minor differences concerning theology or practices, or to embarrass unbelievers because of their ignorance concerning the gospel, but to renounce heretical missionaries who rejected the teachings of Jesus.[42] He concluded by explaining that any who lend aid to them participate with their "evil" proselytizing.

The Closing (2 John vv. 12–13)

In closing, John informed his audience of his wish to provide further written instructions, but the time was not right. Last, he relayed cryptic greetings from another unnamed congregation, thus securing anonymity for both churches, while keeping his own location secret as well.[43]

HIGHLIGHTS IN 3 JOHN

Third John is the shortest New Testament letter. It encourages partnering with others who are proclaiming the gospel. It is unlike other New Testament letters because "Jesus" and "Christ" are absent from it. These omissions were probably a safeguard against persecution, if perchance it fell into the wrong hands. Similarly, John withheld his name, again guaranteeing its recipient would never be associated with him. The letter encourages an elder/pastor to remain faithful to Christ by faithfully loving other believers, while also rejecting the poor leadership example of another "Christian" leader. It was delivered by a missionary named Demetrius, who probably also delivered 2 John.

---

[41] Contemporary Christians fail to appreciate these directives because of unfamiliarity about the legal ramifications of first-century cultural practices regarding hospitality. See Kruse, *Letters of John*, 215–16.

[42] Karen H. Jobes, *1,2,and 3 John*, ZECNT (Grand Rapids: Zondervan Academic, 2014), 273–75.

[43] The similarity of the endings in 2 and 3 John indicates they were composed around the same time. For an examination of their commonalities, see Akin, *1,2,3 John*, 235–37.

The Salutation (3 John vv. 1–4)

John described Gaius as one of his "children," indicating that he probably led Gaius to Christ.[44] John had received a report from others that Gaius was living faithfully for Christ. It is noteworthy that John prayed that God would prosper Gaius's well-being in the same manner as his soul. Praying for God's blessings on his faithful workers so that ministry can prosper is a biblical idea, and goes back, as evidenced here, to the beginning of gospel ministry.

The Exhortation (3 John vv. 5–8)

John commended Gaius for abundantly providing for a group of missionaries who beforehand were "strangers." These men had reported to John about the love Gaius displayed toward them. John confirmed that they went out for the sake of "the Name" (3 John vv. 6–7), which is a reference to Jesus.[45] These evangelists refused support from nonbelievers,[46] and John used their example to explain that ministry in Christ's name is the responsibility of God's people. Consequently, missionaries and those who financially support them are "coworkers" in the work of the gospel (3 John v. 8).

> **When Should a Pastor Be Rebuked and/or Removed?**
>
> John referred to a dictatorial elder/pastor named Diotrephes in 3 John. Diotrephes displayed several hallmarks of a dangerous minister, which were: (1) being self-promoting; (2) rejecting apostolic authority; (3) unjustly maligning others that he viewed as threats; (4) inhospitality toward outside believers; and (5) attempting to excommunicate others who refused to obey his inappropriate demands.
>
> Regrettably, sometimes the wrong people enter the ministry and ascend to positions of power. The results are usually disastrous. Godly leadership requires that such persons be confronted and removed if they are unwilling to repent. Ignoring the circumstances is an abdication of leadership that will only lead to the ruin of a church or ministry. Whenever such actions are required, 1 Tim 5:17–22 provides some essential biblical directives that must be followed.

---

[44] Paul also referred to individuals that he led to Christ using paternal terms (e.g., Phil 2:22; 1 Tim 1:2; Titus 1:4).
[45] See Acts 4:12; 5:41; 9:16; Rom 1:5; Phil 2:9; 1 John 3:23.
[46] In the CSB "pagans;" in the NASB1995 "Gentiles."

A Warning (3 John vv. 9–10)

John explained that he wrote a letter to another church,[47] but it was rejected by a dictatorial elder/pastor named Diotrephes.[48] Gaius was familiar with Diotrephes, probably because he led a church in a neighboring city. John explained that he would confront Diotrephes publicly when John arrived.[49] Diotrephes's offenses were public; as a result, John's apostolic responsibility and love for the church (2 John 1) required public action as well.

Ancient pottery from the sixth century depicting the "evangelists"

A Recommendation (3 John vv. 11–12)

Next, John exhorted Gaius to reject Diotrephes's "evil" example. He then recommended Demetrius as one that "the truth itself" had found faithful (3 John v. 12).[50] He encouraged Gaius to welcome Demetrius and to provide abundantly for him as he continued on his mission.[51]

The Closing (3 John vv. 13–14)

Last, John informed Gaius that while he wished he could provide more extensive written instructions, the time was not right. He also notified Gaius of his plans to visit. The letter ends by extending peace to Gaius as well as cryptic greetings to and from other unnamed "friends" (3 John v. 15) known to both.

---

[47] This lost letter was not 2 John, for Diotrephes's rejection of John means that he would not have preserved any of his letters as well. John wrote 2 John in order to provide some brief instructions to Gaius's church, as well as to inform it of his future visit. John's description of this lost letter as merely "something" also suggests that it was not 1 John. Marshall, *Epistles of John*, 88.

[48] John R. W. Stott, *The Epistles of John*, TNTC (Leicester, UK: InterVarsity, 1983), 224–27. Diotrephes ignored John's instructions concerning godly leadership; cf. Mark 10:42–45.

[49] The issues concerning Diotrephes were likely moral, not doctrinal. Jobes, *1, 2, and 3 John*, 316–19.

[50] Truth here is not "truth" personified or Demetrius's "behavior" (Marshall, *Epistles of John*, 93); nor it is the sum total of truth in the Scriptures (Hiebert, *Epistles of John*, 344). John documented Jesus's claim to be "*the* truth" (John 14:6); he later refers to the Holy Spirit as "*the* truth" that testifies to the truth concerning Jesus (1 John 5:6). The intensive "himself" indicates the Holy Spirit's activity in Demetrius's life testified to his devotion to Christ.

[51] Hospitality is required of pastors and elders (1 Tim 3:2; Titus 1:8). Hospitality is also expected of all believers (Matt 10:40–42; Rom 12:13; 1 Pet 4:9).

BIBLIOGRAPHY

Akin, Daniel L. *1, 2, 3 John*. NAC. Nashville: Holman Reference, 2001.

Bauer, Walter. *A Greek-English Lexicon of the New Testament*. Edited and translated by William F. Arndt, F. Wilber Gingrich, and Frederick W. Danker. 2nd ed. Chicago: University of Chicago Press, 1979.

Brooke, A. E. *The Johannine Epistles*. ICC. Edinburgh: T&T Clark, 1957.

Brown, Raymond E. *The Epistles of John*. ABC. Garden City, NY: Doubleday, 1982.

Carson, D.A., and Douglas J. Moo. *An Introduction to the New Testament*. 2nd ed. Grand Rapids: Zondervan Academic, 2005.

Eusebius. *Ecclesiastical History I*. Translated by Kirsopp Lake. Loeb Classical Library 153. Cambridge, MA: Harvard University Press, 1980.

———. *Ecclesiastical History II*. Translated by J. E. L. Oulton. Loeb Classical Library 265. Cambridge, MA: Harvard University Press, 1980.

Hiebert, D. Edmond. *The Epistles of John*. Greenville, SC: Bob Jones University Press, 1991.

Jobes, Karen H. *1, 2, and 3 John*. Zondervan Exegetical Commentary on the New Testament. Grand Rapids: Zondervan Academic, 2014.

Kruse, Colin G. *The Letters of John*. PNTC. Grand Rapids: Eerdmans, 2000.

Marshall, I. Howard. *The Epistles of John*. NICNT. Grand Rapids: Eerdmans, 1978.

Metzger, Bruce M. *A Textual Commentary of the Greek New Testament*. 2nd ed. New York: United Bible Societies, 1994.

Shanks, Monte A. *Papias and the New Testament*. Eugene, OR: Wipf & Stock, 2013.

Stott, John R. W. *The Epistles of John*. TNTC. Carol Stream, IL: Tyndale, 1964.

Yarbrough, Robert W. *1–3 John*. BECNT. Grand Rapids: Baker Academic, 2008.

Wallace, Daniel B. *Greek Grammar Beyond the Basics*. Grand Rapids: Zondervan Academic, 1997.

23

JUDE

CHRIS HULSHOF

CONNECTION POINT

What relevance does this first-century writing have for us today? In 2003 a new athletic clothing brand known as Under Armour set out to create an ad campaign that would establish their presence and disturb their rivals such as Nike and Adidas. In order to accomplish this, they needed a catchy slogan. They settled on "Protect this House." This slogan and the ensuing media surrounding it positioned the brand from upstart to direct competitor with its rivals.

"Protect This House" is not just an ad campaign for Under Armour. It is the theme that underlies the book of Jude. The church that Jude wrote to was under attack, and Jude wanted those believers to contend for the faith. In other words, the book of Jude was a letter meant to be an encouragement to a group of believers to "protect this house." Jude identified their enemies and what they believed, gave examples of how God had dealt with such enemies in the past, provided a few illustrations with regard to those enemies, and finally offered advice on how to go about contending for the faith.

With this in mind, consider making this your prayer as you read and study this chapter:

Father, you are our divine Warrior and Refuge, the One who fights for us and the place that we can run to for safety. As we contend for the faith, first remind us that through the completed work of your Son you have defeated the greatest enemies of our life: sin and death. Remind us that because of this victory, we are called, loved, and kept. In the name of Christ Jesus who holds us fast. Amen.

SETTING

Recipients

Jude seems to have been writing between AD 60 and 80.[1] His short letter gives us no internal markers as to whom he was specifically addressing. They are not identified by their geographic location, as a number of the other New Testament letters identify their recipients. However, given the nature of the decidedly Jewish stories (both noted and obscure), Jude likely addressed a group of Jewish Christians who were well versed in their history and tradition. Jude identified his audience as "the called, loved by God the Father and kept for Jesus Christ" (Jude v. 1).

---

[1] The opening verse of Jude tells us it was written by "Jude, a servant of Jesus Christ and a brother of James" (Jude 1). The two personal and relational connecting points tell us something about the author. First, he was the brother of James. Since the James he was referencing was the half brother of Jesus, Jude was himself a half brother of Jesus. Second, he identified himself as a servant of Jesus. Thus, the servant-driven life that his half brother Jesus led is the same servant-driven life with which Jude identified. Third, that Jude chose to identify himself as a "servant of Jesus Christ" reflects the attitude of a humble leader. Given the weighty and serious nature of the warnings in this short letter, one might have expected Jude to promote his familial relationship to Jesus as the means for acquiring the recipient's attention. However, Jude saw himself as a servant of Jesus first and a brother of James (and Jesus) second.

The context surrounding the letter of Jude is notoriously difficult, given its brevity and lack of clear details about its audience and situation. The earliest manuscript evidence for the letter dates to the third century AD, and the letter is referenced by Clement of Alexandria in the late second century, but details beyond that are difficult. As Reese states, "It is impossible to give an exact date for its production." Ruth Anne Reese, *2 Peter and Jude*, 19 (see chap. 21, n. 3). A reasonable date would range somewhere between AD 60 (Green, *Jude and 2 Peter*, 17 [see chap. 21, n. 1]) and AD 80–90 (Reese, *2 Peter and Jude*, 19).

First, the recipients were "the called." At an individual level, Jude's use of "called" follows Paul's use of the word in Rom 8:28–30. There the "called" are also foreknown, predestined, conformed, justified, and glorified. Jude's intentional use of "the called" also speaks to the active work of God in salvation. He is the active agent who does the salvific work. God does the calling. At a community level, Jude was emphasizing the way in which this community of faith was called in much the same way God called Israel (Exod 3:7–22; Hos 11:1).

Second, the recipients were "loved by God the Father." This phrase presents the rationale for God's love. The recipients were loved not because of who they were or what they had accomplished. They were loved solely on the basis of God's nature as love.

Third, the recipients were "kept for Jesus Christ." This phrase echoes Jesus's prayer in John 17:12 where he noted that he had kept or protected those that the Father had given him. In this same way, Jude identified his audience as being "kept for Jesus Christ."

Practically speaking, these three identifiers also describe believers everywhere. We, too, are the called, loved by God the Father, and kept for Jesus Christ. The salvation we enjoy is not because of our own doing. God has called us. The love he has for us is not because of who we are or what we have accomplished. God's love for us flows from his nature and not our worth. Finally, all of this is kept securely not because of our ability to hang on to Christ but because of his ability to hold us fast.

Theme and Key Passage

What does it look like to "contend for the faith?" This is the theme of Jude's letter. He was writing to a group of believers who were facing opposition. Yet this opposition was not from the outside. Instead, within the walls of their church were those who were actively seeking to undermine the faith with what they believed and how they were living.

Jude 3b says: "I found it necessary to write, appealing to you to contend for the faith that was delivered to the saints once for all."

This verse sets up what Jude will develop throughout his letter. Without naming names, he first identified who believers would need to contend with, based on what they believed. Then Jude both illustrated and described this opposition. He used both Old Testament examples and illustrations to make his point. Finally, Jude provided a strategy for contending for the faith.

Purpose and Occasion

Though Jude apparently had other themes he wished to address, he realized that a greater need had arisen, so his writing plans changed. *The Message* paraphrases it this way: "Dear friends, I've dropped everything to write you about this life of salvation that we have in common. I have to write insisting—begging!—that you fight with everything you have in you for this faith entrusted to us as a gift to guard and cherish" (Jude v. 3). Can you sense the urgency and the importance in the tone of these verses? Jude was not going to sit passively by as a group of people invaded the church and undermined the faith of this group of believers. He wrote with vigor, just as they must vigorously contend for the faith.

Who are the ones seeking to undermine the faith in this community of believers? Jude did not name names. Instead, he offered a description of their presence, judgment, nature, and where they had departed from the faith (Jude v. 4). Curiously, Jude did not present those who were seeking to undermine the faith in this community of believers as false teachers. Rather, he simply addressed them as "these people" (Jude vv. 8, 10, 12, 16, 19). In this way, the book of Jude differs from 2 Peter. While Peter was addressing false teachers in his second letter, Jude addressed outsiders who had slipped into the church and were undermining the faith from inside this community of faith.[2]

As you read the book of Jude, notice the way Jude connected doctrine and lifestyle. According to Jude, these people had distorted the grace of God and denied Jesus Christ. As a result, their lives spiraled downward into sensuality. Once again, Eugene Peterson vividly paraphrases this in *The Message*: "Their design is to replace the sheer grace of our God with sheer license—which means doing away with Jesus Christ, our one and only Master" (Jude v. 4).

---

[2] Two recent studies on the book of Jude by Ruth Ann Reese and Peter H. Davids convincingly argue that there is little in the text to assume that Jude has false teachers in mind. Instead, both authors argue that the book is written to a group known as the "beloved," and in contrast to them is another group, the ungodly. They are commonly referred to as "those people." It is a group that takes advantage of the grace and forgiveness of God and lives a life that lacks godliness, purity, and self-control (Reese, *2 Peter and Jude*, 24.). Davids agrees with Reese, noting that these others are outsiders whose behavior is not in keeping with the community Jude addresses or an understanding of Jesus as Lord and Master. Thus, there is a type of cultural clash between the "beloved" and the "others" underlying the book of Jude. Peter H. Davids, *A Theology of James, Peter, and Jude* (Grand Rapids: Zondervan Academic, 2014), 260–61.

Jude's warning is as pertinent today as it was then. Doctrine shapes your actions. How you live your life is correlated to what you believe. When you downgrade the grace of God you will inevitably downgrade the importance of Jesus in your life. A life of sinful actions and attitudes will surely follow.

HIGHLIGHTS IN JUDE

The Friends, the Foes, the Faith, and the Fight (Jude vv. 1–4)

Jude did not specifically name the foes he identified in this letter. They were ones who had slipped into the church and were practicing a lifestyle that trampled the grace of God and denied the sovereign lordship of Jesus Christ.

Jude wrote, "the faith . . . was delivered to the saints once for all" (Jude v. 3). Jude's expression here notes that the faith is "once, for all time" rather than "once upon a time." The faith Jude was talking about here was not someone's personal and subjective experience of faith. Instead, his focus was on the core beliefs of Christianity. This is characterized in Acts as "the apostles' teaching" (Acts 2:42). We recognize this message today in the inerrant, infallible, and authoritative Word of God. The faith delivered is not the stuff of legends, myths, or fairy tales.

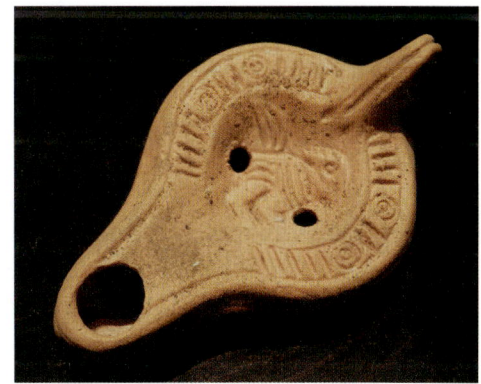

This is an ancient terra-cotta oil lamp. Something like this might have been used by the New Testament authors as they wrote their letters.

The "friends" were challenged to "contend for the faith" (Jude v. 3). For Jude, this contending for the faith was not only a lifelong process, but it would require effort. Contending for the faith is not something done from the comfortable confines of a living room couch. Jude's expression here echoes Paul's personal correspondence with Timothy in places like 1 Tim 4:10 or 2 Tim 4:7.[3]

---

[3] Paul also used similar language in 1 Cor 9:25 when he wrote to the church at Corinth and the church at Colossae in Col 1:29.

These are the remains of a Bronze Age city wall named Bab edh-Dhra, a proposed location for the ancient city of Sodom.

Famous Foes and Their Judgment (Jude vv. 5–11)

The Old Testament contains numerous examples of those whose disobedience led to their judgment. Jude drew on three examples to illustrate the eventual outcome of the people who have "come in by stealth" (Jude v. 4).

First, Jude took the positive rescue and redemption story of the exodus and highlighted the judgment that fell on those who left Egypt but did not trust God. The second example Jude drew on are the fallen angels of Genesis 6 who "did not keep their own position" (Jude v. 6). Because of their rebellion, God's judgment fell on them and they were now bound and awaiting judgment. Finally, Jude pointed to Sodom and Gomorrah as his final example of God's judgment on those whose "sexual immorality and perversions" (Jude v. 7) resulted in the judgment of God.[4] Clearly, Jude

---

[4] Here is the first of two obscure references for modern Christian readers. Jude was using an example from a Jewish intertestamental book known as *The Assumption of Moses* or *The Testament of Moses*. In this story Satan was laying claim to the body of Moses

wanted the friends to know that the testimony of history shows God to be one who judges those whose lives are as willfully disobedient as the lives of those who have crept into this church.

Jude built his case against these foes of the faith by elaborating on three more errors of practice. He wrote that they "defile their flesh, reject authority, and slander glorious ones" (Jude v. 8).[5] Once again there is a connection between doctrine and practice. Their penchant for defiling, rejecting, and slandering is due to their reliance on their dreams rather than "the faith that was delivered to the saints once for all" (Jude v. 3). They have replaced the foundation of pure doctrine with their subjective, personal experience.

Drawing on three more Old Testament examples, Jude noted that their godless actions were similar to the hatred of Cain, the error of Balaam, and the rebellion of Korah (Jude v. 11).[6] What connects all three of these examples to those Jude was warning the friends about? In each of these examples, there was a rejection of the testimony of God and the intent to bring harm to those who followed him. Thus, those who have snuck into this church were seeking to do harm to the friends through their rejection of "the faith."

The Downfall of the Foes (Jude vv. 12–19)

With his case made against "some people who . . . have come in by stealth" (Jude v. 4), Jude then turned to a series of illustrations to magnify the dangers that these foes presented. He called them dangerous reefs (1 Tim 1:19), selfish shepherds (Ezek 34:2–31), waterless clouds (cf. Prov 25:14), fruitless trees (Ps 1:3; Jer 17:6), wild waves (Acts 27; 2 Cor 11:25–26), and wandering stars (Jude vv. 12–13). The first two of these illustrations shines a spotlight on the present danger of those who have mixed in. The final

---

because he had committed murder, but Michael argued that the only authority who can render this kind of verdict is God, who is the true judge. For treatments of Jude's use of this extrabiblical story, see Bauckham, *Jude, 2 Peter* (see chap. 21, n. 1); Giese, *2 Peter and Jude* (see chap. 21, n. 1); Simon J. Kistemaker, *James, Epistles of John, Peter, and Jude*, New Testament Commentary (Grand Rapids: Baker Academic, 2002).

[5] Davids helpfully discusses how Jude's examples here are based not only on the Old Testament accounts but also on familiar narratives that were circulating during the Second Temple period (Davids, *A Theology of James, Peter, and Jude*, 270–72).

[6] Again, Davids is helpful here. He notes that these three examples are rooted in both the Old Testament accounts of Cain, Balaam, and Korah. However, Jude's use of them here is also connected to an understanding of these stories through the lens of Second Temple Judaism (Davids, *A Theology of James, Peter, and Jude*, 274–75).

four illustrations are drawn from the air, the land, the seas, and the sky. Like clouds that have no rain, fruit trees that bear no fruit, waves that lack the proper rhythm of the tides, and stars that wander, the foes who have mixed into this congregation are deceptive, unreliable, and downright dangerous.

Jude drew from both the past and present to remind this community of faith of the impending judgment of these foes. Jude's argument was drawn from the Jewish pseudepigraphal book of *1 Enoch*. He used this text to remind the congregation of God's promised judgment on these tenuous and treacherous invaders. While Jude called them discontented grumblers, who selfishly and arrogantly flattered others for their advantage, the key word that Jude used to describe them is "ungodly," identifying them by this descriptor four times in Jude v. 15.

The friends were also reminded that the apostles predicted the infiltration of these ungodly people. Adding to his previous list, Jude included things such as scoffing, ungodly desires, creating divisions, worldly, and not having the Spirit as further character descriptions of those foes who had mixed in with the friends (Jude vv. 17–19).

Contending for the Faith: A Strategy (Jude vv. 20–23)

With those who sought to corrupt this community of faith identified by their beliefs and actions, Jude gave advice and encouragement to those he called friends. He addressed two ways that the friends could "contend for the faith" or "protect this house." First, he encouraged them to "keep yourselves in the love of God" (Jude v. 21). This is the primary means of contending for the faith. Jude's use of "keep" in reference to the friends here counters his use of "keep" in reference to the friend in the opening verses. The opening use of "keep" addressed the actions of Christ. The concluding use of "keep" addressed the responsibility of believers. It was the responsibility of the friends to keep themselves in the love of God. What does this "keeping" mean? Lenski puts it this way: "To keep oneself in God's love is to stay where God can love us as his children and can shower upon us all the gifts of love that he has for those who are his children."[7]

How do the friends do this? Jude suggested three ways: "build yourselves up in your most holy faith . . . praying in the Holy Spirit . . . waiting

---

[7] R. C. H. Lenski, *The Interpretation of the Epistles of St. Peter, St. John, and St. Jude* (Minneapolis: Fortress Press, 1966), 646.

expectantly for the mercy of our Lord Jesus Christ" (Jude vv. 20–21). It is clear that Jude's strategy for contending for the faith involves human activity, but this activity is trinitarian in its work. Keeping, waiting, and praying are connected to God, Jesus Christ, and the Holy Spirit respectively. This serves to further highlight the connection between the actions of God and the responsibility of human beings.

Finally, contending for the faith means rescuing those in danger. In verses 22–23, Jude identified three groups of people in serious danger and in need of rescuing. Shaddix succinctly summarizes how the friends should deal with those who find themselves swept up in the undertow of these ungodly people. The friends were to deal gently with those who doubt, deal quickly with those who are in danger, and deal carefully with those who are defiled.[8]

Doxological Encouragement for the Battle (Jude vv. 24–25)

Jude wrapped up his letter by reminding the friends that they were protected from stumbling and were able to stand in the God's glorious presence through Jesus Christ. Contending for the faith would not be easy in these circumstances. However, through Jesus Christ they would be able to stand and not stumble. It is to this reality that Jude drew the letter to a close by ascribing glory, majesty, power, and authority for all time to God through Jesus Christ.

BIBLIOGRAPHY

Bauckham, Richard J. *Jude, 2 Peter*. WBC 50. Nashville: Word, 1983.

Davids, Peter H. *A Theology of James, Peter, and Jude: Living in Light of the Coming King*. Biblical Theology of The New Testament. Grand Rapids: Zondervan Academic, 2014.

Giese, Curtis P. *2 Peter and Jude*. Concordia Commentary. St. Louis: Concordia, 2012.

Green, Gene L. *Jude and 2 Peter*. BECNT. Grand Rapids: Baker Academic, 2008.

Kistemaker, Simon J. *James, Epistles of John, Peter, and Jude*. Grand Rapids: Baker Academic, 2002.

Lenski, R. C. H. *The Interpretation of the Epistles of St. Peter, St. John, and St. Jude*. Minneapolis: Fortress Press, 1966.

---

[8] James Shaddix, *Exalting Jesus in 2 Peter and Jude*. Christ-Centered Exposition Commentary (Nashville: Holman Reference, 2018), 180–81.

Reese, Ruth Anne. *2 Peter and Jude*. The Two Horizons New Testament Commentary. Grand Rapids: Eerdmans, 2007.

Shaddix, James. *Exalting Jesus in 2 Peter and Jude*. Christ-Centered Exposition Commentary. Nashville: Holman Reference, 2018.

24

REVELATION

JEFFREY R. DICKSON

CONNECTION POINT

What relevance does this first-century writing have for us today? It does not take long in reading this text to feel as though you are in a different world. Descriptions of beasts, dragons, apocalyptic horsemen, and heavenly seals, bowls, and trumpets may seem like something from the world of fantasy literature. Few books of the Bible have received more attention than the Apocalypse of Revelation. With its kaleidoscope of characters, cosmic events, detailed symbolism, and prophetic elements, it is a work that has proven to be a point of special fascination and speculation for those in and out of the Christian community.

Unfortunately, Revelation's unusual characteristics also leave it susceptible to being misunderstood, misused, and even abused by those who misinterpret its contents. For this reason, many, even in the church, are hesitant to study it or afraid to even open its pages. However, a failure to study Revelation is a failure to appreciate the full message of God's Word and would be similar to reading a compelling novel but never finishing the final chapter.

That said, most are curious about how it all ends—that is, the world and the lives of those in it. Regardless of what side people are on, this world is heading somewhere, and God has provided a preview of what to expect. In our current age of global pandemics, natural disasters, social unrest, and geopolitical conflict, more and more are wondering about ultimate things; and God's people need to be equipped with answers to these questions. Thankfully, the most important questions people have about the future are answered in this book, and these answers focus upon its central character—the Lamb (Jesus Christ).

Revelation reveals that the same Christ who was the agent of creation will be the agent of re-creation (John 1:1–4; Rev 21:5). The same infant in a manger in Bethlehem stands mature at the throne of God (Luke 2:7; Rev 5:6–10). The same rider on a donkey will mount a white horse of victory (John 12:15; Rev 19:11). The same Jesus who humbled himself to the point of death on a cross shares the throne with and is worshipped alongside the Father (Phil 2:5–8; Rev 22:1). The same Savior of the world will return to judge the world (John 3:16–17; Rev 19:11–21). Jesus Christ is the major focus of Revelation, and any investigation of this book that does not ultimately seek him runs the risk of missing the main point. After all, it is "the revelation of Jesus Christ" (Rev 1:1).

If you are looking for answers about the future, this book points to Jesus and the work he will complete in the end. If you are looking for hope, this book unveils the glory that awaits God's people in the new creation. If you are without a relationship with Christ and could care less about what is coming, this book offers a warning to take advantage of what God has done in Christ before it is too late.

With this in mind, consider making this your prayer as you read and study this chapter:

> *Almighty Father, thank you for providing a glimpse of what is to come in the end. We confess our dependency on you to know and understand what you have presented and ask that you would help us become more impressed with Who is returning and why, as we face a world of questions, tribulation, and struggle. Lord, may our understanding of this book either encourage us with what we need to persevere or convict us to repent and be made ready for what is coming. Amen.*

SETTING

Recipients

John's Revelation,[1] probably written around AD 90,[2] is explicit concerning its target audience. The apostle introduces the recipients in passing with

---

[1] Though issues surrounding the specific identity of the author have failed to maintain the interest of a growing number of scholars in recent years, the debate still exists and several possible authors are alleged. These include but are not limited to the following: John the son of Zebedee and the disciple of Jesus Christ, John the elder, John Mark, John the Baptist, Cerinthus, and someone using the name of John the apostle as a pseudonym. Support for John Mark, John the Baptist, and Cerinthus is miniscule at best, and these choices enjoy very little support. That someone wrote Revelation under the name John as a pseudonym possesses little evidence. R. H. Charles, *A Critical and Exegetical Commentary on the Revelation of St. John*, vol. 1 (Edinburgh: T&T Clark, 1920), xxxix. This leaves John the apostle and John the elder as the two most possible options. Those in favor of John the apostle acknowledge there are plenty of similarities both textually and theologically between the Gospel of John and the Apocalypse of John. Grant R. Osborne, *Revelation*, BECNT (Grand Rapids: Baker Academic, 2008), 5. For instance, Mounce reveals that both John's Gospel and the Apocalypse quote Zech 12:10 in the same unique way in the original language. Robert H. Mounce, *The Book of Revelation*, NICNT (Grand Rapids: Eerdmans, 1997), 14. Additionally, Ozanne has uncovered a list of terms that are common to the Gospel of John and the Apocalypse. These include the following: "conquer," "keep the word," "keep the commandments," "dwell," "sign," "witness," and "true." C. G. Ozanne, "The Language of the Apocalypse," *Tyndale House Bulletin* 16 (1965): 3–9. Adherents of this view also cite Justin Martyr and other early church fathers who affirm apostolic authorship. Those arguing for John the elder highlight many idiosyncrasies in Revelation that are not in John's Gospel or other writings—variations and anomalies that seem to overwhelm points of convergence. Donald Guthrie, *New Testament Introduction* (Downers Grove, IL: InterVarsity Press, 1990), 256–58. For instance, Witherington concludes "the difference in diction rather strongly favors the conclusion that the person who produced the final form of Revelation did not also produce the final form of the Gospel of John." Ben Witherington III, *Revelation*, New Cambridge Bible Commentary (Cambridge: Cambridge University Press, 2003), 2. In addition to these distinctions, many who argue against apostolic authorship are quick to remind readers that the author of Revelation never refers to himself as an apostle—he delimits his office to prophet. Not only that, but some point out theological differences between the Gospel and the Apocalypse in an effort to aid this position. However, the many differences between the Gospel of John and the Apocalypse can be best explained by a difference in genre, not a difference in author. For this reason, and given all the evidence cited, John the apostle appears to be the best choice.

[2] Possible dates for the composition of Revelation correspond to who ruled as emperor over Rome: Claudius (AD 41–54), Nero (AD 54–68), Domitian (AD 81–96), or Trajan (AD 98–117). Osborne and Aune observe that most contemporary scholars opt for dates during the time of Nero or Domitian (see Osborne, *Revelation*, 6; David E. Aune, *Revelation 1–5*, WBC 52a [Nashville: Thomas Nelson, 1997], lvii) given the nature of the persecution described in the book and the sophistication of the churches (both their structure and their problems) that are addressed. Price has concluded that in Asia Minor (the region addressed

A modern look at the Isle of Patmos, the traditional location for the writing of John's Revelation.

"John: To the seven churches in Asia" (Rev 1:4), and Jesus himself identifies them more specifically saying, "Send it to the seven churches: Ephesus, Smyrna, Pergamum, Thyatira, Sardis, Philadelphia, and Laodicea" (Rev 1:11). These churches were specific congregations meeting in what is now modern-day Turkey. Interestingly, the order of the list follows the order that you would have passed these churches along the ancient Roman roads in this region beginning with Ephesus (the congregation closest to Patmos) and ending with Laodicea.

---

in the Apocalypse), public expressions of loyalty to the imperial cult were not emphasized to the degree seen in Revelation until the reign of Domitian. S. R. F. Price, *Rituals and Power: The Roman Imperial Cult in Asia Minor* (Cambridge: Cambridge University Press, 1984), 78–124, 155–66, 207–22. Add to this the state of Laodicea described in Rev 3:17 (which appears to have had time to recover from an earthquake it suffered around AD 80) and the phrase "do not harm the oil and the wine" (Rev 6:6), which appears to coincide with an edict passed down from Domitian in AD 92, and a date in the early AD 90s seems to comply with the best evidence. See Colin J. Hemer, *The Letters to the Seven Churches of Asia in Their Local Setting* (Sheffield: JSOT, 1986) 4–5; Guthrie, *New Testament Introduction,* 948–55 for more discussion on the date of Revelation.

These specific addressees elicit an important question: is the message of Revelation limited to these congregations, or does it also speak beyond these ancient churches, and, if so, how? In answering this inquiry, it is important to recognize that these churches were not the only congregations in the region. Instead, perhaps these seven provide a sampling of local bodies dealing with an assortment of issues and challenges that together yield a comprehensive grouping of messages that continues to be relevant today.[3] Some have speculated that perhaps each church represents an era in history, leading to the very end of the last days. However, a better understanding of the relevancy of these individual letters is that the contents of Revelation was directed to these original audiences and is also applicable to congregations dealing with the same issues in any era as they confront their own periods of tribulation. Many of the pressures and persecutions that plagued the church then continue to confront the church now. Furthermore, many of the encouragements and warnings Jesus gives these congregations hold value for today's listeners as well. You might say that Revelation's audience is both specific and general, particular and permanent.[4] It applies wherever and whenever appropriate, but not before it first speaks to these seven churches in Asia Minor at the end of the first century.[5]

Theme and Key Passage

While many elements of Revelation might prove difficult to understand, a theme that connects the major elements of the book is "Forward Thinking in a Fallen World." Ultimately, "the revelation of Jesus Christ" is all about Jesus Christ,[6] who is coming again to usher in a new heaven and new earth

---

[3] Robert L. Thomas, *Revelation 1–7: An Exegetical Commentary* (Chicago: Moody, 1992), 64.

[4] See Edward Hindson, *The Book of Revelation: Unlocking the Future*, Twenty-First Century Biblical Commentary Series 16 (Chattanooga, TN: AMG, 2002), 22–23; and Osborne, *Revelation*, 60.

[5] It is important to remember that these churches were not foreign to the apostle John, as the apostle spent the latter part of his life and ministry in this region ministering to these churches. This also goes a long way in arguing for the apostle John as the author of Revelation, as he would have been both an authoritative and familiar personality for God to use to speak into the lives of these local congregations. For more discussion see Thomas, *Revelation 1–7*, 64.

[6] This opening title—"the revelation of Jesus Christ"—might also be understood, given the grammar used, as "the revelation from Jesus Christ," "Jesus Christ's revelation," "the revelation containing Jesus Christ," or even "the revelation that is Jesus Christ." To limit the translation to just one of these interpretive options fails to appreciate just how

for those who trust what he accomplished when he first came 2,000 years ago. Revelation communicates this future hope to the seven churches and to all people of God so that they may be inspired to persevere in a world of trouble until the day of the Lord.

Revelation 1:1 says: "The revelation of Jesus Christ that God gave him to show his servants . . ."

Purpose and Occasion

Few things create more excitement in popular culture today than a trailer being released for an upcoming major movie. In these heavily produced previews, just enough is revealed to give viewers a taste of what is coming and who they can expect to see in the would-be blockbuster. While not every question one might raise about the film is answered in even the best trailers, the general tone and theme of the movie is communicated in a thoroughly compelling way. The same might be said of the book of Revelation. In this fascinating work, readers in both the first century and the twenty-first century are given a preview of the major events yet to take place and are introduced to some of the major characters involved. What difference did this make for first-century viewers? What difference does this make for a twenty-first-century audience? While Revelation does not answer every question people may have about what is to come, it does provide the kind of sneak-peak that gives believing viewers everywhere hope as they endure through the troubles of this world.

Perhaps this is why, from the very beginning, the book itself encourages its hearers to "[read] aloud the words of this prophecy . . . hear the words of this prophecy . . . and keep what is written in it" (Rev 1:3). In our broken world of many villains, we do well to remember what lies ahead—a perfect and glorious world to come with the greatest hero of all bringing ultimate victory. For this reason, Revelation comes to God's people as a word of hope, expectation, and joy—ingredients necessary to persevere through the trials and tribulations faced in every age of history. This was exceedingly important for the first-century church as it was facing and anticipating severe persecution. In an effort to sustain faithfulness amid mounting pressure, Revelation provides a glimpse of the glory of Christ who will one day come to vindicate those who have suffered for his sake

---

central Jesus Christ is to the contents of the book—both as source, possessor, contents, and major thrust.

and usher them into a perfect, new creation (Rev 2:7, 11, 17; 3:5, 12, 21; 12:11; 19:9; 20:6; 22:14).

However, for those far from God, Revelation provides a word of warning. Viewing its contents from the perspective of the world is more akin to viewing a horror movie trailer, leaving some wondering if they really want to see this all play out. For this audience demographic, the Apocalypse's powerful warning intends to produce conviction and repentance so that they too might be ready for what will take place (Revelation 17–18).

For this reason, the "trailer" found in Revelation is polarizing; embraced by the people of God for triumph it portrays, and criticized by the world for its depiction of harsh judgment. Like a provocative film, one cannot walk away from reading John's Apocalypse without a passionate response one way or the other.

HIGHLIGHTS IN REVELATION

Introduction (Rev 1:1–20)

From the beginning, Revelation establishes itself as at least three kinds of messages in one sophisticated book:

1. An "apocalypse"/ "revelation" (i.e., unveiling of something previously hidden [Rev 1:1]);

2. A "prophecy" (i.e., prediction of future events with persuasive and moral implications [Rev 1:3]);

3. A series of "letters" (relevant both to specific first-century congregations and the church in general [Rev 1:4, 11]).

All these different styles reveal, point to, and are sourced in Jesus Christ who is celebrated in the title of the book ("The revelation of Jesus Christ"—Rev 1:1) and described in glorious splendor (Rev 1:13–16). Everything from the introduction, author (the apostle John), and primary subject matter (Jesus), ultimately reminds the reader that what is disclosed in the remainder of the work is more about Who is returning and why than it is about how and when. A chart or timeline of a "best guess" about coming events does not provide anyone with the kind of compelling conviction

The Churches of Revelation

and comfort that only Jesus can personally bring. Trusting him as the ultimate answer to the world's problem of sin, death, and brokenness goes so much further than misplacing our faith in speculative answers to secondary questions.

Letters (Rev 2:1–3:22)

Can you imagine what it must have been like to receive a letter directly from Christ himself? The seven first-century churches listed in Revelation 2–3 did not have to wonder, as they each received a personal correspondence from Christ that either encouraged, convicted, challenged, or commissioned them to overcome the issues they faced.[7] To the Ephesian church, preoccupied with good things to the neglect of what was most important (love of Christ and commitment to his mission), Jesus said, "Return to your first love" (Rev 2:1–7). To a heavily persecuted congregation in Smyrna with more difficulty around the corner, Jesus said, "Remain faithful until death" (Rev 2:8–11). To an overly accommodating church in Pergamum, Jesus said, "Repent and strive for consistency and truth" (Rev 2:12–17). To a body of believers in Thyatira, poisoned by idolatry and immorality, Jesus said, "Remove the threat and stay strong" (Rev 2:18–29). To a powerless church struggling to stay alive in Sardis, Jesus said, "Rouse to life or I'll blow you out" (Rev 3:1–6). To the persevering congregation at Philadelphia, Jesus said, "Recognize the opportunity before you for the gospel and take advantage of it" (Rev 3:7–13). And to the lukewarm/putrid church at Laodicea, Jesus said, "Reach for the handle of the door and let me in!" (Rev 3:14–22).[8]

Though these letters are highly personal and specific, the principles continue to apply today in churches where congregations face similar dilemmas or opportunities. Overall, Jesus's message to the church both in the first century and in the twenty-first century is to overcome the world by returning to him, remaining faithful, repenting, removing threats, rousing to life, recognizing opportunities, and reaching for the door upon which he is knocking. Certainly, this is a message from which we can all still learn.

Preparation (Rev 4:1–5:14)

Following chapter 3 is a major transition in which Revelation shifts from primarily addressing the seven churches directly to a symbolic revelation that occupies the remainder of the letter.[9] This vision given to John comes courtesy of a new vantage point that the apostle is invited to enjoy—"The first voice . . . said, 'Come up here, and I will show you what must take place after this'" (Rev 4:1). Immediately upon entering this new domain,

---

[7] For a thorough breakdown of historical backgrounds pertaining to the seven churches of Asia Minor listed in Revelation 2–3, see Mark Wilson, "Revelation" in *Zondervan Illustrated Bible Backgrounds Commentary*, Vol. 4, ed. Clinton E. Arnold (Grand Rapids: Zondervan Academic, 2002), 259–78.

[8] Descriptions of these churches have been adapted from Hindson, *Book of Revelation*, 34–51.

[9] This shift is highlighted by "After these things" in Rev 4:1 and the change of context/perspective followed by the vision that ensues.

John interrupted a worship service in which a chorus of four creatures,[10] twenty-four elders,[11] and a multitude of angels joined together to praise the "Lord God, the Almighty" (Rev 4:8), who is worthy of such praise because he created all things.[12] This worship service, along with a host of others throughout Revelation, reminds us that everything taking place is ultimately about God. It is his glory, not our own, which ultimately matters. Realizing this should motivate us to join the chorus of praise that is heard here in the way that we live, speak, think, and so on, directing attention away from ourselves and toward the one who sits on the throne.

> **The Lamb of God**
>
> John appears to be doing something exciting and unique with his use of "Lamb" in Revelation. While this Lamb emerges first in Rev 5:6, he appears no less than twenty-eight additional times throughout the remainder of the book (more than double the number of occurrences of any other title for Christ). Also, the author employs a unique Greek word for "lamb" that is used nowhere else in the New Testament for Christ (*arnion*). Jesus in Revelation is not merely portrayed as the sacrificial lamb identified in places like John 1:29, nor is he merely the Passover lamb Paul mentioned in 1 Cor 5:7. He is all of this and much more! This is ultimately the "revelation of Jesus Christ" (Rev 1:1), and the Lamb is the hero of God's unfolding story.

The worship service of chapter 4 is put on hold upon the emergence of a seven-sealed scroll (Rev 5:1–2) that none could open. Realizing that nothing more could be revealed until these seals are broken, John wept. However, one of the elders nearby directed John's attention to a hero who had overcome so as to open the scroll and continue John's receipt of these divine secrets. This hero is Christ, who is hailed as Lion and Lamb[13]—glorious and humble. He, too, is worthy of worship alongside the One on the throne. This protagonist that emerges takes center stage in the remainder of the apocalypse as God's agent of judgment and re-creation. His special introduction

---

[10] For a more complete description of the four living creatures of Rev 4:6–8, see Osborne, *Revelation,* 232–36. See also the similarities between these creatures and what is described in Isaiah 6 and Ezek 1:10; 10:14.

[11] Though many have speculated as to the identity of these elders, one potential interpretation is that these represent the people of God. The number 24 may be reached by adding the twelve tribes of Jacob (Israel) and the twelve apostles who founded the church. Another option could be that these represent the twenty-four scribes/elders listed in 1 Chr 24:7–19.

[12] Other examples of songs/worship in Revelation can be found in 4:11; 5:9–10, 12; 6:10; 7:10, 12; 11:15, 17–18; 12:10–12; 15:3–4; 19:1–4, 6–7.

[13] For a thorough study on what John is doing with the symbol of "Lamb" and how it is employed in Revelation, see Jeffrey R. Dickson, *The Humility and Glory of the Lamb: Toward a Robust Apocalyptic Christology* (Eugene, OR: Wipf & Stock, 2018).

here and activity in the remainder of Revelation demonstrates that he is coequal with God the Father, reminding us that any worship that we may give to the Father is incomplete without worship of the Son.

Cosmic Conflict (Rev 6:1–19:21)

The revelatory scenes continue in chapter 6 when the Lamb begins opening the scroll, revealing a host of devastating events (i.e., plagues, earthquakes, etc.), which continue with the blowing of the seven trumpets (Rev 8:7–11:19), and concludes with the pouring out of the seven bowls (Rev 16:1–21). God's judgment is unleashed upon the rebellious world and its corrupt kingdoms, focused on "Babylon the Great," which in John's context likely represented the oppressive Roman Empire. Those who have ever asked, "When is God going punish the wicked for the wrongs they have committed?" receive their answer here as ruthless world leaders and spiritual oppressors receive their due.

God's judgment of sin is not in conflict with his love. Rather, a loving God will not tolerate the oppressive and sinful ways of humanity forever. Those who deal in treachery will be judged by the only righteous King. The number of each round of plagues (seven) with three rounds in total suggest that the tribulation experienced in the world during this time is total in its scope as God purges the world before remaking it thereafter.

> **The Second Coming**
>
> The second coming of Christ is a label that can be used to refer to any number of things. For instance, some use it to speak of the unexpected, sudden, and imminent rapture of the church that is described in places like 1 Thess 4:15–18. However, referring to the events of this passage as the second coming may not reflect the best use of the term, given that Jesus meets the church "in the air" and is never said to touch down on the earth in this passage. Others use "second coming" language to describe the entire end-time program described in Revelation (complete with tribulation, return, judgment, etc.). However, "second coming" most accurately refers to the events of Revelation 19, in which Jesus personally, physically, and gloriously, returns to the earth with his church. This event is in stark contrast with Christ's first advent on the earth. In his first coming he came as a baby in a humble manger and years later entered Jerusalem on a donkey to be crucified for the sins of the world, providing salvation for those who trust in him. In his second coming he returns as a glorious king on a white horse of victory to judge the world for its sin.

The world spirals out of control during this period at the hands of the dragon (Satan; introduced in Rev 12:3–4) and his allies: the Antichrist (Rev 13:1–10) and the false prophet (Rev 13:11–18). Together this unholy trinity influences the kingdoms of the world to an oppressive form of idolatry, seeking to dominate the inhabitants of the earth. Ultimately the

The Valley of Jezreel is the traditional location assumed by some to be the site for the battle of Armageddon.

people of God will overcome "by the blood of the Lamb / and by the word of their testimony" (Rev 12:11). But what does this really mean? Victory for God's people, according to Revelation, is rewarded to those who allow God to vindicate them in Christ.

In our increasingly volatile world of hatred, outrage, and activism, Revelation teaches that pursuing faith, hope, and love honors God, not taking matters into one's own hands and seeking revenge. God's people can trust that justice will be done. While we may have to wait for it, we must not carry the load of vengeance ourselves. Aside from all of the complexities associated with the chaos and characters described in this book, in its own way Revelation communicates to both the people of God and to the world a clarifying twofold message: (1) Good news—God and his people win! (2) Bad news—those opposed to God will lose. This all comes to a head in Revelation 19 when, after enjoying a celebratory marriage supper with his bride (the church), Jesus descends from heaven to bring a quick and dramatic end to the evil regime of the Antichrist, false prophet, and Satan. As declared earlier in the book, "the kingdom of the world has become the kingdom / of our Lord and of his Christ, / and he will reign forever and ever" (Rev 11:15). This is the second coming of Christ, and it sets in motion a new era with a new reign. Revelation 6–19 reminds readers of any age how seriously God takes sin, how much God despises evil, and how invested he is in vindicating those who have suffered for his sake. These reminders go a long way in providing reassurance to those struggling to keep the faith and persevering in any number of various trials.

Millennial Kingdom and Final Judgment (Rev 20:1–14)

Following the events of chapters 4–18, John reveals that there will be a 1,000-year period in which Jesus will reign on the earth (Rev 20:1–6).[14] At the beginning of this period, the bodies of the saints who have passed will be resurrected. In the millennial kingdom, Satan will be held captive (in "the abyss" [Rev 20:1]) and Jesus will be ruling from earth. At the end of the 1,000-year reign, Satan will be released for a brief time to deceive many. This insurrection will be quickly snuffed out, and Satan will be relegated to the lake of fire forever. Joining him will be all those who have opposed the kingdom of God, separated forever from the presence of the Lord. The possible two fates revealed in the book force us to consider where we stand with God. Will we be joining Christ in victory? Or will we be judged by Christ in destruction? The message of Revelation is complete with a sobering reminder that the same One who rules and reigns with those who follow him will judge and punish those who do not.

New Heavens and New Earth (Rev 21:1–22:21)

The final frames of the preview that Revelation provides give believing viewers a glimpse of their ultimate destiny. God's people learn they will dwell in a new, glorious city ("I also saw the holy city, the new Jerusalem"

---

[14] Four prominent views exist regarding how these 1,000 years should be interpreted. Those views are premillennialism, amillennialism, postmillennialism, and preterism. Premillennialism also appears in the works of the earliest church fathers: Justin Martyr, Tertullian, Irenaeus, Cyprian, and Victorinus. Amillennialism appears later in the works of Origen and Augustine. One possible reason for a break from premillennial theology later might be that as the Lord continued to wait longer and longer to return after Revelation was written, the church began taking an increasingly figurative/metaphorical view of its contents. Premillennial theology has seen something of a resurgence ever since the reinstatement of Israel as a nation in 1948. For more on this, see William C., Watson, *Dispensationalism Before Darby: Seventeenth-Century and Eighteenth-Century English Apocalypticism* (Silverton, OR: Lampion Press, 2015); Craig Blaising, Kenneth L. Gentry, and Robert B. Strimple, *Three Views on the Millennium and Beyond,* ed. Stanley N. Gundry and Darrell L. Bock (Grand Rapids: Zondervan Academic, 1999).

[Rev 21:2]), free of any death or pain (Rev 21:4). The city's dimensions form a cube (Rev 21:16), similar to a structure found in the Old Testament—the holy of holies (2 Chr 3:8). However, unlike the holy of holies, there are multiple points of entry in the new Jerusalem, which allow entry inside, and the walls are a transparent golden glass (Rev 21:10–27). These details reveal that the heavenly city will be an enlarged holy of holies, in which all of God's people can enjoy uninhibited access into the Lord's glorious presence. The landscaping outside the city includes a river lined with the "tree of life" (Rev 22:2). While this reference alludes to Genesis 2,[15] John quickly points out that, unlike Genesis 3, "there will no longer be any curse" (Rev 22:3). This confirms that paradise has more than been restored. It will be forever protected from ever falling again into sin. This glorious destiny was intended to inspire perseverance among those facing persecution and pressure in the first century. The same inspiration is extended today to those who are in relationship with Christ and who have their names recorded in the Lamb's book of life (Rev 21:27).

> **The Millennium**
>
> The millennial kingdom—both its nature and its place in the scope of God's plan—has been a subject of much debate for centuries. Amillennialism is the view that holds the millennium described in Revelation 20 is symbolic for history in general and that there is no literal 1,000-year period following a seven-year tribulation. Postmillennialism holds that there is a literal millennium in the future but that the second coming will take place after this 1,000-year period. Premillennialism argues that there will be a literal 1,000-year millennium immediately following the second coming of Christ and will conclude at the last judgment described in Revelation 21. Those who tend to read Revelation more figuratively and as a series of repeating patterns tend to hold one of the first two positions. Those who read Revelation more chronologically tend to endorse a premillennial position. The fact that John repeats the phrase "a thousand years" no less than five times in Rev 20:1–6, along with other clues in the context, suggest this period fits immediately after the events of Revelation 19, thus supporting a premillennial position.

Capping off this description of the new heavens and earth is a reminder, invitation, and warning that echoes throughout the millennia. Jesus reminds those who read this book that he is "coming soon" (Rev 22:12), and people ought to make themselves ready so that they might enter the glorious gates of the new Jerusalem

---

[15] In many ways the Bible exists as a story between two trees: the tree of knowledge of good and evil in the garden of Eden, and the tree of life in heaven. Failure to obey God's instructions concerning the first tree renders access to the second tree impossible. However, God sent his Son to die on the cross—also referred to as a "tree" (see Deut 21:22–23; Gal 3:13)—so that believers may overcome the curse and enjoy the tree of life forever in heaven.

(Rev 22:14).[16] Jesus, the Spirit, and the bride invite the world to "come" and "take the water of life freely" (Rev 22:17) so that they might enjoy the many blessings awaiting them in the end. John warns against adding to or taking away from what has been disclosed so that this message is not abused or misrepresented.

These final words disclose valuable information for readers. Given that Jesus is coming soon, we ought to extend the same invitation that Jesus, the Spirit, and the bride share—the invitation to take this preview seriously by accepting what Jesus alone can give. We must proclaim Christ, who is the focus of both John's Apocalypse and the entirety of God's revealed Word. This is a responsibility God entrusts to us today as he did the seven churches in the first century. Will we share the message of Revelation as eagerly as we post the latest movie trailer to our favorite franchise? This apocalyptic preview speaks of the greatest drama ever known and comes with greater implications than any work produced by man. May we appreciate it as such and live in faithful anticipation of the coming of our great God and King!

BIBLIOGRAPHY

Aune, David E. *Revelation 1–5*. WBC 52a. Nashville: Thomas Nelson, 1997.

Blaising, Craig A., Kenneth L. Gentry, and Robert B. Strimple. *Three Views on the Millennium and Beyond*. Edited by Stanley N. Gundry and Darrell L. Bock. Grand Rapids: Zondervan Academic, 1999.

Charles, R. H. *A Critical and Exegetical Commentary on the Revelation of St. John*. Vol. 1. Edinburgh: T&T Clark, 1920.

Dickson, Jeffrey R. *The Humility and Glory of the Lamb: Toward a Robust Apocalyptic Christology*. Eugene, OR: Wipf & Stock, 2018.

Guthrie, Donald. *New Testament Introduction*. Downers Grove, IL: InterVarsity Press, 1990.

Hemer, Colin J. *The Letters to the Seven Churches of Asia in Their Local Setting*. Sheffield: JSOT, 1986.

Hindson, Edward. *The Book of Revelation: Unlocking the Future*. Twenty-First Century Biblical Commentary Series 16. Chattanooga, TN: AMG, 2002.

---

[16] This is the last of seven "beatitudes" found in the book (Rev 1:3; 14:13; 16:15; 19:9; 20:6; 22:7). Many of these beatitudes encourage readers to take seriously the opportunity to pay attention to, learn from, and apply the contents of God's revelation appropriately so that they might be ready for his return.

Mounce, Robert H. *The Book of Revelation*. NICNT. Grand Rapids: Eerdmans, 1997.

Osborne, Grant R. *Revelation*. BECNT. Grand Rapids: Baker Academic, 2008.

Ozanne, C. G. "The Language of the Apocalypse." *Tyndale House Bulletin* 16 (1965): 3–9.

Price, S. R. F. *Rituals and Power: The Roman Imperial Cult in Asia Minor*. Cambridge: Cambridge University Press, 1984.

Thomas, Robert L. *Revelation 1–7: An Exegetical Commentary*. Chicago: Moody, 1992.

Watson, William C. *Dispensationalism Before Darby: Seventeenth-Century and Eighteenth-Century English Apocalypticism*. Silverton, OR: Lampion Press, 2015.

Wilson, Mark. "Revelation." In *Zondervan Illustrated Bible Backgrounds Commentary*, Vol. 4, edited by Clinton E. Arnold, 259–78. Grand Rapids: Zondervan Academic, 2002.

Witherington, Ben, III. *Revelation*. New Cambridge Bible Commentary. Cambridge: Cambridge University Press, 2003.

CONCLUSION

JOHN CARTWRIGHT

Each chapter of this book began by answering one simple question: What relevance does this first-century writing have for us today? Perhaps then, as we wrap up this book, we need to ask a similar question. What relevance does God's Word, as a whole, have for us today? By now, you have been able to interact with each of the twenty-seven books of the New Testament and the unique contribution that each of them makes to the whole. But is there a larger message here? The answer is yes!

If I had to summarize the New Testament in just one word, my choice would be *Jesus*. From beginning to end, the New Testament is about Jesus. "What does that have to do with me?" you may ask. Everything. Let's wrap this book up with a little bit of a review of the New Testament with regard to Jesus.

THE GOSPELS

The Gospels are all about the life, death, burial, and resurrection of Jesus. The New Testament opens with the story of the miraculous birth, the sinless life, the cruel and unjust death, and the ultimate resurrection of Jesus. These Gospel accounts serve to awaken us to the reality of who Jesus is. He was not merely a good person or a wise teacher; he is the sinless Son of God sent to rescue us from our desperate and helpless state of sinfulness.

His death on the cross was the payment for our sin since he had no sin of his own. His resurrection is his ultimate victory over sin and death. Since we are all sinners and in need of this salvation, the beautiful story told in the four Gospels helps us understand that Jesus met our greatest need.

ACTS

Acts is a continuation of the story of Jesus and the founding of his church. Jesus returns to heaven but his promised Holy Spirit comes to indwell those who follow him. In Acts, God is working to build the church of Jesus despite a mountain of opposition. In many ways, the period of Acts is unique. However, in many respects, we can see similarities to today. Is God still using the local body of believers to further his kingdom? Yes. Is the work of the gospel continuing forward despite opposition? Yes. So, even though in Acts Jesus has left this world as it relates to his physical form, his commission for those who love and follow him to be his witnesses to the world continues.

> ### "Born of a Woman, Born under the Law"
>
> What does Paul mean by the curious four-part phrase "born of a woman, born under the law, to redeem those under the law, so that we might receive adoption as sons" (Gal 4:4–5)? Paul is using a common rhetorical device where the first and last phrases should be seen as connected and the second and third phrases should be seen as connected. So, in this context, Jesus being "born of a woman" allows us to "receive adoption as sons." And Jesus being "born under the law" allows him to "redeem those under the law."
>
> Theologically, the first connection reveals the importance of Jesus's humanity, while the second connection reveals the importance of Jesus's sinlessness. In other words, that Jesus was born as a son allowed us to be adopted as sons and daughters of God. That he was born under the law allowed him to fulfill the law on our behalf.
>
> "The Son of God became a man to enable men to become sons of God." C. S. Lewis, *Mere Christianity* (New York: Touchstone, 1996), 155.

THE EPISTLES

The New Testament letters are a reinforcement of the teachings of Jesus. The letters that make up a significant portion of the New Testament are also ultimately about Christ and incredibly relevant for us today. Every letter was written to a group of believers in the New Testament church. One way to view them is as a group of "mini-sermons." Sometimes the authors were dealing with specific problems. Other times the authors were teaching general truths that are profoundly timeless. Think about it. We are able to open these letters written nearly 2,000 years ago and learn in much the same way that the original recipients would have.

These letters are filled with truths that help us learn what it means to be truly authentic followers of Jesus.

REVELATION

Revelation is literally all about Jesus Christ as the conquering Lamb to bring about the new creation. One day, he is coming again to create a new heaven and new earth for those who trust his work on the cross when he came the first time 2,000 years ago. In Revelation we get to read about this future hope as it was written to the seven churches. The goal is to be inspired to persevere in a world of trouble until the day of the Lord. Are we living in a world filled with trouble? Yes. But Christ's kingdom is eternal, and he will return as a victor.

So, what relevance does the New Testament as a whole have for us today? The New Testament is ultimately about Jesus, but it's not just a neat story. We will be held accountable for what we do with these truths. What will you do with Jesus? It is my hope and prayer that if you have never put your trust in Christ's work on the cross for your salvation, you would do that today. And, if you have, my hope and prayer for you is that you will grow in your faith as you allow God to mold you more and more after his Son, Jesus.

SUBJECT INDEX

A

Abraham   6–8, 25, 67, 82, 97, 117, 178–79, 181, 289–90
Abrahamic covenant   6–7, 172–73, 194
acceptance, conditions of   176
Adam   63, 71, 118, 120–21
adoption   121, 123, 180, 192–94, 380
   family of God   192
affliction, perserverance in   239
   See also suffering
Ahab   46
Alexander the Great   11–12, 20
amanuensis   243
Andrew   28
angels   43, 61–62, 68, 123, 222, 285, 287, 329, 331–32, 372
Anna   17, 62
Annas (high priest)   17
Annas the Younger   17
anointing   64, 341
antichrist   241, 342–44, 347, 373–74
Antioch of Syria, church within   188
Antiochus IV   12–13
anxiety   210
Aphrodite, temple of   134
Apollo (god)   188
Apollos   282–83
apostasy   241
apostles
   financial support for   164
   Holy Spirit empowerment of   98–99
   Paul as   174, 176, 233, 267

super-apostles   156, 163–64
Aquila   136
Archelaus   18
Archippus   275
Aristophanes   134
armor of God   197–98
Artemis (goddess)   188
Assumption of Moses, The   358
atonement   292–93
Augustus (Tiberius Julius Caesar Augustus) (emperor)   17
authentic Christianity   335–36, 39, 342–44
authority   64–65, 80, 207, 317

B

Babylon   9–10, 373
Balaam   359
baptism   25, 37, 78, 118, 345
barbarian   223
Barnabas   170–71, 175–76
behavior, belief and   196–97
belief   73–74, 173, 196–97
Benedictus   62
blessedness   21, 28–29
blood of Jesus   340
boasting, sexual immorality and   142–43
body of Christ   112, 127, 143, 148, 197
   See also church
Boulogne, Valentin de   247
branches, the church as   218
brotherly love   235–36
Buoninsegna, Duccio di   325

C

Caesar Augustus (Roman emperor)   18–19
   See also Augustus
Caesarea Philippi   19
Caiaphas   17
Cain   342, 359
called, the   355
Calling of the Apostles Peter and Andrew, The (painting)   325
Cana Cycle   79–80
celibacy   143
Celsus Library   186
Cenchrea harbor   133
centrality of Jesus   219–20
Chalcedonian Creed   219
Champagne, Philippe de   257
children, role of   224
Chloe   138–39
Christ before Pilate   69
Christ hymn   203–11
Christianity   19–20, 23, 36, 58, 76, 111, 148, 196, 223, 262, 277, 290, 314, 317, 331, 335–36, 338, 357
   authentic   335–36, 339, 342–43
   daily renewal within   223
   essence of   127–28
   humility within   137
   personal liberty within   146
   purpose of   139
   world's viewpoint of   228
Christian life
   behavioral examples of   236–38
   brotherly love within   235–36
   characteristics of   246–47
   cruciformity within   210

383

Subject Index

doctrine and *331*
duties within *333–34*
God's provisions within *327–28*
growth within *328–29*
holy living within *257–61, 265–66, 314, 327–28, 331*
home within *224–25*
identity within *223–24*
natural desires within *227–28*
sexual purity *235–36*
significance of faith within *232*
suffering within *220, 234*
work ethic within *242*
Christ, Jesus as *42*
church *102*
as body of Christ *112, 127, 143, 148, 197*
as brances *218*
challenges within *245, 367*
of Colossae *216*
as a community *33–34, 246*
conflict within *258*
of Corinth *153–54, 157*
of Crete *251–52*
culture and *246*
discipline protocols within *242*
divisions within *140–42*
as the elect *347*
of Ephesus *255–56, 371*
establishment of *95*
evil behavior within *142–43*
expansion of *99–106*
faithfulness of *261*
false teaching within *262*
foes within *357*
gatherings within *97*
Gentile presence with *312*
growth of *97*
holy kiss within *238*
holy living within *257–61, 295*
Holy Spirit empowerment of *99–106*
internal conflicts within *338–39*
Jewish presence within *312*
of Laodicea *371*
leadership within *238–39, 246, 260–61, 264*
locations of *188*
marital status and *144*

ministry to troubled *238*
opposition within *355–56*
organization of *252, 255–56*
outsider destruction within *356*
Paul's relationship with *233–235*
of Pergamum *371*
perseverance in affliction by *239*
of Philadelphia *371*
prayer within *101, 258*
prophecy within *148*
public worship disorders within *146–47*
purpose of *245–46*
resource sacrifice within *208–9*
of Revelation *366–67, 370*
of Sardis *371*
significance of *261*
of Smyrna *371*
sound teaching within *246, 265*
spiritual disabilities within *294*
spiritual gifts within *147–48*
theological questions *232*
of Thessalonica *228–30, 234–35*
of Thyatira *371*
unity within *211*
victory of *241*
Cicero *236–37*
circumcision *7, 115–16, 175, 210, 221, 255*
Claudius (emperor) *111*
clay jars, ministers as *154, 160–162*
Colossae *215–16, 221, 275*
Colosseum *127*
Colossian Heresy *217, 221–23*
Comforter, God as *154, 158*
comfort, through suffering *158*
commands, biblical *297–98*
communities *246*
community *23–24*
competition *135, 141, 147–48*
confession *207*
confidence
in Jesus *346*
conflict *151, 258*

contending for the faith *357, 360–61*
Corinth *138, 163*
church within *153–54, 157, 188*
competition within *135*
conditions of *133–135*
destruction of *134*
divisions within *140–142*
Isthmian Games *135*
marriage within *144*
Paul within *112, 135, 231*
religion of *135*
religion within *154*
Temple of Apollo within *154*
Corinthianizing *134*
Corinthians (people)
characteristics of *152*
division within *138*
Paul and *132–33, 138, 155, 159, 163–65*
super apostles *163–64*
super apostles and *156–57*
wisdom viewpoint of *141*
Cornelius *104–5*
cosmic conflict *373–375*
Counselor, Holy Spirit as *99*
covenant *6, 293*
See also specific covenants
Crete *251–52, 255, 263–64*
cross (the event) *51–54, 83–87, 141*
See crucifixion of Jesus
as a way of life *126–27*
cross (the object) *207, 376*
crucifixion of Jesus *36–37, 49–50, 83, 86, 205*
cruciformity *210*

D

darkness, spiritual *341*
David *7–8*
Day of the Lord *240–41*
See also second coming
deacons *261–62*
Dead Sea Scrolls *16, 160*
death *69–71, 79, 117–123, 236–37, 288, 346*
debtor's prison *273*
deity *75–76, 78, 219*
Demetrius *348*
Dente, Marco *222*
Diana *188*
Diotrephes *350*
discernment *238*
disciple/discipleship
characteristics of *48*
dispositions within *28*

Subject Index

essence of 24–25
expectations within 49
fear within 65
growth of 100
humility within 49–51
Jesus's call to 200
journey of 21–22, 30, 33
martyrdom 90
mission of 30–31, 48
nature of 47–51
orientation of 29–30
prayer within 53
preparation period for 36
process of 35
progressive understanding by 47
requirements of 25
restoration within 33–34
righteousness within 29
self-giving 48
self-judgment within 29
suffering within 33
discipline/discipleship
Jesus's call to 28
disenfranchised, the 62, 67
disobedience 58–59
disunity 138
diversity 148
dividing wall 194
divine warrior 197
divinity of Jesus 203–4, 213–14, 287
division 138, 140–42, 147
Docetism 338
doctrine 138, 266, 356–57
double-mindedness 306
dualism 345

E

eating 97, 144–46
elders 260–61, 320, 348–49, 372
Elijah 46
emperor, honoring of 317
empowerment 98–102
emptying, use of term 204–5
enacted loyalty 109
endurance 294, 313, 315–21
Epaphras 217
Epaphroditus 209–10
Ephesian church 371
Ephesians (people) 174, 185, 187–90, 196–97
Ephesus 152, 186, 188–90, 194, 259
Epimenides 264
Esau 17–18, 124, 294
eschatology 238

Eschaton 257
Essenes 16, 20
eternal glory 317
eternal hope 228
eternal Spirit, Holy Spirit as 99
Ethiopian eunuch 104
ethnic groups, within religion 194
exaltation of Jesus 206
exile 9–11, 14
expectations, examples of 124

F

faith 113, 303
  centrality of 180
  contending for 357, 360–61
  as core beliefs 357
  defined 114
  endurance and 284
  examples of 68
  as family trait 7
  good works and 264
  growth within 328–29
  the law *versus* 180
  living by 179
  miracles within 65
  personal 317–18
  response of 62
  salvation through 189
  test of 341
  victory of 345
  works *versus* 114, 302–4
faithful ministry 154
faithfulness
  among God's people 126–28
  of the church 261
  divine 112–17
  endurance through 294, 313
  evidence of 347
  identity of 121
  of God 94
  of Jesus 209
  process of 234
  revealing of 113
  thanksgiving and 140
false prophets 374
  warning regarding 343
false teachers/false teaching
  bondage within 332
  characteristics of 196
  within the church 262
  concern with 217
  within Crete 255, 264
  debating by 254–55
  descriptions of 332

doom of 331–32
effects of 256
examples of 268
identification of 332
methods of 254–55
misuse of the law by 256–57
practices of 222
regarding the resurrection 255
role of 300
warning regarding 261, 329–32, 347–48
family of God 172, 178–80, 276
Father, theme of 80
fear 65
feast table, significance of 97
feeding of the 5000 80
fellowship, love within 148
Festival Cycle 80
Festival of Dedication 14
final judgment 35–36, 375
firstborn, Jesus as 219–20
fleshly desires, denial of 182
foes, judgment of 358–59
foolishness, cross as 141
foot-washing 84
forgiveness 9, 279–80, 293
form, term use of 204
Fountain of Peirene 163
freedom 181
fruit of the Spirit 182, 218, 328
fruit, spiritual 218
fullness of Christ 216, 225
future glory 313
future hope 368

G

Gaius 349–50
Galatia 170–73
Galatians (people) 167, 173–74, 180–81
Galilee 42–47, 63
Gallio 231
Garden of Gethsemane 53
Geburt Christi (Monaco) 61
genealogy, of Jesus 63, 93, 25–26
generousity 162
Gentiles
  accusations to 114
  assimilation of 195
  conflicts within 20, 111
  conversion of 106
  within Corinth 153–54
  divinity viewpoint of 141

Subject Index

guilt of 112–17
Holy Spirit within 96
inclusion of 96–97, 104
Jew division within 194–96
Jews unification and 123–26
law as barrier for 179–80
mystery of 93
Peter and 176
status of 194
giving 149, 154, 162
glorification 123
God 327–329, 345
godliness 234, 269–70, 327–28, 333–43
God's glory within 207
God's promises 60
Golgotha 53
Good Friday 36
good works 257, 264, 266
gospel
  as good news 104, 112–13
  aspects of 265–66
  equality within 276
  foundation of 199
  fruit bearing within 218
  as good news 104, 112–13
  human ministers role within 160
  inclusions within 104
  remembrance of 267–68
  suffering within 268, 270
Gospels, overview of the 379–80
governmental leaders, honoring of 317
grace 140, 217–18, 238, 257
gratitude 221
Great Commission 220
greed 49–50
Greek language 11–12
Greeks 5, 11
growth, through faith 328–29
guardian 180
guilt, Jewish and gentile 112–17

H

Hall of Faith 294
Hanukkah 13–14
hardships 160–61, 185–86
  See also suffering
head coverings 146–47
healings 47, 80, 170
heaven 122
Hebrew, language use of 5
Herod Antipas 19, 33, 46–47

Herod Archelaus 17
Herodian Dynasty 17–19
Herodians 51
Herodias 19
Herod the Great 17–18
Hierapolis 215
high Christology 64
High Priest, Jesus as 84–85, 219, 280, 284–85, 287–88
high priesthood 285
high priests, role of 17
holiness 236, 314
holy kiss 238
holy living 257–61, 314, 327–28, 331, 333–34
  See also Christian life
holy of holies 376
Holy Spirit 99
  activity of 61
  anointing of 341
  enabling by 181
  episodes of 95–96
  fruit of 182
  gentiles and 96
  intercession of 122
  response commands to 175
  role of 84
  submission to 182
  walking by 182
home of a Christian 224–25
honor 135, 141
hope
  within eternal life 266
  future 368
  within physical resurrection 161
  within resurrection 161
  within salvation 186
  of the second coming 237, 342
  within suffering 247–48
  through persecution 314
hospitality 348–49
household of a Christian 224–25
human formation 264
humility
  within discipleship 49–50
  glory within 207
  honor through 141
  of Jesus 84, 139, 154–55, 164, 205
  within leadership 304
  of Paul 164–65
  service within 137
  within spiritual gifts 147
  standard within 137
  submission through 306

within suffering 155
weakness and 155
wisdom and 305
husbands, role of 224
Hymenaeus 268
hypostatic union 219

I

"I AM" statements 24, 65, 75, 80–86, 206
identity in Christ 181
idleness 242
idolatry 49–50, 144–46, 346
idols 346
Idumean 17–18
imperial subjects 319
imprisonment of Paul 190, 202–3
inaugurated eschatology 119
incarnation 205
incest 142–43
inheritance, promise of 180
intercession, of the Holy Spirit 122
Intercessor, Jesus as 84
intertestamental period 11
Isaac 181
Isaiah 64
Ishmael 181
Israel 7, 9–11, 68, 125–26
Israelites 9, 27, 123, 288–91, 294
Jews 9
Israelite worship 7
Isthmian Games 135

J

Jairus 65
James (brother of Jesus) 90, 298–299
Jason 230–31
Jeremiah 8–9
Jerusalem
  destruction of 10, 19–20, 35
  Holy Spirit empowerment within 99–103
  Jesus within 49, 51–54, 67–69
  map of 80, 84
  new 375–377
  Triumphal Entry within 68–69, 83
Jesus 28
  authority of 30
  confidence in 346
  conflicts of 33, 35
  divinity of 203–4

Subject Index

enemies of 288
as fulfillment 24–25
Holy Week actions of 34
as messenger 287–88
ministry of 28, 46, 60–66
Olivet Discourse 35–36
parables of the kingdom
  message of 31–33
power of 43–45, 49
questions of 83
resurrection of 148
return of 35
Sermon on Last Things
  34–36
Sermon on the New Jesus-
  Formed Community
  and 33–34
as spokesperson 286
as teacher 28–29
temptation of 27–28
titles of 64, 217
weakness of 49
within the Gospels
  379–80
Jewish
  religious system 93–94
Jewish Christians 153
Jews 8–20, 23, 62, 75–76,
  80, 82, 93, 95, 97, 104–6,
  111–16, 123–25, 136, 141,
  153, 170–71, 178–79, 194,
  196, 216, 220, 230, 299,
  312, 324
  Diaspora 12
  exile of 11, 111
  gentile division within
    194–96
  gentiles unification and
    123–26
  guilt of 112–17
  hatred toward Paul by
    230–31, 235
  Hellenistic 12
  hopelessness of 93
  laws regarding 178–80
  new sect of 17
  rejection by 123–24
  sects of 14–17
Jezebel 46
John Mark 40–41, 321
John (son of Zebedee)
  31–32, 74
  authorship by 74, 336,
    365–67
  calling of 78
  as the Elder 337, 347
  vision of 371–72
John the Baptist 16, 19, 27,
  33, 45–46, 78

Joseph of Arimathea 36
Josephus 9
joy 210
Judah 9
Judah, kings within
  9
Judaism 20, 111, 173–74,
  210
Judas 53
Jude 354–55
Judea 12–13, 80, 99–103
judge 116
judgment 29–30, 35–36,
  114, 358–59
Julius Caesar 134
justice 112–17, 374
justification 122–23, 171–
  72, 176

K

kingdom 49
kingdom ethic 301
kingdom of God 42–47,
  98–99, 128
kingdom of heaven 31–33
kings 8, 25
Knossos 265
knowledge 3
Korah 359

L

Lamb of God 76, 372
Laodicea 215–16
Laodicean church, letter
  to 371
last days, term use of 269
last hour, metaphor of 341
Last Judgment 240
Last Supper 52–53, 84
Law, the
  as a barrier 179–80
  categories of 177
  family of God and 179
  intent of 257
  interpretation of 117
  limitations of 121
  misuses of 256–57
  purposes of 177, 180, 301
  salvation and 177
  sin and 119
  summary of 128
lawsuits 143
Lazarus 82–83
laziness 242
leadership 238–39, 246,
  260–62, 264, 304
learning, teaching versus
  260
leaven 97

Lechaeum harbor 133
local church 211
  See also church
Lord's Supper 147
Lost Coin parable 68
Lost Sheep parable 68
Lost Son parable 67–68
Lot 332
love
  of believers 341–43, 348
  conditions of 29
  foundation of 223
  nature of 148
  of neighbor 302, 304
  power of 344–45
  sacrifice within 67
  spiritual gifts and 148
  standard of 137
  through salvation 188
  types of 128
love of God 118, 123, 128,
  302, 304, 344–45
Luke (author) 58, 60, 94–95
Luther, Martin 302–4, 329
Lycus Valley 215

M

Maccabean Era 12–14
Macedonia 230
Macedonians 162
Magnificat 62
majesty of Jesus 213
man of lawlessness 241,
  374–75
marital status, within the
  church 144
Mark
  See John Mark
marriage 143–44, 224,
  235–36
martyr/martyrdom 30–31,
  33, 90, 95, 190, 339
Mary 67
Mary Magdalene 86
Mary (mother of Jesus) 26,
  61–62, 79
Mattathias 13–14
Matthew 22, 30
meat sacrificed to idols
  144–46
Mediator Jesus as 219
Melchizedek 291–92
members within 238
memory, Peter's references to
  323–24, 326–27
men, responsibility of 260
mercy 124, 257
messenger, Jesus as
  287–88

Messiah   23, 31–32, 47–48,
  123–24, 141, 176
  See also Jesus
Michelangelo   240
military language   222
millennial kingdom   375
ministers   142, 161–62,
  348–49
ministry   141, 260
miracle(s)   79
mission, instructions on
  30–31
Monaco, Lorenzo   61
money, idolatry within
  49–50
Mosaic covenant   7
Mosaic law   194–95
Moses   7, 116, 288–89
Moses with the Ten Commandments   257
Mount of Beatitudes   300
Mount Sinai   294
Muratorian Canon   58
mustard seed parable   97

N

name of the Lord   206–7
name, term use of   140
Nathanael   78
Nero   41, 190, 311, 317, 338
new covenant   8–9, 154,
  160, 293
new creation   70
new heavens and new earth
  375–77
new life   117–23
Nicene Creed   204
Nicodemus   79–80
North Galatian theory
  169–70
Nunc Dimittis   62

O

obedience   63, 67–68, 188,
  205, 320–21, 347
obligatory obedience   67
Old Testament   5–9, 26–27
Olivet Discourse   35–36
Onesimus   275–80
opposition   235, 355–56

P

Palestine   100
parables. *See also specific parables*   32, 44
parables of the kingdom message   31–33
partiality   115
Passover   52–53

pastoral epistles   248–49,
  254, 262, 264, 266, 269
pastors   348–49
Patmos   366
Paul   8, 248, 253
  Abrahamic covenant   7
  accusations by   114
  apostleship of   174–76,
    267
  authorship by   110–11,
    132, 152, 168, 186–87,
    190, 202–3, 214, 228–29,
    274–75
  Davidic covenant   8
  dialogue partner of   120
  employment of   145–46,
    164
  first missionary journey of
    169–70
  Gentile writings by   9
  Greek language use of   11
  imprisonment of   96,
    202–3, 253
  languages use by   12
  Luke and   58
  map regarding   169
  ministry of   106, 209–10
  name change of   102
  persecution by   102
  second missionary journey
    of   133, 135, 170,
    229–31
  thesis statement of   113
  third missionary journey
    of   112, 132, 138, 152,
    190, 276
  travels of   112
  writing style of   225, 231
pax Romana   19
peace   219, 228
Pentecost   99, 101, 312
perfectionism   342
Pergamum church, letter
  to   371
persecution
  apathy and   285
  disciples and   31
  displacement following
    312–13
  endurance through
    314–16
  examples of   309–10
  gospel expansion through
    96
  by Paul   102
  perseverance through   239
  under Nero   41, 311, 338
  with tribulation   35
perseverance   239, 307
Persia   5, 10–11

personal faith   317–18
personal liberty   144–46
Peter
  See Simon Peter
Pharisees   14–15, 20, 35, 43,
  47, 51, 82
Philadelphia church, letter
  to   371
Philemon   274–80
Philetus   268
Philip (disciple)   78, 100, 104
Philip the Tetrarch   19
Philip II (father of Alexander
  the Great)   11
Philippi   202, 208
physical resurrection   148–49
  237
  hope within   161
Pompey   14, 19
Pontius Pilate   19, 36, 53
post-resurrection   70–71
poverty   307
power   64, 116, 120, 141, 208
practical wisdom   246–47
prayer   53, 84–86, 101, 225,
  242, 258, 346
predestination   192
preparation   371–373
pride   142–43
priests   290
Priscilla   136
prison epistles   187, 214–15
prophecy   148, 369
provision from God   327–29
public worship, disorders
  within   146

Q

Qal Wahomer argument   287

R

Rahab   93, 195
rapture of the church   237
recognition   135
Reconciler, Jesus as   219
reconciliation   154, 160–62,
  219
re-creation   364
redemption   191, 265
rejection
  of Jesus   45, 64, 68, 123–
    26, 341, 345, 347
  as sin   346
  theme of   78
  of truth   74
religion, ethnic dimension
  of   194
restoration   33–34, 45, 64, 87
resurrection

Subject Index 389

allusion to 79
appearances following 86, 90–91
event of 36–37
false teaching regarding 255, 268
hope within 161
of Jesus 69–71
minimal facts argument within 89–91
physical 148–49, 161, 237
self-revelation within 83
significance of 8, 25
revelation 369
reversal 64, 67–68, 99
riches 307
rich young ruler 49–50
righteousness 24, 113, 257, 342–43
ritual impurity 14
rivalry 140
Roman Empire 14, 19, 258, 314, 338, 373
Roman Legion, A 222
the Romans 16–17, 19, 24, 51, 126–27, 135, 170, 194, 202, 215
Roman world 104–6, 134, 180
Rome 17, 188

S

sacrifice 149, 162, 208–9, 292–93
Sadducees 15–16, 20, 35, 51
Saint Paul Writing His Epistles (Boulogne) 247
saint, use of term 316
salvation 173
   assurance of 292
   blessings of 191–93
   conditions of 139
   cultural implications of 194–96
   endurance through 315–18
   fulfillment of 59–60
   God's work within 193
   good works within 188–89
   hope and joy within 186
   human condition before 193–94
   as inheritance 181
   Jesus's response regarding 97
   Judaism and 171
   the law and 177, 179–80
   Paul's picture of 218
   as present reality 186

purpose of 192–93
requirement for 105, 114–17, 126, 178
spiritual blessings within 192
spiritual power of 197–98
teaching varieties of 171
through faith 189
through Jesus 168
transformative nature of 181, 196–97
works of the law and 178
Samaria 96, 102–3
Samaritan 67
Samaritans 102
Samaritan woman 79–80
sanctification 230
Sanhedrin 15, 53
Sardis church, letter to 371
Satan 241, 343, 374–75
Saul of Tarsus
   See Paul
scribe 243
Scripture 269–70, 290, 329, 379
Scythians 223
second coming
   eschatology and 238
   event of 374–75
   Greek Icon of 330
   hope within 237, 342
   instruction within 233
   overview of 373
   perserverance and 307
   reminder of 333–34, 376–77
   timing of 236, 241
Second Temple Period 10, 14–17
seed 179, 316
Seleucid dynasty 12
self-control 265
self-giving 48
self-reliance 164
self-revelation 78–82, 83–87
self-talk 210
Septuagint 283
Sermon on Last Things 34–36
Sermon on the Mount 27–30, 299, 301–2
servant(s) 142, 204–5, 325
service 141, 165, 188
seven-sealed scroll 372–73
sex 235–36
sexual holiness 236
sexual immorality 134–35, 137, 142–43
sexual purity 235–36
shepherding 321

Siemiradzki, Henryk 344
signs 75, 78–82
Silas 321
Simeon 62
Simon Peter
   as disciple 28
   authorship of 310–11, 324
   Barnabas and 176
   boldness of 101
   confession of 65
   death of 320
   denial by 53
   exile writings of 11
   Gentiles and 176
   Gospel of Mark and 40–41
   name choice of 324–25
   rebuke to 102
   resurrection and 86
   sermon of 99–100
   tanner and 104–5
sin 116–23, 143, 192–93, 340, 346
slavery 181, 224–25, 262, 277
slaves, standard of living by 119, 278, 319
Smyrna church, letter to 371
social structures, endurance within 318–19
Socratic Method 83
Sodom and Gomorrah 332, 358
Solomon 7, 9
Son of God, Jesus as 42–47, 43
Son of Man, Jesus as 78
sound teaching 246, 254–55, 267–68
South Galatian theory 168–69
speaking in tongues 99
speech ethics 304–6
Spirit of Christ, Holy Spirit as 99
Spirit of glory, Holy Spirit as 99
Spirit of grace, Holy Spirit as 99
Spirit of Promise, Holy Spirit as 99
Spirit of truth, Holy Spirit as 99
spiritual battle 197
spiritual blessings 185–86, 192, 194
spiritual darkness 341
spiritual discernment 238

spiritual freedom   *182*
spiritual fruit   *218*
spiritual gifts   *147–48*
spiritual slavery   *181*
spiritual world   *343*
Stephen   *95*
stewards   *142*
stumbling block   *141*
submission   *141, 182, 306*
suffering
  as discipleship cost   *33*
  examples of   *247*
  expectation of   *47–48, 319*
  foreshadowing of   *43*
  for the gospel   *268, 270*
  godliness and   *253–54*
  God's comfort within   *154, 158*
  God's glory within   *160*
  hope within   *247–48*
  humility within   *155*
  of Jesus   *65, 69–71, 155, 288*
  of Paul   *182, 209, 220, 247, 253–54*
  power within   *48*
  prayer within   *225*
  purpose of   *316–17*
  questions regarding   *287–88*
  redemption of   *254*
  rejoicing through   *209*
  salvation and   *186*
  significance of   *41–43*
  standard of living within   *319*
  as temporary   *122*
  theme of   *41*
  use of   *158*
  within the Christian life   *220*
suffering Savior, Jesus as   *41*
Suffering Servant   *205*
super-apostles   *156–57, 163–64*
superstitious   *98*
supremacy   *213, 216–17*
suzerain-vassal treaty   *6*
synkrisis   *287*
Synoptics   *78*

T

tabernacle   *7*
table, feast, significance of   *97*
tanner   *104–5*
tax collector   *22*
teaching, learning versus   *260*
thanksgiving   *218, 233*
Theophilus   *58–59*
Thessalonians, the (people)   *228–30, 234–35*
Thessalonica   *232*
Thyatira church, letter to   *371*
Timothy   *209, 231, 235, 250, 261–62, 267–68*
titles of Jesus   *64, 217*
Titus (Paul's fellow worker)   *152–53, 156, 159, 175, 246, 248–49, 251–52, 263–65*
Titus (son of Vespasian)   *19–20*
tongue, speech ehtics and speech ethics and   *304–6*
tongues, speaking in   *147*
Torches of Nero, The (Siemiradzki)   *344*
Tower of Babel   *101*
tree, God's people as   *125–26*
tree of knowledge of good and evil   *376*
tree of life   *376*
tribulation   *35*
Trinity   *206, 315*
triumphal entry   *68–69, 83*
Troas   *159*
true religion   *29*
Tychicus   *191, 277*

U

unbelief   *288–89*
unforgiveness   *280*
unholy trinity   *373*
unity   *123–28, 137, 211*
universal church   *102*

V

Valley of Jezreel   *374*
values   *68*
veil   *146*
veil, worship decorum of   *146–47*
Vespasian   *19–20*
Via Egnatia   *202*
vices   *223*
victory   *222, 345, 374*
vine   *218*
violence   *17*
virtues   *223*
vulnerable, care for   *246*

W

walk by the Spirit   *182*
water   *345*
weakness
  God's power within   *162*
  honor through   *141*
  humility within   *155*
  of Jesus   *49*
  of Paul   *165*
  power within   *30–31*
  service within   *165*
weaknesses
  power within   *45*
  transformation of   *160*
wedding ceremony   *292–93*
Western Wall   *291*
wickedness   *241*
wilderness generation   *289–90*
will, making of   *179*
will of God   *238, 319–20*
wisdom   *141, 246–47, 298–99, 305–6*
wives   *319*
  role of   *224*
woman/women
  education of   *260*
  Gospel of Luke's reference to   *62*
  Jesus as born of   *380*
  Paul's teaching regarding   *258–60*
  of Roman society   *258*
  worship decorum of   *146–47*
Word, Jesus as the   *77–78*
works   *114, 264, 302–4*
works of the law   *176–77*
worship   *146–47, 188, 221–22, 236, 372*

Z

Zealots   *17, 20*
Zechariah   *61–62, 62*
Zeus   *264*